WITHDRAWN

Injustice and Restitution

INJUSTICE AND RESTITUTION

The Ordinance of Time

Stephen David Ross

State University of New York Press

Published by
State University of New York Press, Albany

© 1993   State University of New York

All rights reserved

Printed in the United States of America

No part of this book may be used or reproduced
in any manner whatsoever without written permission
except in the case of brief quotations embodied in
critical articles and reviews.

For information, address State University of New York Press,
State University Plaza, Albany, N.Y. 12246

Production by Dana Foote
Marketing by Nancy Farrell

Library of Congress Cataloging-in-Publication Data

Ross, Stephen David.
    Injustice and restitution : the ordinance of time / Stephen David
  Ross.
       p.   cm.
    Includes bibliographical references and index.
    ISBN 0–7914–1669–0 (alk. paper). — ISBN 0–7914–1670–4 (pbk. :
  alk. paper)
    1. Authority.   2. Reason.   3. Justice.   4. Law—Philosophy.
  5. Science.   6. Political science—Philosophy.   I. Title.
  BD209.R68   1993
  340'.11—dc20   92–42843
                                                                         CIP

10 9 8 7 6 5 4 3 2 1

CONTENTS

Preface		ix
I	Injustice's Debt	1
II	Authority's Rule	13
III	Law's Injustice	37
IV	Economy's Measure	83
V	Subjection's Abjection	105
VI	Monstrosity's Madness	127
VII	Law's Force	159
VIII	Idolatry's Authority	191
IX	Science's Spell	213
X	Witches' Science	253
XI	Justice's Injustice	281
Notes		315
Index		369

Things make restitution to one another for their injustice according to the ordinance of time.

Anaximander

Justice is Strife.

Heraclitus

Which is better, cheap happiness or exalted suffering?

Dostoevsky

Someone must have traduced Joseph K.

Kafka

The political question is truth itself.

Foucault

Why always say of truth that it restitutes?

Derrida

In the measure that responsibilities are taken on, they multiply. The debt increases in the measures that it is paid.

Levinas

What if the "object" started to speak?

Irigaray

What is at stake is not only the hegemony of Western cultures, but also their identities as unified cultures. The West is painfully made to realize the existence of a Third World in the First World, and vice versa. The Master is bound to recognize that His Culture is not as homogeneous, as monolithic as He believed it to be. He discovers, with much reluctance, He is just an other among others.

Trinh Minh-ha

PREFACE

The twentieth century, riven by wars and the collapse of empires, has brought with its close, throughout the world, extraordinary political events marking the reopening of questions of community and identity once thought to be settled under Western law. The second millennium after the birth of Christ, taken to represent Western enlightenment and progress, has brought with its close, throughout the world, extraordinary political writings marking the reopening of questions of authority and law once thought to be settled under Western reason. At the same time, again worldwide, extraordinary circumstances mark the reopening of fundamental questions of nature and technology. The conditions of a just and effective community remain unknown, profoundly disturbed by hidden enmities. The conditions of a just and effective authority remain unsettled, profoundly disturbed by forgotten violences. The conditions of a just relation to nature remain fundamentally political, disturbing science's authority. Writings at the close of our epoch gravitate toward questions of justice, community, and authority, moved by memories of suffering and pain, destruction and oppression, animosity and violence, mourning injustices that cannot be remembered. Western and non-Western writers speak of injustices by nationality, gender, sexuality, race, and class, of violence and oppression. Far-reaching questions of authority and justice explore the possibility that Western reason, at the point perhaps of its greatest triumph, represents another violence, another oppression. At stake is a profound reexamination of the idea of the political, of authority and law.

This book takes up these questions of authority, retracing the ideas of reason and law from ancient Greece to the present. The discussion pursues a line of thought begun with Anaximander, who speaks of the ordinance of time as restitution for immemorial injustice, and Heraclitus, who speaks of justice as strife, through Western literature and philosophy to the present, Western and non-Western. In a voice that repeatedly challenges its own authority, the book explores connections between authority and injustice, rule and law, seeking to understand how ethics and politics can be meaningful where everything in nature is political. The line of thought developed here takes up the possibility that human subjectivity represents repeated subjection to authority, reenacting a timeless and pervasive injustice, throughout nature as well as human experience, providing an understanding of the authority of truth and law as unending restitution for forgotten injustices. Justice, truth, and law circulate as measures of restitution for an injustice older than any measure, an injustice that does not presuppose justice's measure.

The discussion reverses Foucault's understanding that the political question is truth itself, exploring truth's authority as ethical and political. The discussion parallels Trinh Minh-ha's insistence that epistemic authority be delayed to infinity. If political questions repeatedly return us to truth's authority, then both truth and authority demand unending critique, unending deferral, even as we can imagine no way to escape them. Emphasizing twentieth-century continental and pragmatist writings, this book explores alternative voices as challenges to authority, in feminist and multicultural writings, in Greek mythology and African narrative, in Greek drama and twentieth-century literature.

I

INJUSTICE'S DEBT

We[1] struggle to retell Anaximander's tale of an archaic injustice, *adikia*, that inflicts upon us a debt before time; of an archaic injustice whose restitution requires endless time; of a justice, *dikē*, that circulates as strife, *polemos*, within the ordinance of time and law.[2] We begin with questions of law and truth, seeking to touch the limits of their authority. We begin again with questions of justice and the good, seeking to touch their enigmatic limits. We repeatedly contend with our own injustices, the limits of voice and truth.

Do we approach justice's truth? Do we hope to give another measure of justice? Or do we recall an archaic injustice's truth measured by neither law nor reason, especially unmeasured by justice's law? May we imagine that injustice fails to belong to the law that justice always works as Law, an injustice that knows no Law?[3] Here, where injustice honors an age before time, older than memory, before any origin, we think of the circulation of truth and law as the unending forms of restitution that institute Western Law. We think of truth and law as bearing within themselves an injustice before any truth and law that disturbs every measure of justice. We wonder whether the immemoriality of injustice may mark something older than and different from the *logos* and *nomos* of ancient Greece, from Western Reason, something unknown yet present within it. May such an injustice, older and younger than Apollo, than God the Father, emerge from the depths of humanity's inhumanity and reason's madness? May we recall an aboriginal injustice, older and younger than time, unmeasured by law, undiminished by any restitution, unfulfilled by guilt or vengeance, nevertheless repeating law? Could we find hope in such a memory? Could we find *jouissance*?

These enigmatic questions unfold from our inauguration with Anaximander, but we remember Heidegger's reading of the fragment and his relation to the Greeks, a reading we hope to question as we repeat it.[4] Who, more than Heidegger, asks us to think of injustice's immemoriality? Who, more than Heidegger, repeats truth's injustice? For he diminishes the guilt (*Schuldigkeit*) that belongs to *dikē* and the immemorial restitution of things for the *adikias*,[5] the "injustice in things," calling it "thoughtless" (*AF*, p. 43). We read his translation of Anaximander translated into English: "along the lines of usage; for they let order and thereby also reck belong to one another (in the surmounting) of disorder" (*AF*, p. 57). Whatever injustice remains in Heidegger disappears in translation, as if we might read Heidegger without knowing of injustice. Heidegger's German reads very differently: "entlang dem Brauch; gehören nämlich lassen sie Fug somit auch Ruch eines dem anderen (im Vorwinden) des Un-Fugs." The force of need and custom in *brauchen*, the justice in *Fug* and juncture in *Fuge*, the wickedness of lacking *Ruch*, the temporality and twisting of *Vorwinden*, the ethical sense of *Unfug*'s mischief, all fade silently away, following Heidegger's own retreat from *Schuldigkeit* to *Fug*. We wonder that he can so unjustly allow injustice to pass away within the withdrawal of Being.[6] How can Being withdraw without pain, as if revelation might incur no victims? What, more than injustice, reflects the call of Being, requiring inexhaustible time?

In Lyotard's words:

> how could this thought [Heidegger's], a thought so devoted to remembering that a forgetting (of Being) takes place in all thought, in all art, in all "representation" of the world, how could it possibly have ignored the thought of "the jews," which, in a certain sense, thinks, tries to think, nothing but that very fact? How could this thought forget and ignore "the jews" to the point of suppressing and foreclosing to the very end the horrifying (and inane) attempt at exterminating, at making us forget forever what, in Europe, reminds us, ever since the beginning, that "there is" the Forgotten?[7]

What of the silence of the victims, the withdrawal of their suffering? What restitution for their annihilation? Do these questions echo Levinas, or does he open an image of propriety even otherwise than being?

> Transcendence is passing over to being's *other*, otherwise than being. Not *to be otherwise*, but *otherwise than being*.[8]

> In the exposure to wounds and outrages, in the feeling proper to responsibility, the oneself is provoked as irreplaceable, as devoted to the others, without being able to resign, and thus as incarnated in order to offer itself, to suffer and to give. (Levinas, *OB*, p. 105)[9]

What if in the call of Being something echoed that does not belong to Being?

What if in such a call we found ourselves immeasurably indebted, ethically and politically responsible for others? Where in Being can we hear such a call?

What, other than archaic injustice, could mark that responsibility in Being? To what, other than Being, can this injustice belong?

What but archaic injustice can rule against the authority of the proper, against proper authority?

Such questions make us hesitate when Heidegger tells us that the return to Greece bears no particular authority while marking a certain Western destiny (*Geschick*):

> In our manner of speaking, "Greek" does not designate a particular people or nation, nor a cultural or anthropological group. What is Greek is the dawn of that destiny in which Being illuminates itself in beings and so propounds a certain essence of man; that essence unfolds historically as something fateful, preserved in Being and dispensed by Being, without ever being separated from Being. (Heidegger, *AF*, p. 25)

We choose not to emphasize Heidegger's relationship to Hitler. We emphasize instead his saying that the German language (even when most contaminated) is closest to the Greek.[10] We note the dawn of the destiny of Being's Western self-illumination in giving up the injustice of its coming into presence: "the presencing of what is present, is already in itself truth, provided we think the essence of truth as the gathering that clears and shelters; . . . " (Heidegger, *AF*, p. 37). Do we hear a truth that clears and shelters but does not subjugate; a truth without suspicion; a truth in the highest; the injustice of the highest? Do we hear in Being's destiny a refusal of injustice's debt?[11] Do we hear a proper destiny?

Heidegger approaches injustice in things, in himself, in Being, when he says, "Error is the space in which history unfolds." "Without errancy there would be no connection from destiny to destiny: there would be no history" (*AF*, p. 26). Here unfolds the withdrawal of Being—into errant injustice, unending restitution, the injustice of every historical destiny. Yet he recoils: "How is what lingers awhile in presence unjust? What is unjust about it? Is it not the right of whatever is present that in each case it linger awhile, endure, and so fulfill its presencing?" (*AF*, p. 41). He responds with emancipatory language: "Lingering as persisting, considered with respect to the jointure of the while, is an insurrection on behalf of sheer endurance. Continuance asserts itself in presencing as such, which lets each present being linger awhile in the expanse of unconcealment. In this rebellious whiling whatever lingers awhile insists upon sheer continuance" (*AF*, p. 43). We understand this insurrection, this rebellion, to belong to the injustice of lingering in any while, however long, however old, of things together, the lingering of injustice, the inescapability of subjugation. We understand this injustice to require compensation. We take justice as the restitution in time for the injustice of whatever lingers, belongs to time, even in the form of destiny. We take injustice's debt to grow with reparation, with responsibility, defeating any destiny, growing older and younger than itself, exceeding itself as justice's injustice.

Heidegger rejects the penalty, thereby the injustice and law, the vigilance, that threatens destiny's justice: "Surely *tisis* can mean penalty, but it must not, because the original and essential significance of the word is not thereby named" (*AF*, p. 45). He refuses thereby any original and essential significance to the injustice of things and the restitution that they impose. We respond that this injustice, in Anaximander's fragment, may give us a most original and essential truth of things—provided that we resist the propriety of the "most" with another vigilance. Or shall we resist even this original and essential nature as injustice's repetition? The errancy that belongs to things against their destiny—perhaps another assertion of Western privilege—circulates inseparably with their injustice, calling for unending restitution, for insurrection and rebellion in things, neither in us as subjects, nor in Being, nor anywhere in particular. Injustice here precedes and follows the order of time in which truth and justice compose their measure, the injustice into which we find ourselves always already fallen. Injustice grows without measure, older than itself immemorial, younger than itself in deepening restitution, forever mourned.

Does Heidegger repeat a tradition that persists in knowing nothing of its injustices, nothing of others' suffering, nothing of its own subjections, that knows nothing of these in the name of truth, hopes to pay no penalty for that truth? Does Heidegger repeat that tradition even as our thought of injustice echoes the withdrawal of Being? Do we, do we all, repeat that movement even as we struggle with its injustices? If we grant metaphysics its self-authorization to subject us to its dominion, do we at the same time restitute its abjection? The idea of truth, justice's truth, in our tradition belongs mimetically to a certain restitution.[12] Can this truth repeat the restitution that belongs to time? If so, does another truth, perhaps a ghostly, abject untruth, circulate together with injustice's truth, uncanny immemorial recollections,[13] to which truth pays relentless restitution? Do we understand the only restitution of which we can speak as a restoration, or can we repay in different currencies, different countries?

If injustice materializes older than time, what unfolds younger than it? In *Parmenides,* Plato presents two relations of age and youth, one where Zeno says, describing his youthful book, "That is where you are mistaken, Socrates; you imagine it was inspired, not by a youthful eagerness for controversy, but by the more dispassionate aims of an older man, . . . "[14] the other in relation to the one in time:

> So if the one is, it is in time.
>
> (a) Time, moreover, is advancing. Hence since the one moves forward temporally, it is always becoming older than itself. And we remember that what is becoming older becomes older than something that is becoming younger. So, since the one is becoming older than itself, that self must be becoming younger.
>
> Therefore, in this sense, it is becoming both younger and older than itself. (*Parmenides*, 152ab)

The one unfolds as both older and younger than itself while philosophy falls into time as young and old. Justice, in time, perseveres as younger and older than itself, along with reason and law. The one, Being, and injustice, remain older than time but still younger than themselves.

This immemoriality of injustice, with desire and truth, encompasses our concern with the injustice of their authority. We call it "charity,"[15] inseparable from a sacrifice that cannot make injustice whole, without scars.[16] The scars emerge older and younger than time, and we spend endless history paying restitution for forgotten subjections, opening new wounds on top of older injuries. How shall we know such wounds, such injuries and injustices? How shall we think of them except as necessary and justifiable sacrifices? How shall we know happiness together with them? If charity knows of injustice, valor knows the immemorial injustice of sacrifice and the archaic abjection of subjection.

What sacrifice?
What debt?
What restitution?
Can we pay off the debt?
Do we seek endless retribution?

We begin our work again, challenging the authority of its beginning. We begin a second time with questions of the age of authority, which compose the remainder of our discussions.

1. With what authority do we, do I, begin, do I write, do I claim to speak for and with us—or you? What authorizes the we? For that matter, what authorizes this I who begins, who writes as an author, with authority, joining with some others—with you—who read? Does a beginning posit a community of selfsame others or a selfsame authority authorizing itself to institute a community? Does the authority of a beginning inhere in writing and speaking, in language, or does it belong in some way to me or us as human beings, possibly to nature, wherever we find ourselves, *in media res*? Can we—or anything—circulate without authority? Can we or anything avoid authority's injustice?

Whitehead does not think so, and calls it "evil": "The nature of evil is that the characters of things are mutually obstructive. Thus the depths of life require a process of selection. . . . Selection is at once the measure of evil, and the process of its evasion."[17] Selection measures evil, which owns no measure in the good. This understanding provides another view of the sins of the world, older than time, whose laws pertain to the world collectively, while evil pertains to the depths of things in relation, together with its evasion, older and younger than itself. Such a view repeats Leibniz's famous remarks about justice's perfections recast in terms of injustice:

> it follows from what has been said that the world is most perfect, not only physically, or, if you prefer, metaphysically, because that series of things is produced in which there is actually the most of reality, but also that it is most perfect morally, because real moral perfection is physical perfection for souls themselves.[18]
>
> a better law could not be established than the very law of justice which declares that each one participate in the perfection of the

universe and in a happiness of his own in proportion to his own virtue and to the good will he entertains toward the common good. (Leibniz, "Ultimate Origin of Things," p. 353)

Levinas and Whitehead speak against any such proportion. "What meaning can community take on in difference without reducing difference?" (Levinas, *OB*, p. 154). Neither follows Kant's separation of truth and the good under the rule of the unconditioned. Instead, both take things together to compose an immeasurable ethical relation. How, if fallen together, we and others, commanded to belong together in proximity, heterogeneously, can we avoid responding selectively to our proximities and differences? How, if men and women, adults and children, lions and lambs, wolves and sheep, lie down together, can any refuse the task, the work, of responsibility toward the others, avoid obsession with the others, given by the *polemos* of our heterogeneities? We live in proximity, face to face; we suffer wounding by the others close to us, suffer our own obsessions with them. Fallen into nature, things face, care about, each other, stand in each other's way, take on responsibilities toward and through the others. In the others we find our *jouissance*.

Wounding and obsession nonetheless fail to bring us to subjection, fail to speak with suspicion of abject authority and injustice. Obstruction suggests cooperation, community, as injustice suggests justice's measure. Otherwise, selection marks time's circulation in response to obstruction as justice marks time's movement in response to aboriginal injustice.

The differences of things refuse totality, community, even the understanding of community as difference. As Arendt says:

> the reality of the public realm relies on the simultaneous presence of innumerable perspectives and aspects in which the common world presents itself and for which no common measurement or denominator can ever be devised. . . . Being seen and being heard by others derive their significance from the fact that everybody sees and hears from a different position.[19]

In the extreme, agreement cancels itself. "The end of the common world has come when it is seen only under one aspect and is permitted to present itself in only one perspective" (Arendt, *The Human Condition*, p. 53). These words mark the insight that community and publicity rest on, presuppose, differences, in perspective, position, being, nature. Yet from what standpoint does this truth of multiplicity in the one derive its authority, the force of its subjections? Does it, unlike the others, set itself off as true for all, no matter where situated, true without their subjugation and oppression? Or does Arendt's truth of the common world belong within it, unjustly, located somewhere but not everywhere, within or without, exercising a community's authority? Upon what authority does Arendt say "only," and does that authority itself rest within a multiplicity of perspectives? With what authority may we speak of the end of a common world or of modernity, of history or time?

2. Can Arendt's multiplicity within the one avoid the injustices of its heterogeneities, the authority of its commonalities and diversities? Can questions of authority avoid recirculating the injustices of the one, however old or young? We ask whether what appears questionable in law and practice, truth and power, reveals a hidden authority. We ask whether the history of the world—itself a one, perhaps an inoperatic community[20]—may be understood as a struggle over authority, especially truth's authority. Nietzsche calls it the "will to truth," calls authority's struggle the "will to power": a struggle to establish and break authority.

We leave to later, perhaps to others, questions of the authority with which we must struggle against the inescapability of authority.

Instead, we wonder about the measure employed when we speak of questioning authority. This theme of measure belongs to *technē* as norm, propriety, but not perhaps as law, neither *nomos* nor *logos*, *loi* nor *droit*, *Recht* nor *Gesetz*. It represents a questionable Western idea, indeed constitutes our most common understanding of questioning—toward an end, with a measure, capable of fulfillment. Can we imagine a questioning that circulates without fulfillment, without perfectibility? Can we imagine a questioning without authority? Shall we take it as anarchistic, unjust, to question *technē*'s law?

3. We continue to wonder about the oneness of the one that the will to power and truth circulate, the oneness of archaic injustice. "The univocity of being, its singleness of expression, is paradoxically the principal condition which permits difference to escape the domination of identity, which frees it from the law of the Same. . . . "[21] We may elsewhere hear the ring of nature's sonance rather than its radiance, sound rather than light (Ross, *RR*), hoping to escape from the authority of philosophy's luminescence.[22] Here we address the one, the univocity of being, a being containing all differences within itself so that none may escape, a community of differences. Do we hear this totality as the authority of an absolute mastery that fears it will lose everything? Does questioning authority repeat an excess that no authority can contain, not even the totality of the silences of subjection, the reason why Lyotard can claim Kant's superiority over Hegel, always, in virtue of the sublime?[23] The sub-

lime presents the possibility of an unmeasure that does not belong to its sphere of authority, over which it exercises no dominion, even to say, "Here I have no authority." Here and There may belong to no authority. May we hear this lack of authority as the *différend*: that which calls for saying, in a space without authority, what cannot sound?[24] Perhaps we can represent only what belongs to some sphere of authority. And with what authority do we say "only"? With what authority do we say?

We dismantle the dominion of identity by granting the hold of its authority while denying any authority self-authorization. The univocity of identity fragments it, echoes its inexhaustibility. The authority of identity marks its locality, its multiple places, the limits that delimit its work. The lack of authority of that authority marks the limits, the otherwise, of that identity, any identity, the multiplicity of inexhaustible places at which nature works, the otherwise in every place of work. Locality, inexhaustibility, and ergonality (nature's work)[25] represent the otherwise of the dominion of identity. We understand this otherwise as aboriginal injustice, circulating in identity's inescapable authority in the triangle of locality, inexhaustibility, and ergonality.

4. To grant authority provides that something admits no questions, in the extreme the authority of existence and the world,[26] in the median the authority of the judge. Judgment exercises authority. Can we dream of judgment without authority, authority without judgment, endless judgment upon judgment seeking restitution for the violence of its authority?

The endless play of judgment upon judgment[27] restores and breaks the endless round of its authority. With what annihilation of history? What do we forget?

We return to the questionableness of truth's authority. "As long as words of difference serve to legitimate a discourse instead of delaying its authority to infinity, they are, to borrow an image from Audre Lorde, 'noteworthy only as *decorations*.'"[28] What may embrace the center of these reflections? "The political question, to sum up, is not error, illusion, alienated consciousness or ideology; it is truth itself. Hence the importance of Nietzsche."[29] The political question is truth itself. But truth works within its authority, politically. Questioning authority asks about the authority of truth. Authority and truth belong together. Can this conjunction represent the terrain on which Western philosophy has staked its authority, not on a glory beyond sound and touch, but on the autonomy of truth?

Does the truth of philosophy possess no authority while its entire history concerns its authority? Can the truth of authority reveal that it possesses no authority while its entire history concerns its authority? Does truth's authority echo as the propriety of the Master's Voice?

5. Can we understand the history of the West as the play of authority, questioning one authority to establish another? Can we understand it as one of Law? Shall we tell the story of the West's canonical authority in the form of Law?

> Underlying both the general theme that power represses sex and the idea that the law constitutes desire, one encounters the same putative mechanics of power. . . . it is a power that only has the force of the negative on its side, a power to say no; . . . it is a power whose model is essentially juridical, centered on nothing more than the statement of the law and the operation of taboos.[30]

Do we hear this enforcement of the Law as one of the techniques of power, to make itself appear as Power? "Power is everywhere; not because it embraces everything, but because it comes from everywhere. And 'Power' [under Law], insofar as it is permanent, repetitious, inert, and self-reproducing, is simply the over-all effect that emerges from all these mobilities, the concatenation that rests on each of them and seeks in turn to arrest their movement" (Foucault, *History of Sexuality*, p. 95). If this distinction between power and Power constitutes our relationship to Law, how may we understand the distinction between law and Law? Do these questions addressed to authority's unquestionableness circulate in the spaces—the *différends*—between power and Power, law and Law?

Some imposing questions perhaps easier to answer than the others:

6. If humanity is unjust, are we not unjust together, equally guilty? If humanity is unjust, by what standard of justice? We answer that the aboriginal injustice in which we share, to which we belong, older than time, than measure and law, owns no measure of justice, of equality or inequality. The injustice that belongs to law differentiates us as unequals before the law.

7. If nothing human beings do permits them to escape injustice, why attempt to escape it? What freedom, what liberation, echoes within archaic subjection except abjection? We reply that not to attempt to achieve justice under law, even a mythic, imaginary justice, repeats injustice. The impossibility of justice does not relieve the mythic force of archaic injustice. Relief and excuses fall under law, while the inescapable authority of the measure of the law precedes all law, all measure, even the Law.

8. How does archaic, immemorial injustice differ from original sin? If human beings are steeped in sin and imperfection, do they need God to save them? We respond that God cannot save us and, where composing a measure of perfection, falls into time as Law. Original sin marks our falling short of God's commandments. Immemorial injustice marks a vigilance God cannot replace.

9. Does unending restitution mean endless vengeance, retribution? Does justice's strife, *dikē*'s *polemos*, mean opposition, war? What restitution for restitution? What strife against strife but endless deferral? What restitution circulates for losses beyond measure, beyond mourning? What restitution, indeed, but one whose endless circulation silently memorializes immemorial injustice? What of forgotten losses, losses doubly, triply lost?

Finally, two questions *in extremis*:

10. What age comes before time? What before, what aboriginality? With what authority, privilege? Levinas speaks of responsibility to the other[31] as unlimited, inexhaustible: "The unlimited responsibility in which I find myself comes from the hither side of my freedom, from a 'prior to every memory,' an 'ulterior to every accomplishment,' from the non-present par excellence, the non-original, the anarchical, prior to or beyond essence" (*OB*, p. 10) and of

> A past more ancient than any present, a past which was never present and whose anarchical antiquity was never given in the play of dissimulations and manifestations, a past whose *other* signification remains to be described. (*OB*, p. 24)
>
> the very primacy of the primary is in the presence of the present. (*OB*, p. 24)

Do we hear a certain privilege, a primacy of the older, ulterior, prior, over essence, dissimulated as essence, losing its primacy? Do we hear authority's privilege emerge in the heart of immemorial responsibility, in every face to face, in every relation to others, even ourselves?

Can injustice's age demolish the privilege of its priority? Does it circulate as older but also younger than itself, older without authority or privilege? This older and younger, joined with injustice, claim a primacy they undermine. Perhaps one of the restitutions for injustice's injustice may transpire as the endless quest for a fountain of youth.

11. Does the immemoriality of injustice belong to subjectivity, to humanity, as Levinas suggests, or does it belong to beings, perhaps as

their being, perhaps as their otherwise? "Why does the other concern me? What is Hecuba to me? Am I my brother's keeper? . . . in the 'prehistory' of the ego posited for itself speaks a responsibility. The self is through and through a hostage, older than the ego, prior to principles" (Levinas, *OB*, p. 117). He calls it the "despite oneself" (*malgré soi*). Can we hear in the self's being to itself an otherwise beyond being, an injustice that belongs to being as a relation otherwise, a relation to others? "Whether he does anything about it or not, a person who has heard the screams of another person being tortured incurs an obligation?"[32] And for those who have not heard, an obligation to listen, even to what cannot be remembered? Can we hear beyond the self's relation to itself an otherwise, a responsibility, everywhere and in everything? Things pay restitution to each other for their injustices. May we say that injustice and restitution belong to local, inexhaustible beings in their work (*ergon*), a work always circulating toward and away from, in proximity with, other beings? May we say that nature's work undertakes a debt, an injustice, so immeasurable that all of time belongs to its restitution? May we speak of a debt in things, an injustice, a wound, that belongs to beings in their work, a work that wounds them, that endlessly displaces them despite themselves? How could we avoid such a debt, in things, whose otherwise echoes in the triangle of locality, inexhaustibility, and ergonality?

When Levinas tells us of our obsession by "all the others that obsess me in the other," leading to justice, what do we hear as the limits of the others?[33] We add that injustice echoes within this proximity as unassuageable debt. In their proximity, beings take up an unassuageable debt, an obsessive responsibility for each other that exceeds any restitution. Their responsibility imposes inexhaustible reparation, unfulfillable by any work, restored in every work, nature's *ergon*, work, as restitution. Nature's work endlessly repays the debt incurred by the injustice of the being of beings, their locality and inexhaustibility, their work, together.

With these many and difficult questions of the age of injustice and authority, we turn toward a new beginning, to trace the immemoriality of unmeasure as injustice throughout the Western tradition's legislation of truth's measure and law, also to trace the injustice of that legislation. If the age of authority has been repeatedly forgotten, it has endlessly reappeared. We seek to recall authority's oblivion, first in Hobbes, even Locke; then in Western law. We seek restitution for our tradition's injustice by another reading, another truth.

II

AUTHORITY'S RULE

> What is your work?
>   *questions of authority.*
> There's nothing wrong with authority.
>   *perhaps with some authority*
>   *perhaps with lawful authority*
>   *perhaps with every authority*
>   *perhaps every work threatens danger*

May we entertain the thought of an authority before any lawful authority, older than law, neither wrong nor right, in whose shadow every authority appears suspect? Why might we do so?

Consider legitimate, normal authority:

> acceptance of a certain degree of authority—which those subject to it regard as more or less legitimate, which they accept more or less easily, and which they challenge only exceptionally—is the normal state of affairs.[1]

> As an initial formulation: someone or something (X) is an authority if he (she, or it) stands in relation to someone else (Y) as superior to inferior with respect to some realm, field, or domain (R).[2]

We begin with superiority and inferiority as the norm, as legitimate, unquestionable, unexceptional—more or less. The world more or less divides into inferiors and superiors. Never mind slavery and colonization. Never mind race and class. Never mind the subjugation of women's bodies. Never mind subjection. "Executive authority is the right or power of someone (X) to do something (S) in some realm, field, or domain (R), in a context (C). When S is an action that X does to someone (Y), then Y is said to be subject to authority and X exercises his authority over Y."[3] X has a right to do something to Y that Y is justified in challenging only when abused, a right X possesses in virtue of power. At the very heart of this idea of authority lies that of subjection, to authority, to another, within normality. At the very heart of the idea of right lies the authority of superior power. Human life circulates within subjection to authority. It is, has always been, normal to be subject, to be subjected, to be brought under authority. Is it normal to be abject? Is the idea of a practical subject one of subjection? Does abjection lie at the heart of being a subject, within the hope of liberation?

> A crisis of authority exists. . . .
> . . . the structure of authority is crumbling in our society not so much because of injustice and repression as because of the erosion of its intellectual foundations. The philosophical assumptions on which authority as such, not just the authority of our existing institutions, is founded are being rapidly rejected in our culture.[4]

We experience a crisis of authority, not just in our culture, in relation to Western institutions, but authority as such, founded on philosophical assumptions. Do we hear in philosophy the rule of authority "as such"? Does the crisis rest upon suspicion of subjection, an attempt to elude our inescapable abjection? Why might authority as such have a foundation, especially a philosophical foundation? While some authority appears abusive, authority as such is founded. Or rather, Authority Is Founded, Normal, Under Law. Or rather, authority prevails, older than Law if not older than law, older than any norm.

Perhaps the crisis of authority threatens the possibility that authority has reached the limits of its own authorization. Perhaps the authorization of normativity in the normality of authority has become deeply questionable, especially toward those who have normal authority over others—parents over their children, husbands over their wives—who frequently violate others' bodies. Perhaps those who cannot acquiesce to authority cannot be subjected to it, only coerced, placed abjectly in subjection. Perhaps authority always imposes subjection, always coerces; perhaps what authorizes someone to do something to another prevails as subjection or as trust, and trust cannot prevail in general. Perhaps we have accepted as normal a coercive, destructive authority that perpetrates the idea of norms, not to mention normalcy for "us."

What procures normalcy as normativity in what we retain as Normal? What, in agreeing to the normality of subjection do we accept as normal? At one end of (our) history echoes Cicero, for whom "Law is the highest reason, implanted in Nature, which commands what ought to be done and forbids the opposite,"[5] so that "commands shall be just, and the citizens shall obey them dutifully and without protest."[6] No doubt the justice of the laws enacts the ground of their authority, but how can we avoid questioning the most sacred justice and highest reason that would compel citizens to obey commands without protest, to accept authority as normal?

At the other end of (our) history, Dworkin:

> We live in and by the law. It makes us what we are: citizens and employees and doctors and spouses and people who own things. It is sword, shield, and menace; . . . . We are subjects of law's empire, liegemen to its methods and ideals, bound in spirit while we debate what we must therefore do.
> What sense does this make? . . . that our law consists in the best justification of our legal practices as a whole, that it consists in the narrative story that makes of these practices the best that they can be.[7]

Practices that offer themselves as the best that they can be perpetrate a profoundly questionable idea, as if we might procure a supreme tribunal that could balance Job's miseries against his triumphs. The Book of Job speaks more wisely than that. More seductively, more insidiously, Dworkin's movement unfolds from legal practices that are the best that they can be to law's dominion over every facet of our lives except where it permits us otherwise. Dworkin presents a supreme challenge to law in his title, asks how it can possess unquestionable dominion. His answer repeats the privilege of law's authority, grounded in reason, blind to its injustices. Whatever we take as the highest form of reason, there we find law's dominion. Apollo's dominion!

And so we return to Nietzsche's truth, that reason's truth rests on Apollo's authority, that the truth of truth reenacts the will to power. But this truth echoes neither an identity of truth and power nor a fragmentation and dispersal of authority's authority—its crisis. Something strange unfolds within the force of authority, expressed by Derrida in his title, "Force of Law: the 'Mystical Foundation of Authority'"; in Benjamin's essay, "Critique of Violence," where he speaks of "other kinds of violence";[8] also, however obscurely, in Dworkin's view of the empire of law that exceeds any force reason might give it, transforming it into Law, poignantly expressed by Kafka in the story of the doorkeeper in *The Trial*. When the man who has spent his life waiting for admittance to the Law is dying, the doorkeeper, who has repeatedly told him that he may not be admitted at the moment, but may be admitted later, responds to his question with the words:

> "Everyone strives to attain the Law," . . . "how does it come about, then, that in all these years no one has come seeking admittance but me?" The doorkeeper perceives that the man is at the end of his strength and that his hearing is failing, so he bellows in his ear: "No one but you could gain admittance through this door, since this door was intended only for you. I am now going to shut it."[9]

The priest narrating the story denies any contradiction between the fact that the door was intended only for the man and that he could not be admitted at that moment. And we may believe the priest, may acknowledge these truths, though the space between them echoes enigmatically, in the domain of Law where K. finds himself throughout *The Trial*, between the inexplicability of the Law and the force of its authority. It marks a space traditionally filled by reason and justice. We may wonder whether the doorkeeper bellows in the man's ear to exercise an authority that, even in the weakness of death, cannot be challenged because it possesses no authority. The authority of authority, the force of law, presents a void, filled by reason and justice in their nothingness in general, but practically speaking filled by noise and shouting, by the force of orders and commands; by duress, coercion, subjection; by pain of law.[10] In the language of the Old Testament, "thou shalt" obey proper laws; "thou shalt not" do anything improper.[11] This truth—coercion, commandment, subjection—at the heart of law marks the ancient history of its Law. We may not agree that laws are commands, coercive, thereby granting them an authority that both carries the weight of the public force and repeats it, since that force, even when directly coercive by torture and death, presupposes and wields authority, an authority of fear exceeding any implementation.

So we return to Nietzsche's truth, wondering what the truth of authority may represent if anything but fear, anything but violence, whether the force of Law's authority persists as something beyond fear but resembling it, repeating it in its mysteriousness. Can anything institute authority but the means of its constitution: coercion, duress, subjection, violence?

A narrative awaits telling of the movement from the authority of Law to the law of reason, a narrative, Foucault suggests, of reason's madness.[12] Much of its nature mayderived from a careful look at Hobbes, who plays no minor role in this narrative, presenting authority's hidden face to us where reason no longer claims right as its due.

When we read Hobbes instrumentally, as in part we must, his argument reads persuasively, though it is drastically limited in scope. In the state of nature, "the life of man [is] solitary, poor, nasty, brutish, and short" (*L*, chap. 13, p. 107).[13] Several "laws of nature" follow, in particular, the "right of nature" that

> *every man ought to endeavor peace, as far as he has hope of obtaining it;* . . . .
> . . . *a man may be willing, when others are so too, as far forth as for peace and defense of himself he shall think it necessary, to lay down this right to all things, and be contented with so much liberty against other men as he would allow other men against himself.* (Hobbes, *L*, chap. 14, p. 110)

It follows that all enter into covenant with the sovereign "to be their *representative*—every one, as well he that *voted for it* as he that *voted against it*, shall authorize all the actions and judgments of that man or assembly of men in the same manner as if they were his own, . . . " (Hobbes, *L*, chap. 18, p. 144) and that the sovereign rules with indisputable and undivided authority. "Thirdly, because the major part has by consenting voices declared a sovereign, he that dissented must now consent with the rest—that is, be contented to avow all the actions he shall do—or else justly be destroyed by the rest." Because and justly. "Fourthly, because every subject is by this institution author of all the actions and judgments of the sovereign instituted, it follows that whatsoever he does, it can be no injury to any of his subjects; nor ought he to be by any of them accused of injustice" (*L*, chap. 18, p. 146).

Instrumentally, because the state of nature looms as terrible beyond belief, beyond thought, human life requires absolute sovereignty as if entirely voluntary to every subject, entailing absolute and unbroken authoritarian rule except for the preservation of that subject's life. Equally instrumentally we reply that it does not follow from the extremities of the state of nature that we must pass to the extremities of autocracy, that to achieve the end of peace we must employ authoritarian means. Democracy may represent the most effective instrumentality for achieving a stable peace within the imperative of political stability.

This reading and reply seem compelling—instrumentally. They ignore, or interpret entirely instrumentally, Hobbes's remarkable extremes. "Nature has made men so equal" (Hobbes, *L*, chap. 13, p. 104) that none can hope to possess any differential claim in relation to others, leading to insecurity and danger. Equality, security, danger, hope, desire—later, law, power, authority; representation and renunciation—pass from normal, instrumental limits to somewhere beyond all limits. Instrumentally, technically, each of these notions unfolds only under limits (while the "only" itself requires limits). Hobbes's undiminishing appeal reflects the inability of human beings to accept the limits of danger when caught up within them, the tendency for fear to become excessive. The unlimited dangers of insecurity and instability must match an equally unlimited power and authority with the purpose, again apparently instrumentally, of promoting order from within disorder. But no instrumentality can join such extremities.

Hobbes repeatedly writes *in extremis* as if that were normal, while normality and instrumentality presuppose everyday limits. It does no good to respond to Hobbes that at the present moment normal and stable conditions prevail, for danger, security, and authority represent extreme threats without measure, and we must place ourselves at the extreme, must guard against utmost disaster, must imagine the worst, imagine unimaginable terrors. Hobbes writes measuredly of what has no measure without telling us that unmeasure occupies the center of his writing. Of course, writing, with representation, has no measure—or a measure *in extremis*. Hobbes writes in a time of what has no time. In his understanding of the state of nature we find expression of Anaximander's fragment, of the age of injustice. Injustice, not justice, prevails older than time, older than what comes into being and passes away. Things must make reparation for the violence of their being, where this violence belongs together with their necessity and contingency. Birth and death transpire as violent, unjust, demanding endless reparation, mourning. Hobbes's state of nature unfolds, in its mythic and poetical being, from an injustice outside time. Inside time, inside civil society, justice falls under sovereign authority. Yet we remain within the state of nature.

How can the state of nature be terrible beyond measure, but still nasty, brutish, and short, traits of measure? How may we understand the order of time as reparation, except where Sovereignty and Law retain the archaic violence that composes them within their claims to reason and normality? Hobbes's instrumentality presupposes measure. So does the evil of the state of nature. Yet from the immeasurable authority and sovereignty of the state of nature law emerges, with justice, in a state of nature before Law and Justice.

If human beings were divided by their virtues and abilities in clear and measurable ways, if such divisions corresponded to discernible metals in the soul or to recognizable bodily configurations, if hope and desire were limited by such discernments and recognitions, then no absolute authority would be required to provide hierarchical social order. Do these represent the dreams of differences by birth, class, race, and gender that inhabit the West (and non-West)? Hobbes's extraordinary truth tells that none of these differences serves the slightest purpose, instrumentally, in providing social order, that, politically speaking, traditional forms of social hierarchy and privilege have no efficacy, no ground, that hierarchy rests on an unfathomable ground, for human beings are so equal that . . . : "Nature has made men so equal in the faculties of the body and mind as that, . . . when all is reckoned together, the difference between man and man is not so considerable as that one man can thereupon claim to himself any benefit to which another may not pretend as well as he" (Hobbes, *L*, chap. 13, p. 105). Hobbes distracts us from the enormities of this extreme view of equality by presenting us with another extreme: "the weakest has strength enough to kill the strongest, . . . " (*L*, chap. 13, p. 105). And still others: "And as to the faculties of the mind, . . . I find yet a greater equality among men than that of strength." "From this equality of ability arises equality of hope in the attaining of our ends" (*L*, chap. 13, p. 105). Returning to the extremity of danger: "And the invader again is in the like danger of another" (*L*, chap. 13, p. 105).

He seems unable to grasp, certainly to accept, the idea of temperance, of limits, in relation to authority and danger any more than to equality. And perhaps this truth in Hobbes represents something about the Enlightenment that speaks within its contemporary critique, against the critique of its technicality. For the equality of which Hobbes speaks, belonging to all human beings and deriving from nature, does not mark something essentially human, under law, but something contingent and empirical, capable of belonging to any creature, any thing. Nature threatens beyond all law. Human beings are so equal in mind and body, in power and desire, that none has any rights over others not divided by sovereignty and authority. Equality ensues without limit and without equal itself. No measure, it measures nothing. Correspondingly, power and desire persist without limit, without measure. Unlike those who see equality as a measure resistant to privilege, Hobbes takes equality to represent a condition that without measure resists privilege absolutely in virtue of the truth that desire and power have no measure, move beyond limits. In Hobbes, all those terms that have been repeatedly interpreted in the Western tradition as technical and measuring possess and impose no measure. They contrast in this respect with justice, which Hobbes makes a measure under sovereignty, recoiling from the possibility that an unlimited justice, without norms, might undermine the normality of natural law's equality.

We are speaking of slaves and servants, subordination by birth and by embodiment—women, blacks, yellows—every subordination except by history's contrivance. We are speaking of an equality so great that every measure of difference that would exercise a claim persists as arbitrary and unfounded except by sovereign authority. We are speaking of the danger, the terror, that such an equality imposes, a continuing, inescapable, irresistible war of every person with every person, founded on unlimited desire. And we are speaking of an unlimited authority in relation to which desire might reach its limits, for it has no limits within. All in Hobbes.

If equality provides and has no measure, if it derives from contingent, empirical human history while inescapable in its *extremis*, then no specific oppressions and dominations—themselves lacking measures—can follow from inequality. They belong to particular institutional structures arrived at through contingent histories and choices. Equality represents a pervasive condition without limiting sovereignty and authority. Rather, these persist as unlimited themselves, unmeasured, while particular privileges and oppressions contingently fall under particular histories. If equality provides no measure, then it neither supports privilege nor subverts it, but imposes historical representations of individual privileges in their contingencies and subversions.

May Hobbes's irresistible fascination lie within his excessiveness, marking the extremes of authority and order? May there lie at the dark heart of Hobbes's view of sovereignty an unassuageable terror of disorder, one that we find ourselves mirrored within? Even if we agree that this fear, of anarchy, assuaged by Law, by the *archē*, belongs to us all, including those who seem to lack it, what of this extreme equality that Hobbes does everything but give us? How does this belong to Hobbes except as another terrible fear—of the mob?

Do we find in Hobbes an idea of such an equality belonging to human beings, an utter equality beyond all measure, physical and mental, tangible and epistemic, that nothing whatever follows? This nothing composes the enigma of the state of nature—not a universal essence that pertains to all human beings essentially. For Hobbes tells us nothing about the essences of humanity, tells us only about the equalities that pertain to any human essences, in strength, capacity, intelligence, and so forth. Whatever human traits there may be, however these may be related to mind or body, human beings are effectively equal politically and juridically. Perhaps animals are equally equal; if not, they might be—again, except for human sovereignty. Perhaps every creature is so equal.

This utter, enigmatic equality presents itself without limits even where it appears to fall within limits, where its limits echo their names, for Hobbes acknowledges that human beings differ somewhat in strength and size, intelligence and experience. This "somewhat" means nothing at all, and nothing follows from it; a somewhat that gives way to unfathomable equality; an equality that does not stand under law.

Nothing follows except an utter, total fear leading to a total authority almost without limits. Almost, for this sovereign, who represents the people of his country even where they have not chosen, whom they authorize even where they have not authorized themselves, have not marked their names, gives rise to no resistance, no questions, up to the point, no matter what path or traversal, whether voluntarily or resistantly, whether in speech or writing, through fear or celebratively, up to the point at which the sovereign may perform any act without opposition— up to but not including their death, for the sovereign owes them their protection. "The obligation of subjects to the sovereign is understood to last as long and no longer than the power lasts by which he is able to protect them" (Hobbes, *L*, chap. 21, p. 179). Almost, for this sovereign does not, cannot, disperse the threat of war, which remains between sovereigns and states if displaced from civil society. If war presents the ultimate threat, then Hobbes's sovereign quite fails to diminish it.

Instrumentally, we may read Hobbes as asserting that protection of life represents the supreme human end, subordinating everything else. What danger to life, we wonder, could entail so extreme a subordination? Could life possess supreme instrumental worth? Hobbes approaches the possibility that, as human, the sovereign is subject to the same conditions as his subjects, and recoils: "But a man may here object that the condition of subjects is very miserable, as being obnoxious to the lusts and other irregular passions of him or them that have so unlimited a power in their hands" (*L*, chap. 18, pp. 151–52). He gives two replies, one instrumental: "the greatest in any form of government that can happen to the people in general is scarce sensible in respect of the miseries and horrible calamities that accompany a civil war, . . . ," the other something else again: "the power in all forms, if they be perfect enough to protect them, is the same. . . . the greatest pressure of sovereign governors proceeds not from any delight or profit they can expect in the damage or weakening of the subjects . . . " (*L*, chap. 18, p. 152). The sovereign represents his subjects—another unrepresentable—and exercises their authority, but not as a subject, not as a human being, free from subjection. The sovereign's authority, like his subjects' equality, exceeds any humanity, works beyond any normative authority. The equality, claimed as human, appears so incomplete, so indecisive on any account or practice, as to work without limits. The sovereign's authority unfolds with no limit, save one that appears fully instrumental except that Hobbes refuses any empirical implementation. The power of protection, the authority vested in it, possesses no limits, save death. It doesn't matter if the sovereign rules as nastily and brutishly as anyone in the state of nature—as a human being. The sovereign wields his power as a fictive person devoid of every human trait, wielding unbroken authority derived from unbroken equality leading to unbroken fear. The divine right of kings, unbreakable in Hobbes, rests on the king's absolute inhumanity.

Nothing follows, therefore, from equality, fear, authority, and sovereignty, nothing positive, nothing instrumental; above all, nothing superior. Hobbes rejects the idea of an intrinsic superiority from which instrumental authority might follow. Nature's authority, like its equality, destroys every superiority, moral or epistemic. Yet something follows, however noninstrumental, unspecific: resistance to whatever might threaten such equality, fearfulness, and sovereignty. The unbroken equality in humanity resists any instrumentality in inequality, exceeds every differential measure. Everywhere else, inequality of humanity justifies privilege and oppression, yet in Hobbes it resists any practice founded on inequality and injustice. These, inequality and injustice, like falsity and pain, move us without a measure, more like the sound of a musical instrument than a measuring rod. We can resist inequality and injustice without the slightest idea of equality and injustice, without the slightest idea of perfectibility.

We will think more of this enigma later. It expresses something fundamental in the idea of authority, another idea whose complement—liberty—moves us in powerful ways without perfectibility or instrumentality. This enigmatic authority lies at the extreme danger point of liberty and authority, where the principle that all human beings are equal works hand in hand with slavery, and where the freedom of those in authority leads others to gas chambers. The danger that we cannot draw a line to prevent these horrors by law repeats in reverse the saving grace that the lines we cannot draw protect us equally in our humanity or sentience. For equality and justice belong to animals and other creatures as well as humans, except by right and law.

Because equality, desire, hope, and power possess no intrinsic limits, only local limits, an arbitrary and unlimited sovereignty is required. Unlimited sovereignty is required to limit unlimited desire. Or rather, nothing can provide such limits while unlimited desire pervades unlimited authority. Hobbes largely ignores this proximity of authority and desire. Natural law permits him to do so, enacted as a covenant never instituted but binding, older than any institution. From the equality and fear that have no limits to an authority without measure, Hobbes's thought moves to an utter, total law from which nothing follows but resistance. Law repeats in its extremities the excesses of equality and humanity. It resists the instrumentality of Law.

The natural condition of mankind prevails as unrestricted equality and fear. The right of nature—*jus naturale*—repeats the unrestriction, still in a voice free from universality. "The liberty each man has to use his own power, as he will himself, for the preservation of his own nature—that is to say, of his own life" (Hobbes, *L*, chap. 14, p. 109). This liberty echoes in a voice free from measure, from Law, from perfectibility. This liberty, unlike the "liberty of subjects," has no measure, moves beyond law (but not beyond limits) while "Liberty, or freedom, signifies properly the absence of opposition . . . " (Hobbes, *L*, chap. 21, p. 170). "And according to this proper and generally received meaning of the word, a FREEMAN *is he that in those things which by his strength and wit he is able to do is not hindered to do what he has a will to*" (*L*, chap. 21, p. 171).

Human beings are so equal that . . . —an equality beyond measure, beyond Law, but not without limits, not Infinite. This equality unfolds beyond measure, because nothing follows from it that qualifies humanity, no properties, characteristics, or traits of human beings except for power, desire, and war, themselves beyond measure. Nevertheless, to belong to history, human beings' equality must possess proper limits.

Although no properties of humanity follow from this equality, some things follow, namely, a fear beyond measure, also beyond Law, without limits but not Infinite, a terror and an evil, beyond all measure, leading to a covenant and an authority, also without measure, in both cases almost without limits, but limited nevertheless. The immeasurability of the covenant reflects the Western scriptural tradition, for God's covenant with his chosen people belongs to them as if they chose it even where they would repudiate it.

Hobbes does not accompany these extremities beyond measure with a justice equally extreme. He does not follow Heraclitus, for whom justice, *dikē*, belongs together with war and strife, all beyond Law.[14] Hobbes places justice entirely under Law, in the human sphere of authority. In the state of nature, of war, justice rules by absence. "To this war of every man against every man, this also is consequent: that nothing can be unjust. The notions of right and wrong, justice and injustice, have there no place. Where there is no common power, there is no law; where no law, no injustice" (*L*, chap. 13, p. 108). No opposition holds between justice and injustice, right and wrong. These fall under Law. But justice, in Heraclitus, circulates with injustice, right with wrong, beyond measure and opposition. Justice in Hobbes circumscribes the limits of human life, under Law, echoing together with equality and war, even law, a justice beyond Law. It appears in the idea of natural law.

From an equality beyond measure accompanied by unmeasurable, excessive desire, the state of nature circulates as one of fear and war *in extremis*. What could temper, limit, such extreme strife and desire? Nothing can limit utter equality—though Hobbes beautifully marks the immediate transition from utter equality to utter authority, the greatest inequality possible except for God. He moves from an absent superiority to institutional autocracy and subordination, sovereignty undivided by privilege, a movement without mediation, magical, despite the famous arguments. For these represent instrumentality, depend on measurable security, and possess little plausibility. The instrumental arguments provide little plausibility. Terror needs no argument to support its dispersal at any cost, without measure.

Among the natural rights and laws that appear in Hobbes, one defines a liberty without social and institutional value, entirely vanishing in civil society; a liberty functioning solely to establish, through its unlimitedness, the unlimitedness of sovereign authority. From it follows the first natural law. "It is a precept or general rule of reason *that every man ought to endeavor peace, as far as he has hope of obtaining it; and when he cannot obtain it, that he may seek and use all helps of war*" (*L*, chap. 14, p. 110). The second natural law makes this establishment secure: "*that a man be willing, when others are so too, as far forth as for peace and defense of himself he shall think it necessary, to lay down this right to all things, and be contented with so much liberty against other men as he would allow other men against himself*" (*L*, chap. 14, p. 110). We return to natural law in general: "A LAW OF NATURE, *lex naturalis*, is a precept or general rule, found out by reason, by which a man is forbidden to do that which is destructive of his life or takes away the means of preserving the same and to omit that by which he thinks it may be best preserved" (Hobbes, *L*, chap. 14, p. 109). Natural laws regulate in general, universally. They impose a measure based on preserving life.

Even so, two things seem strange, one that Hobbes does not tell us what a law of nature may represent in general, only what it may represent in relation to human life. We might find this a logical error, after Plato, who tells us that every intelligible idea must fall under a generic heading. Such a heading suggests that a natural law provides a precept of reason as to what we may and may not do in general, regardless of civil institutions, in our nature or the nature of reason. Yet if we pursue the generic heading, we must find a way to move from the general to a particular law of self-preservation. Equality represents the only general we find in Hobbes. Similarly, the right of nature marks the liberty each (male) individual has to use his power for whatever he wills, but in particular to preserve his life in civil society. A gulf opens between natural liberty and the liberty of (male) subjects (in Hobbes).

The second strange thing emerges here, for from the right of nature and self-preservation Hobbes concludes that human beings have a duty to give up their rights and to enter a covenant beyond all covenants, without limits, based on a law without limits. For the sovereign may, with impunity and without challenge, enact any law whatever except that which would dissolve his sovereignty. So nothing concerning any individual law follows from natural law in general. Nothing remains forbidden except lawlessness, defiance of authority. Here we may distinguish law in general from Law as authority, where law in general materializes, like justice, inseparable from and unmeasured by unlaw, while Law concerns itself primarily with its own dissolution. Unlike Law, fallen into measure, law belongs to injustice, older than measure.

Archaically, in the state of nature, human beings have the right to pursue and repel. This pursuit—desire—and repulsion—power—belong generically to action, not specifically to humanity. And there prevail no limits of any kind to what we may desire or oppose, except the limits that reason introduces. But if desire and power, along with equality and war, circulate beyond measure, then reason cannot limit within the absence of measure, but must somehow introduce measure. The question emerges whether reason, of itself, in its nature, can impose measure, or whether reason finds itself beyond measure.

In Hobbes's extraordinary discussion we find the suggestion that reason as such knows nothing of measure. Reason's concern rests with natural law, and natural law repeats the unmeasured movements of desire and power in the state of nature, leading to the covenant *in extremis* upon which unlimited and unmeasured authority rests. Sovereignty represents unlimited and unmeasurable authority. This we read in Hobbes; and, further, that that authority provides the ground of measure. That explains why there prevails no Justice, no Law, in the state of nature, in reason as such, but justice under sovereign authority. Put another way, the right of nature supports no right at all if it protects whatever an agent might choose to do, for such a right protects nothing at all. Only under civil authority can such protection be instituted, can a differential right apply. If effective rights define differentia under Law, then in Hobbes no such rights appear implicit in nature or reason themselves. Rather, reason and nature, like desire, equality, liberty, and power, possess no intrinsic measure, belong to no art or *technē*.

Needed for measure, where law becomes Law, the authorization of sovereign authority rules, the sovereign as representative of all. Power works by representation, constituting a subject. The ambiguities of representation and subjection forcibly emerge in Hobbes: "A person is he *whose words or actions are considered either as his own or as representing the words or actions of another man or of any other thing to whom they are attributed, whether truly or by fiction*" (*L*, chap. 16, p. 132).[15] Fiction belongs to the idea of a person, of a subject, inherent in representation, where authority requires authorization. The entire idea rests on fiction, where representation joins misrepresentation.

> The word *person* is Latin, . . . which signifies the *face*, as *persona* in Latin signifies the *disguise* or *outward appearance* of a man, counterfeited on the stage, and sometimes more particularly that part of which disguises the face, as a mask or vizard; . . . So that a *person* is the same that an *actor* is, both on the stage and in common conversation; and to *personate* is to *act* or *represent* himself or another. (*L*, chap. 16, p. 132)

Authority emerges from this space of misrepresentation: "Of persons artificial, some have their words and actions *owned* by those whom they represent. And then the person is the *actor*, and he that owns his words and actions is the *AUTHOR*; in which case the actor acts by authority" (*L*, chap. 16, p. 133). Authority belongs to action in a sphere of appearance as if on the stage, where the performance receives authorization by the author. Sovereign power receives authorization from the covenant in which all find themselves whether they agree or not, a contract without concurrence. The authorization that grounds authority in Hobbes works as a fiction, an artifice belonging to its truth. Fiction, artifice, impersonation belong to representation as misrepresentation and to authority as to . . . —and here we stop. Does the other that belongs within authority, as misrepresentation belongs to representation and untruth belongs to truth, present itself as absence of authority, as resistance in power, or does it maintain authority in the ways that resistance belongs to power?[16] Can we find ourselves outside authority in its ordinance, its history? Or do we find the other to authority in the reader who understands the authorization, who belongs to history, succeeded by other readers?

Hobbes cancels the right of nature in each human being to resist sovereign authority, as if such a right and liberty had an instrumental limit falling under *technē*. We have noted the unpersuasiveness of his technical arguments when avoiding extremity. His fascination turns on the extremities of liberty and authority beyond *technē*. If liberty and authority rule beyond measure, always *in extremis*, then nothing can limit them, no *technē*, art, reason, law, or end. Rather, reason belongs to them immeasurably, as they belong to it. It follows that authority remains divided by liberty in general, including the liberty of subjects, who remain equal enough, excessively equal, to retain responsibility for understanding the work of authority. Authority's work becomes exclusive under Law as if belonging to a measure. According to a metrical, technical understanding, sovereign authority perfectly fits its purpose of protection and perfectly fulfills the covenant that establishes it. According to the idea that authority, sovereignty, and reason prevail archaically, beyond and older than measure, imposing responsibility on time, sovereign authority remains, as in Heraclitus' view of *dikē*, inescapably contested, challenged, resisted, because resistance belongs to the *polemos*, unmeasure, that no instrumentality can resolve. The unity of the state and the authority of the sovereign persevere subject to no measure, deriving from a truth, an authorization, an act of representation, without measure, themselves deriving from a state of war and fear beyond measure.

Part 1 of *Leviathan* ends with this immeasurability, concludes with an injustice older than time and *polis*, and with the ancient justice of strife and war. We require an equally aboriginal act in which this archaic justice outside time and sovereignty passes into civil order. Hobbes reenacts in his own terms the immemorial movement in which justice becomes a *technē* and in which authority becomes measurable, accountable. This act unfolds beyond any *technē*, any measure, as Hobbes virtually says in opening part 2. "For the laws of nature—as *justice, equity, modesty, mercy*, and in sum, *doing to others as we would be done to*—of themselves, without the terror of some power to cause them to be observed, are contrary to our natural passions, . . . " (*L*, chap. 17, p. 139). This terror of some power irrupts as a founding violence beyond all other violences, founding civil society, implementing justice and mercy. These belong to civil society while the violences from which they emerge derive from an injustice older than they, older than time. This terror, this violent power, that brings them into time's ordinance as measure, perpetrates itself as surpassing any measure. Hobbes, in the name of reason, repeats what Plato shows in book 1 of *Republic*, though Plato obscures it in the rest of the dialogue, obscures it because even this violence at the heart of state power cannot avoid challenge. Socrates' reply to Thrasymachus's claim that justice is the advantage of the stronger belongs to, presupposes, both civil society and *technē*. But to the possibility that the *polis* and *technē* both appear in an act in which the "stronger" has given up all advantage and authority, we find no answer.[17] We reflect upon justice, advantage, strength, and authority under *technē*, but there lies in each of them something that surpasses any art, any measure. *Technē* circulates in time and requires from us endless reparation to know the truth of the violence of its founding. This founding of *technē*, of measure, appears in *Oresteia*, where we may say the Erinyes represent the dark forces that nothing in human life can lay to rest. We find it also in Kafka's understanding of the Law.

Thus, the opening words of part 2 of *Leviathan* tell that we have moved from the archaic beyond measure to *technē*: "The final cause, end, or design of men, . . . is the foresight of their own preservation, and of a more contented life thereby— . . . " (*L*, chap. 17, p. 139). The movement from the state of nature to civil society, from natural authority to sovereignty, from a desire beyond limits to a power establishing limits upon every desire, rests upon a final cause or design of men. This final cause expresses a human *technē*, and comes from nowhere. For if we accept purely technical and instrumental considerations, and if the goal of human life is contentment, then the abuse of sovereign power offers grounds for its overthrow. In Hobbes, the founding of sovereign authority, beyond challenge, beyond limits, must rest on a design beyond limits, a design brought forth by an archaic movement, beyond measure, older than time, older than *technē*. The design of the *polis*, the founding of its authority, emerges as older than measure, older than design under *technē*, comes forth as fundamentally, inescapably unjust.

Hobbes brings the inherent violence in the measure of being to the foreground, as if it belonged to measure, placing it in the proximity of *technē*. Part 2 of *Leviathan* makes the transition from the state of nature to sovereign power based on an absolute and irrevocable act of violence and terror, contenting itself thereafter with instrumentalities deriving from the absoluteness of that terror. The violence at the heart of the instrumentalities of civil and political life materializes everywhere, unmasked. The reply to Hobbes (and Locke), that there has never been a state of nature, however fearful, that we have always found ourselves within civil authority, misses the point. The fiction of the state of nature expresses the archaic violence in the representation of being—where representation authorizes the exercise of authority. The most ordinary of hopes in relation to Hobbes, to overcome war and violence, persists as but a dream. The state of nature remains, injustice older and younger than itself. "[T]he law of nations and the law of nature is the same thing." (*L*, chap. 30, p. 277).

At the heart of sovereignty, of Authority, Power, and Law, lies a violence, an authority, power, and law beyond measure: the rending of *technē* from *poiēsis*. Once *technē* institutes Law, it offers instrumentality after instrumentality, testing the rules of conduct and governance. Inviolable human rights offer the same instrumentality as the calculation of goods and evils. Archaic authority and power, without and beyond measure, pass under rule and measure. More completely perhaps than anyone else writing on authority, Hobbes places us at the edges of authority's violence, where authority's law opens onto the abyss.

We then read Hobbes very differently, depending on whether we take him to present the formation of a commonwealth as an archaic violence, beyond rule, or the structure of a commonwealth after the institution of public sovereign authority. He makes the transition himself repeatedly; for example: "Having spoken of the generation, form, and power of a commonwealth, I am in order to speak next of the parts thereof" (*L*, chap. 22, p. 180). He can speak of the parts, the order, the system, the laws, of a commonwealth only upon assumption of its sovereignty, where the latter possess no truthful representation, no rules, no *technē*. Civil laws belong to a commonwealth as commonwealth. "By CIVIL LAWS I understand the laws that men are therefore bound to observe because they are members, not of this or that commonwealth in particular, but of a commonwealth [in general]" (*L*, chap. 26, p. 210). The generality and universality of a commonwealth do not distinguish civil from natural laws, authority under law from authority in the state of nature. The distinction does not turn on generality or universality, both falling under rules, under *technē*. It represents the authority of the state as resting on the authority of reason's truth, where reason rests on unspoken and irrational measurability.

Shall we protest that without *technē*, without measure, reason would have no truth—at least, no authoritative truth? The question of truth's truth—the reason why Foucault can say that the political question is truth itself—addresses truth's authority. Reason grants certain truths authority over others, establishing the authority of truth over untruth, knowledge over false opinion. In this respect, science represents a supreme violence founded on the archaic movement establishing its authority, calling for unending reparations, some of which we hope to repay here. The founding ensues as a fiction, together with the war in the state of nature, telling us of the inescapability of the violence. If it occurred, it took place before time, with time the ongoing working of the violence. We hope to found, bring forth, a certain reparation, always within and yet somehow beyond reason's authority. Always within, not only because we find ourselves inescapably within the law, but because we must grant some authority, belong to some commonwealth, and any would contain within itself a similar violence. We hope to find a way to interrogate the inescapable extremity in authority, every authority, including our own, including the writing that would challenge that authority, without giving up all authority.

When Hobbes speaks of civil laws, he speaks within the commonwealth, of the debate over whether civil laws represent commands or whether they presuppose civil and rational authority.

> CIVIL LAW *is to every subject those rules which the commonwealth has commanded him, by word, writing, or other sufficient sign of the will, to make use of for the distinction of right and wrong—that is to say, of what is contrary and what is not contrary to the rule.* (*L*, chap. 26, p. 210)

> And first it is manifest that law in general is not counsel but command; nor a command of any man to any man, but only of him whose command is addressed to one formerly obliged to obey him. (*L*, chap. 26, p. 210)

Can we find a right and wrong outside the commonwealth, beyond the commonwealth? That question represents one form of a continuing debate with Hobbes, found in Locke and continuing in contemporary debates on justice, in Rawls, for example.[18] It represents a very different question from whether we can address justice and injustice, right and wrong, from outside reason, outside *technē*. Hobbes presents us with a fictive narrative of the formation of the authority underlying the rules of practice and reason. Justice and injustice in general, reason and unreason in general, may still fall under *technē*. Under *technē*, right and wrong do not express "mere" commands, but originariness. Socrates replies in this way to Thrasymachus, Locke to Hobbes, Dworkin to Austin. All these replies miss the point. For in some sense, before, if not chronologically before, a rule can rule, a civil law can authorize, Authority and Law must authorize. What transpires as this before, this formerly, this archaic immemoriality?

Here we may deplore Descartes's deceptiveness, founding modern reason, as if within reason itself there might emerge an answer to questions of reason's authority, as if that authority were not violent. Descartes's predecessors were more truthful: Even God's authority, finally, cannot justify itself. Modernity came into being, with Descartes, as if the ultimate authority at the heart of Authority were indistinguishable from it, as if Authority could establish itself in God or Reason. Before that movement in Descartes, in the Greeks and Scholastics, authority's authority lay outside itself. In our time, we seek to challenge both modernity's authority and its view of authority—but not by giving up authority, which we cannot do. We cannot give up authority, we cannot desire to give up authority, but we can refuse to reauthorize its self-authorization.

Hobbes repeatedly brings to our attention the abyss between the founding of authority and its exercise. While he reasserts the authority at the heart of civil law, he reestablishes the authority of *technē* as if the abyss must hide itself within civil law. Civil laws express the sovereign's commands, but, once commanded, they obscure the strangeness of authority and law. "The law of nature and the civil law contain each other and are of equal extent" (Hobbes, *L*, chap. 26, p. 212). "The law of nature, therefore, is a part of the civil law in all commonwealths of the world." He plays out the drama that lies at the heart of the archaism of injustice. For once *technē* appears as the measure of all things, once reason falls under law, then the natural law—hitherto archaic, injustice and strife, demanding unending restitution—falls under measure and rule, rules us as reason and law. Where archaic injustice presupposes no justice, at least no Law of Justice, civil justice claims to belong to reason and law, even in Hobbes. Yet in Hobbes we see the possibility of confronting the archaic, the beyond, of authority's *extremis*.

We find ourselves resisting two things in Hobbes: (1) the movement beyond law as a founding, an origin, as if reason and law began, rather than as a continuing movement within law against itself; (2) the identification of lawlessness beyond and outside law with breaking laws. In a time in which we think of our history as a founding of laws by lawlessness and violence, we recognize that our time also presents the unforgettable memory of the destruction of peoples by colonizing violence.

We must not forget (or forgive) violence in oblivion to its originary foundation. The founding of law upon its breaking, its violence, does not justify its destruction. Lawlessness has no justification, as if it somehow belonged to law. Rather, the unmeasure of authority and violence belongs to law inescapably, within its measure. Something in law—in Law—surpasses any measure. That is Kafka's Truth.

We may follow the tradition in reading Locke as presenting the great historical reply to Hobbes, undertaking to consider that reply from the standpoint of the immemorial authority we have explored in Hobbes. Locke begins his second *Treatise of Government* in two ways:

> 3. Political power, then, I take to be a right of making laws with penalties of death, ...[19]

> 4. To understand political power aright, and derive it from its original, we must consider what state all men are naturally in, and that is a stage of perfect freedom to order their actions and dispose of their possessions and persons as they think fit, within the bounds of the law of nature, without asking leave, or depending upon the will of any other man. (Locke, *T*, II, p. 404)

We find in Locke the themes we found in Hobbes, if somewhat less clearly demarcated. Locke defines political power under Law, within a sovereign power, speaks of the state of nature as perfect freedom, a condition without measure or *technē*, since no rules apply, except for three qualifications: (1) This perfect freedom pertains to actions but especially to possessions and their dispositions; (2) this freedom is bounded by the laws of nature; (3) it is related to the will of other human beings, not to nature's circumstances. Locke appropriates Hobbes's unrestricted view of liberty and equality, but with a striking difference. "A state also of equality, wherein all the power and jurisdiction is reciprocal, no one having more than another; . . . " (*T*, II, p. 404). For Hobbes, human beings are so equal that no measure follows. For Locke, equality is reciprocal, "no one having more than another," so that "the state of nature has a law of nature to govern it, which obliges everyone; and reason, which is that law, teaches all mankind who will but consult it, that, being all equal and independent, no one ought to harm another in his life, health, liberty, or possessions" (*T*, II, p. 405). Equality and authority, in Hobbes, rule beyond measure. In Locke they possess intrinsic measure, expressed authoritatively in the following passage: "For men being all the workmanship of one omnipotent and infinitely wise Maker . . . " (*T*, II, p. 405). Human beings are made, along with nature, by their Maker; the law of nature follows *technē*, represents a measure, in this case their equality and, consequently, law and justice. Reason in Locke belongs to measure, falls under *technē*.

For this reason, Hobbes and Locke, though they appear contradictory concerning the state of nature, do not conflict. Can one doubt that concerning justice and community Locke has it over Hobbes, by justice's measure? I do not think so. Where we may challenge Locke concerning property and slaves, we cannot exempt Hobbes. But Locke's superiority falls under measure, as superiority must. Equality and authority in Hobbes impose no norm to which practice may be restored, but exceed every norm. Equality and authority in Locke unfold always tempered by the norm of good work. He distinguishes liberty from license though "man in that state have an uncontrollable liberty" (*T*, II, p. 405). And he denies absolute or arbitrary power in nature. "And thus in the state of nature one man comes by a power over another; but yet no absolute or arbitrary power, . . . " (*T*, II, p. 406). Liberty in Hobbes proceeds free from control except under an equally extreme authority. In this way, authority and liberty emerge younger in Locke than in Hobbes. They fall under Law.

In the same way, Locke can distinguish the state of nature from a state of war in terms of measure: "Men living together according to reason, without a common superior on earth with authority to judge between them, is properly the state of nature. But force, or a declared design of force, upon the person of another, where there is no common superior on earth to appeal to for relief, is the state of war; . . . " (*T*, II, p. 411). Hobbes and Locke, against subsequent international rules of war, agree concerning the state of war, that it exceeds all measure, that the violence, destruction, and arbitrariness within it, beyond reason, have no bounds, though they differ on whether the state of nature and absolute authority materialize beyond reason. We may agree with Locke only if we accept the limits of conflict in the state of nature to fall under reason's measure. International law, more than Locke and Hobbes, seeks to repudiate the excesses of violence beyond measure by bringing war under Law. We reply that, despite Hobbes, not only does war exceed Law, but so do reason and the good. Justice surpasses measure along with injustice, though in both Locke and Hobbes justice belongs to Law. Union represents excess along with conflict and war. This excess repeats the violence older than law.

Slavery represents one of its historical appearances, and when Locke repudiates slavery as entering into a illegitimate compact, he hopes to bring it under law: "For a man not having the power of his own life cannot by compact, or his own consent, enslave himself to anyone, nor put himself under the absolute arbitrary power of another to take away his life when he pleases" (*T*, II, p. 412). He does not repudiate the lawful slavery that places the slave's life in arbitrary jeopardy, expressing the fundamental difficulty of authority under law, continuing today. "I confess, we find . . . that men did sell themselves; but it is plain this was only to drudgery, not to slavery, for it is evident the person sold was not under an absolute, arbitrary, despotical power, for the master could not have power to kill him at any time, . . . " (*T*, II, p. 412). Leaving aside the movement from selling oneself to being sold, the issue addresses authority. For Locke, authority always falls under law—never absolute, arbitrary, despotic; never excessive—presenting him with the question why a restricted authority over a slave could not be just. He equates the excessiveness of authority with its unlawfulness, its being beyond law and measure with violating law.

This raises Hobbes's question, whether in thinking of authority and humanity we must think beyond, outside measure, outside all laws and norms, even as we always fall under laws, in order to grasp the unlawfulness of law's measures. We question whether injustice always falls under Law, in the history of Law's emergence, or whether injustice perpetrates an age before, older than Law, if not older than authority or law—an injustice that belongs together with justice in the strife that joins them.

Authority and injustice persist older than time, founded on violence immemorial, inescapable today in the generic violence of Law and the monopoly on violence demanded by state authority. What follows law tests authority by violence—capital punishment against self-preservation—in Benjamin[20] and Hobbes; by slavery, indenture, or institutional subordination, all representatives of inferiority under authority, subjected to its superiority. In Locke, however obliquely, the test of authority lies in property, not because, but in spite, of its youth. Natural law presupposes property. "[W]e must consider what state all men are naturally in, and that is a state of perfect freedom to order their actions and dispose of their possessions and persons as they think fit, . . . " (*T*, II, p. 404). This perfect and unrestrained freedom to dispose of one's possessions obtains beyond law, reflecting at least with respect to property (but not one's body) that one has total and unmixed authority. Yet such an authority belongs to one in virtue of one's body, labor: "Though the earth and all inferior creatures be common to all men, yet every man has a property in his own person; this nobody has any right to but himself" (*T*, V, p. 413). "It is allowed to be his goods who hath bestowed his labor upon it, though, before, it was the common right of everyone" (*T*, V, p. 414). Property, then, along with authority, belongs to everyone beyond measure in the state of nature, but belongs to one in particular based on bodily labor. Labor moves us from unmeasure to measure, presupposing a bodily measure. "The measure of property nature has well set by the extent of men's labor and the conveniency of life. No man's labor could subdue or appropriate all, ... Which measure did confine every man's possession to a very moderate proportion, and such as he might appropriate to himself without injury to anybody in the first ages of the world, . . . " (*T*, V, pp. 416–17). The first ages of the world work without measure, while all subsequent ages presuppose measure. For Locke, even beyond measure, labor determines limits to property. Property's attraction depends on its limitation by an intrinsic measure having to do with bodily size. Like Hobbes, Locke takes the physical limits of human bodies to constitute a rational basis for measures of power and desire.

This marks the point at which unlimited authority in Hobbes, beyond measure, becomes ordinary authority in Locke, intrinsically limited, measured. Property sets the crucial limits, what one can properly own within the range of one's strengths and labor. The propriety of one's individuality turns around the notion of property, based on two important characteristics, one its inherent limitation, the other its reflection of no particular traits of human beings. Even labor cannot make a piece of property properly one's own.

Foucault's reading of labor in the nineteenth century unfolds in relation to this intrinsic measure of human differences.

> *Homo oeconomicus* is not the human being who represents his own needs to himself, and the objects capable of satisfying them; he is the human being who spends, wears out, and wastes his life in evading the imminence of death. He is a finite being; and just as, since Kant, the question of finitude has become more fundamental than the analysis of representations (the latter now being necessarily a derivation of the former), since Ricardo, economics has rested, in a more or less explicit fashion, upon an anthropology that attempts to assign concrete forms to finitude.[21]

Labor defines finitude in Locke in the sense indicated by Foucault: "By this very fact, need and desire withdraw . . . " (Foucault, *The Order of Things*, p. 257). Need and desire, violence and authority, equality and injustice, all withdraw from their agelessness into the measured ages of the world where civil life and science exercise normal authority.

The Order of Things professes to be "an archaeology of the human sciences." We may take Foucault seriously, perhaps extending his reach, by asking how our questions of the ages of authority, old and young, apply to science and its authority—not merely the human sciences, as if the human were an essence without an essence and as if authority in the physical or natural sciences were unconflicted. Science presents itself as much younger than injustice. Yet we cannot avoid asking whether science perseveres unjustly, either under or away from law, along with any law of science. In reply, we ask whether a thought of science may emerge away from measure, an anarchical science, where anarchy moves away from any first principles, but not from principles.

We wonder about a science of the otherwise, otherwise than science, seeking the laws of authority as their injustice, refusing them authorization.

We have moved twice in the direction of archaic injustice's unmeasure, first in relation to Anaximander, where the injustice of all things haunts endless time and where time pays unending restitution. Truth and justice give the measure of an injustice without measure. Second, we have retraced in Hobbes a remarkable tracing, through the state of nature to civil laws, from unmeasure to measure. Hobbes echoes nature's archaic injustice, leading from *poiēsis* to *technē*. Locke, in reply to Hobbes, echoes the same traces, giving precedence to measure. Now we may hope to retrace the entire movement, going back again to Greece to trace a movement in which measure repeatedly seeks its unmeasure, in nature as well as *poiēsis*, Apollo's Dionysian soul. We hope to disturb the history of Law, especially natural law, as containing archaic law.

III

LAW'S INJUSTICE

If injustice befalls us older than time, and time's ordinance, its law, demands restitution by things to one another for their injustices, then it seems inevitable that justice be strife.[1] We hope to remember the injustice within justice and law, within every proportion and measure, remember that "all things take place in accordance with strife and necessity."[2] All things; and justice is strife. If strife perished from the world, all things would pass away. For things take place in accordance with their limits, struggling, working, together in proximity, in the limits of their limits. How can we doubt that this struggle in things belongs to their secrecy, to nature's love of hiding? How can we avoid wondering whether, if justice be strife, then injustice be peace: the joining of justice with injustice, war with peace.[3]

When Zeus gave Justice to humanity, demanding that they forsake violence,[4] did he forsake his own violence? Or does Justice presuppose a founding violence, mythic or divine,[5] within its prohibition against violence? How to understand this prohibition except as a violence demanded within the institution of law as part of Zeus's rule? Does this demand, this rule of justice over injustice, impose another violence, another injustice?

> That other road is better
> which leads toward just dealing;
> for justice conquers violence,
> and triumphs in the end.[6]

37

Does justice conquer violence, all the while enmired in violence? Does the peace it offers, as Nietzsche says, impose another violence? By what measure do we find justice better, and does the presence of a measure impose another of justice's violences?

Athena recoils before the blood spilt upon the house of Atreus:

> Too mighty is this matter, whose'er
> Of mortals claims to judge hereof aright.
> Yea, me, even me, eternal Right forbids
> To judge the issues of blood-guilt, and wrath
> That follows swift behind.[7]

No measure of judgment rules, no justice, not one divine, within eternal Right. Yet time and fate hold us in their grip.

> Yet, as on me Fate hath imposed the cause,
> I choose unto me judges that shall be
> An ordinance for ever, set to rule
> The dues of blood-guilt, upon oath declared.
>
> *Look on this cause, discriminating well,*
> *And pledge your oath to utter nought of wrong.*
> (Aeschylus, *E*, p. 288)

No measure holds, no law, but injustice calls upon us to discriminate well and utter no wrong. These seem simple tasks, within law, but utterly beyond fathoming when instituting law. The Furies know:

> Now are they all undone, the ancient laws,
> If here the slayer's cause
> Prevail; new wrong for ancient right shall be
> If matricide go free.
> (Aeschylus, *E*, p. 288)

Ancient justice will be destroyed if Orestes prevails. And it represents the only justice we know. The measure of right and wrong, of blood and guilt, shall be cast down. No measure, no justice, can weigh the moment of destruction. Justice here is war, not bloodshed once more, for we hope to do no wrong, but is strife against norms, anarchy, destroying ancient laws. Justice repeats injustice.

The Erinyes, in their fury, pursue Justice unrelentingly, creatures of its authority.

> Yea, whatso'er befall, hold thou this word of mine:
> *Bow down at Justice's shrine,*
>   (Aeschylus, *E*, p. 289)

Bow down to Justice's rule and law, thereby undertaking its violence.

> Venom of vengeance, that shall work such scathe
> As I have suffered; where that dew shall fall,
> Shall leafless blight arise,
> Wasting Earth's offspring,—Justice, hear my call!—
>   (Aeschylus, *E*, p. 298–99)

The Erinyes reenact the violence of ancient law, venomous vengeance without mercy. Mercy here does not repeat ancient authority, does not institute another power allowing those who obey it to escape destruction, but exercises a right to impose another authority, another justice. The Furies understand another authority, another power, to countermand their own, the very nature of authority. They understand its injustice.

> Woe on you, younger gods! the ancient right
> Ye have o'erridden, rent it from my hands.
>   (Aeschylus, *E*, p. 288)

For the judges' vote ties. No rule can measure justice. The rule of justice belongs to injustice. Yet time permits no escape from judgment—from justice or injustice. Athens covenants with injustice in the name of justice, implementing another rule of law.[8]

The emergence of a new community would be impossible without a new law, a new justice, inseparable from the injustices that institute it, that it must retain within it, demanding unending restitution, paid by mourning. The measure of law repays the violence that lies at its heart by continuing violence against injustice and by accepting its own contingencies. In the name of another justice, every rule of justice shall be brought down, restitution for its injustice. In the name of justice! In the name of its authority! Brought down! "For god delights to put down all those who are exalted."[9]

The truth of justice repeats the injustice of the Same. The age of injustice echoes the aboriginal injustice in every authority, including the unjust authority of every law. This represents the One in every law. Returning to Heraclitus:

> To god all things are beautiful and good and just; but men suppose some things to be just and others unjust.[10]
>
> The way up and the way down are the same.[11]
>
> Listening not to me but to the logos, it is wise to acknowledge that all things are one.[12]

And Parmenides:

> Along this road there are very many indications that what is is unbegotten and imperishable; for it is whole and immovable and complete. Nor was it at any time, nor will it be, since it is now, all at once, one and continuous.[13]

If the *logos* represents measure, then its Same represents Law. Yet the One, in Heraclitus and Parmenides, has no law, no measure, institutes itself in unending, unmeasured repetition. The One of the *logos* stands in the strife of injustice and justice that gives rise to measure. The One of Parmenides stands beyond measure, beyond the strife of opposition and negation, held fast by the goddess of Justice not "to allow it to come into being or pass away."[14] In Parmenides, then, justice endures older than time—forever older, and forever one, undivided. Does this represent the Same as Injustice, at least before the ordinance of time?

Even Protagoras, in Plato's account, presents the coming of justice as an event outside form and law, outside *technē*: "Hermes asked Zeus how he should give justice and respect to men. 'Shall I distribute them as the arts were distributed . . . or to all alike?' 'To all alike,' said Zeus; 'let all have their share'" (*Protagoras* 322cd). This share, all alike, leaves the one—injustice—outside rule, outside norms, outside *polis* and law. Justice and law presuppose not a law of justice, as if such a law might impose a measure of humanity and law, but injustice without law or measure, from which justice emerges as measure, retaining its injustices. Injustice persists as a One, in every law and form, but not as form or law. This injustice, this one, silently echoes when we speak of the inescapability of war and violence—the violence of justice, law, and peace. For inside law, we do not remember its lawlessness. Inside justice, we do not recall its injustices. The violence that follows and undermines violence, the domination after domination that imposes justice, express the oblivion within Justice and Law to the truth of their injustice. This truth expresses why the political question is truth itself, the truth of the oblivion of the Truth of Law to the injustices to which it owes restitution.

The history upon which we are here embarked seeks to recall this truth of law's oblivion as if we do not, might not, forget, as if we never have forgotten. And it remains essential to recall, as we trace the surfaces of violence and domination in law's emergence, that we cannot trace the violences of that emergence, only its surfaces. For the greatest violence of all, the most fearful, looms as the unknown domination, the authority, according to which nothing is wrong. We are tracing law's immeasurability in the Western tradition as if it had not been forgotten, back to Greece and forward, through the work of its forgetting. We recall forgotten injustice. We pay restitution.

A dark question emerges at the heart of our thought of injustice to ourselves and others, of our oblivion. Before we persist in our remembrance of the unfolding of Western truth, justice, and law as restitutions for the injustices of things, should we question the truth with which we have begun, the Greek understanding of justice as restitution? What perpetrates its injustice, and how shall we repay it? If we demand that we remember injustice in our acts of restitution, resist injustice as our restitution, how may we make restitution against the injustice of our own beginning, Western and Greek, the injustice of any beginning? What privilege do we grant the West if we restate questions of justice in the words of Anaximander and Heraclitus, Plato and Aristotle, Nietzsche and Heidegger, Whitehead and Foucault, Benjamin and Derrida, even Arendt and Beauvoir, Lorde and Trinh? With what injustice do we, can we, speak, with what authority and with what rebellion against authority, any authority? With what authority, Western, non-Western, or other, can we repudiate Western authority in the name of restitution?

To return to the Greeks in the name of justice: does that repeat Western injustice? Shall we follow in the footsteps of those for whom oblivion belongs to the West, to the Greeks, perhaps the Hebrews or Egyptians, asking us to recover our Western roots? Can we hope to question every footstep's silent tread, to question a following that we cannot avoid but do not wish to forget? Arendt, after Heidegger, set her model of the *polis* in Greece and never grasped the horror of slavery.[15] Heidegger accepted Hitler as the German leader and never paid restitution for gas chambers.[16] Do we find it incongruous to wonder if the Greek model, especially in Germany, in its "highest" or "proper" forms, betrays a certain privilege?[17] Do we find it incongruous to suspect every form of propriety, Greek or other, again especially German, even Nietzsche's?

We have noted Heidegger's denial that his return to the Greek imposes injustice.[18] "What is Greek is the dawn of that destiny in which Being illuminates itself in beings and so propounds a certain essence of man; ... " (Heidegger, *AF*, p. 25). Yet why repeat this certain essence in order to overcome it? Maybe "we Europeans" have no choice. But the others? If we understand the errancy that belongs to the nature of history as its injustice, how do we understand its destiny (*Geschick*)? "Without errancy there would be no connection from destiny to destiny: there would be no history" (Heidegger, *AF*, p. 26). Do we repeat the injustice of Western privilege in every movement toward the injustices that institute it?

A tradition rules in which The West belongs to Plato. "The safest characterization of the European philosophical tradition is that it consists of a series of footnoes to Plato."[19] If we allow ourselves the play of irony, remembering Kierkegaard, we must smile at the extremes framed by this hyperbolic claim, from Nietzsche to Heidegger to Whitehead. No doubt it is an equally safe general characterization of the Western philosophic tradition that every major philosopher sought to break with (and within) that tradition, from Descartes through Kant and Hegel to Kierkegaard, Nietzsche, and Heidegger. All proclaimed the end of traditional philosophy. Whitehead unashamedly claims to continue it, no less heretically. None of these self-definitions removes any of these authors from the tradition or repeats it.[20]

Santayana calls the same tradition "heretical."[21] He means by heresy an extremity difficult to associate with the idea of tradition, an excess much closer to the image of a history that owes unending compensation for its injustices, where every compensation both exceeds measure and enacts other injustices. Santayana's view of heresy leads him to question whether the authority of the Western tradition might lie in its unending challenges to authority, and how we may understand heresy itself to belong to that tradition. What if heresy represented philosophy's restitution for its injustices? What restitution might we demand for heresy's injustice?

Were we to follow Santayana,[22] we would hold that the works of the Western tradition have been excessive, granting us a certain oblivion in collecting them under the authority of that tradition while at the same time imposing endless reinterpretations of their excesses. Two forms of authority appear here, that of the tradition as a tradition, and that of the tradition's repeated challenges to every authority, including its own. The Western tradition institutes canonical authority in virtue of its repeated rebellion against authority. This represents Santayana's view. It also represents modern science, whose authority lies within its demand for rational authority, its demand for evidence and proof. The form of thought in our tradition that would repudiate every authority rules as our supreme authority.

The critique of Socratic or Enlightenment reason inverts this play of authority and insurrection without disturbing it. The liberating side of reason presents us with the greatest hegemony, that of science, technique, and law. Even in Nietzsche and Heidegger, the challenge repeats the play of authorization and departure: The critique belongs to and furthers the rebellious side of a tradition that seeks authoritativeness. It may provide comfort to think that this circulation of authority and insurrection belongs intrinsically to tradition, any tradition—and in a sense it does, except that every expression of this fragmentation and discontinuity engenders heresy.[23] Moreover, such a view of tradition did not always exist; it arose in time.

Tradition represents an interplay of belonging and departing, continuity and fragmentation. This truth possesses as much certainty in our time as any truth of tradition might, with the provisos that it belongs to our time, repeating the circulation of tradition, and that we do not think within it of its injustices and untruths. This truth came into existence and will pass away. It offers too reassuring an expectation that the tradition will remain secure in its departures. Heresy becomes orthodoxy. Restitution becomes reassurance. We enter another oblivion in which we cannot entertain the possibility of certain thoughts or actions because they do not belong to our tradition, as if we knew for all time what that tradition might become, as if we possessed its measure.

Our tradition belongs to the Greeks (leaving open for the moment whose identities circulate as "we" and "the Greeks"), while in that fact lie aboriginal injustices and violences. For the idea of origin belongs to the tradition of the Greeks (as does the idea of the "non-West"), and we would avoid its repetition while we attempt restitution toward it. Yet within that tradition, perhaps in others, the idea of restitution works its justice, restoring what has been lost in that tradition and compensating for that tradition's injustice, committing other injustices. We hope to remember, within this restitution, that it belongs to that tradition, leading to further restitutions, that this restitution disrupts itself. We remind ourselves repeatedly that we cannot take comfort in injustice. This restitution, against the injustice inherent in our tradition, in our writing, in every act or deed, institution or authority, promotes further restitution. But we cannot take comfort from that reassurance. Restitution cannot become another measure of retribution toward injustice, but always works within its own injustices, expressing why we cannot escape retribution, even retribution against retribution. The age of injustice belongs together with the immemoriality of retribution, each unforgotten, each unimplemented.

Against the Enlightenment view of reason as law, to which we will turn, some branches of Western thought have responded with defiance, hostile to law and reason; others have responded with grave suspicions of law's authority. This authority represents the Law under whose sway classes of human beings, not to mention animals and other creatures, have been oppressed. Law here represents subjection. One reply within the Enlightenment tradition circulates as insurrection, rebellion against the excessive authority present in Reason or Law, going back, as we have here, to the beginning in our tradition of authority and law, a beginning in the Greeks. Yet how can we avoid thinking of this reply as prototypically Western? Did the Greek view of authority originate elsewhere?[24] With what authority does Greek philosophy compel us?

Certainly Plato, if we continue to cite him, has no difficulty citing Egyptians and others as authorities.[25] Does this resolve our questions of traditional authority, or do those questions remain as they displace themselves? For if the Greek tradition expanded elsewhere in the Mediterranean, or if humanity began in darkest Africa, do we find ourselves present within this tradition still, in whatever divided way its authority imposed itself on us? If the earth was once a Western colony, and if it is no longer, does it remain Western as it ceases to work as a colony?

Gayatri Spivak criticizes the insurrectional repudiation of Enlightenment authority under law, in Foucault and Deleuze (she exempts Derrida), as reinaugurating the European Subject: "I am suggesting, rather, that to buy a self-contained version of the West is to ignore its production by the imperialist project."[26] This self-containment seems crucial to the West, both as a tradition and in the insurrections its injustices demand. Our question here, posed by Spivak out of her Western and non-Western authority, asks how to speak or depart from a Western self-containment that both colonizes its others and rebels against itself.[27] Yet while she questions the construction of the subject, Spivak hesitates at the possibility that the social realities explored by a critique of imperialism might represent another construction. For that the ideas of Reality and Construction, not to mention Critique, might belong to Greece calls for a reexamination of the idea of critique.

Spivak calls attention to the fact that "The West" represents a manufactured product in its self-containment and relation to its non-Western others. The recentered European Subject presupposes the construction both of a Subject by the European tradition and of Other Subjects elsewhere who may not Be European. The Non-Western Female Subaltern materializes here as constructed, Western, in any of her representations, as constructed as the European in any of his. This does not deny any subaltern's truth, but represents it as a truth dispersed throughout different constructions, awaiting others. Nor does it deny the justice required by the subaltern woman, but represents suspicion of her construction as either Western or non-Western. "What must the elite do to watch out for the continuing construction of the subaltern. The question of 'woman' seems most problematic in this context. Clearly, if you are poor, black, and female you get it in three ways."[28] To let the subaltern speak for herself remains within the injustices of law, for we know of no Justice and must beware of Law.

Our response to speaking for the poor, black, female subaltern or letting her speak from within the immemoriality of injustice marks both practices as belonging to a West whose members seek recompense toward her for the injustices she has suffered. One difficulty is that she has suffered injustices at many hands, not only at theirs. They cannot, then, bring justice to her, but must first seek to understand the conditions of her suffering. A second difficulty is that "we" do not possess authority to rectify the subaltern's silence, but must know it as another question of authority, hers as well as ours, but others' also. The forms in which justice and rectification may circulate, as emancipation, belong to a context in which we cannot avoid further restitution.

How comforting to accept the reading of Anaximander that to the conflict that lies within everything we can find a proportionate compensation! How comforting to believe that time will heal all wounds or at least make them no longer relevant! The age of injustice tells us that time has no such power, that its healing endlessly yearns for compensation without proportion. And this dark truth presents us with no new proportion. We cannot escape from time, but must, in justice and truth, refuse to belong only to time, as if only through time justice can prevail. Such a justice, in and through time, repeats the only justice we can find, but it cannot prevail against an injustice whose age exceeds all time, demanding a justice that exceeds all measure and a truth whose untruth exceeds every bound. No comfort rules in injustice, no comfort but that of injustice in justice.

We remember what happens to Western authority when every authority is delayed to infinity: "The West is painfully made to realize the existence of a Third World in the First World, and vice versa. The Master is bound to recognize that His Culture is not as homogeneous, as monolithic as He believed it to be. He discovers, with much reluctance, He is just an other among others."[29] As we hesitate at recognizing ourselves as "just" an other, we find ourselves impelled to recognize the fragmentation of the First World, the authority of The West in response to other cultures. The West's authority unfolds as one authority among others, dissolves into a multiplicity of cultures pervaded by heterogeneity, a heterogeneity that applies to The Greeks as much as to Us.

This heterogeneity of Western culture expresses a heterogeneity within the Same of West and Non-West. It suggests another Truth of Culture, except that we hope to defer its authority to infinity, to defer even the authority of deferral to infinity: deferral's inexhaustible deferral, with and without authority. Discovering the West's heterogeneity discloses an archaic truth covered over by Truth and Culture. Yet Heterogeneity does not represent another such Truth. And, perhaps more strangely, the Master possesses no Authority.

Yet The Master and His Culture belong to the authority of some culture, if without Authority. The unity and dividedness of The Master's Authority retain the injustices of their authority. The "just an other" repeats the exclusion of an only that appears in the rule of Western authority, claimed as Authority. Reason appears and reappears, again and again, on both sides of its authority. The Non-West marks the heterogeneity of The West by marking its own heterogeneity, thereby dismantling its authority in its challenge to the West.

Here, Greece as The West offers no more and no less Western hegemony than any other, while Greece as the recovery of the injustice (and justice) in Western authority offers no less and no more injustice or authority. The more and less belong to measure, while we address an authority older than measure. Once The West's Authority, Law and Master, shows its heterogeneity, the injustice lies in heterogeneity as well as in justice. The line dividing subjugation from authority constantly shifts in a tradition that seeks authority through reason and truth but finds that every such authority becomes Hegemony, Authority, Reason, and Truth. Whatever voice the female subaltern may discover, for herself, whatever heterogeneity it may disclose within Our Master's Voice, it will exercise excessive authority within a play of injustice and restitution, demanding another restitution beyond its powers.

To let the subaltern speak, as if we could, acknowledges that she possesses a truth without acknowledging the difficulties of authority and jurisdiction facing her. That she might, and does, speak, for herself and with authority and jurisdiction, falls into the heterogeneities and deferrals of truth, authority, and jurisdiction or law, all demanding restitution in the name of injustice. Law, here, speaks of authority and jurisdiction, filled with injustice. Justice and injustice relate as young and old, where each twists and turns around the other. The critique of Western hegemony calls for critique. The emancipation of the subjugated calls for emancipation. Our complacency at the thought that They as well as We exercise hegemony in their jurisdictions calls for critique and emancipation. Our critique of authority and justice after we have repudiated Authority and Justice, our critique of Critique, calls for critique, the age of its injustice.

And so we return to ancient law, seeking the alchemy of its injustice into Law. Read after Nietzsche and Whitehead, Plato offers an extraordinary example. For following our previous discussion, responding to Plato's double role, we may say that European philosophy represents a series of footnotes to Plato, because no footnotes begin to plumb the limits of his philosophy, of any philosophy, of any culture, that we determine our philosophical limits by how we read and reread Plato, along with others, as Western and non-Western. We return to Plato seeking archaic injustice.

In *Apology* Socrates appears before the Athenian court accused of breaking the laws of Athens. Against Meletus's claim that laws make the young good (*Apology* 24de), Socrates responds that human beings do so. Yet he never tires of the refrain that parents may not possess the skill to teach virtue to their children; in *Meno*, for example: "If anything—not virtue only—is a possible subject of instruction, must there not be teachers and students of it?" (*Meno* 89d). "All I can say is that I have often looked to see if there are any, and in spite of all my efforts I cannot find them, . . . " (*Meno*, 89e). We may read this in many ways, but one seems worth emphasizing: nothing makes human beings virtuous, Nothing makes human beings knowledgeable, where this making belongs to *technē*. Virtue does not belong to *technē*; nor perhaps does philosophy. If they possess authority, that of the good or truth, it does not rule by art or law, knowledge or truth. Truth and goodness belong to magic more than to rule, produce fascination more than efficacy. "At this moment I feel you are exercising magic and witchcraft upon me and positively laying me under your spell until I am just a mass of helplessness" (*Meno*, 80ab). Socrates, in the production of truth, produces helpless perplexity by enchantment. Here, in *Meno* at least, truth belongs not to rule, to law, to *technē*, possesses no authority, but wrestles with and against every authority. The towering achievement of the Athenian court of law was to put Socrates to death rather than—in Plato's language—"to escape from doing wrong," to avoid injustice. In Plato's earliest writings, injustice precedes and follows justice and law, whose courts represent models of wrongdoing.

Socrates' death makes mockery of any justice in law, reasserts the primordiality of injustice. Can we imagine that, after Socrates, Plato might take justice to be ruled by law, by rule? Can we imagine that Plato might suppose that some truth possessed such authority that it might rule over the life of Socrates? Must not Plato's writing, must not our philosophical writing, endlessly mourn Socrates' death, not by providing means ensuring that it will never again occur—for no such means prevail—but by paying tribute to it, compensating for it, seeking restitution?

Like *Phaedrus*, *Laws* takes place outside the city, outside law and justice. We speak on law from outside law—though without finding any such location. We speak on law as if it might belong to *technē*, though like justice it moves closer to chance than purpose.

> Man never legislates at all; our legislation is always the work of chance and infinitely varied circumstance.... In view of such facts one might be moved to say, as I have just done, that no law is ever made by a man, and that human history is all an affair of chance. (*Laws*, 709ab)

> That God is all, while chance and circumstance, under God, set the whole course of life for us, and yet we must allow for the presence of a third and more amenable partner, skill. (*Laws*, 709c)

Technē comes third after God and chance. How, we ask, can justice and law move from third to first, to the best and most authoritative of all, except by injustice? Does this language of first and third repeat the injustice of things before time?

"There are two different kinds of good things, the merely human and the divine..." (*Laws*, 631c). We have the dependence of human law on the divine, but divine laws include not only wisdom but sobriety (*sōphrosynē*) and righteousness, all given precedence over health and wisdom. Yet *sōphrosynē* clips the wings of desire in *Symposium* and *Phaedrus*, repeating to excess in *Laws* the form of *Republic*'s truth:

> In the first place, we shall absolutely prohibit the taste of wine to boys under eighteen.... In the next, while we permit a moderate use of wine to men under thirty, we shall absolutely forbid carousing and free potations. But when a man is verging on the forties, we shall tell him, after he has finished banqueting at the general table, to invoke the gods, and more particularly to ask the presence of Dionysus in that sacrament and pastime of advancing years—I mean the wine cup. (*Laws*, 666bc)

The ages repeat the restrictions on the stages of instruction in *Republic*, in a comical context of sobriety, drinking, and singing. Singing is mandatory here, as philosophy was mandatory in *Republic*. And we recall Dionysus. The result appears as excessive righteousness, repeated in relation to virtue.

> The spell we have described must be recited without intermission by everyone, adult or child, free man or slave, man or woman; in fact the whole city must repeat it incessantly to itself in forms to which we must somehow contrive at all costs to give inexhaustible variety and subtlety, so that the performers' appetite for their own hymnody and enjoyment of it may persist unabated. (*Laws* 665c)

We wonder at the enjoyment. And we may wonder even more whether this incessant thirst for righteousness without intermission does not belong intrinsically to law, to *technē*'s injustices, repeated later. "The life of the aspirant to victory at Olympia or Pytho leaves no leisure for any other tasks whatever, . . . " (*Laws* 807d).[30] This, under *Technē*, expresses a Righteousness to kill a Socrates. Here, in *Laws*, Plato mocks those for whom the righteous life might be happy, presents us with a frenzy, an excess, of Righteousness in the name of Dionysus. If Law unfolds as Dionysian, if Justice, under *Technē*, represents excess, then what it exceeds, what it destroys, represents restitution for its own injustice. Restitution becomes "Restitution," marked for us by a dose, a *pharmakon*, of hemlock.

This excess, which appears in one form in *Symposium*, *Phaedrus*, and *Republic*, appears again in *Laws*, but differently. For philosophy exceeds *technē* in *Republic* as desire for beauty exceeds all ordinary desires in *Symposium* and *Phaedrus*. Here, in *Laws*, such excesses fall into righteousness, into justice, into the restitutions they purport to offer for their own injustices. They procure more and excessive virtue to the point of injustice. The form of the mandate, of the demand, to sing, to obey law, to be righteous, that very form, that law, represents supreme injustice. Righteousness itself, within law, law itself, represents injustice, exceeds law.

On such a reading, the passages in *Laws* and *Statesman* that speak to the authority of law rewrite themselves. For that authority, Plato tells us, again and again, is unjust; and the authority with which that claim is made is unjust. "In one sense it is evident that the art of kingship does include the art of lawmaking. But the political ideal is not full authority for laws but rather full authority for a man who understands the art of kingship and has kingly ability" (*Statesman* 294a). If there rules an art of kingship, his citizens must grant the king full authority, as in *Republic*. If there rules no such art, then the citizens must grant lawmaking full authority. "Then so long as men enact laws and written codes governing any department of life, our second-best method of government is to forbid any individual or any group to perform any act in contravention of those laws" (*Statesman* 300c).[31] Yet even if such an art exists, based on a scientific truth (*epistēmē*) (a mighty claim), and even if it is joined with law, its best marks a distinction indistinguishable from its worst:

> The rule of one man, if it has been kept within the traces, so to speak, by the written rules we call laws, is the best of all the six. But when it is lawless it is hard, and the most grievous to have to endure. (*Statesman* 302e)

> If therefore all three constitutions are law-abiding, democracy is the worst of the three, but if all three flout the laws, democracy is the best of them. (*Statesman* 303b)

Here, in *Statesman*, excess is kept within the traces by law. In *Laws*, however, law itself becomes excessive, with nothing to keep it in bounds. The excess belongs to authority, whether scientific or political. Plato expresses exquisite sensitivity to the excessive force of authority and its relation to truth. *Meno* suggests that no authority, epistemic or ethical, can authorize itself. *Statesman* and *Laws* suggest that every authority becomes excessive. The dream of liberation pertains not only to freedom from the tyranny of excessive authority and desire, but to the tyranny of its own authority. Laws inhabit this extraordinary space of authority, enforcing rules and bounding rule.

Reality tempers the dream of a true art of rule: "In one do we find a willing sovereign with willing subjects; in all a willing sovereign is controlling reluctant subjects by violence of some sort" (*Laws* 832c). We may interpret these words to represent the resistance of subjects to being ruled. We may interpret them instead to represent the unboundedness of every authority, subjecting us to limits' dangers. Authority's injustice calls for restitution after restitution, appearing in time as reluctance and violence.[32]

The most famous belief ascribed to Plato in relation to injustice is that everyone must seek the good.[33] It follows, for a Socrates faced with exile or death, that one cannot defy the laws. "Do you imagine that a city can continue to exist and not be turned upside down, if the legal judgments which are pronounced in it have no force but are nullified and destroyed by private persons?" (*Crito* 50b). Yet the laws do not define right and wrong but represent the unending demand injustice places upon us to resist, to rectify and restitute. Socrates cannot both belong to and violate the *polis*. One cannot pick and choose among injustices, among laws, as if we possessed a measure. Socrates was taken to have violated Athenian law. Our revulsion to his death shows that law does not set the standard of justice and injustice, does not define the limits of authority. Socrates' role as gadfly represents unending restitution in time, in the *polis*, for the unending play of injustice that belongs to things beyond measure. The wrong that we must not return represents the injustice that exceeds all measure, in which we find ourselves inescapably caught in the form of unending restitution, again exceeding all measure, including our own death, where law as measure contains within its authority something beyond all measure.

This understanding represents how we may understand *Minos*, spurious or not. Law materializes here as neither institutional nor authoritative: "Law, therefore, is not things established by law."[34] Rather, law (*nomos*) "wishes to be the discovery of being,"[35] "is the invention of being."[36] *Nomos* exceeds any standard in things, even one given by being. It inhabits the region where being opens to us, the region of its injustice and our striving for restoration. *Minos* represents this unending struggle as a movement from the disclosure to the invention of being, to the incessant play of justice's injustice.

Wherever nature's law appears in Plato, authorizing political undertakings, it appears in profoundly questionable forms. No truth, no law, follows from nature; in their injustice they require from us repeated compensation for any authority, any standards or norms, that arise as compensation for their injustice.

> Law can never issue an injunction binding on all which really embodies what is best for each; it cannot prescribe with perfect accuracy what is good and right for each member of the community at any one time. The differences of human personality, the variety of men's activities, and the inevitable unsettlement attending all human experience make it impossible for any art whatsoever to issue unqualified rules holding good on all questions at all times. (*Statesman* 294bc)

Plato never repudiates this view of law, never overcomes these deficiencies of any invariable and unqualified standard in relation to time. The repeated appearances of such laws cannot, then, represent standards, but express the excesses of any temporal standard. The idea that nature and ideas represent standards against which all human standards receive their measure cannot on our reading be Platonic. Rather, we read Plato as following the Anaximander fragment closely, where the norms and authority of human laws do not receive authorization from the Ideas, but where the latter represent the injustices for which all time pays restitution. On this reading, the indefinite dyad, beautifully expressed in *Philebus*, speaks to law directly without a standard. "And we must do the same again with each of the 'ones' thus reached, until we come to see not merely that the one that we started with is a one and an unlimited many, but also just how many it is" (*Philebus* 16d). The how many speaks to a measure in the one and many, and we read this passage as acknowledging the truth of measure. Yet it continues:

> But we are not to apply the character of unlimitedness to our plurality until we have discerned the total number of forms the thing in question has intermediate between its one and its unlimited number. It is only then, when we have done that, that we may let each one of all these intermediate forms pass away into the unlimited and cease bothering about them. (*Philebus* 16e)

We do not stop with the intermediate, with the number of forms between, however exactly we can determine them, but let them pass away into the unlimited, to which they pay restitution! The indefiniteness of the dyad pervades it and remains at every moment within it, pertaining to the One, the Many, and the Intermediate in different forms of indefiniteness. The definite, here, compensates the indefinite, following the deficiencies of the invariable and unqualified in relation to time. These represent the continuing injustice and strife in nature, temporal or invariable.

The injustice that belongs to things, to which we and others pay unending restitution, circulates older than time. This theme of age and youth in relation to law echoes throughout Plato's writings, but perhaps most explicitly in *Parmenides*, where it echoes repeatedly.[37] The young Socrates receives rebuke from the older Zeno and the much older Parmenides for his naive view of Ideas, but especially for neglecting nonbeing: "If you want to be thoroughly exercised, you must not merely make the supposition that such and such a thing *is* and then consider the consequences; you must also take the supposition that that same thing *is not*" (*Parmenides* 136a). Youth plays out repeatedly in Plato in relation to philosophy, in *Republic* and *Laws* as unreadiness and inexperience, in

Socrates' history in relation to corrupting the young and the impossibility of imparting virtue to them, in *Parmenides* twice, first in relation to truth, where a youthful eagerness for philosophy appears as *polemos*, strife, against the more temperate, nonpolemical pursuits of the older philosopher, second in relation to being, whose self-sufficiency cannot be accepted, always riddled and undermined by what is not, by what is younger and older.

Here, in philosophy's self-relation and relation to nature, we find age and youth pertaining to philosophy itself, whose beloveds belong to it differently in virtue of their age and youth. Without youthful exuberance, how could philosophy find itself moved by desire? Without mature dispassion and compassion, how could truth come to light? Age and youth meet *philia* and *sophia*. As age and youth circle around each other in time, so love and wisdom circle around each other—in time, as restitution for something older than time.

For young and old relate to each other outside time, where injustice and nonbeing circulate older than time. This older belongs to nature in a strange way. *Parmenides* is full of this strangeness. Socrates speaks of it directly, speaks explicitly of the enigmatic restitution for the age of injustice, when he responds that "there would be no end to such an undertaking" (*Parmenides* 136c). There persists no end to the restitution of things to their injustice, of being to nonbeing, both because they unfold older than time and because there rules no measure of compensation.

In time, under law, truth opposes falsehood and injustice, evil. The age of injustice, before time, falls somewhere else, away from this opposition, into unending restitution. Time, here, belongs to justice and injustice, truth and untruth, being and nonbeing, in an incessantly unfamiliar way. Parmenides speaks of this strange temporality several times in the dialogue, where he pursues the nonbeing of the One, a discourse both unsuitable for and required by "a man of his age" (*Parmenides* 136e). The themes of younger and older echo among the protagonists of the dialogue, but they ring in the very heart of the One. Under the hypothesis that "there is a *one*" (*Parmenides* 137c):

> Such a thing cannot, then be either older than, or of the same age with, anything.
> Therefore the one cannot be younger or older than, or of the same age with, either itself or another. (*Parmenides* 141a)

> Therefore the one has nothing to do with time and does not occupy any stretch of time. (*Parmenides* 141e)

But also:

> So if the one is, it is in time. (*Parmenides* 152a)

> So, since the one is becoming older than itself, that self must be becoming younger.
> Therefore, in this sense, it is becoming both younger and older than itself. (*Parmenides* 152b)[38]

In time, the one prevails as older and younger than the others. But how both? How older and younger than itself? How older than time?

At the end we return to the point from which we departed, appearing to give up the intelligibility of discourse: "It seems that, whether there is or is not a one, both that one and the others alike are and are not, and appear and do not appear to be, all manner of things in all manner of ways, with respect to themselves and to one another" (*Parmenides* 166b). The alternative remains that all manner of things in all manner of ways, younger and older than themselves, do not destroy discourse, indeed, that the possibility of discourse depends on this excess of injustice.

The Anaximander fragment tells that the ordinance of time as *polemos* pays unending restitution for the injustice, the *adikia*, of things before, outside, or exceeding all time. Injustice, for which justice pays unending restitution, inexhaustible compensation, belongs to no time, no measure, but makes measure possible, gives rise to law. Law belongs to justice with its restitutions and measures. Truth, Law, Justice, belong to the ordinance of time, and pay unending restitution. But no truth circulates except with an untruth that exceeds any measure of truth, an untruth that does not presuppose truth, an untruth that pertains to all manner of things in all manner of ways.

Parmenides tells two things in the dialogue. First, that essence and form, especially in relation to being and virtue, occupy a conflicted space in which discourse repeatedly echoes on the edge of collapse, either into the unwarranted authority of a form or essence that cannot withstand critique, or into the absence of all authority.[39] The polemical space belongs to authority, here to *technē*, which does not overcome the strife though its unending task pursues restitution. Essence and form persist as necessary, inescapable, and conflicted. Second, however, we find ourselves accepting the challenge of *technē* always too soon, requiring a thought of something older, before *technē*, older and younger than itself. This older and younger fall outside *technē*, outside essence and form, fall away into the indeterminate together with *technē*. They do not replace it. No thought of injustice obtains that does not fall into time, under law, toward an essence of justice. No truth unfolds that does not seek establishment in time. But this establishment in time belongs to Truth, and will forever come forth too soon without the untruth from which it emerged.

Our reading of Plato in relation to the age of injustice barely touches on the play of the dialogues at the edges of the city where justice and law meet the injustice of Law.[40] It may yet enable us to review the appearance of justice in those who footnote Plato without reflecting on the injustice's age, as well as the appearance, in Plato as in Hobbes, of authority's excesses beyond law.

Against, or alongside Plato, we find Aristotle's law, repeating one side of Plato, the *polemos* within *technē* between necessity and insufficiency, in the voice of *epistēmē*: "All instruction given or received by way of argument proceeds from pre-existent knowledge" (*Posterior Analytics* 71a);[41] "the proper object of unqualified scientific knowledge is something which cannot be other than it is" (*Posterior Analytics* 71b). Scientific knowledge (*epistēmē*) concerns what cannot be otherwise, what is necessary, under law. Yet the knowledge itself cannot in the same way be necessary; it presupposes a necessity before necessity, a propriety before propriety. What proceeds from preexistent knowledge represents an age before all knowledge, all truth and science. Before something can be known by way of argument, something must be known without argument or ground, without necessity. Something with authority must precede any establishment of authority. Science, here, repeats the age of injustice in the form of authority for its own authority. For while the objects of science may be necessary, scientific knowledge might not be, though Aristotle calls it "unfailingly true" (*Posterior Analytics* 100b). "All men by nature desire to know" (*Metaphysics* 980a). "Clearly then Wisdom is knowledge about certain principles and causes" (*Metaphysics* 982a). All men desire by natural necessity to know something certain without necessity. The *polemos* falls between necessity and otherwise, between certainty and variability. Necessity brings us directly to lack of necessity.

> We all suppose that what we know is not even capable of being otherwise; of things capable of being otherwise we do not know, when they have passed outside our observation, whether they exist or not. Therefore the object of scientific knowledge is of necessity. Therefore it is eternal. (*Nicomachean Ethics* 1139b)[42]

> The virtue of a thing is relative to its proper work. (*Nicomachean Ethics* 1139a)
>
> Wisdom must be intuitive reason combined with scientific knowledge. (*Nicomachean Ethics* 1141a)
>
> Practical wisdom on the other hand is concerned with things human and things about which it is possible to deliberate. (*Nicomachean Ethics* 1141b)

Scientific knowledge belongs to necessity and certainty, universality and eternity, except that not everything can be demonstrated, but some things are known by intuition, something certain and true without authority. Moreover, even the virtue of science emerges relative to its proper work, where both the proper and the work possess unscientific authority. For in Aristotle, however ambiguously, wisdom bears authority. "[F]or the wise man must not be ordered but must order, and he must not obey another, but the less wise must obey [*peithesthai*] him" (*Metaphysics* 982a). Truth carries authority—in Greek, Peithō's authority, the goddess of persuasion. In the extreme, authority without wisdom has no truth; truth brings authority. No wonder questions of authority echo those of truth. We wonder by what force.

After Aristotle, we may ask, by what authority beyond truth does science gain ascendancy over virtue? The answer in Aristotle proceeds by no authority, while science establishes truth's authority. Our question does not address the discipline and practice of *epistēmē*, with its authority—though we may find ourselves persuaded more by Plato's *Meno* than by Aristotle that all knowledge worthy of the name, like virtue, exceeds any authority, whirls in confusion, as science.[43] Even by means of science's discipline, establishing truth's authority under Peithō, such a truth and such an authority cannot establish virtue's authority, because virtue intrinsically possesses no authority, but inhabits the space of work, nature's *ergon*, where work belongs to *poiēsis* as much as *technē*, to *tychē*, fortune, as much as law.

> We must, as in all other cases, set the observed facts before us and, after first discussing the difficulties, go on to prove, if possible, the truth of all the common opinions about these affections of the mind, or, failing this, of the greater number and the most authoritative; for if we both refute the objects and leave the common opinions undisturbed, we shall have proved the case sufficiently. (*Nicomachean Ethics* 1145b)

This, perhaps more than *epistēmē*, represents the state of human authority. Truth's authority belongs to law as it falls away from *technē*: "And surely he who wants to make men, whether many or few, better by his care must try to become capable of legislating, if it is through laws that we can become good" (*Nicomachean Ethics* 1180b). Yet neither virtue nor laws can make one good with necessity or certainty.

Here, in Aristotle as in Anaximander and Plato, nature appears in doubled garb. One repeats the authority of justice; the other counters it:

> Things are just either by nature or by law.[44]

> For that which continues for the most part can plainly be seen to be naturally just. As to what we establish for ourselves and practise, that is thereby just, and we call it just according to law. Natural justice, then, is better than legal. (Aristotle, *Magna Moralia* 1195a)

Whatever sense better possesses here belongs in just as divided a way to nature and law. Natural justice rules better than law where political justice belongs to law. But the better prevails both by nature and by law, together and in strife. This becomes clear in a deeply contaminated form:

> Hence we see that is the nature and office of a slave; he who is by nature not his own but another's man, is by nature a slave; and he may be said to be another's man who, being a human being, is also a possession. (Aristotle, *Politics* 1254a)

> Where then there is such a difference as that between soul and body, or between men and animals . . . the lower sort are by nature slaves, and it is better for them as for all inferiors that they should be under the rule of a master. (*Politics* 1254b)

Aristotle is not alone: "I . . . exclude women and slaves, who are under the authority of men and masters, and also children and wards, as long as they are under the authority of parents and guardians";[45] "one may assert with perfect propriety, that women have not by nature equal right with men."[46]

How can the Aristotle for whom "*nature is a source or cause of being moved and of being at rest in that in which it belongs primarily*, in virtue of itself and not in virtue of a concomitant attribute" (*Physics* 192b) and the Spinoza for whom "nature has set no end before herself, and . . . all final causes are nothing but human fictions"[47] find in that same nature so abhorrent, detestable, and pernicious a doctrine?[48] How can we find satisfactory the claim that Aristotle was Greek and slavery was acceptable to the Greeks, the superiority of men over women acceptable in the Renaissance? As we emphasize their historical location and the impossibility of escaping from any location, do we relinquish the force of our own repugnance? Or may we experience a repugnance, an abhorrence, critique, that can challenge the force of Law from within a domain of law without positing another Law?

We may find our way by considering a variety of responses.

1. Nature does not establish slavery's authority but authorizes another authority, perhaps that of equality among all human beings.
2. Nature establishes no authority, has nothing to do with authority.
3. Nature's movement from itself, its plenitude and inexhaustibility, defies the measure within authority. Nature moves by necessity and by chance.

1. That nature might authorize one law over another presupposes that nature possesses both measure and authority, for either without the other lacks authorization. The nature that moves from itself rather than from a concomitant cause, as Spinoza emphasizes, knows no end even when regarded teleologically. Nature's movement from within expresses a natural plenitude in which whatever belongs to nature moves. We need not understand such a plenitude to belong to a cold and indifferent world in which human beings struggle to promote the good, but as expressing charity, nature's inexhaustibility, excess. Everything owns a stature beyond and apart from measure, older than measure. Measure belongs to *technē*, to law.

Law possesses measure and authority. Yet nature—the nature whose movement from within departs from *technē*—possesses, establishes, no authority. Equality possesses authority within *technē*'s measure. Otherwise, even where slavery represented the essence of injustice, equality would own no overarching authority. We may find slavery repugnant even where we hesitate to promote another authority of equality under law.

May we find slavery repugnant, as subjugation and oppression, where we have no authority to authorize another authority, where we know others have implemented slavery? May we find slavery unjust where we have no ideal to put in its place? May we insist on abolishing slavery where we have no knowledge of reconstruction? The age of injustice demands that we seek restitution for injustice where we have no just law, no equality, where no alternative measure possesses authority.

2. Equality, within nature, either repeats the authority of a nature within *technē*, without excess, or echoes as another excessive univocal before law and *technē*, away from measure.[49] The realm of authority, after Hobbes, exceeds any measure, exceeds any law, but somehow belongs to the authority of law as it exceeds it.

For if all authority belonged to law, if justice and injustice presupposed a natural and universal measure, then in our repugnance for Aristotle's and Spinoza's affirmation of natural superiority over slaves and women we would have to presuppose another authority, another absolute authority, as if we, like they, could legislate for all time from within our particular times. We would impose on a contingent and discontinuous history an authority for all time. We would disrupt the inexhaustible plenitude of nature.

Another authority, for all time, reaffirms the authority of authority, within nature, and frames the debate as one of Law. Nature holds absolute authority as we chafe under the weight of lawful authority. Yet this absolute authority belongs to a particular time and place, and vests itself, its will and power, in a liberation that oppresses some. Why should we accept the authoritarian premises? Why not give up all authority in nature, give up the authority of nature's plenitude? How can we do so with authority? How can we repudiate authority, and with what authority?

3. The phrase, "under the authority of," presupposes superiority and inferiority, mastery and subjection. We concern ourselves with the authority of authority. We cannot deny the presence of authority—too much authority. Nothing can make authority disappear. We understand the state of nature, in Hobbes and Locke, to question authority's authority, not the possibility of authority's disappearance, but the unbounded fear within this possibility that gives authority absolute authority—abyssal unlimits that betray the arbitrariness of authority.

Children's size and dependency places them under the authority of their parents or other adults temporarily, contingently. This contingency receives expression in the mythology of the rebellious child who defies adult power, thereby defying every natural authority. In virtue of their dependency, children fall under the authority of adults, too frequently an abusive authority. As soon as children are no longer small, no longer dependent, that authority, however legitimate or enabling, vanishes. Nature, here, gives authority no authority, supports it contingently. Nature possesses no authority to authorize law or any other authority. Yet nature cannot free itself from authority, even as it cannot authorize authority.

Children fall under the authority of adults for a while but not thereafter, a term short compared with the continuing oppressions of women and subalterns. And what of the injustices borne by children, thrown down too far under adult authority? Suppose all subjection were for the moment, contingent rather than necessary, authority without authorization, without a nature. Would authority survive without authorization? Or does too much authority circulate?

Slavery, oppression, subjugation persist as reprehensible, unjust, with or without Law, without Justice. Injustice exceeds any Law of Justice, where justice, possessing no authorization, exercises proximate, contingent authority, and where every such authority inhabits a world of constant danger. We place ourselves in danger when we oppose authority, oppose slavery and oppression. We place ourselves in danger when we participate in slavery and oppression, even acquiescing without participation. Our opposition does not represent a greater danger than slavery except to those who benefit from it. Rather, the danger of injustice at every moment within the ordinance of time has no measure. We know the repugnance of injustice, including its attractions, without knowing, without believing, that its abolition—any form of restitution—makes life safer, less unjust. The danger prevails in every practice that its just laws will impose another oppression, injustice, that restitution does not guarantee the disappearance of injustice. For this guarantee fails twice: on the one hand, that *praxis* gives no guarantees, offers proximateness and contingency, and on the other, that injustice remains no matter what. Yet this no-matter-what, this inescapable danger, reveals proximateness and contingency, falls outside law, has no measure.

We see in Hobbes one side of the immeasure of authority, its terrible risk and danger. The other side, also visible in Hobbes, promotes the realization that authority does not easily expire, that once established, law takes on a life of its own, exceeding the proximate dangers of lawlessness. The discourse of nature frames the discourse of *technē*, both discourses of law, to make present the danger of authority authorizing itself. Here nature possesses no authority. The discourse of nature falls into *technē* as law and measure to counter every law's authority. The discourse of nature falls outside, away from *technē*, whatever the proximity of nature and *technē* to each other and law, to undermine the authority of every challenge to authority as if it possessed another supreme authority.

Even the dialectic of authority, positive or negative, takes on too great an authority. Every authority imposes oppression, demanding challenge. Every challenge takes on another authority, must possess authority for its effectiveness. Yet with what authority do we accept a challenge to every authority? That of history—the story of authority's contingency—or that of nature, which possesses no authority?

Nature's absence of authority possesses no authority but represents the lack of authorization in every authority without establishing another, without authorizing itself, replacing nature's necessity with nature's chance, *technē*'s necessity with *tychē*'s fortune. This nonauthorization of self-authority expresses a countermovement to authority and self-authority without promoting another authority, another measure, without *technē* or law. Nature's plenitude, self-movement, univocity, *tychē*, represent a challenge to *technē* that cannot authorize its rejection. We cannot live without law, without authority, but we hope to sustain vigilance against their authority. One of the forms of such vigilance develops as the age of injustice and plenitude of nature without authority, while its lack of authority cannot lie within it. The lack of authorization within every authority cannot come from self-authorization, but belongs to *tychē*. This failure represents why nature and injustice exceed *technē* and law, why the injustice of slavery cannot lie in law, cannot fall under measure, why at great risk we must resist oppression. The risk persists that resistance repeats, augments, oppression. The risk persists that resistance cannot oppose oppression, in virtue of repetition and chance.

What Socrates says in *Republic* about women, even where we find it abhorrent, places us at risk in a way unknown to Aristotle and Spinoza. "The one sex is far surpassed by the other in everything, one may say. Many women, it is true, are better than many men in many things, but broadly speaking, it is as you say" (*Republic* 455d). Whatever "broadly speaking" may mean, it cannot be true that women are superior to men in many ways and still surpassed by them in everything. What follows sounds equally ambiguous: "the natural capacities are distributed alike among both creatures, and women naturally share in all pursuits and men in all—yet for all the woman is weaker than the man" (*Republic* 455e). How does nature function here? Not perhaps to name the ways in which men and women, human beings, do their work, their *ergon*, achieve virtue, *aretē*, but to designate a univocal, indeterminate all: All men and women share all human excellences, whatever they—any of them—may be. Perhaps this idea of *aretē* pertains restrictedly to human beings; perhaps it imposes a single, masculine ideal on men and women; perhaps it perpetrates univocity, indeterminateness, inexhaustibility. Men and women share alike in the determinateness and indeterminateness, lawfulness and lawlessness, of *aretē*. If a woman possesses whatever virtues guardians require, she may possess authority. Even so, women are weaker than men. Even so, women and children are possessions, maintained by "considerable use of falsehood and deception for the benefit of their subjects" (*Republic* 459d). "[O]ur guardians and female guardians must have all pursuits in common, . . . these women shall all be common to all these men, and that none shall cohabit with any privately, and that the children shall be common, and that no parent shall know its own offspring nor any child its parent" (*Republic* 457d). How can we read these passages but as placing women and children under the authority of men? How can we avoid recognizing in return that where men share women in common, and none cohabit privately or possess wealth, the women also share men in common? Children, still under the authority of adults, also belong to none in particular.

The *aretē* set forth in *Republic* falls entirely under law lacking human complexity.[50] Even so, its implementation challenges authority repeatedly and complexly. Whatever human excellence may be, men and women share it and the same measures (and unmeasures). Even if women were inferior to men in everything—and they cannot be—men gain no intrinsic authority over them, and whatever authority comes to pass disperses when held in common. Even so, women and children are possessions.

The enormous risk to which Plato subjects us tells us that no differences between women and men hold, no sexual differences, that could establish just laws differentiating them, and even if such differences held, they could confer no Authority or Law. Plato challenges both the subjugation of women based on their inferiority and any alternative based on equality. Perhaps women are (in some contingent and empirical ways) inferior to men—smaller, physically weaker; some women and some men. And perhaps some are in other ways superior to men. Nothing whatever follows in relation to authority and subjugation.[51] The authority vested in parents over their children possesses no intrinsic authority.

All this finds expression not as the superior authority vested in nature over human contingency, but where what belongs inexhaustibly to nature resists every authority—we have called it "the age of injustice." In apparent contrast, as Aristotle takes authority for granted in truth, wisdom's authority, he takes supreme authority for granted in the state, rule's authority. "There is also a doubt as to what is to be the supreme power in the state" (*Politics* 1281a). "The discussion . . . shows nothing so clearly as that laws, when good, should be supreme" (*Politics* 1282b). Laws should be supreme as if something must be supreme, as if authority presupposes superiority.

This good falls either into or beyond law. If into law, then law establishes its own goodness, its own authority. We have seen that self-authorization repeats tyranny, arbitrarily overcomes the arbitrariness of authority by its repetition. If the good falls beyond law, then the authority of law exceeds law's authority, where excess represents the measure of the authority of authority. To this excess of authority, Aristotle gives Plato's traditional response to Socrates' fate: "In the perfect state . . . all should joyfully obey such a ruler, according to what seems to be the order of nature, and that men like him should be kings in their state for life" (*Politics* 1284b). Here, not laws but men, not men in their wisdom, in the nature of their truth, but according to what seems the order of nature, kings' authority, shall be obeyed joyfully. Here, in Aristotle, in the face of the evidence, we find authority vested with the greatest possible authority, greater than that of truth: not authority as such, over others, force and compulsion, but subjects' joyful acquiescence in the dominion over them. Does this represent the dream of authority, to be powerful in virtue of appearing not to enforce any authority—to be authorized by truth and wisdom, to possess authority without authority, without desire, to be supreme without force? "The law is reason unaffected by desire" (*Metaphysics* 1287a). And similarly, presenting law as governed by Authority: "For law is order, and good law is good order; . . . to introduce order into the unlimited is the work of a divine power—of such a power as holds together the universe" (*Metaphysics* 1326a). The goodness in law that grants it authority, that makes it Law, in a plenitudinous universe, in nature, prevails as divine, infinite, excessive, inexhaustible. Authority in law or truth exceeds law and truth inexhaustibly. Natural law, nature's law, exceeds any measure.

And so, where Cicero speaks in the highest of Law, we find the highest represents both the authority of Authority and the injustice within the Justice of Law. "Law is the highest reason, implanted in nature, which commands what ought to be done and forbids the opposite" (Cicero, *Laws* I, VI); "for Law is a natural force; it is the mind and reason of the intelligent man, the standard by which Justice and Injustice are measured" (*Laws* I, VI). Law measures Justice and Injustice, based on Supreme Law: "which had its origin ages before any written law existed or any State had been established" (*Laws* I, VI). The age of injustice reemerges as Cicero argues for the age of justice. Here, Nature's relation to itself and us persists as one of Law and Authority, vested in the singing of the birds, reminding us of Plato's cicadas![52]

> Do you grant us, . . . that all Nature is governed? For if you do not admit it, we must begin our argument with this problem before taking up anything else.

Surely I will grant it, if you insist upon it, for the singing of the birds about us and the babbling of the streams relieve me from all fear that I may be overheard. (Cicero, *Laws* I, VII)

If we cannot discuss law without positing Nature's Law, then by all means do so, leaving Nature's Authority unauthorized, even in Rome, "by the might of the immortal gods" (Cicero, *Laws* I, VII). If right reason appears as law or Law, then "we must believe that men have Law also in common with the gods" (*Laws* I, VII), in common with nature's plenitude. We are led by this splendor of law in nature to question nature's *technē*. "Now that we have admitted the truth of these conclusions, and rightly, I think, how can we separate Law and Justice from Nature?" (*Laws* I, XIII). Why would we wish to do so except to question the deficiencies of law against the perfections of nature?

But the most foolish notion of all is the belief that everything is just which is found in the customs or laws of nations. (Cicero, *Laws* I, XV)

For Justice is one; it binds all human society, and is based on one Law, which is right reason applied to command and prohibition. Whoever knows not this Law, whether it has been recorded in writing anywhere or not, is without Justice. (*Laws* I, XV)

Human, implemented, laws do not represent justice but find themselves judged by a law older than writing, older than justice, older than human law. We foolishly think just any law within human history, still measured against an ancient Law. We ask whether this ancient Law belongs to measure, or whether its ancient age represents the foolishness in all Law.

When we add that "if a State lacks Law, must it for that reason be considered no State at all?" (Cicero, *Laws* II, V), we supplement the foolishness of the State's authority, which would impose nature's law but can only foolishly write itself as *technē*'s Law.

Yet authority must rule within this foolishness, the madness of authority: "*Commands shall be just, and the citizens shall obey them dutifully and without protest*" (Cicero, *Laws* III, III). What repeats itself before us, again and again, represents the movement from the madness of human law, founded upon something far older than it, to an authority that forces without authorization, in the guise of nature.

The voice of authority:

> By now, it is clear . . .
> We see . . .
> I have shown . . .
> All within the ordinance of time.

Listen to its lack of authority:

> For if not yet, then perhaps later . . .
> If we do not see, perhaps others see . . .
> Perhaps I have not shown yet, but soon . . .
> If this is not clear, then perhaps something else is . . .
> Perhaps . . .
>
> All within nature's plenitude.

If justice and injustice have not yet shown themselves clearly, then perhaps we can make them clearer—still within the ordinance of time. Yet the injustice older than time and the nature whose plenitude exceeds time and law reveal themselves unclearly in a different way, without a not-yet whereby they may become clear. It may be impossible to see clearly, to show definitely, the injustice to which we must pay unending restitution. Yet we must pay restitution, where truth and justice, clarity and temporality, belong to restitution. Yet we may not accept this law of restitution as the last word, the truth of restitution.

In the history of philosophy, truth, and law, there persists an inescapable presence, alongside and within law and truth, cutting across and into them, another history outside truth and law, older and younger than they, named sometimes "nature," sometimes "law," for Anaximander, named "injustice," for others named "gender," "sexual difference,"[53] always expressing authority's truth, that it lacks authority. Perhaps it does not matter which name has primacy, for to make any form predominant places us again under law. What matters represents the excesses in law and truth, lawlessness and untruth, whereby they receive authorization. What matters expresses that this unauthorized constitution of authority requires restitution, endlessly circulates as restitution, cannot escape from restitution. We call this inescapability "injustice," distinguishing it from injustice under law, injustice in time, from morality and virtue. These belong to the ordinance of time, presupposing authorization of their authority even where that authorization lacks authority. We call this lack "charity." Others call it "nature" and "right," "power" and "desire," "women" and "jews." We temper its call by sacrifice, the injustice of authority.

In this sense nature, law, power, and desire appear in our discourse twice—within an already established authority, and also marking the excesses of every authority. History and *praxis*, among other discourses, constitute themselves in the midst of inexhaustibility.

We have found this inexhaustibility between Hobbes and Locke; we have found it again in Cicero. Natural law falls outside Law as law, the authorization of authority. The very ground of law, to present itself as rational and necessary, falls into nature twice, as reason's necessity, and as a plenitude beyond all reason, another necessity. The theme of the ground of law exceeds every law and ground. Here law meets truth. "Laws, in their most general signification, are the necessary relations arising from the nature of things. In this sense all beings have their laws; the Deity his laws, the material world its laws, the intelligences superior to man their laws, the beasts their laws, man his laws."[54] This passage, opening Montesquieu's *The Spirit of the Laws*, represents law's excesses multiply, excessively, in the laws that belong to all things, to nature everywhere, and in nature's inexhaustible plenitude. The excesses belong to God and nature, to humanity and animals. All fall under, obey, laws. Authority and obedience, superiority and inferiority, pertain to God and nature, and even God obeys his laws. "God is related to the universe, as Creator and Preserver; the laws by which he created all things, are those by which he preserves them. He acts according to these rules, because he knows them; he knows them, because he made them; and he made them because they are relative to his wisdom and power. . . . " (Montesquieu, *Spirit of the Laws*, p. 161). Law possesses an authority that cannot reside within law, cannot work by law, an authority authorized by something beyond all measure.

This theme of beyond all measure that weighs upon law's authority represents the authoritative power vested in *technē*, for measure works by law's excesses. God, the universe, Creator and Preserver, human superiors and inferiors, all express law's excesses and those excesses' excesses. Law can rule with authority only where *technē*'s measures overcome law's excesses. For without authorizing measure, without *technē*'s authority, law's excesses repeat nature's plenitude, ruled any way nature moves by necessity. And even this necessity falls under law and exceeds it, since the necessity of nature, in all things and ways, exceeds any reason.

A striking example appears in Leibniz, for whom nature's plenitude exceeds all multiplicity, still lawful and rational. For moral perfection and metaphysical greatness coincide, nature's movement as the ground of law.

And in order that no one should think that we confound here moral perfection or goodness with metaphysical perfection or greatness, and that the former is denied while the latter is granted, it must be known that it follows from what has been said that the world is most perfect, not only physically, or, if you prefer, metaphysically, because that series of things is produced in which there is actually the most of reality, but also that it is most perfect morally, because real moral perfection is physical perfection for souls themselves.[55]

Perfection in Leibniz exceeds all limits, in the whole and in the parts, except for certain qualifications that resist explication:

As in a well-constituted republic as much care as possible is taken of the good of the individual, so the universe cannot be perfect if individual interests are not protected as much as the universal harmony will permit. And for this a better law could not be established than the very law of justice which declares that each one participate in the perfection of the universe and in a happiness of his own in proportion to his own virtue and to the good will he entertains toward the common good. (*OUOT*, p. 353)

Things are the best they can be, in the whole and in the part, except that the harmony of the whole takes precedence over the parts. For Leibniz does not say that the whole might achieve whatever harmony it may achieve proportionate with the perfection of the parts. "[W]e discover in numbers, figures, forces, and all measureable things of which we have an adequate conception, that they are not only just and perfect but also quite harmonious and beautiful, in short, that they cannot be improved nor can anything conceivably better be hoped for."[56] This better beyond all conceivable goodness belongs to nature and to God as the justice in law that orders all things for the best. It represents a best beyond all others, beyond measure. If we assume a measure of justice, known to God, if not to us, then the goodness of things in the whole and in the parts will be good to that degree and in that measure. In Leibniz, the good, the best of all possible worlds, inexhaustibly transcends any measure, even God's.

We find ourselves led similarly by Rousseau and Kant, Bentham and Mill, to a measure of authority beyond all measure. In Rousseau, the general will exceeds all law: *"Each of us puts his person and all his power in common under the supreme direction of the general will, and, in our corpo-*

rate capacity, we receive each member as an indivisible part of the whole."[57] Authority and force exceed law.

> The strongest is never strong enough to be always the master, unless he transforms strength into right, and obedience into duty. . . . To yield to force is an act of necessity, not of will—at the most an act of prudence. In what sense can it be a duty? . . . Clearly, the word "right" adds nothing to force: in this connection, it means absolutely nothing. (Rousseau, *SC*, p. 6)

Rousseau shows an understanding of force and right—the absolute impoverishment of right—unknown to others.

> There is but one law which, from its nature, needs unanimous concent. This is the social compact; for civil association is the most voluntary of all acts. Every man being born free and his own master, no one, under any pretext whatsoever, can make any man subject without his concent. To decide that the son of a slave is born a slave is to decide that he is not born a man. (*SC*, p. 105)

No representation, no legitimation, can weaken this absolute liberty: "Sovereignty cannot be represented, for the same reason that it cannot be alienated. It consists essentially of the general will, and will cannot be represented. Either it is itself or it is different. There is no middle term. . . . the moment a People allows itself to be represented, it is no longer free: it no longer exists" (Rousseau, *SC*, p. 96).

The key term is "People," the repositors of the general will. We can read Rousseau as repeating Hobbes, repeating the absolute authority that repeats the absolute liberty of the state of nature, vested in a People with a General Will. We can also read him as repeating the lawlessness of absolute liberty and authority, vesting not in tyranny but in absolute accountability, so that nothing can authorize the transfer of authority. It remains inexplicable, before all law, vested in the People who legislate, where the law repeats, expresses the authorization within an untransferable authority.

We come again to tyranny. For Rousseau's vision of the People foreshadows the Terror, and Hobbes's vision of authority lies in the most tyrannical of dictatorships. We question not that vision or its result, but the movement from the arbitrariness of authority into absolute, tyrannical authority, as if what lies beyond all law—an authority beyond all intelligibility—somehow falls into absolute law. This law beyond law does not represent Law; this authority beyond authority does not stand for Authority, for the presence within the State of Absolute Authority under Law. Rather, as in Kafka, it expresses the inescapability of an inexhaustible authority that has no beginning and no end, that does not belong to time, an authority always and forever unjust but that justice cannot live without, except that in requiring that authority, justice must always pay for it. Hobbes recognizes, we may say, the injustice in justice, the arbitrariness of authority. The sovereign, however, does not owe unending debt for the authorization of his authority. Rather, his citizens own him unending obedience. Hobbes does not recognize restitution.

The same is not true of Rousseau, but it is easily true of his followers, of any followers of a general will and liberty that fall into time profanely, where the profanity expresses distance not from God but from unending restitution to injustice. The general will never finds itself in time, any more than does absolute liberty. Time, rather, spends itself, its order, seeking to restore disorder to the order of the general will, an order profoundly contaminated by archaic injustice.

Whatever the cost, the Western world of law divides into pairs of oppositions whose debates define its terrain: Hobbes and Locke, Rousseau and Mill, Kant and Bentham, Hegel and Marx; individuality and community, rights and utility. These oppositions, under the masks of enduring debates, fall into law, belong to justice, but appear to know nothing of the age of injustice, do not mourn its aboriginality.

This fall of justice into law, becoming Justice and Law, knowing nothing of the ordinance of time's unending debt, of unending vigilance toward violence, marks the Enlightenment in certain ways, though it fails to hold in any text we have so far considered. If Our Western tradition exemplifies the rule of *technē*, authority seeking authorization, every text we have read to authorize legitimacy as the foundation of authority resists legitimation. We find ourselves exploring the twin truths of Western Authority: that authority falls entirely into law, while every canonical authority repudiates the lawfulness of authority. Excess rules everywhere, the twin of injustice. Justice echoes an archaic injustice; authority reflects its enigmatic lack of authority.

This inscrutable excess of authority appears in German as *Recht* and in French as *droit*, words that are largely unknown in English. Yet something akin does appear, in Bentham and Mill, for example, which in its differences may show us something about the Authority of Right. It appears in Bentham in relation to utility.

> By utility is meant that property in any object, whereby it tends to produce benefit, advantage, pleasure, good, or happiness, (all this in the present case comes to the same thing) . . . to the party whose interest is considered: if that party be the community in general, then the happiness of the community; if a particular individual, then the happiness of that individual.[58]

We address the happiness of the community: "the interest of the community then is, what?—the sum of the interests of the several members who compose it" (Bentham, *PML*, p. 263). This sum appears to fall under *technē*, under measure, into being without remainder.[59] Communities, collectives, aggregates, nations, societies, experience no pain and pleasure however collective their practices. Why should we assume that the sum of individual utilities into an aggregate, the calculus upon which exchange and substitution rest, represents anything but the arbitrariness of the authority vested in it? For utility defines right and wrong, repeating authority.[60] How can a sum of utilities be calculated without imposing suspect technical assumptions, and how can such assumptions give social violence its authority?

This question arises within a critique of utility as a ground of justice among those who advocate a theory of rights, as if Right provided a clearer and more defensible authority to law. Of this, more in a moment. We add the implausibility of a social practice without a social good. We question the subsumption of the social good under law, under measure and calculation, as if the authority it confers might no longer belong to the immemoriality of injustice.

The collectivity of utility does not escape measure but repeats the enigma of utility itself with authority and law. Each decision repeats the impossibility of the calculation, the sum, that Bentham describes as present in every encounter with interest and utility. Bentham offers us an image of a perfect calculus: "Sum up all the values of all the *pleasures* on the one side, and those of all the pains on the other. The balance, if it be on the side of pleasure, will give the *good* tendency of the act upon the whole, with respect to the interests of that *individual* person; if on the side of pain, the *bad* tendency of it upon the whole" (*PML*, p. 266). The impossibility of performing this calculation can be expressed in two ways: the difficulty of making a decision, in which the summary tables Bentham describes are largely irrelevant; and the preponderance of one or another practice over the others, as if duty, however unpleasant, might triumph over every pleasure.

The second difficulty shows again in Mill, who seems to accept Bentham's view of utility exactly: "The creed which accepts as the foundation of morals *utility*, or the *greatest happiness principle*, holds that actions are right in proportion as they tend to promote happiness, wrong as they tend to produce the reverse of happiness."[61] Yet he adds a distinction between higher and lower pleasures: "It is quite compatible with the principle of utility to recognize the fact, that some *kinds* of pleasure are more desirable and more valuable than others. It would be absurd that while, in estimating all other things, quality is considered as well as quantity, the estimation of pleasures should be supposed to depend on quantity alone" (*U*, p. 901). Utility cannot work without a distinction between higher and lower pleasures, but that distinction destroys utilitarianism, undermines any calculation. Higher and lower pleasures express a distinction of authority without a measure. They repeat the age of injustice, outside time and law. Those who suffer injustice suffer! And what they suffer belongs to no system of exchange, no system of calculation. Rather, we seek throughout all history to redeem that suffering without repeating it. And still we repeat it endlessly in our general economy.

With this understanding of the good, individual or collective, beyond law, we come to Kant and Right. If the history of Right knows an age older than him, Kant nevertheless, with Hegel, expresses something profound about the authority vested in Law over law.[62] Let us set aside the different formulations of the categorical imperative, whether they coincide or represent excesses of moral authority in their differences, between a universal law whose form represents obligation in general and a kingdom of ends without practical exemplification. Let us set aside the purity of form and end, universality and finality, which may express the age of authority over and beyond any exemplification. Let us set aside the aporia at the heart of Kant's system—that the supersensible exceeds knowledge yet constitutes the ground of freedom, cannot be represented yet appears in representation in the form of the sublime.[63] And let us set aside the relation between scientific knowledge and natural law, which bears no weight in relation to freedom yet constitutes epistemic authority. We set aside all those other points in Kant where we may find traces of the age of injustice, every appearance of the abyss. We restrict ourselves here to Right, the foundation of authority. "The conception of RIGHT,—as referring to a corresponding Obligation which is the moral aspect of it,—in the *first* place, has regard only to the external and practical relation of one Person to another, . . . " (Kant, *SR*, p. 241). In our time, institutional authority has become invasive and pervasive throughout human experience; it repeats archaic injustice unknown to itself. The idea of restricting authority to practical relations between people, the idea of an only in relation to authority, expresses the relation of philosophy's authority to itself—nothing whatever. We have seen this in relation to Plato's *Laws* where virtue's excesses betray themselves. How could this insight, of the excesses of desire in relation to authority, the will to power, be overlooked in Kant, in relation particularly to Right? "RIGHT, therefore, comprehends the whole of the conditions under which the voluntary actions of any one Person can be harmonized in reality with the voluntary actions of every other Person, according to a universal Law of Freedom" (Kant, *SR*, p. 242). The only disappears into one totality after another: the whole of the conditions, every person, a universal law of freedom. Nothing receives exemption. And so we ask: How can any totality within the inexhaustible plenitude of nature and imagination construct a measure, or must such a totality, such a plenitude, exceed any law and measure? Right, here, speaks not of what Kant calls "positive law" and measure, what falls under a concept, into representation, but of obligation and authority beyond any representation, any knowledge. It reveals another "indeterminate object," lacking "any appropriate intuition."[64] In particular, how can the totality of what falls outside the totality of knowledge compose a measure? Or should we read the repeated references in Kant to the limits of representation and knowledge, and beyond, to speak to the age of authority beyond the limits of law's authority, a beyond where we endlessly encounter the abyss?

If the latter, we may understand that the very excesses, indeterminatenesses, of the authority of Right in Kant, as the ground of authority, make it impossible to authorize its authority: "It follows also that it cannot be demanded as a matter of Right, that this universal Principle of all maxims shall itself be adopted as my maxim, that is, that I shall make it the *maxim* of my actions" (Kant, *SR*, p. 242). No maxim, no law of laws, can confer upon law its authority.[65]

From the unmeasured authority beyond measure, Kant, like Locke, quickly arrives at the fundamental Western measure: mine and thine. "Anything is 'Mine' by Right, or is rightfully Mine, when I am so connected with it, that if any other Person should make use of it without my consent, he would do me a lesion or injury. The subjective condition of the use of anything, is *Possession* of it" (Kant, *SR*, p. 245). Suffering belongs to possession, to property, as something Mine. The body becomes a possession rather than a site of excess. Yet the Right in Property makes both excessive, again following Locke. Here use does not contain authority, but exceeds itself in virtue of its authority.

Suppose there were things that *by right* should absolutely not be in our power, or, in other words, that it would be wrong or inconsistent with the freedom of all, according to universal Law, to make use of them. On this supposition, Freedom would so far be depriving itself of the use of its voluntary activity, in thus putting *useable* objects out of all possibility of *use*. (Kant, SR, p. 245)

We set aside the possibility that within law's measure, every possession lessens another's freedom, that for one person to own something, others would have to relinquish their freedom to it. Authority begins here with the inescapable injustice of property. We emphasize instead that the authority of Right belongs to use, to *technē*, falls into measure. Kant repeats Locke's technical view that human beings' relations to themselves are fundamentally possessive, that from the point of view of right they represent properties and commodities. Mine and Thine repeat the asymmetries of authority, as if we cannot be human without superiority and inferiority.

Why should we accept this as the Truth? Why should we accept supremacy as the truth of power? "The Origin of the Supreme Power is *practically inscrutable* by the People who are placed under its authority" (Kant, SR, p. 256). This acknowledgment of authority's inscrutability within Authority and Law becomes an affirmation of rule: "In other words, the Subject need not *reason too curiously* in regard to its origin in the practical relation, as if the Right of the obedience due to it were to be doubted" (Kant, SR, p. 256). The authority of sovereignty must not be questioned, as if it rested on a Right impervious to reason. We find an authority within the State without rational justification that leads to, justifies, force upon those of its citizens who question it. "For, should the Subject, after having dug down to the ultimate origin of the State, rise in opposition to the present ruling Authority, he would expose himself as a Citizen, according to the Law and with full Right, to be punished, destroyed, or outlawed" (Kant, SR, p. 256). This view, absent on our reading from the Plato traditionally credited with it, belongs to Kant, though his view of rights seems at odds with it. In both, against the practical exemplification of reason's authority to question authority, the Authority of the State rests on no authority. In Kant, it rests in a Right that moves between excess and instrumentality. "It is a Duty to obey the Law of the existing Legislative Power, be its origin what it may" (*SR*, p. 256). Punishment, destruction, belong intrinsically to Right. "The Penal Law is a Categorical Imperative" (*SR*, p. 257). "This is the Right of

RETALIATION" (*SR*, p. 258). If we recall the movement in *Oresteia* from vengeance to sovereignty and law, we may discern in Kant a similar acknowledgment of an authority (here in Right) that exceeds any relation to measure, even within the State. The State's power rests on a retaliation, a justice, that does not rule within the law.

If right and law receive extreme representation in Kant, their authority appears in its glory in Hegel, between sovereignty and reason. Framing the *Philosophy of Right*, from beginning to end, reason's authority looms with universality and necessity: "Right and ethics, and the actual world of justice and ethical life, are understood through thoughts; through thoughts they are invested with a rational form, i.e. with universality and determinacy."[66] Three ideas present themselves to us here in the form of Right: thought, universality, and determinacy. Universality represents the form, determinateness the authority, of law. We ask about the authority of universality. Hegel tells us of the authority of sovereignty: "Sovereignty, at first simply the universal *thought* of this ideality, comes into *existence* as subjectivity sure of itself, as the will's abstract and to that extent self-determination in which finality of decision is rooted" (*PR*, p. 181). Sovereign authority invests in monarchy, the individual vested with power derived from subjectivity and self-assurance. Power must rule supreme, must hold sure, and must work individually. Subjectivity sure of itself presents itself as undivided authority. The arbitrariness of sovereign authority in Hobbes, the terrible truth of authority, appears in Hegel as "sure of itself."

Why must authority be sure rather than strong? Why must it be individual rather than dispersed, and would that make it any less authority, less authoritarian? Does the certainty of authority's relation to itself make that authority more or less acceptable? The myth of legitimation echoes here, where authority imposes itself not only as authority, absolute authority, but as absolutely absolute.

Paraphrasing power's famous couplet in the name of authority, may we suggest that if authority rules, then absolute authority rules absolutely, where the "absolutely" exceeds all authority, all normality—its corruption—even all truth. It persists as absolutely sure of itself where its nature forbids assurance. Its absolute assurance passes into absolute individuality, so that only an individual with absolute authority can possess authority absolutely.

We ask Hegel what we would ask Hobbes: what of dispersed authority, divided among the people and their institutions, courts and legislatures? Do we find a democracy less authoritarian when so dispersed? Might it govern more authoritarianly in the dispersion of its authority? The more and less here belong to measure, and within measure neither Hobbes's nor Hegel's view of sovereignty possesses plausibility. To the contrary, both because authority emerges everywhere, divided by divided authorities, and because unbroken authority represents such danger, absolute authority finds itself regulated by other authorities, the authority of the sovereign dispersed over other sovereignties. All this falls within *technē*. Hegel and Hobbes mark the arbitrary excessiveness within authority that gains fulfillment within a sovereignty beyond measure. Sovereign authority without measure represents the unlimitedness of authority.

Here we find the monarch's Right to Rule:

> This ultimate self in which the will of the state is concentrated is, when thus taken in abstraction, a single self and therefore is *immediate* individuality. Hence its "natural" character is implied in its very conception. The monarch, therefore, is essentially characterized as *this* individual, in abstraction from all this other characteristics, and *this* individual is raised to the dignity of monarchy in an immediate, natural, fashion, i.e. through his birth in the course of nature. (Hegel, PR, p. 184)

Authority, derived from universality and necessity, falls into subjectivity in the form of a human being with absolute power. Authority, here, derives from nature, as if one might be born with supreme authority belonging to nature's laws. Human authority reflects natural authority, an authority beyond measure, older than *technē*. "The basis of right is, in general, mind; its precise place and point of origin is the will. The will is free, so that freedom is both the substance of right and its goal, while the system of right is the realm of freedom made actual, the world of mind brought forth out of itself like a second nature" (Hegel, PR, p. 20). Nature's freedom belongs to its plenitude. The actualization of what has no measure, older than measure, appears, falls into time, as measure. The age of injustice appears in Hegel after Hobbes as the age of authority, something older than humanity, threatening its fall into *technē*.

The immense dark pool into which Hobbes's view of power throws us ripples under Hegel.

> The state in and by itself is the ethical whole, the actualization of freedom; and it is an absolute end of reason that freedom should be actual. The state is mind on earth and con-

sciously realizing itself there. In nature, on the other hand, mind actualizes itself only as its own other, as mind asleep. Only when it is present in consciousness, when it knows itself as a really existent object, is it the state. (Hegel, *PR*, p. 279)

Sovereignty and self-actualization meet in the state, in the person of the sovereign, authority incarnate. In nature, mind sleeps, as if nature's authority sleeps, as if authority cannot belong to nature as absolute. Self-certainty authorizes authority, establishes sovereignty, as absolute, over nature's truth, asleep, entirely lacking self-certainty. The age of injustice, belonging to nature's authority beyond or beside the state, possesses no assurance whatever.[67]

The absoluteness of an authority beyond measure derives in Hegel from a freedom beyond measure. "Only in freedom of this kind is the will by itself without qualification, because then it is related to nothing except itself and so is released from every time of dependence on anything else" (Hegel, *PR*, p. 30). The will, in its freedom, relates only to itself. Fallen into time, the will's authority relates to itself even as its actualization requires relation to others—other individuals, states, times, and places. The univocity of authority breaks the hold of authority upon itself. It cannot break its hold upon others because that hold represents the force of its authority. What it can break represents its self-authorization, its legitimation.

Like Locke, Hegel marks abstract right as property:

> Right is in the first place the immediate embodiment which freedom gives itself in an immediate way, i.e. (*a*) possession, which is *property*-ownership. (*PR*, p. 38)

> A person has as his substantive end the right of putting his will into any and every thing and thereby making it his, because it has no such end in itself and derives its destiny and soul from his will. This is the absolute right of appropriation which man has over all "things" (*PR*, p. 41)

This theme, of the exteriorization of will into things as property in the form of mastery, runs through Hegel's discussion of the will. It may be read as the authorization of *technē*, of exteriorization as measure in the form of appropriation. Yet property also marks one's relation to oneself and one's body. "I possess the members of my body, my life, only so long as I will to possess them" (Hegel, *PR*, p. 43).[68] We may contrast this sense of life as property with life in *Phaedrus*: *erōs, mania,* and *pharmakeia*.[69]

Within the play of immediacy and possession, we hear subjectivity forming itself as property: "But from the point of view of others, I am in essence a free entity in my body while my possession of it is still immediate" (Hegel, *PR*, p. 43). We possess ourselves in the form of property, possess our bodies. And not only as the externalization of our wills, in things, but doubled possession. For charity toward things promotes no less an external, no less a free will, than possession. It manifests the injustice in property older than their possession.

We cannot question, in Hegel, whether something other than human will can possess authority. "An animal acts on instinct, is driven by an inner impulse and so it too is practical, but it has no will, since it does not bring before its mind the object of its desire" (Hegel, *PR*, p. 227).[70] This view returns in Heidegger as *Geschlecht*.[71] Animals have no body, or at best only an animal-technical body that can grasp, but that cannot mean—that is, a body (paws, claws, fangs) that can pull and push, but that does not—cannot—represent; or if it represents, does not autoerotically represent its own representativity.

We, in virtue of the gift in our hand, the freedom of our will, possess things as our property, including animals and our own bodies, possess ourselves, thereby exercise authority over them. We, in virtue of our wills, exercise authority. But animals and things do not. Authority here rests on the greatest possible injustice, rests on it where we accept the authority of reason grounding the authority vested in our hand and will. Nothing can overcome this injustice, not even God's will, that we are given dominion over all things by nature. To the contrary, our authority, by nature, belongs to it and us as the profound injustice in, the terrible if inescapable nature of, authority. It appears in our relation to ourselves as one of authority. We possess, possess authority over, ourselves. We do, however monstrously wrong that it should be so, even though all justice rests upon it—not that others should possess authority over us, but that "a free entity in my body" should be anyone's property, even our own, that we, or anything, should in its nature fall under any authority, even its own.[72]

Hegel joins Hobbes in the Absoluteness of Authority, grounding both sovereign authority and institutionalized injustices. As history falls under law, the absolute self-certainty of Law works against the rule of law, however dangerously and obliquely. The critique of reason's law after Hegel represents a critique of its Authority under Law. Its form represents positive law, the unfounded authority of the state, receiving implementation in courts and police actions, turning the arbitrariness of their authority into terror, owing no debt to any injustice.

This inescapable danger of Law's Authority, its violence and terror, calls for new strategies in response. We pursue a strategy affirming the truth of terror and violence, of the unauthorization of every authority, of imperviousness to reason where reason demands its own authority. Emancipation calls for action against violence and oppression in the name of, not escape from injustice, but restitution for an injustice older than any justice, any restoration, any law, and infinitely younger, inescapable. Liberation calls for action against injustice without possessing justice, since that may belong to law and demand resistance.

This emphasis upon the lack of authorization of every authority does not represent the only strategy of liberation, of justice and justification, and terror and melancholy do not represent the only possible results. If one side of Hegel and Hobbes represents the passage from the unfounding of Authority into law as if giving its foundation, then the other side represents resistance to Law within law, refusal of law's Authority. The American pragmatists offer such a resistance, especially Dewey. In relation to philosophy, to reason's authority:

> Philosophy, like politics, literature and the plastic arts, is itself a phenomenon of human culture.[73]

> Thus philosophy marks a change of culture. In forming patterns to be conformed to in future thought and action, it is additive and transforming in its rôle in the history of civilization. Man states anything at his peril; once stated, it occupies a place in a new perspective; it attains a permanence which does not belong to its existence; it enters provokingly into wont and use; it points in a troubling way to need of new endeavors. (Dewey, *Philosophy and Civilization*, p. 8)

The key words here are "culture," "transformation," and "peril." To state, to enact as law, is to belong to and constitute history and culture, to bring change about and undertake risks. Authority circulates as dangerous and troubling, threatens in its use and opens troubling directions for different undertakings.

Authority, here, rules as dangerous, transient and risky. New perspectives, new spheres of life and practice, impose themselves with a perseverance opposed to their temporality. Authority and law represent both order and coercion. Dewey responds by incorporating this understanding into law, meeting the risk of authority by temperance and temporality: "If we trust to an experimental logic, we find that general principles emerge as statements of generic ways in which it has been found helpful to treat concrete cases" (*Philosophy and Civilization*, p. 133). And no more. We meet the threat of practice by adaptability. "As habits set in grooves dominate activity and swerve it from conditions instead of increasing its adaptability, so principles treated as fixed rules instead of as helpful methods take men away from experience."[74] We respond to the transience of rules with the thrill of experience. "In fact, situations into which change and the unexpected enter are a challenge to intelligence to create new principles" (Dewey, *Human Nature and Conduct*, p. 239). Intelligent practice mediates between past and future, between the inescapability of rules and their impermanence and risk. "Yet the choice is not between throwing away rules previously developed and sticking obstinately by them. The intelligent alternative is to revise, adapt, expand and alter them. The problem is one of continuous, vital readaptation" (*Human Nature and Conduct*, p. 240). Within time and *technē*, we grant law the authority intelligent reason can give it, constantly undergoing revision and alteration.

How could anything within time and law improve upon Dewey's understanding of practice? We meet the force of danger by care and adaptability, avoid the rigidity of law by emphasizing the impermanence of rule. The future remains a sphere of danger and promise. The order and authority of law belong to local spheres, extended to other spheres only through revision and alteration. The future remains indefinitely open, dangerous and risky.

Does this represent the only possible relation practice can have to the future? Two things seem missing. One represents the injustice of the past, past sufferings and oppressions. Can an adaptable intelligence take up the demands of aboriginal injustice, the hope of mourning? The other represents the continuing risk of practice, that however intelligent and self-aware, practice may repeat past injustices and embark upon new ones, some too horrible to anticipate, others too horrible to remember. Does Dewey assume that intelligence mitigates the risks of terror or that terror becomes acceptable when brought about by adaptive intelligence? Shall we think of war as something amenable to rational intelligence, where all risks can be moderated, or as practice beyond the limits of rationality, where reason faces infinite risks within its spheres of moderation? How are we to respond with intelligence to gas chambers and slavery? How do we take responsibility for colonial oppressions, women's sexual objectification? Can we respond intelligently to either without placing ourselves at risk? Can those oppressed?

Law always stands at risk, always places us at risk in its permanence and authority. We respond by diminishing its authority, acknowledging a fundamentally finite authority to law, social or natural. And so the foundations of science remain tentative and proximate, epistemic authority always exceeds any grounds, any foundation—until we build a bridge or skyscraper, where lives and public safety are at stake. Does the public authority for human life extend only to a humane and rational engineering? Or does the monstrosity of every rule apply to rationality and engineering?

Two themes in Dewey speak to these issues. One appears in the idea that philosophy—and by extension, literature and science, all forms of knowledge and truth—represent a change in culture, belong to culture intrinsically and contribute to it, without another separate end.

> Philosophy is criticism; criticism of the influential beliefs that underlie culture; a criticism which traces the beliefs to their generating conditions as far as may be, which tracks them to their results, which considers the mutual compatibility of the elements of the total structure of beliefs. Such an examination terminates, whether so intended or not, in a projection of them into a new perspective which leads to new surveys of possibilities.[75]

What if this understanding applied to Dewey's own writings, to every writing, to every form of truth? What if our work belonged to culture as criticism, critical of its influential beliefs, critical therefore of itself, passing into new perspectives? It would express something true of every philosophy, every authority. Epistemic authority represents critique, including its own authority, critical of itself. One way to speak of this side of Dewey is that everything in pragmatism falls under erasure. The extreme limits of this idea of erasure pertain to suffering, violence, domination, and oppression, the danger that in erasing resistance and critique, we erase the oppressions and sufferings that gave them birth.

Another theme in Dewey offsetting the authority of reason's law, however humane and self-critical, establishes another proximate perspective on law, not only its impermanence and danger, but its utility. Intelligent methods

> not only draw their material from primary experience, but they refer it back again for test.[76]

If we start from primary experience, occurring as it does chiefly in modes of action and undergoing, it is easy to see what knowledge contributes—namely, the possibility of intelligent administration of the elements of doing and suffering. (Dewey, *Experience and Nature*, p. 22)

Primary experience represents the beginning and end, the source and test, of knowledge, from science to philosophy to art and practice. Law here possesses no authority except the authority of experience, administering the elements of doing and suffering. If we take the suffering to include both undergoing and pain, then doing and undergoing, including violence and oppression, perpetrate an age older than reflection, older than understanding.

Again we erase the authority of law before an experience and a practice without authority, an origin without aboriginality, a test without law. Laws and norms prevail within any practice, but they possess only that authority that experience gives them, where its amorphousness and transience undermine any authority. Authority disappears twice, into its own representation of its lack of authority, the absence of authorization for any authority within human practice or culture except that of the culture's authority, and also in the force of critique, the groundlessness of experience, formed by reflection but never totally formed, never entirely subservient to any form of reflection, that grounds any law of reflection upon doing and suffering.

The possibility of law in Dewey rests upon that which has no law, intrinsically, but only proximate law, something outside and older than law. Authority lacks authority. It also lacks justice and injustice. Our entire discussion circulates around the question of whether the arbitrariness and proximity, the locality, of authority and law can be instituted within *praxis* and *technē*, or whether something absolute in authority, however dangerous and repellent, defines authority's locality. If we accept Dewey's *technē*, do we resolve the oppressiveness of Authority and Law? Can we think of *technē* as anything but *Technē*?

Our tracing of authority's unmeasure in the very tradition that established its measure, from universality to reason, has traced a disturbing side as well, a Dionysian moment in this Apollinian narrative. We have made restitution for our tradition's injustices twice, by recalling both some of the heinous moments in its most remarkable works, and where those works show archaic injustice in the force of their authority. We have taken the measure of what in our tradition marks unmeasure, the arbitrariness of authority, even as it imposes its own authority. We hope to have disturbed the authority of the history of philosophy, of Western metaphysics, to have traced some of its injustices, known and unknown. We now undertake a different project, to trace some of the forms that surround authority, especially Western authority, to give them weight, to unfold their injustices in the forces that bear down upon justice's authority, to unmeasure their measure.

IV

ECONOMY'S MEASURE

When Leibniz speaks of the excess of the essence of body over extension, he appeals to the activity of substance: "All of this shows that there is in matter something else than the purely Geometrical, that is, than just extension and bare change. And in considering the matter closely, we perceive that we must add to them some *higher or metaphysical notion, namely, that of substance, action, and force;* . . . . "[1] This classical idea of activity beyond extension appears in Leibniz and Berkeley, later in Whitehead, representing a certain view of the limits of extension. In Berkeley's words: "By *matter*, therefore, we are to understand an inert, senseless substance, in which extension, figure, and motion do actually subsist. But it is evident from what we have already shown, that extension, figure, and motion are only ideas existing in the mind, and that an idea can be like nothing but another idea, ... "[2] He offers two kinds of argument, one that we think only of ideas: "For what are the forementioned objects but the things we perceive by sense? and what do we perceive *besides our own ideas or sensations?* and is it not plainly repugnant that any one of these, or any combination of them, should exist unperceived?" (*PK*, p. 524). We can know, think of, only what we find in our minds, a principle of epistemic authority. The other argument recalls Leibniz, emphasizing the activity of mind contrasted with the passivity of matter.

> This perceiving, active being is what I call *mind, spirit, soul, or myself.* (Berkeley, *PK*, p. 523)

> 25. All our ideas, sensations, notions, or the things which we perceive, by whatsoever names they may be distinguished, are visibly inactive: there is nothing of power or agency included in them. . . . Whence plainly follows that extension, figure, and motion cannot be the cause of our sensations. (Berkeley, *PK*, p. 531)

Being, substance, is active, while matter is inactive. Material things cannot exist except in and through an active substance, mind or spirit.

Matter and extension rest within their inactivity in virtue of their divisibility. "I do not believe extension alone constitutes substance, . . . For we can analyze it into plurality, continuity, and co-existence (that is, simultaneous existence of parts)."[3] Plurality and continuity represent the measure of activity and force together, where measure represents collectivity. The individuality of substances, of monads, becomes measure in their togetherness as the togetherness of ideas becomes abstraction for Berkeley.

> 8. Again, the mind having observed that in the particular extensions perceived by sense there is something common and alike in all, . . . it considers apart or singles out by itself that which is common, making thereof a most abstract idea of extension, which is neither line, surface, nor solid, nor has any figure or magnitude, but is an idea entirely prescinded from all these. (Berkeley, *PK*, p. 512)

Extension expresses the alike in a plurality of particular extensions, their commonality and togetherness, represented as abstract, divorced from their particularity. Commonality, community, togetherness, publicity, compose abstraction, extension, passivity, and measure. Things in their active natures persist as unique and particular, without parts as Leibniz says.[4] Even so, the plenitude of nature in every part has no end.[5] Matter represents confusions in monads relative to each other collectively in the form of representation.

> Because God, in regulating all, has had regard to each part, and particularly to each monad, whose nature being representative, nothing can limit it to representing only a part of things; although it may be true that this representation is but confused as regards the detail of the whole universe, and can be distinct only in the case of a small part of things, that is to

say, in the case of those which are nearest or greatest in relation to each of the monads. (Leibniz, *Monadology*, p. 545)

Monads circulate together representationally, with their mutual relations graduated into distinct and confused perceptions. Moreover, God's Law rules their relations together.

In this view of extension, something precedes, something multiply active comes before extension, before measure, which belongs to the collectivity, while individual monads as such have no measure, no extension. Even so, representation belongs to monads, defines monads, composes their activity. Something older than extension and measure, plenitudinous and inexhaustible, gives birth to them, circulates in and disturbs their economy. Measure represents the law of the collective, Community's Law, where something older marks the limits and injustice of collectivity.

Whitehead similarly speaks of "two metaphysical assumptions" in relation to "presentational immediacy," the contemporary world available for perception:[6]

> (i) That the actual world, in so far as it is a community of entities which are settled, actual, and already become, conditions and limits the potentiality for creativeness beyond itself. (*PR*, p. 65)

> (ii) The second metaphysical assumption is that the real potentialities relative to all standpoints are coordinated as diverse determinations of one extensive continuum. This extensive continuum is one relational complex in which all potential objectifications find their niche. It underlies the whole world, past, present, and future. (*PR*, p. 66)

The actual world composes time and place, conditioning and limiting what falls into time and place beyond itself in the form of order and continuity, exercising collective authority, leading to measure.

Our concern, explicit in Whitehead, addresses the authority of this measure as it defines law. If the first condition represents determination under law, the second represents collectivity: the coordination of all standpoints as diverse determinations of one extensive continuum underlying the whole world, past, present, and future. The entire world, everything circulating in time, falls under a comprehensive rule of One Law. Even so, this Law is not prior to the world but arises out of its general character.[7] It does not circulate older than time's succession, but represents a condition for it, belongs to it, representing the solidarity of actual entities. Actual entities in their succession and inheritance, in their multiple heterogeneity, give rise in their circulation to extension and measure. In their togetherness, composing a universe, all actual entities compose a "most general scheme of real potentiality."[8] Repeating Whitehead's insight into the conditions of a universe: "An actual entity cannot be a member of a 'common world,' except in the sense that the 'common world' is a constituent of its own constitution. It follows that every item of the universe, including all the other actual entities, is a constituent in the constitution of any one actual entity" (*PR*, p. 148). The extensive continuum represents the most general fact expressing this commonality of the world present in each actual entity, not before time, but circulating within it. The universe in its public truth conditions every future as extensive in its real potentiality. Measure emerges from this publicity. It represents nature's collectivity. We are concerned with the rule of measure over its inexhaustibility.

Whitehead offers a remarkable understanding of the relation between public and private:

> The theory of prehensions is founded upon the doctrine that there are no concrete facts which are merely public, or merely private. The distinction between publicity and privacy is a distinction of reason, and is not a distinction between mutually exclusive concrete facts. The sole concrete facts, in terms of which actualities can be analysed, are prehensions; and every prehension has its public side and its private side. (*PR*, p. 290)

Publicity and privacy circulate everywhere, in every individual fact or entity, inseparably. Every actual entity is for itself and for others. Extension and measure express this publicity.

In Leibniz, exempting God, monads mirror each other representationally. Each is individual in virtue of the others it represents. In this representational plenum, nothing is older than representation, than monads, except God and representation itself. Again, while God and preestablished harmony are older than time, than representation, there circulates no injustice. What is preestablished is orderly and harmonious, determining God's authority over all. Measure presupposes community, publicity, derived by a sacrifice, a selection and exclusion, which Whitehead calls "evil." The inescapable conjunction of public and private contains a primordial injustice.

Whitehead expresses the inescapable condition of a single universe of diverse actual entities: to belong to a common world and to represent that world in each actual entity—to belong to space and time under law and measure. This commonality imposes evil in the incompatibility of heterogeneous things that cannot circulate together without loss. With respect to law itself, Whitehead rejects a single Law for all time, speaks of a multiplicity of epochs, a close relative of Nietzsche's Eternal Return of the Same, working against the sameness of the Same. "The arbitrary, as it were 'given,' elements in the laws of nature warn us that we are in a special cosmic epoch. Here the phrase 'cosmic epoch' is used to mean that widest society of actual entities whose immediate relevance to ourselves is traceable" (*PR*, p. 91). "We" are in a special epoch constituted by certain "arbitrary" laws of nature. This insight concerning the arbitrariness of the authority of the most general natural laws and the truths relevant to them, representing and presupposing a multiplicity of other epochs, other worlds (not just possible worlds), expresses the age of authority—an authority older than any time to which we belong. It less clearly expresses this authority's injustice.

The theme of "older than time" appears throughout Whitehead, in the arbitrariness of time and law, in the multiplicity and heterogeneity of different epochs, different universes and times. One General Scheme of Potentiality establishes the condition for the togetherness of all things in One Universe. Whitehead presents the truth that we can find no sense of One World, of a Universe, that does not rest on an arbitrary condition of order. "The primordial created fact is the unconditioned conceptual valuation of the entire multiplicity of eternal objects. This is the 'primordial nature' of God" (*PR*, p. 31). Before all time, before all fact, there transpires an unconditioned envisagement of every possibility of form: Form before form; within the creativity of time. We wonder with what injustice. For the inescapability of conditions imposes arbitrary limits. "God is the ultimate limitation, and His existence is the ultimate irrationality. For no reason can be given for just that limitation which it stands in His nature to impose.... No reason can be given for the nature of God, because that nature is the ground of rationality."[9] Before all time, before all fact, there transpires an unconditioned imposition of form. We wonder with what injustice. For the other primordial condition is Creativity.

> Creativity ... is that ultimate notion of the highest generality at the base of actuality.... is always found under conditions, and described as conditioned. (Whitehead, *PR*, p. 31)

> "Creativity" is the principle of *novelty*. An actual occasion is a novel entity diverse from any entity in the "many" which it unifies. (Whitehead, *PR*, p. 21)

Before time and measure, we find two arbitrarinesses, one the primordial nature of God, the first imposition of order, as if without injustice, the other the freedom within each entity to depart from any of its conditions, again as if without injustice. Yet the disturbance of the first by the second represents evil. We call it "injustice." Our question concerns the injustice of God's authority as the ultimate irrationality, the injustice of any collective authority, God, Law, or Measure. Does God's authority, in its primordiality and collectivity, compose immemorial injustice?

The arbitrariness and irrationality of God's nature express the limits of determinateness, the disorder older than order. We nevertheless hesitate at any "ultimate limitation," as if the limits of reason and order repeat reason and order.[10] Perhaps ultimacy brings injustice, disturbance and unlimitation rather than limitation's authority. Reason's arbitrariness, unreason, may represent not another reason, God's rather than ours—as in Leibniz—but madness and injustice. God's authority over nature must be unjust, whatever authority we vest in "must." Where in Whitehead can we hear this possibility?

The extensive continuum represents the most general condition of potentiality for the circulation of actual entities together, given their creativity. We question the privilege, granted the authority of greatest generality and ultimate limitation. We do not thereby reject the possibility that the limits of reason lie in indeterminateness and unreason, the limits of truth in untruth, of justice and authority in injustice, perhaps in another, unlawful authority. We question the restoration of these indeterminatenesses, madnesses, untruths, and injustices to determinateness, to law as Law, to truth as Truth and Fact. We question every form in which the ultimate limits of reason may be represented. Above all, we question why the primordial nature of God, the condition of intelligibility as form, does not belong to Creativity, to time, to disorder as well as order, to injustice.

We are on the crux of Anaximander's fragment, both the age of authority and its injustice. In its age, older than time, authority circulates in time seeking recompense for its injustice, always receiving restitution, never achieving its due. We have seen Whitehead's evil, apparently within time, belonging to limitation and exclusion. We have seen that such a view of limitation must pertain to God, while Whitehead represents the primordial nature of God as imposing a selection without evil. Can we understand this aboriginal valuation of all possibilities, all forms, the circulation of inexhaustibly heterogeneous things together, to rest on an arbitrary, unjust selection, sacrificing untold possibilities? Can we understand the primordiality of God as injustice? Can ultimate limitation, in its arbitrariness, represent injustice? Can measure represent its restitution?

When Nietzsche corrects *The Birth of Tragedy* in his "Attempt at a Self-Criticism," he tells us that the question was always one of truth, the Dionysian in the Apollinian order of truth. If we take these gods to represent disorder and order, without injustice, we repeat an understanding of truth with nothing at stake. Dionysus risks nothing in confronting Apollo. Or else truth risks itself in unending violence and domination, in the claims of its authority. In Foucault's words: "Humanity does not gradually progress from combat to combat until it arrives at universal reciprocity, where the rule of law finally replaces warfare; humanity installs each of its violences in a system of rules and thus proceeds from domination to domination."[11] We understand this thought to represent the possibility that the installation of violence belongs to science, to physics and the natural world, to nature. Nature circulates domination after domination, violence upon violence—again, older than time—in the institution of authority. This truth pertains to science even if science does not represent its own age as older than time. Science's measure imposes a rule on nature instituting Authority.

Lyotard speaks of science (or Science) as producing

> a discourse of legitimation with respect to its own status, a discourse called philosophy. I will use the term *modern* to designate any science that legitimates itself with reference to a metadiscourse of this kind making an explicit appeal to some grand narrative, such as the dialectics of Spirit, the hermeneutics of meaning, the emancipation of the rational or working subject, or the creation of wealth. . . .
> Simplifying to the extreme, I define *postmodern* as incredulity toward metanarratives.[12]

Incredulity toward metanarratives suggests that we seek a postmodern science free from science's legitimation, from its authority, as if we might give up the project of legitimation once and for all, either give up the project of science or avoid its injustice. The age of authority and its injustice, the inescapability of authority—including Lyotard's authority—vanishes into our incredulity. For how may we temper the inescapable authority of science? Does science remain Science in its Nature, under measure and law, as if there could rule no science older than Science, older than law?

When Lyotard speaks of *le différend*, he defines it in terms of wrong, seeking resolution: "As distinguished from a litigation, a differend [*différend*] would be a case of conflict, between (at least) two parties, that cannot be equitably resolved for lack of a rule of judgment applicable to both arguments."[13] What if we could find an equitable resolution? What if we could promulgate a rule? Would we then incur no *différend*? That returns us to questions of injustice's age, to which we return again and again. Injustice cannot be resolved, under rule, while judgment has no rules. Injustice materializes before judgment's lack of rules. Injustice transpires older than science's authority. Judgment rules older than itself, older and younger than itself as judgment's judgment. "The history of the world cannot pass a last judgment. It is made out of judged judgments" (Lyotard, *D*, p. 8). We may give the name *semasis* to this circulation of judgments and their judgments.

What if the impossibility of a last judgment, the call in judgment for further judgment, marked the *différend* in judgment and authority? What if not conflict but authority represented the *différend*, the lack of authority of authority? What if that represented the age of injustice? What becomes of authority in general circulation?

Science's authority sets our model of self-governing authority, delimits the problem of reflection, defining measure's authority. The remoteness of the world, of nature, from representation, seems to contradict the privilege granted to representation against which Heidegger and Derrida speak, the privilege granted science's *mimēsis*. We may question Heidegger's view of science:

> Science is not an original happening of truth, but always the cultivation of a domain of truth already opened, specifically by apprehending and confirming that which shows itself to be possible and necessarily correct within that field. When and insofar as science passes beyond correctness and goes on to a truth, which means that it arrives at the essential disclosure of what is as such, it is philosophy.[14]

As we question science's authority in the voice of another authority—truth setting itself into work, the original happening of truth—do we repeat authority's injustice? Does our challenge to science's authority acknowledge its injustice, an injustice older than time? And what of the injustices science tells?

How can science's truth, however concealed, rest upon an injustice older than any authority? Whitehead's understanding of the primordial nature of God expresses this injustice in reverse: the unconditioned valuation of all possibilities, but not of all equally, without privilege or rank. The primordial nature of God privileges some orders over others, imposes hierarchy, in relation to any actualities, within time, and before any actualities, before time.[15] These hierarchies belong to form intrinsically, as if form imposes hierarchical order before all other orders, as if authority and complexity lend their precedence to actualities, imposing aboriginal priority upon them.

In Spinoza we similarly find two principles of order and two principles of individuality. The two principles of order appear together:

> In Nature there is nothing contingent, but all things are determined from the necessity of the divine nature to exist and act in a certain manner. (Spinoza, *Ethics*, I, Prop. 29)

> An individual thing, or a thing which is finite and which has a determinate existence, cannot exist nor be determined to action unless it be determined to existence and action by another cause which is also finite and has a determinate existence; . . . and so on *ad infinitum*. (Spinoza, *Ethics*, I, Prop. 28)

Everything follows from God necessarily; everything follows from other things. If the latter expresses the ordinance of time, then the former expresses the immemoriality of what belongs aboriginally to time. What comes before time imposes God's ordering of all things, existent and non-existent. "The ideas of nonexistent individual things or modes are comprehended in the infinite idea of God, in the same way that the formal essences of individual things or modes are contained in the attributes of God" (Spinoza, *Ethics*, II, Prop. 8). What belongs to time possesses another infinitude, a plenitude or inexhaustibility.

Everything follows from God; everything follows from other finite things; everything possesses its own essence and strives to endure. "The effort by which each thing endeavors to persevere in its own being is nothing but the actual essence of the thing itself" (Spinoza, *Ethics*, III, Prop. 7). Something persists older than time, before things struggling to persevere, exercising power and desire. God and the totality prevail older than time. Yet in Spinoza, they lack injustice even where things conflict. Anaximander tells us that God and Nature in their totality, within which each individual thing has its place, grounded in hierarchy and privilege, betrays injustice. The *conatus*, on this reading, expresses injustice in things striving to persevere, the violence of their persistence. Such a reading expresses Nietzsche's truth, that order, including justice and truth, rests on a truth of violence. Heterogeneity, inexhaustibility, and plenitude contain injustice within themselves, the inescapability of sacrifice.

Truth belongs to a sacrifice whose injustice circulates older than any enfranchised truth, including the authority of science—especially including the authority of the truth of science. Science's violence rests first on the violence of being, then second on the violence of truth. The age of authority tells of the violence of any authority, especially that of science's truth. The inescapable germ of truth in Heidegger's view of science does not represent the originariness of the others but the violence of science's standard of truth.

Something dwells within us older than science, immemorially, the age of injustice. Science expends its time seeking restitution for the injustice that presses within it. Rule and measure represent the restitutions composing justice that constitute the order of time.

Here science's restitutions circulate as rule and measure. We ask how epistemic authority belongs to injustice and composes violence. We ask what it means to challenge the authority of science from the standpoint of an injustice older than time. We look to the circulation of science in time as nature's measure.

Certain answers emerge within time. Desire and power materialize older than truth where power and desire compose truth—though, reciprocally, truth composes authority within desire and power. Our age, Foucault points out, is one based on truth's authority.

> Truth is a thing of this world: it is produced only by virtue of multiple forms of constraint. And it induces regular effects of power. Each society has its régime of truth, its "general politics" of truth: that is, the types of discourse which it accepts and makes function as true.[16]

We take up this general politics as a circulation, as truth's economy.

Suppose we heard the general economy, politics, and hedonology of truth as situating truth in time, under law and measure. In doing so, we would place truth in no jeopardy whatever. Instead, we question truth's authority, older than it, older than science, in the form of injustice. What if truth's general economy expressed this injustice?[17] By *restricted economy*, we mean a circulation under rule, as if disturbed by no primordial injustice. By *general economy*, we mean a circulation whose heterogeneities disturb every restricted authority. Law and measure belong to, circulate in, time, under rule, possessing an authority so old, an excess so immeasurable, as to circulate uselessly in time. We may hear this age and injustice of authority to speak against any truth, but Foucault cannot mean, in speaking of truth as a thing of this world, that it might disappear. To the contrary, in belonging to this world, truth's circulation, however multiply dispersed, bears weight and age. We may hear this age and injustice of authority to speak against any authority, yet authority remains so old that we cannot escape it. We may hear this age and injustice of authority to speak against a younger authority, one that establishes itself without question, without challenge. And we may hear the authority of science's truth to rule without question in every question. In Peirce's famous definition: "The opinion which is fated to be ultimately agreed to by all who investigate is what we mean by the truth, and the object represented in this opinion is the real."[18] Everything turns toward ultimate agreement, as if questioning might guarantee a limit constituting its authority, as if the guarantee might possess ultimate authority. Yet a guarantee possesses only the authority of the practices backing it. Science's authority belongs to its institutional stability, not to the form of its inquiry, belongs to the forces that back its guarantees with law and might. These guarantees, this law and might, entail that science circulate in a restricted, not a general economy. We take up measure as a restricted, not a general economy. We respond with truth's general economy, the incessant injustices of its authority.

An irony of the Western tradition is that science's authority emerged in profound challenge to authority—that of God and the Church. Reason's authority counters God's Authority—understandably, an equal or greater authority. What might be construed as a challenge to overweening authority established itself as another authority.[19] God and Reason impose Absolute Authority. Yet if authority's injustice befalls us older than time, then every authority that would place us at risk of injury, of ourselves or others, that would place us in risk of sacrifice, presents us with grave injustices. Every authority! The side of Plato's dialogues where virtue's authority repeatedly circulates in question falls beneath the side of the dialogues establishing the Authority of the Good as God and Law. Similarly, the iconoclastic side of empiricism that would reject any absolute authority disappears beneath the side that would establish the absolute authority of representational experience. The possibility within empiricism that what experience presents us with lacks authority passes into the authority of sensory representations.

Nothing can grant science authority except observation, yet observation lacks authority. How, then, does science gain authority? What authorizes science's circulation? That question befalls us older than time, but its answer falls into time again and again, circulating around law and measure. We will return to science's authority. We turn back to the authority of measure's law. Does science possess a measure that composes its authority without injustice?

Whitehead recognizes two conditions constituting measurement's authority, counting and stability: "Measurement depends upon counting and upon permanence. The question is, what is counted, and what is permanent" (*PR*, p. 327). Yet these do not give us measurement, even in relation to Whitehead's sense of measure. What can be measured, counted, must be stable. It cannot be permanent in time. But measurement also presupposes repetition, quite different from permanence, repetition of units in an economy of exchange. Centimeters, inches, light years, arcs, measure space where stable units can be counted again and again and where one unit of space can substitute for another. This, more than mathematical form, may define science's traditional authority. Yet fractal theory tells us that the repetition of multiple variations reappears at every level of scale, so that form endlessly repeats but cannot be counted, and each differs enough from every other not to be replaceable by it. Chaos theory tells us that small changes at one level may produce such immense changes at another that comparable units of comparison and substitution cannot be found. Strong and effective scientific theories can be found that do not presuppose measures of substitution and equivalence. We wonder if science's economy might circulate without authority.

Measure and exchange circulate in their most influential substitutive forms in relation to wealth, and measurement inhabits a restricted economy of circulation. We take iron atoms as equivalent, each substitutable for any other without loss, each electron for any other. Atoms and electrons, inches and grams, represent units whose individual specificities vanish into an economy of substitution, each exchangeable for any other. Money represents the basic currency of scientific authority. "The two functions of money, as a common measure between commodities and as a substitute in the mechanism of exchange, are based upon its material reality. A measure is stable, recognized as valid by everyone and in all places, if it has as a standard an assignable reality that can be compared to the diversity of things that one wishes to measure: . . . ."[20] These remarks on an economy of exchange and substitution come from Foucault's chapter on "Exchanging" in *The Order of Things*. We will read it as directed to measure's injustice. Yet we hesitate to accept Foucault's view of the materiality of money, of units of exchange, since substitution and exchange pervade our thinking, giving rise to economies of life and practice. We take up matter's economy.

Foucault identifies equivalence as the fundamental basis of exchange: "The standard of equivalence is itself involved in the system of exchanges, and the buying power of money signifies nothing but the marketable value of the metal" (*OT*, p. 171). The "buying power" and "marketable value" represent "nothing but" equivalent exchanges. In this "nothing" do we hear the circulation of economies of substitution everywhere?

> All wealth is *coinable*; and it is by this means that it enters into *circulation*—in the same way that any natural being was *characterizable*, and could thereby find its place in a *taxonomy*; that any individual was *nameable* and could find its place in an *articulated language*; that any representation was *signifiable* and could find its place, in order to be *known*, in a *system of identities and differences*. (Foucault, OT, p. 175)

Systems of identities and differences involve the circulation of units of exchange and substitution, like coins, but also of pleasure, sound and meaning, and truth, composing restricted economies.[21]

The presence of such economies within the Western tradition marks *technē*'s perfectibility as measure. We seek to understand the movement from such economy and measure to authority. Or rather, we seek to understand how such a measure, circulating in time, can have vested in it an authority older than time. This, perhaps more than any other, represents the limits of measure's relation to authority.

If we question the establishment of the authority of science's truth, to what does such a question lead us? If to observation, then to units of data that circulate within an economy of experimentation and report. If to scientific practice, then to units of apparatus that reliably and repeatedly reproduce the same results. If the authority of science's truth rests on reliability, then that reliability rests on an economy of measure, not perhaps on counting and permanence, as Whitehead suggests, but on the reproducible functions of units within a system of exchange and substitution.

Science's authority, on this reading, traditionally belongs to a restricted economy of measure and scale; scientists exchange reproducible units with each other throughout practices divided by space and time. Time, here, belongs to the authority of law but also to an economy of practice. We take up the possibility that modern authority, like law, requires and circulates within units of exchange and substitution. In imposing its authority, as against the king's authority, law creates an economy of legislation and execution where each individual represents the same under the law and where the authority of the law defines an economy of rule. Similarly, science's authority, grounded in truth, depends on an economy of exchange and substitution of reproducible experiments, units of apparatus and experimentation, where each apparatus and result matches the others so well that differences may be regarded as irrelevant. Can we imagine a science without units of circulation? Can we restrict science to measure's economy?[22]

The authority of law becomes Law where an economy of exchange circulates in time representing authority and where that authority circulates in time imposing an economy with no knowledge of its injustice. This authority of equivalence may be compared with narratives of great acts of vengeance, the House of Atreus for example, where each act's grandeur vests in a unique horror, or with the narrative of the execution of Damiens "the regicide."[23] The horror represents injustice here, for it expresses a refusal to fall into a reciprocity of vengeance and punishment even where these circulate endlessly. The Erinyes represent the plenitude and excess, the inexhaustibility and general economy, of guilt and punishment, reappearing in Kafka, the excess of authority and guilt before time. What replaces them circulates in time as an economy of human equivalence, where each unit of crime and transgression stands equivalent in measure to any other. In this way, the principle of justice, to fit the punishment to the crime, defines a restricted economy of justice into which the immemorial age of authority vanishes: the ordinance of time.

What does it mean to recognize the arbitrariness of what circulates in time? What injustice befalls such arbitrariness, and how can it do so out of time? How, when it does so, can such an injustice belong to truth, especially to the truth of science? What truth can science circulate except within a restricted economy? These mark questions of authority, whether the age of authority speaks against any authorization of authority, speaks of its arbitrariness and its injustice.

Money, once gold and silver, now a printed currency without material value, defines the economy of identities and differences within which power and desire circulate, delimits the force and limits of their authority. Authority becomes Authority in such an economy where money represents wealth and where wealth implements authority and desire. "[I]n a general fashion we use gold and silver because they contain hidden within themselves 'a peculiar perfection.' A perfection that is not of the order of price, but is dependent upon their endless capacity for representation" (Foucault, *OT*, p. 176). Gold and silver provided "a privileged instrument for the representation of all other kinds of wealth" (Foucault, *OT*, p. 176); paper currency supplanted them in virtue of its surpassing representativity and replaceability. Foucault emphasizes the durability of gold and silver. Whitehead emphasizes permanence in measurement. In a material economy, permanence and durability impose too great a price, remain too much with us, demand replacement under new technologies by economies whose units approach the limits of perfectibility: pure differences without identity. Such a purity exceeds perfection, undermines equivalence. So does materiality.

The interweaving of activities of production and representation constitutes a restricted economy when based on substitutability. Currency plays a role, in relation to production, similar to the role that words play in relation to things, expressed in *Gulliver's Travels* in the story of Lagado, where members of the Academy hope to replace words with things, carrying things themselves about to escape the indeterminatenesses of representation. Yet to carry things about instead of words, to show them in place of names, carries the indeterminatenesses and excesses of representation into the very things themselves where that indeterminateness belongs, older than representation. Words do not introduce ambiguity into representation, but present representation's ambiguities in a general economy of linguistic differences. The very perfection of things as their own representations destroys their authority.

> For Classical thought in its formative phase, money is that which permits wealth to be represented. Without such signs, wealth would remain immobile, useless, and as it were silent; in this sense, gold and silver are the creators of all that man can covet. But in order to play this role as representation, money must offer properties (physical and not economic ones) that render it adequate to its task, and in consequence precious. (Foucault, *OT*, p. 177)

That wealth requires representation to function as wealth, as meaning requires language, appears to place us in a restricted economy, the circulation of signs and things as goods. Yet the representation, where both material and economic, the precious representation of irreplaceable goods, both reinforces and disrupts the constraints of restricted economy. On the one hand, money represents wealth, possession, and production, in terms of an economy of signs divided into units of exchange and substitution. On the other hand, the material properties of gold and silver disrupt the system of exchange and substitution. One can hold on to gold, enforcing its value, beyond any currency. One can hold on to currency, augmenting its value, beyond any substitution. Gold and silver, coins and currency, both represent and embody wealth—as things themselves, in Lagado, both represent and embody themselves—opening an imponderable breach within nature and representation. This doubling repeats the impossibility of any stringent distinction between restricted and general economy.

In a restricted economy, wealth circulates in a system of identities and differences based on equivalent and substitutable units of exchange. Measure belongs to such an economy. In such terms, it grants authority to wealth and science through the representation of power and desire. In relation to measure, we wonder whether the properties of things may fall into time, may be mathematically representable, except within a system of equivalence, whether representation circulates in general economy. In relation to wealth and production, we wonder whether these can fall into time, into representation, except within an economy of equivalence, or whether production, *poiēsis*, composes a general economy. In relation to science, we wonder whether the form of scientific knowledge—its universality and reproducibility—presupposes an economy of exchange and substitution based on units of equivalence. In this form, scientific knowledge offers itself as multiply anonymous, in that sense "objective": concerned with no differences except those marked by the general economy of truth. We wonder how truth's general economy can escape disrupting all these works by its lack of equivalence.

Michael Polanyi speaks of knowledge in terms of personal commitment:

> It is the act of commitment in its full structure that saves personal knowledge from being merely subjective. Intellectual commitment is a responsible decision, in submission to the compelling claims of what in good conscience I conceive to be true. It is an act of hope, striving to fulfil an obligation within a personal situation for which I am not responsible and which therefore determines my calling. This hope and this obligation are expressed in the universal intent of personal knowledge.[24]

Within the tradition, it would be absurd to ask why Polanyi is threatened by merely subjective knowledge, why the intent must be universal. If what is subjective is true, is that not good enough? If it works, have we not made an achievement? Even more, are local knowledges, belonging to one or a few of us, in special ways, not knowledge at all, excluded from science? Polanyi answers in terms of authority: "When I speak of science I acknowledge both its tradition and its organized authority, and I deny that anyone who wholly rejects these can be said to be a scientist, or have any proper understanding and appreciation of science" (*Personal Knowledge,* p. 164)[25]

Let us suppose, despite their endless differences, that universality and objectivity, the rejection of mere subjectivity, circulate together. When Polanyi moves from personal commitment to science, staking everything on the risk of failure, he moves through the notion of authority—science's authority over itself and its truths. Two questions emerge in the above passages. First, is to learn, to *submit*—and if so, to authority? Do trust and authority belong together, or does one live in intimacy while the other inhabits privilege, superiority and inferiority? The other question has to do with the conditions of commitment to traditional authority. What would it mean for a tradition's authority to be unconditional? Can such an authority, unconditioned, circulate in time, or does it, as Hobbes suggests, fall outside, before time?

We have been led to think of the law of authority, in time, as concerned with circulation, after Foucault, who distinguishes it from accumulation.

> Just as in the order of representations the signs that replace and analyse them must also be representations themselves, so money cannot signify wealth without itself being wealth. But it becomes wealth because it is a sign; whereas a representation must first be represented in order subsequently to become a sign.
>
> Hence the apparent contradictions between the principles of accumulation and the rules of circulation. At any given moment of time, the number of coins in existence is determined. (Foucault, *OT*, p. 177)[26]

In neither money nor representation does authority circulate, except in a time under law that grants, that grounds, their authority. Money authorizes practice insofar as it represents wealth in circulation. Knowledge authorizes practice insofar as it represents truth in circulation. The circulation of knowledge and truth, of history and practice, expresses the timeliness, under law, whereby these gain authority.

Can we pursue this hypothesis further? Can we think of authority before law and time as the injustice whereby authority institutes itself in general circulation? Perhaps what appears as common among things determines their intelligibility, common among different things, accumulates their differences as identity. Perhaps what circulates in and around things determines their essences, thereby their intelligibility. Polanyi asks us to submit to authority by example so that science may circulate. Can we say that authority in time belongs to and falls under circulation, in economies of exchange and substitution, so that justice under law finds its measure in equivalence and exchange, while the authority older than time seeks recompense for injustice that has no measure because it does not circulate, or circulates in general economy?

Language and representation circulate, along with measurable units of materiality. Our account of circulation points to the immeasurability and uncirculability of materiality—its immateriality. We think of matter circulating without units of circulation and of a general economy of production and display measured by no units and circulating none. How can an economy of substitution grant authority, and how can authority circulate within a restricted economy? How can knowledge and truth belong to circulation as an economy demands, how can they always belong to circulation and reciprocity? Foucault answers: "When goods can circulate (and this thanks to money), they multiply, and wealth increases; when coinage becomes more plentiful, as a result of a good circulation and a favourable balance, one can attract fresh merchandise and increase both agriculture and manufacturing" (*OT*, p. 178). When goods circulate—goods of every kind, including knowledge and truth—they multiply, become more plentiful. Levinas tells us of the immeasurable debt of responsibility. We find ourselves repeating the immeasurability of authority. The assumption, circular in its circulation, represents goods such as possessions, knowledge, truth, beauty, and authority as becoming more plentiful, more heterogeneous, as they multiply, multiplying into an inexhaustible circulation, a general economy. We add that in such a circulation, goods conflict, engendering evil. In such a circulation, what transpires older than all these goods, however plentiful and multiplying, rules as injustice. Their multiplication makes endless restitution for injustice.

The age of authority circulates far older than equivalence, filled with injustice, to which restricted economies pay endless tribute. We wonder if a productive interrelation of human beings can arise, of animals and plants, of natural things, that does not presuppose a system of equivalence. The restricted circulation of which we speak expresses where animals and plants, human beings, divide into units that may be substituted for each other without loss or sacrifice. If a thief steals a tool, an instrument, a typewriter, we demand recompense as replacement. Where love, or our sweat, has left the imprint of our desire upon others, replacement achieves nothing—because nothing equates with what we have lost, and beloved things cannot circulate, exceed circulation. The trauma of theft forces itself upon us because even after restitution what we have lost has no equivalent, and the idea that in the circulation of like things we will find our security restored fails to represent the limits of our economy. In this failure appear the limits of time's and law's authority, an authority older than any exchange. We circulate with others in an injustice beyond any restitution, always seeking compensation.

Life and practice exceed any economy, as any economy exceeds its own circulations—in accumulation and loss, for example. The "economy of circulation" no more truly represents economic relations than it represents truth and beauty. Nor, for that matter, does the failure of circulation and equivalence in things appear in the substitution of universality for their individuality. No doubt what the demands of exchange circulation impose, their overweening and excessive authority, tramples upon the individuality of individuals, who cannot circulate without sacrifice. But conscious subjects do not represent the only individuals. Every thing shows itself as individual in this sense, animals, plants, and microorganisms, atoms and electrons. All circulate together. Have we proved that each electron is exactly the same as any other? Such a proof has no importance whatever in the system of circulation describing modern physics. In a sense, who cares? In a sense, the individuality of atoms and electrons circulates a residue of no scientific importance whatever, no importance in nature.

Shall we respond that such unimportance has always shown itself, finally, to possess unlimited importance, that the residue exceeding any notion of natural law eventually presents itself demanding recognition? Or shall we respond that the residue tells us of the limits of circulation, but that circulation has no authority and vests in none? Why should truth materialize in a form that circulates within a restricted economy? Why should value vest in authority, especially in an authority of exchange? "The theory of money and trade responds to the question: how, in the movement of exchange, can prices characterize things—how can money establish a system of signs and designation between kinds of wealth?" (Foucault, *OT*, pp. 189–90). How in the movement of exchange do values get represented? And why represented for circulation? Why do objects of desire and need require representation (in circulation), and why can one affirm their worth with authority? Why and what authority?

An answer lies in the sacrifice that constitutes circulation on the one hand, and authority, on the other—the sacrifice Whitehead identifies with evil. "The creation of value is therefore not a means of satisfying a greater number of needs; it is the sacrifice of a certain quantity of goods in order to exchange others. Values thus form the negative of goods" (Foucault, *OT*, p. 192). Exchange and equivalence materialize in virtue of a sacrifice of goods, a sacrifice of things and their worth, to achieve a certain worth and measure. The goods exceed their worth in general circulation. Excess appears on both sides, in what gets sacrificed for exchange circulation and in the economic life unleashed within a restricted economy. "What is the origin of this excess that makes it possible for goods to be transformed into wealth without being effaced and finally disappearing altogether as a result of successive exchanges and continual circulation?" (Foucault, *OT*, p. 192). Exchange cannot circulate without loss, yet goods grow through circulation, representing the excesses of general circulation, the life of an economy unto itself. Here nature passes from plenitude and generation into circulation, from general to restricted economy: "The whole system of exchanges, the whole costly creation of values, is referred back to the unbalanced, radical, and primitive exchange established between the advances made by the landowner and the generosity of nature. This exchange alone is absolutely profitable" (Foucault, *OT*, p. 195). Nature's plenitude passes through representation into economic circulation as if that movement expressed its definitive representation, as if equivalence and exchange belonged intrinsically to *technē*. Even so, nature's excesses in relation to such an economy cannot be avoided. "It would be untrue to say that nature spontaneously produces values; but it is the inexhaustible source of the goods that exchange transforms into values, though not without expenditure and consumption" (Foucault, *OT*, p. 195). Thus, we may say finally, to represent the closure within which we fall, value and exchange become indissociable[27] in a restricted economy.

Value and exchange become indissociable as we represent the closure of their mutual representation. What permits us to recognize the excess of value in relation to exchange and the life of circulation beyond its elements? Foucault grants this role to Sade:[28]

> Sade attains the end of Classical discourse and thought. He holds sway precisely upon their frontier. After him, violence, life and death, desire, and sexuality will extend, below the level of representation, an immense expanse of shade which we are now attempting to recover, as far as we can, in our discourse, in our freedom, in our thought. but our thought is so brief, our freedom so enslaved, our discourse so repetitive, that we must face the fact that that expanse of shade below is really a bottomless sea. (*OT*, p. 211).

The immense expanse of shade does not circulate, does not allow us to circulate within it, but lies underneath every circulation, perhaps older than time. The "prosperities" of which Foucault speaks, however solitary and endless, represent violences and sacrifices.[29] He does not speak of the endless circulation of women as commodities, sacrifices to male authority.

What kind of economy might we inhabit without exchange? What kind of knowledge and truth, of science, might circulate without equivalence? The reproducibility central to science marks the repetition and circulation of its representations. We take a scientific truth to circulate without regard to its provenance and circumstances. Polanyi rejects this view of science, yet maintains its authority within another circulation, that of the authority of art. Within art, a teacher's authority does not circulate in virtue of its reproducibility, but possesses disciplinary authority only in virtue of its circulation.[30]

Tradition's authority marks the point where art and science meet, where science establishes its claim to authority. Without circulation, for example, of texts and commentaries, without endless circulation in endless circularity, tradition could possess no authority. The circulation of texts, of writings and reports, in their equivalence, lends a certain authority to tradition. Suppose each version, each printing of a text, differed and exercised a different authority? Suppose each text resisted its author's authority because we knew of no such author and no such authority? What kind of authority could tradition have? We may compare the circulation of texts with archaeological remains that do not circulate. We may compare circulation of exchangeable units with an inexhaustible circulation exceeding any units whatever.

Measure authorizes reproducible units, while the injustice of its authority disrupts exchange and equivalence. The forms of this disruption show themselves in the circulations of authority, around the subject, thrown down abjectly into subjection, into idolatry, and in nature, ruled by science, pervaded by monsters. With these themes of subjection, monstrosity, idolatry, and science we trace the economy of authority's injustice. We pursue the unjust authority of authority into the abjection of our subjection, the monstrosity of reason, the mystic force of law, and the inescapability of the idols in their twilight. We follow these themes into the unjust and monstrous authority of science's truth, whose dangers we cannot live without.

V

SUBJECTION'S ABJECTION

"Man" appears, in the narrative of *The Order of Things*, at a certain point in the "analytic of finitude," defining "our modernity":

> Man, in the analytic of finitude, is a strange empirico-transcendental doublet, since he is a being such that knowledge will be attained in him of what renders all knowledge possible. (Foucault, *OT*, p. 318)

> For the threshold of our modernity is situated not by the attempt to apply objective methods to the study of man, but rather by the constitution of an empirico-transcendental doublet which was called *man*. (Foucault, *OT*, p. 319)

This irruption of Man constitutes a certain Subject, grounded in finitude, at the same time—its doubling—constituting and completing the ground of knowledge. The subject here—clearly The Subject—comes to possess knowledge in Himself of what makes knowledge possible, closing the circle of objective truth within the sphere of subjectivity.

What spheres compose the orbit of The Subject? Shall we suppose that the entire narrative of "our" postmodernity appears in Heidegger's words in *The Origin of the Work of Art*, speaking of "the thingness of the thing" and "the basic Greek experience of the Being of beings as presence"?[1] "The process begins with the appropriation of Greek words by Roman-Latin thought. *Hupokeimenon* becomes *subiectum*; *hupostasis* becomes *substantia*; *sumbebekos* becomes *accidens*" (Heidegger, *OWA*, p. 23). We have noted the unbroken privilege granted this basic Greek experience, vanishing into "our" Latin-Roman oblivion to Being—an absolute privilege rescinded by Heidegger while granting another privilege to German, in the highest *Geistlichkeit* of *Geist*.[2] *"Roman thought takes over the Greek words without a corresponding, equally authentic experience of what they say, without the Greek word"* (Heidegger, *OWA*, p. 23).

Yet within the Latin word something appears, that has already appeared, that seems to vanish obscurely into *hypokeimenon*'s thingliness:[3] that before The Subject is placed under things as their foundation, supporting their weight, their *subjectum*, the subject as *subjectus* is thrown under the dominion of others' authority, pressed down by injustice. If Man finds himself thrown down—*projected*—as the ground of whatever knowledge we may have of things in virtue of the empirico-transcendental possibility of knowledge residing in Himself, Subject and Object of all knowledge, that projection transpires in virtue of masking, obscuring, in the closure of the circle of power, the authority vested in Him as a subject thrown under the dominion of others. Masked, hidden in Heidegger, present only obliquely in Foucault's understanding of "Man,"[4] rules the inescapable truth that the constitution of the subject—especially as The Subject—constitutes our subjection.[5] The story of the "We" here represents the subjugated narrative of subjection whose insurrection we strive to promote.

The Subject, the ground of knowledge, of thingliness, upon whom all beings, objects, rest, unfolds repeatedly as a site of subjection. That truth, more than any other, composes Hobbes's insight, what makes him in a certain way inevitable in our understanding of political authority, in relation to the authority that constitutes authority's truth. From the state of nature to absolute sovereignty, subjects find themselves already subjected to unlimited authority. Certain aspects of this truth appear in Foucault, strange perhaps in the suggestion that this immemoriality of power constitutes a new truth, emergent within the development of a new subject, Man, in relation to power: "The 'man' that the reformers set up against the despotism of the scaffold has also become a 'man-measure': not of things but of power."[6]

Foucault describes this emergence of a measure of power in terms of rules capable of "reducing the whole diffuse domain of illegalities" (Foucault, *DP*, p. 94). They appear in Foucault as irruptions, discontinuities and breaks; we think of them here as present within the Roman order of law and authority, from the beginning, before the beginning, within the relation between subject and *technē*. Among the rules, in particular, presides *the rule of lateral effects*: "The penalty must have its most intense effects on those who have not committed the crime; . . . " (Foucault, *DP*, p. 95). This does not express the only rule, and we may suspect that each technology of discipline imposes a different instrumentality and ideality. For example, the other rules of "the semio-technique with which one tried to arm the power to punish" (Foucault, *DP*, p. 94) appear as follows:

> The rule of minimum quantity.
> The rule of sufficient ideality.
> The rule of perfect certainty.
> The rule of common truth.
> The rule of optimal specification.
>   (see Foucault, *DP*, pp. 94–98)

Minimality, sufficiency, optimality, truth, all speak of a certain moment in Western reason where exchange value and substitutive equivalence take precedence over injustice, moments of instrumentality and measure in relation to truth. Even here, the moment at which exchange value takes a certain precedence over and within discipline marks the economy of exchange and instrumentality.

The rule of lateral effects tells another story. For within the restrictive economy of punishment as example and deterrent, an economy restrictive enough to give rise to a counterreaction based on the rights of human subjects not to be subjected to punishments unfairly, instruments for the regulation of others, circulates the unyielding truth that humanity emerges within systems of authority and regulation, that human beings materialize as human subjects, not as *hypokeimata* but as sites of subjection, thrown under others' authority, wounded by history's discontinuities. Here discipline and punishment define a certain epoch's dynamic of subjection where, within the idea of a Subject as citizen within a realm of Ends we find presupposed the authorities of Reason, Truth, and Law under whose rule every citizen falls subjected, the rule of *technē*. Older than any kingdom of Law and Ends rule the injustices of authority and reason, any authority and any reason, dominions of power to which We find ourselves subjected.

Dostoevsky's *Underground Man* speaks famously to this point of subjection from within its abject paradoxicality:

> Oh, tell me, who first declared, who first proclaimed, that man only does nasty things because he does not know his own real interests; and that if he were enlightened, if his eyes were

> opened to his real normal interest, man would at once cease to do nasty things, would at once become good and noble because, being enlightened and understanding his real advantage, he would see his own advantage in the good and nothing else, and we all know that not a single man can knowingly act to his own disadvantage.[7]

This critique of Socrates' repeated claim in the dialogues that no one knowingly acts against the good divides in two. In the first place, that of the advantage of the good, the two competing claims fall within instrumentality, address its force and authority. The second place speaks to the "within" of instrumentality, granting the force of authority.

> Why, one may choose what is contrary to one's own interests, and sometimes one *positively ought* (that is my own idea). (Dostoevsky, *NU*, p. 23)

> And, after all, that is not all: even if man really were nothing but a piano key, even if this were proved to him by natural science and mathematics, even then he would not become reasonable, but would purposely do something perverse out of sheer ingratitude, simply to have his own way. (Dostoevsky, *NU*, p. 28)

Reason, instrumentality, and law, whether or not we can or ought to defy them perversely, work by imposition, authority, and power, and we fall under them, subjected to them, at their best and worst, in their very nature. The Underground Man displays his perversity as monstrous and ineffective, abject, proffers his conviction that human beings might choose perversely to oppose reason without historical confirmation. Western human beings have chosen rationality. The truth he represents marks this choice and rationality to belong to authority and to impose themselves upon us as subjects, subjecting us to their rule. The truth he indicates shows that authority imposes itself inescapably in the joint forms of abjection and subjection. "And, indeed, I will at this point ask an idle question on my own account: which is better—cheap happiness or exalted sufferings? Well, which is better?" (Dostoevsky, *NU*, p. 114). We ask instead, which is more abject? Even so, "who, I ask you, would agree to call himself abject, subject of or subject to abjection?"[8]

Shall we so quickly give up the dream of a *praxis* free from subjection, from rule? Can we hope for life without subjugation, domination?

Nietzsche and Foucault do not think so. "In a sense, only a single drama is ever staged in this 'nonplace,' the endlessly repeated play of dominations."[9] This play of domination upon domination manifests the injustice of history's *praxis*, caught up in the dream, but not the possibility, of resolution and universality, in the "always more" that persists within the injustices of violence and domination. Here the injustice of violence and domination gives rise to justice, to violence and domination but also to resistance, to violence against violence and domination of domination.[10]

We may hear these repeated circularities of violence and domination as expressions of the force required of *praxis* for its effectiveness, repulsing the ineffectiveness of a utopianism too weak to make a difference. If we hope to engage in moral and political practice, we must achieve efficacy, utilizing the instruments of effective practice, violence and domination. Here we with Nietzsche give up the pretense of escaping violence and power in the name of *technē*.

Yet the repeated movements to instrumentality, to effectiveness and efficacy, speak of the inescapability of the domination and violence of *technē* in the voice of its inescapability. No resistance to *technē*, to instrumentality and measure, persists in such a view of *praxis*. Yet the injustice older than time perseveres older than measure and law, older than *technē*, as *technē* itself prevails older than time. Its authority and its injustice fall within it, befall it always and everywhere, circulate in the form of measure and law, instrumentality, *technē*, subjection and abjection, and resistance.

"The *Erhabene* persists, not over and beyond, but right in the heart of the *Aufgehobenen*." Either the Absolute belongs to "the universe presented by your phrase, and is relative to it"; or the Absolute must, as Absolute, be unpresentable. "This is why the absolute is not presentable."[11] Either the Absolute includes all silences, falling beyond presentation into silence, or, if presented, cannot take account of all silences, all *différends*, silences and possibilities. Lyotard asks us to consider that "What is not presented is not. The presentation entailed by a phrase is not presented, it is not" (Lyotard, *D*, p. 77). The silences and untruths brush against the what-is-not, while Being speaks through language in the silence of withdrawal. The *Erhabene*, the sublime, presents an unpresentable, a forgotten, that must not be forgotten—a "must" belonging to the *différend*, marking endless restitution.

What might this truth of presentation—if a "truth"—have to do with authority and subjection? Lyotard tells us it presents the unpresentable as a silence whose inexpressibility speaks in proximity to subjugation and victimization. The Absolute heals all scars as it silently repeats their pain. The Absolute includes all scars, all sacrifices, as it reconstitutes their wounds. Injustice asks us to think of sacrifices and sufferings that cannot be gathered up, cannot be remembered or mourned, of subjection to a catastrophic history without absolution. The recurrent threat of history, eloquently attested to by Hegel, unfolds as the identity it imposes on the heterogeneity of victims.

The *différend* belongs to a site of authority and subjection. "As distinguished from a litigation, a differend would be a case of conflict, between (at least) two parties, that cannot be equitably resolved for lack of a rule of judgment applicable to both arguments" (Lyotard, *D*, p. xi). We may read this definition as marking a moment of conflict outside, beyond, the economy of rule and law, of measure, where we have not established a measure, a rule of judgment. Such a reading suggests that within the rule of law, a conflict possesses no *différend*; that within the sphere of legitimacy, litigation succeeds according to criteria and rules; that within an economy of judgment, equitable resolution may be possible in spite of archaic injustice. Yet the *différend* belongs to nature's heterogeneity. "[A] universal rule of judgment between heterogeneous genres is lacking in general" (Lyotard, *D*, p. xi). Lacking in general, like the difference of masks, suggests an absence of rule older than any rule, as if genres, rules, law, legitimation, all circulate as heterogeneous in general: judgment without criteria, a general circulation. That truth marks the importance of Kant: judgment without criteria; judgment beyond presentation, beyond judgment; endless, heterogeneous judgment, semasis, a general economy of judgment, with its victims.

Beyond judgment, in its general economy, in the uncanny spaces among heterogeneous spheres of judgment, conflicts open without rules for adjudication, where every adjudication presents a wrong, an injury, injustice, calls for further judgment, semasis, in resistance, restitution. In the name of the *différend*, Lyotard repeats what we have borrowed from Anaximander, tells that judgment belongs inescapably to history, to time, that injustice unfolds older than time, always present in time, in every justification and measure. History moves as the rectification of the injustices already present in its movement: the injustices of justice. The economy of judgment upon judgment, semasis, circulates as unceasing *différends* demand endless reparations within archaic injustices. The archaic endlessly reappears, endlessly repeats itself as new injustices, calls for endless restitution.

We may hesitate at Lyotard's presentation of a *différend* as a wrong lacking restitution, as if a wrong under rule might escape injustice, as if a *différend* inhabited a different space entirely from *le différend*.[12] As if to have the means, the rule of law, to prove, to say, to testify to an injury might eliminate its injustice. As if, under law, injustice might give way to justice. As if an economy might eliminate all victims. As if the Erinyes might no longer haunt the city, howling for retribution. Have the Furies been domesticated, or do we hear their execrations as we speak? "Kafka warned us about this. It is impossible to establish one's innocence, in and of itself. It is a nothingness" (Lyotard, *D*, p. 9). A nothingness of silence, unpresentable, or an empty nothingness in relation to archaic injustice, circulating in time, based on measure? Innocence presents itself as nothing because we find ourselves, in time, always already guilty—or rather, find ourselves always already within a general economy of violence and injustice as we seek our innocence under law. Judgment lives in two worlds at once, judgment's injustice and justice's judgment. Innocence bears no distinction from guilt, justice from injustice, except under law, time, fallen under the responsibility for restitution for immemorial injustice.

This irruption of the unpresentable as the *différend* expresses the archaic immemoriality of injustice, that it cannot be replaced—substituted or exchanged—by any rule of justice, by any rectification, as the untruth from which science arose, in its splendor, does not disappear with the achievements of science. Nor does it render those achievements null, destroy its truth.[13] That the *dommage* of the *tort* might be blunted by testimony, by truth, represents truth within an exchange economy. Nothing blunts archaic and immemorial injustice, nothing blunts it and nothing measures it. It gives forth unfailing suspicion of every authority where judgment falls under authority, imposes and suffers subjection.

We struggle, in the name of the *Erhabene*, between remembering and forgetting, archaic and restitutive justice. We struggle to bear witness to the forgotten *différend* (Lyotard, *D*, p. xiii), hoping to make it reappear, knowing that it is a *différend* only as forgotten. We struggle to bear witness to, to remember, what cannot be remembered, while it circulates everywhere around us. We struggle to say what we are called to say, to represent, by archaic injustice. We struggle toward the victims.

This struggle shows itself repeatedly in Lyotard,[14] who speaks of judgment as phrasing, linking, where these fall under necessity, subjected to authority. "The only one [object] that is indubitable, the phrase, because it is immediately presupposed. (To doubt that one phrases is still to phrase, one's silence makes a phrase)" (Lyotard, *D*, p. xi).[15] Never mind the reappearance of the absolute authority of the *cogito*, as if its necessity may be displaced but not escaped. Phrasing, linking, belong to necessity, indubitably. We may read this as mirroring our view that we respond to judgments by successive judgments, to what falls into history by further history, as a representation of what we call "semasis," judgment's general economy, but with a difference. For semasis falls into a time already fallen, already broken by past and future injustices, circulates in time in restitution for something time cannot represent, owes and pays unending restitution, thereby marks authority's contingency.

What of the inescapability of injustice? What of the necessity of excess? *"La réalité comporte le différend"* (translated as "Reality entails the differend").[16] And what if reality were composed of *les différends*, circulating as *différends*? What if *les différends* composed nature's economy, if heterogeneity composed nature's necessity? Would that compose injustice? Does archaic injustice compose the necessity of linking? Do victims compose *les différends*?

When Aristotle says of *physis* that *"nature is a source or cause of being moved and of being at rest in that to which it belongs primarily,* in virtue of itself and not in virtue of a concomitant attribute" (Aristotle, *Physics*, 2.192b), he makes no mention of nature's necessity. When he discusses the ways in which nature moves of itself, he includes necessity "for the most part," together with chance (*tychē*) and spontaneity (*automaton*).[17] The nature that moves from itself to itself moves by necessity, sometimes or mostly, or by chance. The completeness of nature's self-movement, to and from itself, entails chance and necessity. Can each be the other's injustice? Do they compose a general economy?

This remarkable insight in Aristotle appears almost nowhere else in the Western tradition until Hegel, for whom necessity and freedom belong together, where the "truth of necessity, therefore, is *Freedom*,"[18] and where it represents a mistake "to regard freedom and necessity as mutually exclusive" (Hegel, *Logic*, p. 283). After Hegel, Whitehead can say in his *Category of Freedom and Determination* that "the concrescence of each individual actual entity is internally determined and is externally free" (Whitehead, *PR*, p. 28). To be determined is to be free, and conversely. We have spoken of the victims.

If nature moves of itself, by necessity, it also moves by chance and spontaneity. The completeness of nature's self-movement transforms the identity of the Same into a univocal that undermines the dominion of identity, transforms the totality into a general economy. This economy composes our acknowledgment of nature's injustice, for if we take nature to move entirely by necessity, we may be tempted to overlook the victims of that necessity, accepting its authority as inescapable. Yet if within nature, some things move by necessity, others move by chance, if under authority, within the play of power, authority works by necessity, where that necessity works by chance, then that authority cannot impose necessity even if inescapable. It cannot turn from its victims.

What of time's necessity? We may think of Aristotle, for whom necessity belongs to chance, of Hegel, for whom it belongs to freedom. If time, if nature, exercise necessity, they do so in virtue of their freedom or arbitrariness, the arbitrariness of that necessity. If phrasing possesses necessity, if we must link no matter what, if not to link repeats linking, then judgment authorizes itself by necessity within the broken freedoms of judgments without rules. In what can phrasing's authority and necessity lie, given that it has no nature? In what economy?

Necessity circulates in time within measure and *technē*. Foucault's univocals, Being or power, our univocals, injustice and authority, identity and representation, possess no measure or *technē*, exercise no necessity, even where inescapable. We wonder whether necessity, like authority, may represent another univocal, whether the definite article transforms heterogeneous *différends* into the univocity of *Le différend*, and by what injustice. We return to Anaximander to remember that each univocal belongs to injustice, to authority's and necessity's injustice. Beware of authority! Suspect every rule! Resist necessity's injustice within our necessity!

To have a rule, to fall under criteria, to achieve legitimation, do not spare us injustice. These do not follow from victimization, but on the contrary constitute it. That we are not spared has nothing to do with necessity but everything to do with subjection. Lyotard asks us to think of a victim who has no way to testify to a wrong, who lacks authority to name injury. In the extreme, animals represent the utmost victims:

> 38. Some feel more grief over damages inflicted upon an animal than over those inflicted upon a human. This is because the animal is deprived of the possibility of bearing witness according to the human rules for establishing damages, and as a consequence, every damage is like a wrong and turns it into a victim *ipso facto*. . . . That is why the animal is a paradigm of the victim. (Lyotard, *D*, p. 28)

Yet what could grant an animal or deprive it of this possibility of witness? Fairy tales imagine animals who speak and testify, who act and suffer. What if a silent victim gained standing in a court of law to testify; what if one's speaking in the world aroused miscomprehension; what if one gained comprehension but found oneself still abused? Would one find oneself less of a victim? Is the victimization of animals that they cannot bear witness to wrongs or that every such witness would make no difference? Do concentration camp survivors become less victims as we build memorials to their suffering? Or does our testimony, which victims of concentration camps may not be able to give themselves, make them more victims, make them more explicitly victims? Do we subject animals to our authority as victims or do we coerce them as objects, not even subjects, coerced without objection, subjected to abjection? If the victim cannot object, what marks the measure of the oppressor's sovereignty? If victims cannot stand abject, cannot measure their oppressors, what marks the measure of their oppression?

In most Western criminal systems, victims have no standing. Can this wrong be righted, as if by granting a certain instrumentality in punishment, victims would be less damaged? Or may the victim's wrong have no remedy except the Erinyes, howling their fury in the streets? Perhaps the shrieking of victims who have suffered gives us their truth without remedy, the injustices of their subjections before all authority, while remedy belongs in vain to time. Perhaps subjection can never find a remedy. Oppressed subjects can be liberated; as victims, their wrongs remain abject wrongs even when righted.

We may wonder where in Lyotard's *différend* we may find abjection, wonder at victims' proclivity to blame themselves. The Underground Man represents utter subjection for us in virtue of his debasement. Animals represent the paradigm of victims for us because we take them to represent subjection without abjection. Human beings do not fulfill the same paradigm, because of the contamination of their abjection, as victims, no matter how subjected, how oppressed. This expresses the measure and circulation of subjection against which the immemoriality of injustice wages endless retribution—against another possibility that subjection may show itself to be Right in virtue of the victim's abjection. Animals never give us that respite, never liberate us from the injustice of their subjugation. We cannot blame an animal as victim when we do not take the animal to blame itself. And what if we found animals to know abjection, perhaps without exalted suffering?

The age, the immemoriality, of injustice tells that subjection and subjugation circulate everywhere and always without justification within the measure of historical time whose ordinance consists of one justification after another; never immemorially, never archaically, for that injustice has no measure. Tribal narratives tell that to kill an animal for food one must pay recompense, for nothing, not even hunger, can bring justification. The Enlightenment West appears to know nothing of this injustice except in fragmentary moments. The sweep of instrumentality, under *technē*, compels us to imagine that every action might attain justice, might have justification, under reason's law, oblivious to the possibility that life, existence, being, togetherness in proximity and community, might rest on pain and suffering, exclusion and domination, on authority and more authority, especially the authority of justice. A general economy of pain and suffering inseparable from joy and pleasure: our abject *jouissance!*[19]

We may go further. For the archaic injustice, older than time, within which justice imposes a measure, coincides with justice's *archē*. In this respect, if animals represent a paradigm of victimization because they cannot testify to a wrong, cannot obtain standing, cannot speak, provide a paradigm of subjection free from abjection, free from any tendency on their part, we suppose, to blame themselves, other creatures and things also suffer subjection. Objects, not just subjects, suffer subjection. We dream that animals might speak, might tell us of their subjugation. How could rocks and stones, broken under foot, how could leaves of grass, speak up? And if they could not, would they be less subjected, less victims, freer from archaic injustice, from evil[20]?

Could the speaking that defines a *différend* uphold another hegemony under which subjects alone suffer subjection, under law, where the "subject" marks less the irruption of subjection than a moment within the sovereignty of Law? "It is in the nature of a victim not to be able to prove that one has been done a wrong. A plaintiff is someone who has incurred damages and who disposes of the means to prove it" (Lyotard, *D*, p. 8). This proof and means propel themselves as moments in time and law. If damage appears normal, under measure, belongs to law, if the community recognizes it, does the victim's victimization cease? Lyotard grants animals standing as victims because they cannot speak, in their silence. Would he (or we) grant rocks and stones the same standing? What authorizes us to grant standing at all? What composes language, speaking, or representation as moments of legitimation? Does every distinction, under law, every representation, divide along lines of authority, victims from victimizers, unprivileged from privileged? Does every distinction, every measure, define Humanity as a site of propriety? Do we tell a story of humanity as one of authority and subjection in our most dispassionate representations, moments of the will to power? "I would like to call a *différend* [*différend*] the case where the plaintiff is divested of the means to argue and becomes for that reason a victim" (Lyotard, *D*, p. 9). *Différends* compose reality as *Le différend*. The *différend* composes nature's authority.

We cannot live without incurring injuries, without injustice, without the pain of past injustices. The entire system of law exists to bring an injury to measure, to bring about its recognition, its standing before the law. What grants the law such authority except something archaic, before the law? How can the law overcome its own victimization? It cannot restore what has been lost, cannot make life whole. Those who suffer injury remain injured when they have healed. A mother is raped and murdered before her children. A mother is murdered alone at night, unknown to her children. The murderer is executed. A child is molested. A house is vandalized. A woman is stolen from her home and taken thousands of miles away into servitude. Two parents are taken hundreds of miles away where they are starved and killed. An entire people has its land sold to others, is taken hundreds of miles away to another place. A child is killed by a drunken driver. A child kills herself driving at night. A child kills herself. A parent dies. A parent molests his children. And more.

The narrative of psychoanalysis tells how difficult, how impossible, we find it to recognize, to know, to speak of such injuries, as they circulate as traces in later life,[21] representing this impossibility in the language of blame and guilt.[22] Freud tells his narrative in causal and instrumental terms as the superego represents excess. Guilt and punishment exceed any rational measures, any norms the ego can provide. Civilization depends on guilt's excesses. The outcome leads to war.

The narrative of traces tells that wrongs can never be extirpated, that they remain in further life, in history, as wounds for the injured and as influences upon the future. History, in Freud and Nietzsche, circulates a residue of violence and injury, leaving victim after victim, endlessly seeking a restitution without fulfillment, without a name, yearning for silence amid the cacophonies of life. Standing, legitimation, acknowledgment before the tribunal of the law, do not undo the injury, unvictimize the victim. Endless time means endless restitution, in every work, from art to science, endless *mimēsis* and mimicry, restorations with no chance of succeeding against the injustices that gave rise to them and the injustices of the reparations. They have no chance of succeeding where no measure of success prevails. They succeed, as they must, succeed and fail, within the measure of time.

The narrative of guilt and blame in *Civilization and Its Discontents* tells of archaic injustice in a voice that reassigns injustice into time, a voice of Law, as if what we have done in time, in our lives, might merit blame and punishment. This restoration into time of an ancient Law identifies that Law with immemorial injustice as if that Law did not itself impose countless injustices, as if it were not unjust at its heart. Even so, civilization for Freud, at this point of his career, reflects the inescapability of injustice though we resist conceiving it as the inescapability of the Law. Even more, perhaps, than Freud, Kafka represents this inescapability, where the Law's force upon us imposes our guilt and our blame, demands the most extraordinary punishments, in no way acknowledging its own injustices.

Here we approach the dividing point of archaic injustice in relation to time and law, to measure. For while Kafka's and Freud's Law appears to impose no measure, it imposes blame and guilt, requires punishment, names it as a measure. Archaic injustice, as Nietzsche knew, may be fulfilled in Dionysian terms, far from blame and guilt, in exaltation, provided that we do not turn our back on its abjection, on the Underground Man suffering the glory of his suffering. Immemorial injustice may fall under Law, demanding punishment; it may fall away from Law, recognizing that no law, no punishment, can eliminate injury. Victims remain victims, abjectly.

Dostoevsky speaks of this explicitly in *The Brothers Karamazov*, where Ivan brushes against the nihilism whose proximity to suffering cannot be avoided.[23] Ivan dreams of the end of injustice, dreams that all scars may be healed. "I believe like a child that suffering will be healed and made up for, that all the humiliating absurdity of human contradictions will vanish like a pitiful mirage, ..."[24] Ivan's dream belongs to Hegel, his nightmare to Nietzsche.

> With my pitiful, earthly, Euclidian understanding, all I know is that there is suffering and that there are none guilty; . . . What comfort is it to me that there are none guilty and that cause follows effect simply and directly, and that I know it—I must have justice, or I will destroy myself. And not justice in some remote infinite time and space, but here on earth, and that I could see myself, I have believed in it. (Dostoevsky, *BK*, p. 289)

As if God or readers care that Ivan cannot accept the world with its injustices. As if God's role rested on instrumentality, seeking to make a better world. Yet what if God were as archaic as injustice, marking history's memory of injustice? If no harmony can compensate for one child's suffering, perhaps we must call upon ourselves to remember. Yet remembrance, fallen into time, under law, conspires with evil. "If all must suffer to pay for the eternal harmony, what have children to do with it, tell me, please?" (Dostoevsky, *BK*, p. 290). We cannot accept suffering and subjection under law, must resist them with all our heart, staking everything on their overcoming. Yet under archaic injustice, suffering cannot be overcome as we circulate in endless restitution. This impossibility marks why we resist Hegel and Nietzsche, even Heidegger, while we credit them for telling us again and again of sacrifice against its oblivion. We resist their oblivion, that scars might be healed within the Absolution of the Absolute,[25] the joyous forgetfulness of superhistory, in oblivion to the injustice of Being and Care. Charity belongs to me; suffering and injustice belong to others.

Children continue to suffer, and nothing can make that suffering right, no instrumentality, no law, no god. Nothing can remedy the suffering, not even time's endless restitution. Even so, time provides restitution in the forms of law and truth, joy and love, work and play, provided that we do not forget archaic injustice, and provided that we do not equate it with truth and law, as if we might achieve immemorial justice. Alyosha's smile at Ivan's despair can be taken to express this truth: that injustice has no truth, but still, somehow, the truth of justice bears upon that archaic injustice without falling under Law.

We return to Foucault's suggestion that discipline and punishment work most effectively upon those who enforce the rules, suggesting that within immemorial subjection, the irruption of the Subject defines a unique site where privilege joins subordination. Victimization does not work upon victims alone, even where we grant them voice and standing. Victimization belongs to "us" as we refuse to countenance any antecedent community. This way of circulating represents what we hope to discover in our recognition of immemorial injustice.

The power that circulates everywhere, together with injustice, can do so in virtue of its proximity to its other, resistance.[26] "Where there is power, there is resistance, and yet, or rather consequently, this resistance is never in a position of exteriority in relation to power. . . ." (Foucault, *HS*, pp. 94–95).[27] Power works together with injustice, each older than time, while time represents the unending circulation in which power's dominations seek restitution and injustice calls for restoration. The most important Western forms of restitution emerge as Truth and Law: "'Truth' is linked in a circular relation to systems of power which produce and sustain it, and to effects of power which it induces and which extend it. A 'régime' of truth."[28] This *régime* will come to an "end," posing a dilemma. "[O]ne day, perhaps, in a different economy of bodies and pleasures, people will no longer quite understand how the ruses of sexuality, and the power that sustains its organization, were able to subject us to that austere monarchy of sex, so that we became dedicated to the endless task of forcing its secret, of exacting the truest of confessions from a shadow" (Foucault, *HS*, p. 159). Leaving aside the "perhaps" and "quite," even the "shadow," we may someday find ourselves freed from the confessional truth of sexuality, with its endless task—to what? To a no-longer-endless task? To a task no longer associated with truth? To a truth of sexuality that no longer employs ruses? Or to other truths, other endless tasks, other ruses, where truth still circulates with power and resistance, injustice and restitution? To other injustices and restitutions?

Truth and Law represent traditional Western forms of restitution for immemorial injustice, together with power and its resistances. This truth of injustice and law belongs to their archaic memory, archaic long before the Greeks, dividing Greek law as it is divided within itself by non-Western and other laws. Truth and law represent the endless restitutions whereby the archaic injustices in authority and power receive their resistances, restitutions that cannot annul the arbitrarinesses and oppressions of the authorities that give rise to them.

The unyielding form of this oppression for the West, within the endless circles of injustice and restitution, prevails as subjection, constitutes the subject as a site of liberation and subjection. The archaic truth of injustice represents the subjection to authority vested in every subject, under law, as its truth, as resistance to authority. The hidden truth of power everywhere shows that injustice cannot be overcome, that power cannot disappear, that oppression belongs to the most enlightened and liberated. Conversely, law and truth, as restitution, represent resistance. Power and resistance represent injustice as subjection.

We are exploring the truth of subjection that it belongs not only to those subjected, but to subjects elsewhere, that the most privileged of human beings materialize as most subjected if not most oppressed, circulate in their abjection. The everywhere of power works everywhere by subjection to authority, and the most manifest, vivid signs of regimentation appear at one social and political site while working elsewhere, prevail as one's subjection, the other's abjection.

This displacement of power's efficacy belongs to archaic injustice, defines the nature of its subjections. The subject constituted by authority works as many subjects, many different kinds of subjects, who occupy different sites in any *régime*. One of classical Marxism's essential contributions to our understanding of ideology, while at the same time one of its greatest limitations, represents class distinctions as differential sites of constitutive power. We follow this insight with the qualification that the differential sites circulate everywhere, do not represent class distinctions alone, "go right down into the depths of society" (Foucault, DP, p. 27)

"The body" (too close, perhaps, to The Body) constitutes the site of this subjection. "[I]n our societies, the systems of punishment are to be situated in a certain 'political economy' of the body: . . . " (Foucault, DP, pp. 25–26).[29] This usefulness of the subjected body mirrors the strategy inherent in the disposition of sexuality: "Sex was a means of access both to the life of the body and the life of the species" (Foucault, *HS*, pp. 145–46). As the subject finds itself constituted by subjection, the subject's body, with its disciplines and *régimes*, constitutes a site of subjection circulating around the spheres of sex and sexuality, where reproduction abjectly meets desire. The subject's body falls within the spheres of regulation to which the subject finds itself subjected. This subjection circulates older than time and measure, along with the subject and its bodily subjections. Even if biology represented the sole regulation of the body, it experiences its biology, the Underground Man testifies, in the form of abjection. But biology does not represent the only regulation of our embodiment. Our reproduction owns too great an importance.

The subjection of our subject bodies to natural biology speaks of archaic injustice, that we find ourselves already fallen under law. Shall we gladly acknowledge our anatomical natures, against the Underground Man's resentment and spite, along with their laws? If we do, do we replace the injustice of their authority by justice without injustice? The justice of our acceptance still belongs to authority's injustices. This takes us back to the injustice of phrasing's necessity—let us call it the "inescapability of time and judgment." How can necessity escape its own abjection, where time offers unending restitution?

The *différend* occupies the site where injustice falls into time as authority and law, the site between rule and law, every system of rule and law. It falls where necessity collapses, where the necessity of law and rule fall apart. We may think of this instability as a point of language, its monstrosity: "The differend is the unstable state and instant of language wherein something which must be able to be put into phrases cannot yet be" (Lyotard, *D*, p. 13). Instead, we may think of it as belonging to time and law, where language and judgment circulate in time. Between every past and any present, any present and its futures, there circulate the instabilities of further judgments. The instabilities of judgment belong to it as judgment, not just fallen into time. The instabilities pertain to its injustice, not just to its fallenness into time. The site of the *différend*, always between, makes it unstable everywhere. The *différend* composes reality, everywhere as injustice. Putting it into words expresses one of its injustices.

This marks the narrative we might tell of animals' victimization. Not because they cannot speak, cannot defend themselves. Socrates' *Apology*, as it shapes its future, does not erase his victimization. Animals cannot speak; consequently they become victims of human beings, as if their silence could justify any abuses. This does not mark them as victims accepting their victimhood. It represents our injustice and our oppressions, marks oppressors who rule by legitimacy, law's abjection. Victims stand as victims whether they can speak or not, whether we speak of them or not. But insofar as we can silence them, we may succeed in marking our own injustices. Insofar as we can subject others' bodies to our powers, we fall abjectly into our injustice.

Subjection belongs to subjects insofar as they are subjects; it works through and upon their bodies, conspiring with their silences. In this sense, the silence of animals falls upon them through the mechanisms of their regulation, for we cannot mistake their suffering. Lyotard speaks of the possibility that all the victims in the concentration camps might have been silenced, as if there could have been a double victimization—their murder and the erasure of their traces. In the last stages of the Second World War, the Germans destroyed record after record, exterminated witness after witness. They did not destroy every record; they could not have exterminated every witness, since that would have meant destroying themselves.

But suppose they had succeeded. They do not represent the only official murderers who attempted to expunge all records of their crimes. All through Latin America, in Argentina, Brazil, and El Salvador among others, police and army officers tortured and murdered their political enemies, frequently innocent people, to show their power. When their governments fell, they pleaded innocence. In some cases, virtually all the evidence was gone. Suppose they had succeeded. Suppose there were no witnesses, no records, no memories, no evidence. Suppose all traces had disappeared.

"Every wrong ought to be able to be put into phrases [Tout tort doit pouvoir être mis en phrases.]" (Lyotard, *D*, p. 13; *Le Différend*, p. 29). What force in this "ought"? With what law, authority? Lyotard speaks of *Müssen* more than *Sollen*. We find ourselves within the call of judgment to further judgment, the *responsiveness* of semasis as restitution for inexhaustible injustice.

Human beings cannot live without judgment; judgment represents their activity. Other creatures, every thing, belongs thereby to judgment, falls into and under the responsibility to respond, in judgment and further judgment. Semasis, here, represents the responsiveness of judgment upon judgment, an ethical-political response to the call of injustice.

In the erasure of the records of injustice, we encounter its archaic truth. For reason seems to suppose that truth leaves a record, that science's and justice's laws depend on evidence and proof. Yet history's truth tells of supreme sacrifice and loss, where all records may be expunged, every trace of truth and injustice, into oblivion. History tells of hidden traces within oblivion and of oblivion nevertheless, where forgetfulness marks in its nothingness traces of an aboriginal injustice without marks, without record, before all measure and sign, death and loss without mourning. Proof here falls into time while injustice has no proof or measure, falls away from time. One measure of the measure of archaic injustice resides in the privilege we grant to proof within the privilege we grant to truth.

Lyotard suggests that we may give the measure of the record justice imposes upon its history so that the victim may be authorized to speak. He asks us to respond to the impossibility of response with proof.[30] What of this requirement of proof, of measure under law? Leaving aside the contamination of the claim that if there can be found no proof, we must relinquish the claim of murder by gas chamber, the contamination of the demand for proof. Let us imagine that the demand for proof belongs to reason, under its authority. What kind of authority rules? What authorizes its authority?

Before we dwell upon this question of proof, though we will postpone it till later, we may read this demand for reference, whatever we may think of the limits of reference, as a demand for showing, showing the reality of gas chambers, of suffering and subjections. The question here, to be postponed, concerns the relation of showing, not to proof, but to subjection, of speaking to authority. The question of proof falls entirely within, under, the dominion of authority in general. The demand for proof falls into time; judgment's judgment echoes an age before time.

The question of injustice for Lyotard appears at times to turn on the authority with which the victim speaks. The danger ensues of an injustice that finds itself placed in jeopardy where it can achieve no standing, cannot be heard or is not granted authority when heard. The *différend* takes its force from the silence with which injustice's authority comes to light. Yet in both cases, addressed by archaic injustice, time's injustices can fall away from the light, no longer noticed, no longer relevant. Lyotard asks how an injustice deprived of all the mechanisms of appearance can circulate, can establish authority, *or remain forgotten*. One answer we have been exploring, Lyotard's answer, tells that archaic injustice bears upon everything in time, with or without silence, bears upon it as forgotten, always in a particular voice, takes the forgotten's injustice as the call of nature. If we do not hear injustices against those whose voices are too weak or covered over, we owe it to ourselves and them to seek to amplify them, where the debt represents the impossibility of success. The *différend*, here, owes nothing to silence, to *régimes* and genres, to rules and regulations, but circulates among the multiplicities of time's orders, law's justices, the injustices that haunt the edges of every just order. The *différend* falls between as a site of excess, belonging to injustice's law.

If we always belonged to the *différend*, then the wrong that belongs to it might reflect an ancient injustice toward us, an abject wrong before all time, an injury, a violence, that pertains to judgment. That wrong, that injustice, before and along with all time, for which judgment and law pay restitution, passes into justice in time. In Lyotard, this justice in time circulates among regimens and genres, as if they might escape the *différend*, and as if we might escape injustice. It seems to know nothing of its own abjection.

It all depends on the authority we grant to genres and regimens. Does the emergence of the *différend* as a site of conflict, lacking equitable resolution, indicate heterogeneity opposed to homogeneity, a breakdown of rules alongside the authority of rules, or does it show the heterogeneity within the homogeneity, the conflict that belongs to every rule: "a case of conflict . . . that cannot be equitably resolved for lack of a rule of judgment applicable to both arguments" (Lyotard, *D*, p. xi)? We seek the rule of resolution, the regimen whose authority pacifies the conflict, as if by a phrase we subject ourselves to rules. "A phrase . . . is constituted according to a set of rules (its regimen)" (Lyotard, *D*, p. xii). Can we escape the injustice of the conflict, of the *différend*, by the sovereignty of rules, by our subjection, or does the *différend* remain, does its remainder and our witness to its supplement, show ancient, abject wrong? "Can we hope to bear witness to the differend" (Lyotard, *D*, p. xiii) as the conflicted site of time and law and justice, where these echo something time and law and justice cannot contain? Rules of discourse and production, *technē*, persist as problematic, not just in what we do not know that undermines their authority, but in the presence of authority—its injustice. The site of the *différend* lies where authority's inescapable presence represents an injustice unmeasurable by law.

If a phrase is constituted by a set of rules, it falls under law's authority, opening questions of its fallenness and of the injustice of that authority. If law provides equitable resolution of a wrong, then the measure of that equity belongs to law, while, as we have seen in Hobbes, equality has no measure, but provides the possibility of a measure that always fails to bring equity. Equity and law remain problematic. Weak phrase! They abjectly belong to the *différend*'s injustice, to reality everywhere. They circulate within the authority to which we find ourselves subjected.

Our questions echo in the silence of archaic injustice, which haunts the repetitions of time and law, but which cannot be measured by law or reason. The silence of what does not fall under a regimen differs from the displacement of what has no measure, what constitutes any measure. Both arouse questions of necessity. We return to Lyotard's understanding of the necessity of phrasing, linking, as temporal movements belonging to the general economy of judgment. We wonder whether this necessity might free itself from heterogeneity, might be pure. On one line of thought, the necessity of the *cogito* reflects its purity, speaks against the heterogeneity of the rational soul. Following this line, we might wonder, with Nietzsche, whether the two "I"s" of the *cogito* were homogeneous or heterogeneous. Can the "I think" speak to the "I am" without injustice?

On another line of thought, necessity belongs to freedom as freedom belongs to it, so that each opens the other to the other's heterogeneity. Shall we think of this heterogeneity as fulfilled in Absolute Spirit, or shall we understand the latter not as a *différend* but univocally as The *Différend*? This may represent the utmost question in our reading of Hegel, the injustice of the healing of wounds. Does the belonging together of universal and particular, the Idea and the individual, freedom and necessity, reflect a healing or a scar? Does this question betray a yearning for a rule, a measure? Does the heterogeneity of the *différend* tell too much of its measure? What of the injustice of the Other? Lyotard speaks to this directly in his utmost critique of Heidegger: "But remaining anchored in the thought of Being, the 'Western' prejudice that the Other is Being, it has nothing to say about a thought in which the Other is the Law" (Lyotard, *HJ*, p. 89). The law falls upon us as the measure of the forgotten.

Yet this measure, of the heterogeneity that escapes all measure, named as the *différend*, forces us under its subjection, imposes a certain authority, a certain too-great and wrongful authority. Perhaps to acknowledge the authority of the *différend*, the call to witness, appears after all to gain a measure of emancipation. Perhaps nothing shows itself abjectly in our subjection to the law that within every rule and measure heterogeneous conflicts wrongfully impose themselves. Perhaps the difficulty represents subjection to a law and measure blind to its own abjectness as forgotten, as if the only question of injustice, in relation to subjection, concerned right and wrong. Yet right and wrong, true and false, belong to law, circulate in time. In what may we find their restitution to injustices older than they? In what ways might we escape restitution, the restitution of forgetting? Where can we find in the *différend* the possibility of its subjection, an abject subjection? What abjectness belongs to the witness to the *différend*? What of the abjection of the forgotten?

Witness to the concentration camps, to the gas chambers, screams in a voice of abjection, of culpability, either as torturer or as aide, as monstrous or complicitous. No one survived without shame, without abjection. That imposes the monstrosity under which all of us fall. We would like a dignity free from abjection as we know that more powerful forces overcome us. We may be subjected to their rule, but we yearn to do so without shame. We would escape from abjection into necessity, as if necessity did not thoroughly, pervasively, rule abjectly.

We find ourselves here in the beginning, middle, and end. The dignity for which we yearn belongs to the Subject and His Humanity, as if no matter what forces come to bear upon us, we can respond with human dignity. Yet dignity belongs to time and law, circulates with the *différend*, unfolds shamefully and wrongfully under the shadow of archaic injustice. Without abjection, the *différend* has no shame, owes no restitution for ancient wrong. Witness to the *différend* calls for abjection to every subjection, including its subjection and the shame of our subjugation. We have come to nature's monstrosity in the abjectivity of our subjection.

VI

MONSTROSITY'S MADNESS

When Lyotard speaks of the four silences of the *différend* that must be answered, he speaks of the victim's proof of injury. "How can the reality of the referent be subordinated to the effectuation of verification procedures, or even to the instructions that allow anyone who so wishes to effectuate those procedures?"[1] Does this question bring us to injustice's unmeasure, or does it propose another measure? In asserting the reality of suffering against its proof, we resist the entrenched authority of canons of justification. Do we thereby institute another authority? Lyotard explores that possibility. "This inverts the idea of reality we spontaneously have: we think something is real when it exists, even if there is no one to verify that it exists; . . . " (Lyotard, *D*, p. 32). The injury is real; the wrong exists. With their reality and existence, injustices possess authoritative relevance. Being precedes reference and proof, law and measure, as if we might not institute another authority by dismantling their authority. And what of the injustice of authority, Being's authority, the injustice older than Being, that asks us to question Being's rule? What authority remains after we depose the authority of reason? Do the "is it happening?" "there is," and "giving" of "the event" take precedence, and with what authority? With what injustice does Being's *Ereignis* claim priority? With what authority does authority claim authority? With what monstrosity?

Within the law of proof, something monstrous emerges as the injustice of proof. Lyotard represents it as the four silences: *"This case does not fall within your competence, This case does not exist, It cannot be signified, It does not fall within my competence"* (*D*, p. 13). Without the sound of the victim's voice, whatever injustice pertains, whatever injury or wrongdoing, has no standing, possesses no authority, need not be listened to, even where the wrong has silenced the victim, has taken away the victim's voice, even where the wrong wrongs. This joining of voice with authority, where the force of unjust authority silences the victim, represents justice's monstrosity, in the French sense of *mon(s)tre*, including monstration, demonstration, measure, proof. Without the monsters, demons, in demon-stration, the victim's wrong exerts no claim. Justice calls for proof. It seeks a voice whereby to fear witness to injustice. "What is at stake in a literature, in a philosophy, in a politics perhaps, is to bear witness to differends by finding idioms for them" (Lyotard, *D*, p. 13)

And what if injustice knew no witnesses? What if the witnesses disappeared? What of that immemoriality of time, of finiteness, that covers over every right and wrong, that immemoriality of loss? Does something monstrous belong to the trace, to the disappearance of right and wrong, something monstrously forgotten in Being?

Perhaps injustice's silences find monstrosity at the limits of witness, the meeting of authority and testimony. Our tradition, under law, makes everything of testimony, bringing evidence before the tribunal of law in the form of proof. We remember that Socrates failed to convince the Athenian court of his innocence. Except for Plato, we might forget. Shall we think of Socrates' innocence as a reality, a fact, to which Plato bears witness? Shall we think of innocence and guilt as having nothing to do with evidence, but as reality nevertheless? Shall we think of guilt and innocence as something monstrous, obscure, to which we might bear witness without the facts, without the measure of truth's authority?

Lyotard explores the possibility of saving the reality of the wrong by saving the referent from its law, the name from its regimen. "[The name] actually acts as a linchpin and endows its referent with a reality . . . " (Lyotard, *D*, p. 43). "The name fills the function of linchpin because it is an empty and constant designator" (Lyotard, *D*, p. 44). Our witness to injustice dwells in the *différend*. "Let us wage a war on totality; let us be witnesses to the unpresentable; let us activate the differences and save the honor of the name."[2] What monstrosity lies in this name, as if it might designate but not represent, might link without force, without regimen, as if there might be reality without discourse, without the other of the *différend*? What monstrosity circulates where being meets language, language meets representation, truth meets injustice?

What if we had no witness to the honor of the name? Would monstrosity disappear? Would we escape injustice, save the victims from their fate?

The honor of the name calls us to remember lost and vanquished individuals and events, calls us to memorialize by naming that of which we have no memory, victims whose traces have disappeared. To fall into history represents falling into traces, language's and representation's traces, monstrously. The monstrosity belongs to representation, to the voice, but not to names' authority in opposition to the authority of representation. Such an idea, the honor of the name, restores the virtue of the name's authority, the respect, the authority of authority, the monstrous authority of authority, within the name's self-authorization.

By monstrosity we return to archaic injustice, where silence meets authority. Within monstrosity we join several thoughts, one following Derrida, the monstrousness (*monstre*) of representation (*montre*), the injustice of its authority, another thought following Foucault, reason's madness and monstrosity, where life meets representation, including Foucault's linking of power with monstrosity. "The monster ensures in time, and for our theoretical knowledge, a continuity that, for our everyday experience, floods, volcanoes, and subsiding continents confuse in space.[3] We add two thoughts that bear kinship at some remove from monstrosity, one from Foucault on reason's madness: "We have yet to write the history of that other form of madness, by which men, in an act of sovereign reason, confine their neighbors, and communicate and recognize each other through the merciless language of non-madness; . . . ,"[4] the other by Kant on the colossal, followed by Derrida:

> An object is *monstrous* if, by its size, it destroys the purpose which constitutes the concept of it. But the mere presentation of a concept is called *colossal*, which is almost too great for any presentation (bordering on the relatively monstrous), because the purpose of the presentation is made hard [to carry out] by the intuition of the object being almost too great for our faculty of apprehension.[5]

> How can the category of the "almost too" be arrested? The pure and simple "too" would bring the colossal down: it would render presentation impossible.[6]

Writing in 1966, Foucault speaks of the relation between classification and monstrosity in classical representation, in the middle of the eighteenth century, where monsters delimit the limits of representation as madness defines the limits of reason. The monster ensures the continuity of that which taxonomy has sundered. We must look elsewhere for injustice, first within classical representation's inception, emerging against the plenitude of similarities and resemblances that Foucault calls "The Prose of the World":

> First and foremost, the plethoric yet absolutely poverty-stricken character of this knowledge. Plethoric because it is limitless. Resemblance never remains stable within itself; it can be fixed only if it refers back to another similitude, which then, in turn, refers to others; each resemblance, therefore, has value only from the accumulation of all the others, and the whole world must be explored if even the slightest of analogies is to be justified and finally take on the appearance of certainty. It is therefore a knowledge that can, and must, proceed by the infinite accumulation of confirmations all dependent on one another. And for this reason, from its very foundations, this knowledge will be a thing of sand. (Foucault, *OT*, p. 30)

That the world, in every thing and everywhere, teems with mirrors, resemblances and affinities, of every thing, everywhere, gives not the slightest certainty, drifts all over the place like a thing of sand blown in the wind. Does the world drift in a general economy?

Why does the teeming of things, the plenitude everywhere and in the smallest thing, war with "the appearance of certainty"? We have listened to Anaximander; what of Anaxagoras? "In everything there is a portion of everything. . . . " "For of the small there is no smallest, but there is always a smaller; for it is not possible for what is not to be. But of the great there is always a greater also. And it is equal in number to the small, each thing being with respect to itself both great and small."[7] Things teem of each other, each in everything, each containing a portion of everything, each without a smallest or a greatest, each greater and smaller (older and younger) than itself. What do we find inadmissible in so truthful a representation? What do we find monstrous? Two inadequacies expressed by Foucault:

> sixteenth-century knowledge condemned itself to never knowing anything but the same thing, and to knowing that thing only at the unattainable end of an endless journey. (*OT*, p. 30)

> the whole world must be explored if even the slightest of analogies is to be justified and finally take on the appearance of certainty. (*OT*, p. 30)

Both express the dispersion of identity, the latter identity's authority, the former identity's heterogeneity. We remind ourselves of the "gift of the gods," in *Philebus* passed on "in the form of a saying" that "all things . . . have in their nature a conjunction of limit and unlimitedness" (Plato, *Philebus* 16d).[8] The conjunction of limit and unlimit repeats the plenitude of the prose of the world, lacking measure. Having gained measure, Socrates tells us to let each pass away into the unlimited and cease bothering about it. Intermediate things take us to the heart of their injustice, at which point we may forget them. The "how many" of measure and law pay endless restitution to the one and many for their injustice. The "how many" of measure and law work within the monstrous economy of limit and unlimit.

The second inadequacy concerns uncertainty, repeats the circulation of injustice within authority. The prose of the world teems with mirrors and similitudes in relation to which no identity can be given authority. The task of identity, then, represents two sides of a general economy, one the many in the one, requiring unlimit and unmeasure, the other the authority of measure and law, of identity, that falls into unlimit as injustice. Both may be expressed as identity's monstrosity.

Monstrosity represents the unlimit within the limits of taxonomy and classification. If Foucault appears to have classical representation and the seventeenth century in mind, we may find in our own century a similar play of monsters. In his review of Stephen Jay Gould's book on the Burgess Shale,[9] R. C. Lewontin describes the shale as follows:

> The Burgess Shale is a deposit of fossil-bearing rock about 530 million years old in Yoho National Park in the Canadian Rockies. In this one very small quarry, indeed in a layer only seven to eight feet thick, is a collection of invertebrate fossils that shows more diversity of body plan than is encompassed by all living marine invertebrates. (*G*, p. 4)[10]

The Cambrian explosion includes more of all known types of living things, but also more diverse, monstrous forms, than all modern kinds together. Lewontin pictures several of what Gould calls the shale's "weird wonders," describing them as "shocking to zoologists" and "unlike anything else ever seen."

The Burgess Shale confronts two important icons of the organic evolutionary mystique, one the "tree of life," the slow diversification from a narrow range of types at the bottom of the trunk to more and more branches and subbranches as the tree grows; the other the "cone of increasing progress and diversity" (Gould, *WL*, p. 45): "Yet the Burgess Shale, and indeed the entire Cambrian explosion, contradicts this metaphor. All the main branches of the 'tree' of invertebrate life seem to have emerged at ground level like a lilac bush and some, perhaps, most, were nipped in the bud at an early stage" (Gould, *WL*, p. 45). This immense plenitude of forms burst on the scene in a variety far exceeding any evolutionary pressure toward species development or diversification. Within any taxonomy of normal forms, the Cambrian period's plenitude represents monstrosity. More generally, the economy of forms requisite to biological taxonomy rests on the monsters it cannot accommodate, its efficacy in direct proportion to their exclusion.

The Burgess Shale was discovered by Charles Doolittle Walcott, described by Gould as "one of the most extraordinary and powerful scientists that America has ever produced" (Gould, *WL*, p. 240), a biologist of deserved eminence. "Walcott was the most powerful scientific administrator in America. He not only ran the Smithsonian Institution from 1907 until his death in 1927; he also had his finger—or rather, his fist— in every important scientific pot in Washington" (Gould, *WL*, pp. 241–42). Nevertheless, "his reaction to the Burgess Shale fauna was to see them as a collection of conventional organisms. In Gould's often-repeated metaphor, Walcott 'shoehorned' the fossils into the standard classification of animals" (Lewontin, *G*, p. 6). Gould interprets this aberration as a war of ideologies.[11] Lewontin interprets it in relation to the sociology of science.[12] Both understand it to involve status and success.[13] Both accounts, as different as they may be, represent the issue in terms of science's authority. They present a romantic view of science's embattlement, the one of conflicting ideologies where truth must struggle against social and institutional impediments, the other a struggle over the enervation of age and success.

Gould and Lewontin tell their narratives of classification and misclassification entirely in terms of the autonomous agent struggling to liberate truth from the impediments of bureaucracy and history, as the triumph of a particular authority. Neither considers the possibility that Walcott's ideology and desire for status belong to science, inhabit its authoritarian structures, that we may suspect the triumph because of the discipline, not its impediments.

Lewontin's and Gould's accounts assume that we have finally got the Burgess Shale straight, in the large if not in all its details. The narrative of biology for both unfolds as an epic of the victory and triumph of truth's sovereignty over its obstacles. Odysseus reaches port. Gould and Lewontin differ on the shamefulness of Walcott's blindness, the former as if his background and character were to blame, the latter ascribing his fault magnanimously to disciplinary pressures and human foibles. For both, however, the narrative is moral and belongs to Walcott. Truth represents the sovereign prize won by her suitor's extraordinary efforts against temptation. The hero of the story is Harry Whittington, his story Horatio Alger's, won by hard work and pluck. Whittington "painstakingly stripped apart the squashed layers of the fossils and succeeded in making three-dimensional reconstructions. The result was that by 1975, with his reconstruction of the five-eyed *Opabinia*, Whittington began to see the Burgess fauna as radically different from what had been previously known" (Gould, *WL*, p. 251).

This Greek-Judeo-Christian narrative surrounds our understanding of truth, and we may resist succumbing to it too quickly by warning ourselves against another moralizing narrative, as if we would replace this truth by another, perhaps non-Western, perhaps post-Western. Rather, we may consider two narratives, not as competitors for a single prize, as if one might win, but coexisting narratives resisting each other's authority. For the prince wins the princess and kingdom by his bravery and pluck. Can we forgo the kingdom of truth without forgoing truth's monstrosity?

Gould interprets the monstrous plenitude of Shale life as proof of his own thesis of discontinuity and contingency, imposes upon this narrative an epic of inevitable triumph: "[I]f we wish to assert human centrality in a world that functioned without us until the last moment, we must somehow grasp all that came before as a grand preparation, a foreshadowing of our eventual origin" (*WL*, p. 45). A certain privilege and authority of humanity within the natural world, a mark of Our *Geschlecht*, echoes within this natural necessity. Yet Gould gives us another necessity and another authority in his own narrative, an authority derived from superior proof, as if any proof over so political a domain as human supremacy might provide the slightest security, but also an authority derived from the necessity of contingency. He offers a different inevitability. "The iconography of the cone made Walcott's original interpretation of the Burgess fauna inevitable" (*WL*, p. 45). If continuity is not inevitable, its resistance to discontinuity is. Both necessities rest on authority, and Gould prefers one authority over another.

He offers seven "possible world" scenarios to support his reading of the record, still within the narrative of authority. He speaks of the contingency of the eukaryotic cells, imagining an extension of the delay of the development of mind for half the known history of life, so that, within the expected lifetime of the earth, human beings' reflective capacities might not have arisen. "Run the tape again, and even if the same general pathways emerge, it might take twenty billion years to reach self-consciousness this time—except that the earth would be incinerated billions of years before" (*WL*, pp. 310–11). Do we possess a tape to run again? Would it resemble the current scenario within known laws of nature? Does Gould presuppose two continuing kinds of authority within his view of contingency: that of a "record"—however different it might become, it would still comprise an intelligible and discernible representation even in the absence of human reflections; and that of the authority within human reflection, given by his own considerations?

Gould focuses his possible-world narratives on what he calls "the biological object that most excites our parochial fancy—*Homo sapiens*" as if another narrative perspective, emphasizing humanity less, might be truer and more authoritative. Thus, within the "contingency" of human life, humanity might not have arisen.

> In other words, we are an improbable and fragile entity, fortunately successful after precarious beginnings as a small population in Africa, not the predictable end result of a global tendency. We are a thing, an item of history, not an embodiment of general principles.
>
> This claim would not carry startling implications if we were a repeatable thing—if, had *Homo sapiens* failed and succumbed to early extinction as most species do, another population with higher intelligent in the same form was bound to originate. (Gould, *WL*, p. 319)

The language of necessity and authority—"was bound to"—repeats itself elsewhere, as we give up humanity's evolutionary necessity but not its logical necessity. If contingency entails monstrosity, might it not entail the monstrosity of logic, reason, truth, and goodness? Or are these monsters impossible for science to contemplate?

> And so, if you wish to ask the question of the ages—why do humans exist?—a major part of the answer, touching those aspects of the issue that science can treat at all, must be: because *Pikaia* [the world's first known chordate (Gould, *WL*, p. 322)] survived the Burgess decimation. This response does not cite a single law of nature; it embodies no statement about predictable evolutionary pathways, no calculation of probabilities based on general rules of anatomy or ecology. The survival of *Pikaia* was a contingency of "just history." I

do not think that any "higher" answer can be given, and I cannot imagine that any resolution could be more fascinating. We are the offspring of history, and must establish our own paths in this most diverse and interesting of conceivable universes—one indifferent to our suffering, and therefore offering us maximal freedom to thrive, or to fail, in our own chosen way. (Gould, *WL*, p. 323)

A narrative, an scenario, without injustice, as if contingency posed no monstrosity.

Consider two narratives Gould and Lewontin neglect in their praise of Harry Whittington's success. One tells that Whittington's reversal of Walcott's classification will itself later be reversed, that the presiding narrative does not represent victory but caution. The second tells that science circulates by stumbling from one anomaly to another,[14] that the Burgess Shale's monsters belong not to biology's errors but to its truths. What disappears when we accept Whittington's reading is not the weirdness of the Shale's "weird wonders," as Gould describes them, but our relation to their monstrosity.

On one narrative, what makes the Burgess Shale remarkable is its contrast with prevailing evolutionary understanding. Since Gould has carried on what he regards as a long and in some ways successful struggle within prevailing orthodoxy for his unorthodox views, it is not surprising that he would regard Whittington's painstaking labor toward reclassification as a triumph of imagination over orthodoxy. Yet in the larger view, successes have their reversals, and another taxonomy may be expected, replacing the image of life gone mad.

This refusal of a narrative of triumph and liberation tends in many circles to be read as skeptical, nihilistic, destructive to scientific truth. Such a metanarrative lays the groundwork for Lyotard's rejection in *The Postmodern Condition* of metanarratives in his exploration of postmodern possibilities in science. Yet except for refusing a certain view of truth's authority, based on a narrative of sovereignty, nothing circulates as pessimistic or nihilistic about this narrative for biology. We do not have to grant too strong a thesis concerning disciplinary authority, in Kuhn the rule of a paradigm over its anomalies, in Foucault, belonging to a discipline "within the true."[15] The narrative we are addressing takes the passage of time seriously in relation to science, expecting every claim to be overstated, every authority to be excessive. Since truth's authority always imposes itself excessively, every advance anticipates a diversion. At any moment in science, the very young make the major advances, because authority does not hold them in an unbreakable grip. Such an account may work against the idea of a single direction of progress, but in no other way wars with success and truth.

The authority of entrenched science gives rise to our two narratives, one that such an authority upholds the walls whose breaching defines scientific progress, whose recurrent anomalies mark the possibility of new understandings and truths, the other that the anomalies and monstrosities mark truth itself, the excesses without which no system of order can circulate within the plenitude, a general economy of truth. Here the anomalies and monsters of the Burgess Shale and the Cambrian period mark the limits and truths of the order of evolutionary biology. After Foucault's remark above, taxonomy is possible within the continuity and plenitude of nature because of the monsters and anomalies to which it gives rise.[16]

Irigaray's critique of Freud, taking up the importance of sexual difference within Freud's own critique, follows similar lines. "'When you meet a human being,' he says, they say, first of all, 'the first distinction you make is "male or female?" and you are accustomed to making the distinction with unhesitating certainty' (p. 113)."[17] Freud specifically rejects the specificity and stability of the distinction. "For of course 'the other organs, the bodily shapes and tissues, show the influence of the individual's sex, but this is inconstant and its amount variable' (p. 113)" (Irigaray, *Speculum of the Other Woman*, p. 14). Irigaray's point turns on the authority vested in the distinction, not its grounds. With what authority does the distinction between male and female come into play from the first? What first and what distinction, not to mention with what unhesitating certainty? Freud questions the certainty but not the authority whereby we make the distinction from external signs in a relation based on an original repetition. Males and females may at best be distinguished for the most part. This undermines in no way the distinction, only the authority of its significance. The authority of its significance rests on the testimony of the monstrosities and perversities that inhabit sexual life.

The anomalies and monstrosities of sexual difference—here joined with gender—belong to that difference itself, define and delimit it. It appears marked as difference—gender marks itself as gender—in virtue of the monsters to which it gives birth. Similarly, the Burgess Shale, taken as a natural plenitude, returns us to a system in which nature not only possesses a large in every large and a small in every small, as if these were relations of continuity, but a very different in every different, a monstrous departure in every departure. Plenitude as continuity threatens nothing, offers no order. Plenitude as monstrosity brings the authority of order under attack from the standpoint of another order. Monstrosity represents the stakes of truth.

In this sense, truth's plenitude represents monstrosity, and its monstrosity reflects the age of injustice. The monstrosity of truth, its anomalies, mark the price we pay for the circulation of that truth. The monstrosity of truth marks the pain of belonging to organic nature, to life, for created things, for natural beings, not for subjects alone.

Gould speaks of contingency in a language that glories in nature's fecundity, takes on the role of speaking for the vanished possibilities in evolution's contingencies. The reemergence of vanished forms of life indeed represents a triumph, if only in our remembrances. The vanishing is monstrous, something Gould seems to have difficulty grasping in his eponymous cinematic imagination.

> The greatest expression of contingency . . . comes near the end of Frank Capra's masterpiece, *It's a Wonderful Life* (1946). . . .
> The wily angel, clinching his case, then pronounces the doctrine of contingency: "Strange, isn't it? Each man's life touches so many other lives, and when he isn't around he leaves an awful hole, doesn't he? . . . You see, George, you really had a wonderful life" (Gould, *WL*, pp. 287–88)

George discovers that he really mattered, that what happened in many people's lives depended on him, that he was necessary to them. The necessity Gould opposes expresses an order of development and history, of natural law, in which nothing in particular matters because the laws of nature make the outcome secure. Yet who could possibly hold that view, since natural laws require initial conditions for their outcomes? Gould replaces one mode of necessity and authority with another, and contingency becomes a repetition of injustice with no memory of injustice, of nature's waste, death and destruction, disorder. The latter indeed composes a threat:

> I am not speaking of randomness . . . but of the central principle of all history—*contingency*. A historical explanation does not rest on direct deductions from laws of nature, but on an unpredictable sequence of antecedent states, where any major change in any step of the sequence would have altered the final result. This final result is therefore dependent, or contingent, upon everything that came before—the unerasable and determining signature of history. (Gould, *WL*, p. 283)

Substitute *vanishing* for "unerasable," *disorderly* for "determining," and *blind* for "dependent": every pole of authority displays itself. Gould recognizes that "historical explanations take the form of narrative" (Gould, *WL*, p. 283), without considering the monstrous possibility of narratives without authority. "If any of these earlier stages had not occurred, or had transpired in a different way, then E would not exist (or would be present in a substantially altered form, E', requiring a different explanation" (Gould, *WL*, p. 283). What of the contingency of E's dependency, so that it might have come about anyway from any number of different conditions—without necessity and unreachable by any epistemic authority?

> When we realize that the actual outcome did not have to be, that any alteration in any step along the way would have unleashed a cascade down a different channel, we grasp the causal power of individual events. We can argue, lament, or exult over each detail—because each holds the power of transformation. Contingency is the affirmation of control by immediate events over destiny, the kingdom lost for want of a horseshoe nail. (Gould, *WL*, p. 284)

Here contingency represents power, marked by this cascade of transformations. Archaic injustice presents us with questions of what matters and of the lost who made no difference. Gould speaks in a language of power, control, and destiny. The language of authority evokes a language of destiny. With trepidation, we wonder if the language of destiny always evokes a language of authority, the authority of contingency. "Contingency is a license to participate in history, and our psyche responds" (Gould, *WL*, p. 285). We will participate in history wherever we find ourselves in history and under whatever circumstances. Some of these will be far from glorious.

Frost suggests such a truth in a poem Gould quotes with enthusiasm, revealing his deafness to archaic injustice. He suggests that we should read the poem for "solace": "For anyone who feels cosmically discouraged at the prospect of being a detail in the realm of contingency, I cite for solace a wonderful poem by Robert Frost, dedicated explicitly to this concern: *Design*" (*WL*, p. 291). Gould does not recognize the monstrosity of the order Frost describes:

> I found a dimpled spider, fat and white,
> On a white heal-all, holding up a moth
> Like a white piece of rigid satin cloth—

> Assorted characters of death and blight
> Mixed ready to begin the morning right,
> Like the ingredients of a witches' broth—
> A snow-drop spider, a flower like a froth,
> And dead wings carried like a paper kite.
>
> What had that flower to do with being white,
> The wayside blue and innocent heal-all?
> What brought the kindred spider to that height,
> Then steered the white moth thither in the night?
> What but design of darkness to appall?—
> If design govern in a thing so small.[18]

Design appalls by its evil, a witches' cauldron, appalls by its necessity and authority, imposing within nature terrible things. Frost's poem speaks of the monstrosity of archaic injustice with no restitution whatever except natural design. Time and law mark nature's, not human, law, and we see in nature's appalling and monstrous workings injustice and restitution. Monstrosity marks the general economy of nature's injustice and time's restitution.

Madness's monstrosity repeatedly appears in *Madness and Civilization*. One appearance we have noted, madness as reason's monstrosity, belonging to reason itself: "reason's madness." Closely related we find Descartes's repudiation of the unthinkability of madness:

> Can I deny that these hands and this body are mine, save perhaps by comparing myself to those who are insane, and whose brains are so disturbed and clouded by dark bilious vapors that they persist in assuring us that they are kings, when in fact they are in extreme poverty; or that they are clothed in gold and purple when they are in fact destitute of any covering; or that their head is made of clay and their body of glass, or that they are pumpkins. They are mad; and I should be no less insane were I to follow examples so extravagant.[19]

They think they are kings, when in fact they are poor; that they are clothed in gold, when in fact they are destitute. When the facts are otherwise, the plain facts, with their authority, there lies madness. Descartes cannot consider certain possibilities, else he would be insane. Certain possibilities against the plain facts, against the authority of the plain facts, belong to madness. Madness belongs to a certain sphere of multiple authority, where the authority of truth meets the authority of life. Perhaps only in the Enlightenment West does this conjunction coincide with the authority of reason.

This relation of madness to reason seems one of opposition, at least in Descartes: against the plain truth of the facts, "they" persist in their folly; madness against reason. We equate madness with unreason even as reason evinces its own madness. This madness, belonging to reason, seems worlds apart from madness "itself," though Foucault speaks of such a madness, of a madness "before" reason's regulation: *"We must try to return, in history, to that zero point in the course of madness at which madness is an undifferentiated experience, a not yet divided experience of division itself"* (*Madness and Civilization*, p. ix). How, Derrida asks, may we confront this "zero point" of madness, madness *itself*? How we may think this zero as a confrontation with madness, with its monstrosity, represents our greatest achievement, however impossibly. "In writing a history of madness, Foucault has attempted—and this is the greatest merit, but also the very infeasibility of his book—to write a history of madness *itself. Itself.* Of madness itself. That is, by letting madness speak for itself."[20]

What offense does madness itself commit, compared with the offenses of Being Itself or the *archē*-trace of *différance*? Does not each present its own disruptions? For madness surely, and forcibly in Foucault, appears before us in its monstrosity, doubles its monstrosity. The madness that would speak for itself, "older than reason," speaks of reason's limits, thereby of its own limits, acknowledges its limits in a discourse that always hides its limits from itself as it seeks to control them.

Against Foucault, Derrida questions madness itself, obscuring madness's monstrosity, the monstrosity of the univocity of the itself. Against Levinas's critique of Heidegger, Derrida questions the privilege of Being, thereby asserting Being's monstrosity—itself.

> Therefore, the "relation to the Being of the existent" cannot possibly dominate the "relation to the existent." . . . Being is not elevated, is not the land of the existent, for elevation belongs to the existent. There are few themes which have demanded Heidegger's insistence to this extent: Being is not an excellent existent.[21]

Monstrously, Being is not an existent. Monstrosity here belongs to injustice, to the ethical, something Levinas tells us repeatedly, speaking of obsession toward the other. "Itself," "otherwise," "responsibility" meet in the monstrosity of madness. Derrida seems to accept this while he condemns it in others. "Thus, the thought of Being could not possibly occur as ethical violence. On the contrary, without it one would be forbidden to let be the existent, and one would enclose transcendence within identification and empirical economy" (Derrida, "Violence and Metaphysics," p. 142). Itself, otherwise, monstrosity, and madness all resist the consolidation of Being, as does Being itself. Here monstrosity's madness represents our oblivion toward Being in another voice, the monstrosity of its economy.

Madness presents its monstrosity to us twice, doubled, marking that which makes no sense, where no sense shows its monstrosity, also marking the monstrosity of the sense that madness possesses. Both of these appear in Foucault. Both appear elsewhere, marking Foucault's recognition of insanity's monstrosity.

They appear in Descartes, though we have acknowledged only one side of their emergence. Foucault presents the site in Descartes where madness threatens monsters, where the facts might mean nothing at all, where everything might irrupt in question. Descartes's demonic threat might threaten intervention within the circulation of reason, threatening this movement with a monstrosity Descartes refuses as he accepts lesser monsters—if indeed lesser. For everything we perceive may be untrue, may be imposed upon us as if in a dream, by an alien, monstrous power, but still we perceive and think within this dream with our minds intact. Madness threatens the monstrosity of the possibility that who and where we find ourselves hold no security, that who and where offer no integrity, vanish into the chaos of deranged thought. Hume suggests that experience offers us testimony of whatever appears before us, no matter how alien and monstrous, tempered by the order of repetition. Descartes suggests that demonic doubt might pervade the fabric of thought, tempered by a refusal to admit madness's unique disorder into his doubt.[22]

Can we be mad and deceived, or are madness and deceit opposed, the latter reflecting a certain plan of work, the former beyond work? We may imagine a madness that simulates deception, as Descartes suggests, not knowing my hands and legs are mine. We may consider a different testimony of madness's monstrosity. Oliver Sacks worked as a neurologist with patients who described profound alienation from their bodies, losing "proprioception." In one case, a young man had a brain tumor causing him to "lose his left leg":

> The experience, he told me, was the most uncanny and frightening in his life, and he wouldn't have believed it possible unless he had experienced it. . . . What was so awful about

this sort of loss was that the leg hadn't been "misplaced," but had in fact lost its place. And since there was no longer any place it could come back to, he just didn't see how his leg *could* come back.[23]

"I swear to God, cross my heart, I haven't. . . . A man *should* know his own body, what's his and what's not—but this leg, this *thing*"—another shudder of distaste—"doesn't feel right, doesn't feel real—and it doesn't *look* part of me." (Sacks, *H*, p. 57)

Sacks himself undergoes a climbing accident, precipitated by proximity to a different monstrosity:

The huge white face seemed to swell and swell, and the great bulbous eyes became radiant with malignance. The face grew huger and huger all the time, until I thought it would blot out the Universe. The bull became hideous—hideous beyond belief, hideous in strength, malevolence and cunning. It seemed now to be stamped with the infernal in every feature. It became, first a monster, and now the Devil. (Sacks, *L*, p. 20)

He remains calm for a moment, then: "Blind, mad panic!—there is nothing worse in the world, nothing worse—and nothing more *dangerous*" (Sacks, *L*, p. 20). He cripples his knee in his panicked flight, undergoes an operation with monstrous dreams in convalescence.[24] Much more alarmingly: "The flesh beneath my fingers no longer seemed like flesh. It no longer seemed like material or matter. It no longer resembled anything. The more I gazed at it, and handled it, the less it was 'there,' the more it became Nothing—and Nowhere" (Sacks, *L*, p. 73). He begins recovery with the same monstrous quality: "It was as if I suddenly remembered how to walk—indeed, not 'as if.' *I remembered how to walk*. All of a sudden I remembered walking's natural, unconscious rhythm and melody; . . . " (*L*, p. 145). Sacks was never mad—or "never" "mad." He found himself disconnected from his leg, alienated from his body, as others with neurological disorders find themselves. The experience is uncanny, monstrous, an alienness indescribable as deception.

The madness to which Sacks calls our attention[25] does not fit the Cartesian model of deception and truth. This madness—or neurological disorder, for these people may otherwise be sane—consists of an alienation beyond cure by the will. Derrida speaks of the "subversion" of pure thought in Descartes when "I" imagine that I cannot add or count correctly. What happens when counting and thought become alien, when space and time cannot be imagined at all? Descartes sets madness aside when considering sensory deception. "They are mad; and I should be no less insane were I to follow examples so extravagant." This mad extravagance reappears in the very heart of the *cogito*. "Let him deceive me as much as he will, he can never cause me to be nothing so long as I shall be thinking that I am something" (Descartes, *M*, p. 183). Unless I am mad, quite mad, in thinking that I think and am. This madness does not present deception, that I might think of illusory things, but contaminates the "I" and the thought beyond reparation, an alienation from myself that the *cogito* could not begin to repair.

In imagining God's imperfection or a demon's deception, we imagine a certain kind of intention that "subverts" the object. But the intention preserves the objectivity and order of some object, however different. In imagining madness, we imagine the disruption of intention and order to the point where they might belong to others rather than oneself. What if the "I" that thinks were like Sacks's leg, felt as belonging to another, or no one, or not a leg, to belong to no self, alien and unintelligible, to reside in the abyss without anything looking back.[26]

If Derrida rejects madness itself as a zero point, he offers another point much closer to Sacks's. "And if madness in general, beyond any factitious and determined historical structure, is the absence of a work, then madness is indeed, essentially and generally, silence, stifled speech, within a caesura and a wound that *open up* life as *historicity in general*" (Derrida, *CHM*, p. 54). The generality represents everything: "madness in general, without determination except for the absence of work. Not a determined silence, imposed at one given moment rather than at any other, but a silence essentially linked to an act of force and a prohibition which open history and speech. *In general*" (Derrida, *CHM*, p. 54). Yet what of madness in general, Being beyond authority, general economy?[27] Do these impose their own authority against which we seek restitution in law and time, to prevent madness from becoming Madness, injustice from becoming Injustice under Law, as being becomes Being?[28] "I think, therefore, that (in Descartes) everything can be reduced to a determined historical totality except the hyperbolical project. Now, this project belongs to the narration narrating itself and not to the narration narrated by Foucault. It cannot be recounted, cannot be objectified as an event in a determined history" (Derrida, *CHM*, pp. 57–58). Does this narration represent monstrosity, the monstrosity of madness itself, where the before lends itself to time archaically? Derrida resists the archaism of madness as it reflects the monstrosity of injustice, but does not, cannot, resist the archaic.[29] What of Being's injustice, injustice's injustice? What saves injustice from its own injustice as every restitution repeats injustice? What keeps madness in check as the mark of the abyss?

What would happen if we admitted such a madness as the monstrosity of Being, nature's work? Every argument and proof would lose its authority, including the proof of the *cogito* and the existence of God. Nature would work in a general economy; things would circulate without authority. We may understand this loss in two ways. One is that these proofs are threatened by the point where madness meets reason, repeating madness as unreason, Foucault's reading of Descartes, where the monstrosity of madness belongs to reason. Here Descartes's project, of establishing authority on reason without faith, presupposes escape from reason's monsters, authorizes rational authority. Yet faith was threatened by those monsters at other times, at Descartes's time, when Satan threatened reason demonically with proofs indistinguishable from God's, so that faith collapsed under its own monstrosity. Here reason and faith share their monstrosity, marked by the monstrosity of madness. Here madness threatens us with the monstrosity of truth, as reason or faith, threatens truth with the monstrosity of every proof, monstrously threatens truth.

Madness threatens reason's truth, threatens every truth, as if madness, as Foucault tells us, possessed its own truth. Here madness itself appears. Yet Descartes also presents us with madness's monstrosity, not another truth, but the madness of truth and reason within and madness's monstrosity without. We find here our second understanding of the loss of rational authority. Monsters appear in madness, circulate of their own volition, regardless of reason's authority. Madness, in this monstrosity, tears truth away from reason, circulates truth in a monstrosity without testimony or proof, far from order, opens an economy in which truth might have no authority, where authority possesses no authority, where reason's authority belongs to madness and monstrosity.

The age of injustice, older than time, belongs to time in the endless restitution justice pays for immemorial injustice. Law and Reason represent some of the forms of this compensation. Madness suggests endless formlessness together with madness's order. Within the disorder of madness, where restitution may have no meaning, authority rules.

A striking appearance of madness as monstrosity emerges after Descartes in Locke. What Locke calls "mad" his followers took as the principle governing relations of ideas among themselves, guaranteeing the order of experience.[30] Locke introduces the association of ideas as unrecognizable in us, but "in itself really extravagant, in the opinions, reasonings, and actions of other men."[31] He calls it "madness." (Locke, *Essay*, p. 528). Reason belongs to nature and truth; madness belongs to custom, falsity, and chance. Chance, *tychē*, returns in the garb of madness, while Locke's example threatens to overcome his view of reason, if it had not already collapsed under the naturalness of madness and the association of ideas.

> The death of a child that was the daily delight of its mother's eyes, and joy of her soul, rends from her heart the whole comfort of her life, and gives her all the torment imaginable: . . . Till time has by disuse separated the sense of that enjoyment and its loss, from the idea of the child returning to her memory, all representations, though ever so reasonable, are in vain; and therefore some in whom the union between these ideas is never dissolved, spend their lives in mourning, and carry an incurable sorrow to their graves. (Locke, *Essay*, p. 532)

Excessive sorrow, unto madness, mourning, and melancholia (Caruth, *Empirical Truths*, pp. 33–43), belong to nature within the association of ideas. In empiricism, from Hobbes to Hume, persist uncontrollable and insatiable monsters and madness, ungoverned by rule. The testimony of experience presents us with madness as if indistinguishable from reason, where reason falls to pieces with madness within.

Madness threatens reason with at least three blows: (1) as unreason, reason's other, falsely appearing before us as illusion, deception; (2) as reason again, its other, where fiction belongs to the self as its appearances; (3) as monstrosity, repeating reason and unreason but also something else, something even Derrida does not wish to acknowledge, since acknowledgment repeats the hold of reason upon its monsters. Yet the monstrosity of madness not only persists at reason's edges, at the brink of the abyss, but casts us down deep into its recesses.

In (1), as Locke says, we take everyone compared with us as not only wrong but mad, their minds associating ideas in the most unnatural or idiosyncratic ways. Madness here represents unreason against reason's universality circulating in the name of nature. In (2), reason repeats madness while madness echoes reason, the former the arbitrariness of every authority, its injustice, the latter the astonishing order found within mad disorder, anarchy and chaos. In (3), madness's monstrosities become familiar, the break in our relations to our bodies and things around us. We come to know and feel, in ourselves or others, the alienation of thought, not as a moment in its intelligibility and truth, but in the belonging of thought to *us* or *me*. Here, madness places us not at or over the abyss, but thrown down into it. We experience the hold of illusions and falsehoods without giving up the sense of belonging to truth. The extreme possibility Descartes imagines, emphasized even more in Locke, shows that madness might strike at thought itself, no longer owning the familiar garb of thought, even so still true.

With the belonging together of reason and madness, we return to one of the pivotal points of their separation in the tradition, in *Phaedrus*, where the tradition separates what Socrates denies can be separated, belittles what Socrates claims as the highest call of desire.[32] *Mania* here shines and soars, approaching Beauty and the Good as if the Good means nothing apart from madness's desire, monstrous desire, nothing in cold reason, nothing in unimpassioned writing. "[I]f any man come to the gates of poetry without the madness of the Muses, persuaded that skill alone will make him a good poet, then shall he and his works of sanity with him be brought to nought by the poetry of madness, and behold, their place is nowhere to be found" (Plato, *Phaedrus* 245a). Madness belongs to poetry's truth, and may belong to reason's truth. Such a madness cannot appear as madness "itself," but as madness's madness, in myriad forms, chimeric, monstrous. Madness's truth appears as a gift of the gods, a gift that exceeds everyday gifts. The gift of Being, of beings' excesses, exceeds any gift.

Today, after the death of the gods, does madness become unreason, clinically circumscribed as pathology? Does it take a special ear to hear the gift of madness as disorder's truth? "The twins, who were then twenty-six years old, had been in institutions since the age of seven, variously diagnosed as autistic, psychotic, or severely retarded" (Sacks, *H*, p. 195). "They are . . . serene contemplators of number—and approach numbers with a sense of reverence and awe. Numbers for them are holy, fraught with significance" (Sacks, *H*, p. 208). Perhaps such a sense of awe approaches madness, the awful monstrosity of madness, not here an estrangement from one's body but a strange attachment that separates one from other attachments.

Madness's excesses belong to desire, to *erōs*, marked by *Phaedrus* and *Symposium*, but also by *Republic*, where the love of wisdom knows no bounds. Desire as *erōs* knows no bounds, circulates around us as excess: desire exceeding itself. This excess exceeds itself, whether as desire or power, madness or truth, more than any other excess. In *Phaedrus*, we may call excess "desire" or "madness," *erōs* or *mania*. The name matters less than the monstrosity, where excess shows itself. As desire, love can become monstrous, overpowering, destructive. As madness, truth and goodness display their own monstrosity. In *Phaedrus*, the form of this monstrosity inscribes itself as writing, where desire yearns to show itself as excess. Only in relation to madness's excesses can we understand how writing might be desire's *pharmakon*,[33] or why Phaedrus and Socrates carry on their discussion of love outside the city's walls.[34]

These themes of excess unto madness belong to Greek writing, belong indeed to writing, but especially to the Greeks. Athena sends madness upon Ajax so that he thinks he is killing Odysseus and the Atreans when he is killing sheep:

> But in he came, driving lashed together
> Bulls, and shepherd dogs, and fleecy prey.
> Some he beheaded, the wrenched-back throats of some
> He slit, or cleft their chines; others he bound
> And tortured, as though men they were, not beasts.
> Last, darting through the doors, as to some phantom
> He tossed words, now against the Atreidae, now
> Taunting Odysseus, piling up huge jeers
> Of how he had gone and wreaked his scorn upon them.[35]

Ajax is already mad, with monstrous rage and fury. The great warrior comes home from war in a frenzy, brings the injustices and hatreds inescapable in war to peace, where their monstrosity cannot be tolerated. Athena saves Odysseus and Agamemnon from Ajax by diverting his madness, saves the peace, through a madness already diverted. Athena repeats in *Ajax* the transformation of archaic injustice into justice she undertook in *Eumenides*, again in the form of madness. The Furies and Ajax repeat the monstrosity of madness as a form in which archaic injustice reappears in time and law.

What is Hecuba to him, or he to Hecuba?[36] What but another repetition? What indeed, in Greek, but the unspeakableness of injustice passing into the unspeakableness of vengeance and then of madness?

> How to utter a tale of unspeakable things?
> For disastrous as death is the hap you will hear.
> In the darkness of night madness has seized
> Our glorious Ajax: he is ruined and lost.
>   (Aeschylus, *Ajax*, p. 322, lines 214-17)

The unspeakableness of madness as vengeance, the slaughter of the Greek chiefs, passes into another madness. The monstrosity of madness goes beyond speaking, calling to us in Ajax's name the archaic injustice he seeks to redress and the injustices to which he gives rise.

Ajax and Hecuba speak in the same mad voice of injustice:

> No, but she the strong
> Zeus-born deity
> Miserably tortures me.
> Whither should I then flee?
> Whither seek for rest?
> Since my former glory is gone, my friends,
> With younger victims, yonder spoils by frenzy won,
> Since all the host with swords uplifted
> Sternly would slay me.
> (Aeschylus, *Ajax*, p. 328; 401–09)

When Hecuba discovers that her daughter, Polyxena, must be sacrificed to Achilles' memory, she chastises Odysseus for his betrayal.[37] When she discovers that her son, Polydorus, has been murdered by Polymestor, whom she trusted as a friend, she speaks in madness's language of monsters and betrayal: "O awful crime! O deed without a name! beggaring wonder! impious! intolerable! Where are now the laws 'twixt guest and host? Accursed monster! how has thou mangled his flesh, slashing the poor child's limbs with ruthless word, lost to all sense of pity!" (Euripides, *Hecuba*, p. 823, lines 709–12). And after she has blinded Polymestor, he speaks in an identical voice, that of a monster made so by monstrousness—his and Hecuba's: "Ha! hush! I catch their stealthy footsteps here. Where can I dart on them and gorge me on their flesh and bones, making for myself a wild beasts' meal, exacting vengeance in requital of their outrage on me?" (Euripides, *Hecuba*, p. 834, lines 1070–73). Polymestor curses Hecuba to become mad as a dog, though again, she is already mad: "Though wilt become a dog with bloodshot eyes" (Euripides, *Hecuba*, p. 838, line 1265). The voice of vengeance echoes madness whether victim's or oppressor's. Archaic injustice represents the wild unspeakableness of authority and goodness, appearing for us as the monstrosity of madness.[38] It appears, in *Hecuba*, in the form of Polydorus's ghost, opening the play.[39] Hecuba is Locke's mourning mother, torn apart by the monstrosities of revenge and grief, by archaic injustice. We do much worse than to become monsters of injustice.

Hecuba's and Ajax's madness belongs, we think, to the terrible circumstances in which they find themselves, creatures of injustice. Eros's *mania* brings another madness before us as a gift of the gods. This madness, as well as the madnesses of which Sacks speaks, with Foucault before him, represent madnesses with another meaning, calling reason's own madness into question. This madness may be romanticized, glorified, and perhaps we should with Derrida resist the temptation to think it gives us madness itself. We resist romanticization by denying another privilege to madness's truth.

Yet the maddest madness, without meaning, the saddest instances of madness before which we weep for others and ourselves, mark the limits of reason again, in a different way. This madness resists all attempts to seize it, to know its truth, either from within reason as its other, or any other truth. This madness, itself, breaks the hold of reason's law, dissolving all authority into the abyss. It does not represent the only such dissolution: we find dissolutions of "the body" that mark the same limits. Yet history tells of great achievements in broken, deformed bodies. The deformation of the mind marks an infinite injustice, beyond all other injustices, with or without intelligibility. Madness itself does not mark pure madness unframed by reason, but the most alien madness, whose alienness marks the alienness of reason's authority. Joined with Hecuba and Socrates, the monstrous truth persists that reason's rationality can be rational only in madness.

Monstrosity shows up in Derrida in the form of *montre* and *monstre*: representation and excess, a nonmathematical, finite form of the sublime intimately related to the abyss, where monstrosity meets monstration and the demonic undergoes demonstration, proof.[40]

> *Monstrer* is *montrer* (to show or demonstrate), and *une monstre* is *un montre* (a watch). I am already settled in the untranslatable idiom of my language, for I certainly intend to speak to you about translation. *La monstre*, then, prescribes the divisions of a line of verse for a melody. *Le monstre* or *la monstre* is what shows in order to warn or put on guard. In the past *la montre*, in French, was written *la monstre*.[41]

Reading Hölderlin's "Mnemosyne," after Heidegger, Derrida continues:

> We are a "monster" void of sense
> We are outside sorrow
> And have nearly lost
> Our tongue in foreign lands.

> We are a monster, and singular, a sign that shows and warns, but all the more singular since, showing, signifying, designating, this sign is void of sense (*deugungslos*). It says itself void of sense, simply and doubly monster, this "we": . . . display [*montre*] that deviates from the display or monstration, a monster that shows [*montre*] nothing. This gap of the sign to itself and to its so-called normal function, isn't it already a monstrosity of monstrasity [*monstrosité*], a monstrosity of monstration? . . . But this we, the monster, is it man? (Derrida, *G*, p. 167)

Monstrosity, born of injustice, meets monstration, transforms itself into demonstration, the proper demon of evidence and proof, wherein we hope to hear the victims of science's *technē*. Here, as in *Phaedrus*, the monstrosity of madness belongs to writing, writing the mad monstrosity of demonstration, demonstration the monster of writing—always "we"; the monster in our gifts:

> the name of man, his *Geschlecht*, becomes problematic itself. For it names what has the hand, and so thinking, speech or language, and openness to the gift.
>   Man's hand then will be a thing apart not as separable organ but because it is different, dissimilar from all prehensive organs (paws, claws, talons); man's hand is far from these in an infinite way through the abyss of its being. This abyss is speech and thought. (Derrida, *G*, p. 174)

We find the gift of language, speech, or thinking not given to animals or machines, but only to "us." *Geschlecht* shows as always "ours." The difference between humans who do not think and other creatures marks the absolute limit of Man. "Apes, too, have organs that can grasp, but they do not have hands. The hand is infinitely different from all the grasping organs—paws, claws, or fangs—different by an abyss of essence. Only a being who can speak, that is, think, can have hands and can handily achieve works of handicraft."[42] The monstration in the hand belongs to language in its monstrosity, its temporality and privilege, marking the essence of humanity, of Man, its unending injustices. Monstrosity, here, belongs to French as *Geschlecht* belongs to German.

In the monstrosity of our *Geschlecht*, we find again that we humans, as always, represent the proper measure of justice, where every measure marks archaic injustice. Here we approach the abysmalness of the sublime, where measure reveals its proximity to madness, where justice owes everything to law. In Kant's words:

> An object is *monstrous* where by its size it defeats the end that forms its concept. The *colossal* is the mere presentation of a concept which is almost too great for presentation, i.e. borders on the relatively monstrous; for the end to be attained by the representation of a concept is made harder to realize by the intuition of the object being almost too great for our faculty of apprehension.[43]

Derrida asks two questions: "How are we to think, in the presence of a presentation, the standing-there-upright [*Darstellen*] of an excess of size which remains merely *almost* excessive, at the *barely* crossed edge of a limiting line?"[44] Compared with the infinite, with the sublime, "everything is small" (Kant, *Critique of Judgment*, p. 91). The colossal, in its "almost too," surpasses itself, falling into the abyss, dragging the mathematically sublime with it. The second question addresses the sublime's excess directly in relation to magnitude.

> Why can magnitude, which is not a quantity, and not a comparable quantity in the order of phenomena, let itself be represented under the category of quantity rather than some other category?. . . In short, why is the sublime large and not small? (Derrida, "Parergon," p. 136)

Why is excess great rather than insignificant, infinite rather than finite, pleasing rather than disgusting?

Madness unfolds in relation to reason, the sublime in relation to magnitude, mediated, measured, by the *colossus*, by the looming figure of Man, by the essence, nature, of Humanity, in one case by Human Reason, in the other by The Human Body. Humanity stands up in close proximity with its nature, its law and measure, the measure it brings to things, and with its excesses, what exceeds its nature, its law, exceeds any measure. Why, Derrida asks, must we take excess as large rather than size, why *anything* at all?

The colossal, the almost-too in its monstrosity, pressing against the excess of the sublime, recoils into a familiar measure. "Everything is measured here on the scale of the body. Of man" (Derrida, "Parergon," p. 140). Monstrosity and measure meet at the edge of the sublime and recoil, the colossal falling back into its measure, a human measure, privileging humanity as Our *Geschlecht*. We see a repetition, perhaps in a distorted mirror, of the play of humanity and animality that marks *Hecuba*'s monstrosity as bestiality. Humanity must forbear falling into animality, as if that represented a falling back, and as if humanity's divinity, approaching the excesses of desire, seems almost too animal, too bestial, to be sublime. What if Hecuba's and Polymestor's madness, their animality, represented divine excess? What if, as the Greek dramatists suggest, madness's bestiality belonged to the gods, were a gift of the gods, belonged to their divinity? What if the gift of the gods had no measure, surely not a human measure, perhaps not a divine measure? What if madness's monstrosity represented the absence of measure to either madness or reason and every measure repeated injustice?

In close proximity to these monstrosities, Derrida addresses animal sacrifice:

> there was a time, not long ago and not yet over, in which "we, men" meant "we adult white male Europeans, carnivorous and capable of sacrifice." ("Force of Law," p. 951)

> carnivorous sacrifice is essential to the structure of subjectivity, which is also to say to the founding of the intentional subject and to the founding, if not of the law, at least of law (*droit*). ("Force of Law," p. 953)

When we ask about this "essential," whether Jewish, Greek, or Christian, possibly German as *Geschlecht*, we find ourselves in that uncanny space of injustice in which humanity repeats the fetish of The Human in the form of monstrous sacrifice, sacrificing monsters.

The theme of animal sacrifice appears in Greece, sometimes inseparable from human sacrifice, where authority and injustice meet the divine. We recall the sacrifice of Hecuba's daughter, Polyxena, who meets her death with words not unlike Iphigenia's, sparing their slayers' injustice.[45] Vengeance must come to an end. Even so, injustice reigns. The two young women can spare their murderers vengeance—in vain in Agamemnon's case—but cannot spare the punishment. Some deeds, however noble, however necessary and inescapable, however part of history's triumph, remain crimes, recall injustice. The Greek chorus knows this better than we do, knows the inescapability of punishment that belongs to injustice, as the highest virtue.[46]

> 'Tis enough
> That Cadmus' clan should strive with Argos' host,
> For blood there is that can atone that stain!
> But—brother upon brother dealing death—
> Not time itself can expiate the sin!
> (Aeschylus, *The Seven Against Thebes*,
> I, p. 108, lines 676–80)

> But blood of man once spilled,
> Once at his feet shed forth, and darkening the plain,—
> Nor chant nor charm can call it back again.
> (Aeschylus, *Agamemnon*,
> I, p. 200, lines 1016–18)

For the Greeks nobility belongs to injustice, demanding punishment for even the greatest deeds.[47] Closely allied we find animal sacrifice, marking the monstrosity of human justice.[48] Hecuba and Polymestor become bestial, the monstrosity of what they must take on to survive the injustices that surround them and to whose superior force and authority they must submit regardless of what they do.[49]

Monstrosity marks the "almost too" where goodness and justice possess no measure as they circulate around one measure after another. The absence of measure within every measure, the arbitrariness of authority's authority, especially in the form of monstrosity and madness, represents archaic injustice. The madness and monstrosity of goodness and truth, appearing in the obsessiveness and oppressiveness of proof, of reason as demonstration, the demonic monstrosity of demonstration, all measure the almost-too of every restitution against endless injustice. Here writing as reason marks its own monstrosity and madness, wandering without a home, without a measure, where every truth circulates as monstrous in its monstration.

And yet it marks truth. And goodness appears in its monstrosity. Or rather, goodness and truth persist in virtue of their monstrosity, in virtue of their guilt and responsibility, their victims. Not in the innocence of goodness and truth but in the monstrosity of their injustice.

Bloch speaks of monstrosity as a "species of servitude" associated with self-hatred, found above all in Kafka: "Kafka gave it its final and fundamental form: that of naked violence, which is the most veiled, yet open and perfidious violence—only in the monstrosity that is the court is the punishment that hunts men down rendered visible, while the crime is never disclosed."[50] All our themes appear here together with a certain view of monstrosity, as perfidious and naked violence. The monstrosity of the court makes punishment visible in the silence of its accusation. Just a twist shows that justice requires, depends on, monstrosity, belongs to the monsters that devour it, while injustice remains silent as it haunts law.

Bloch identifies a mythology of culpability without quite hearing Anaximander's voice: "Where life is not regarded as punishment, death is; Anaximander summarized in a single phrase the entire missing mythical complex when he said that all things must return to the primal stuff from which they have arisen 'in order to give reparation and pay penalty for their injustices according to the order of time'" (*NLHD*, p. 249). He may not hear the injustices that call for punishment within great deeds that strive not to repeat punishment. He appears to identify injustice with guilt. Yet what has archaic injustice to do with guilt? What has its immemoriality to do with vengeance or offense? "[T]he idea [is] that arrogance and defiance merit punishment, because the death sentence for the 'injustice,' the *adikia* (even insult, affront, and illegal possession), is levied against the already intrinsically criminal being of being-separate. Death is the wage of sin; . . . " (Bloch, *NLHD*, p. 249). That death or any other punishment measures the crime of injustice forfeits its own injustice in the measure it provides to justice. The "merit" of punishment repeats measure.

Bloch seems to give us another measure in his critique of this punishment of *adikia*. Yet if we withdraw to other places in his text we find a reversal of this mythology of culpability without forfeiting culpability. "The authority crushes its head, posits *metaretaliation* in the place of retaliation as the effect of the mythology of guilt" (*NLHD*, pp. 250–51). We call it "monstrosity." It belongs to tragedy. "Tragedy portrays people who were both culpable and declining, but equally portrays them as victorious" (Bloch, *NLHD*, p. 251). Hecuba's monstrosity marks her greatness. The mythology of culpability reverses in tragedy from the punishment that belongs to guilt to the ambiguity of victory. Some crimes, some triumphs, even when required by injustice, merit punishment, reenact injustice. Bloch seems to give us a standard of justice as he recognizes that tragic triumph and fulfillment has no measure. "In sum: out of the destructions of destiny tragedy paves the constancy of a great person who is victorious even in defeat. The death sentence of the tribunal becomes the scene of an irrefutable glory, the glory of the guilt itself" (*NLHD*, p. 252). This glory in injustice reflects its other side as it marks the monstrosity within the achievements of justice. The other side of injustice marks guilt and glory. The glory of archaic injustice appears as guilt, with and without punishment. The other side of injustice, its justice, circulates as goodness, truth, and law.

The glory of guilt and atonement in relation to immemorial injustice appears in the Old Testament and Greece (as well as contemporary Africa)[51] in the form of the curse. The curse and the glory reenact monstrosity, the appearance of injustice in the form of justice, as punishment or atonement. When Bloch speaks in his utopian voice, he expresses this monstrosity again, however differently: "A Marxism that was what it was supposed to be would be a radical penal theory, indeed the most radical and at the same time most amiable: It kills the social mother of injustice" (*NLHD*, p. 263). Its radicality belongs to the matricide that engenders it. It is cursed by its own violent injustice.

What justifies it, if it needs justification, represents the possibility of the future. "The basic tenor of radical natural law against the state is the classless society, the realm of freedom; it only grows insofar as it is a prelude" (Bloch, *NLHD*, p. 275). To what a prelude? To its future injustices? Does radical law exceed any future, any injustice, by its own injustice, in this way always a prelude, to some what, however imponderable, to some future in relation to the silences of the past?

We face the impossible task, in time, of restitution for the injustices of time and law, especially of truth, reason's truth, marked for us and Bloch by our glorious Greek heritage, represented repeatedly at the height: justice, injustice, war, strife, victory, destiny, goodness, truth, law, guilt, vengeance, retribution, and so on. These "highest" terms, in our language, mark our tradition's injustice, where that injustice—with its justice, strife, truth, and law—represents a difference from these highests in time, a difference requiring endless time, inexhaustible deferral, for its expression, representation, implementation, restitution, its circulation. Within this injustice, immemorial and archaic against its measure under law, against any measure including guilt, atonement, violence, punishment, glory, we speak, we act, against, alongside, together with, the rule of law, represent, however obscurely, the lack of authority of authority, the injustice of every just authority. We hope to turn the forces of justice and authority against themselves, to represent a force already turned, to mark unknown, unrepresented violences, lost, forgotten oppressions, not as guilt-ridden offenses, demanding punishment—if that would institute other offenses—not as retributions repeating old offenses, but to remember the injustices that made us and the injustices we will institute within every act of liberation and justice.

We struggle to remember injustice against any narrative of justice. This struggle, against war and violence, a struggle for, against, and within every good, represents justice's strife, archaic injustice, appearing as monstrosity. We struggle within every silence, the silences of truth and language, with the monstrosity of injustice, the persistence of victims.

The Greek dramas tell of the demand for punishment as restitution for injustice, but punishment opens up its own injustices, rests on arbitrary force and violence. Oedipus and Agamemnon deserve to be condemned for their crimes, though they could have made no better choices. Neither ignorance nor circumstances save us from monstrous injustices, but bring about their monstrosity. The Erinyes walk among us, marking injustice, however much we may have forgotten.

We imagine, under law, that madness and incapacity give excuses for injustice. Under law, in time, we cannot expect punishment to make one less mad, to give one force of character against one's history. History, here, represents the sphere of work against injustice, but always work, where work repeats injustice. Shall we punish someone too mad to know that what he did was wrong—Pierre Riviére, for example.[52] Would it be wrong? Of course. Would it be wrong to do nothing? Of course. Shall we punish criminals who emerge from a life of destitution and poverty, drug users, slum dwellers, creatures of the underworld?[53] What of our need for an underworld, terror of whose monsters helps us recoil from our temptations? What of killing animals instead of people, sea animals instead of mammals? What of letting the urban poor die rather than the wealthy, women rather than men,[54] providing a differential health care system? What of our responsibility for every oppression, every victim's suffering? What if this were our general economy? What if it were the force of law?

We live surrounded by monsters, as the Erinyes circulate around every work, knowing that vengeance marks no restitution as it delimits another sovereignty. The political realm, of justice and law, composes a realm of monsters. The greatest achievements of law, the commonwealth and truth, express their monstrosity together. The show of law and truth appears monstrous, exercises demonic authority, imposes authority on others. Writing, proof, circulate as monstrous. We hear this monstrosity on both sides, the demonic and horrible in authority, the show of truth and goodness in monstrosity. The demand for proof, for evidence and demonstration, in science and law, rules monstrously in the double sense that injustice haunts every demonstration, reason's madness, and that science circulates in historical events of silence and exclusion.

We return to Lyotard with this monstrous insight: phrase regimens and genres, disciplines and forms of knowledge, commonwealths of law, rule in the delimitations of their oppressions and victims. This marks the deepest insight of the Greek dramatists: the victory over Troy in which Greece gained its glory suffused with injustices, large and small. The gods appeared in Greece, not to save justice but to measure the space of human life together with monstrous injustices. Victims do not need proof; archaic injustice guarantees their suffering. Justice's restitution may require proof, but some crimes permit no punishment as the world seeks restitution.

We return to a certain inescapable suspicion of authority, an inexhaustible suspicion of inexhaustible authority, appearing in our memories sometimes as madness, sometimes as monstrosity. The monstrousness of history's memory represents truth and history, goodness and knowledge, science and *technē*, wisdom and law, all belonging to an injustice older than any, where each spends all time seeking restitution without restoration.

    The monstrosity of goodness as the age of injustice.
    The monstrosity of goodness as the restitution of time.
    The monstrosity of goodness as the debt of responsibility.
    The monstrosity of goodness as the authority of law.
    The monstrosity of goodness as the economy of truth.
    The monstrosity of goodness as the circulation of subjection.
    The monstrosity of goodness as the madness of reason.
    The monstrosity of goodness as the force of law.
    The monstrosity of goodness as the propriety of the idols.
    The monstrosity of goodness as the witches of science.
    The monstrosity of goodness as the Erinyes, our Muses.

    . . . .

The monstrosity of goodness as the force of law.

VII

LAW'S FORCE

When Thrasymachus bursts out, unable to contain himself, the room, the world, even Socrates, trembles:

> But gathering himself up like a wild beast he hurled himself upon us as if he would tear us to pieces. And Polemarchus and I were frightened and fluttered apart. (Plato, *Republic* 336b)

> And I, when I heard him, was dismayed, and looking upon him was filled with fear, and I believe that if I had not looked at him before he did at me I should have lost my voice. (Plato, *Republic* 366de)

What could frighten Socrates, who fears not even death? What threat can Thrasymachus offer a just society? Could the justice, the order, of this society rest more on Thrasymachus than on Socrates? Shall we understand Thrasymachus's danger to threaten the city's safety from without or within?

Thrasymachus describes the discussion taking place between Polemarchus and Socrates as "balderdash" and "drivel,"[1] a suggestion, perhaps, that we may take Socrates as no purer in relation to danger than Thrasymachus himself, no philosophy as purer than Socrates. "But if you really wish, Socrates, to know what the just is, don't merely ask questions or plume yourself upon controverting any answer that anyone gives—since your acumen has perceived that it is easier to ask questions than to

159

answer them—but do you yourself answer and tell what you say the just is" (Plato, *Republic* 366cd). Yet Socrates does not say what justice is, not at least here.[2] He suggests that Thrasymachus has prohibited exactly the kind of answer Socrates would give, leading Thrasymachus to take up the dare. "What then, he said, if I show you another answer about justice differing from all these, a better one—what penalty do you think you deserve?" (*Republic* 337d)[3]

Does this language of penalty and prohibition represent the state and law? Does Socrates reply in kind to Thrasymachus, not by presenting reason's greater truth over Thrasymachus's shouting and threats, but with a more effective means of social control? One form of control exerts direct physical force, including intimidation. Another, perhaps more effective and insidious, works by suggestion and persuasion. Shall we regard the latter as less controlling, less forceful? What of the possibility, as Nietzsche says, that reason itself possesses this kind of efficacy and authority, that its authority belongs more to the will to power than to the superiority of its truth?

Thrasymachus's famous answer is "that the just is nothing else than the advantage of the stronger. Well, why don't you applaud? Nay, you'll do anything but that" (Plato, *Republic* 338c). Socrates not only does not applaud but offers a countermovement: "Provided only I first understand your meaning, said I, for I don't yet apprehend it" (*Republic* 338c). Tell me what you mean so that I understand it. Tell me what you mean in my terms. We both speak Greek; nevertheless, you must meet my conditions of discourse, follow my rules. Socrates imposes his authority twice: once in requiring anything at all, the other in setting the conditions of fulfillment.

What gives Socrates the authority to require of Thrasymachus that he speak in terms that Socrates may claim to understand? What gives Socrates the authority to require of his interlocutors—Meno, Euthyphro, Cephalus among others—that they meet the conditions of his discourse, that they satisfy philosophical constraints? Have they already accepted the force of reason? Have they accepted both the force of reason and its terms and conditions? Or do we find, in Socrates, an authoritarian imposition of reason's force? Do we recognize in Socrates' person the masked authority of reason?

Thrasymachus tells us, if we listen, that Socrates does not perform innocent movements but belongs to the same space of conflict and control as Thrasymachus: "You are a buffoon, Socrates, and take my statement in the most detrimental sense" (Plato, *Republic* 338d). "That is because you argue like a pettifogger, Socrates" (*Republic* 340d). When

Socrates "scores" a point, the audience cheers: "Yes, by Zeus, Socrates, said Polemarchus, nothing could be more conclusive" (*Republic* 339e). "Of course, said Clitophon, breaking in, if you are his witness" (*Republic* 340a). Polemarchus asks the crucial question: if reason possesses intrinsic and unambiguous force, "What need is there of a witness?" (*Republic* 340a). Perhaps Socrates needs a witness, needs the crowd's support, because the force he requires to defeat Thrasymachus does not hold, does not belong to reason, to words and discourse, to philosophy, but obscurely belongs to authority and power. The force of reason's law does not rule except as a mark of another force, another authority. The authority of reason's truth and law does not belong to reason as such, nor could it, but, like every authority, requires force, exercises force, possesses no superior force as such.

> You think, do you, that it was with malice aforethought and trying to get the better of you unfairly that I asked that question?
> I don't think it, I know it, he said, and you won't make anything by it, for you won't get the better of me by stealth and, failing stealth, you are not of the force to beat me in debate. (Plato, *Republic* 341ab)

Of course Socrates possesses the force to beat him, with or without the others' support. But Thrasymachus knows, as they do not, that beating exercises force, and that Socrates' authority requires a might that reason does not own if Socrates does. This does not mark reason as defective because it does not intrinsically possess this force. Nothing possesses it and nothing could. This force marks its own injustice.

The argument concludes in consensus, perhaps suggesting reason's universal appeal, perhaps that Socrates requires this consensus to defeat Thrasymachus. Moreover, the conclusion does not end the discussion, for two things follow. In one, Thrasymachus reverts to form, to issues of strength and force. He describes his view of force in a famously vulnerable way: "[Y]ou think that the shepherds and the neatherds are considering the good of the sheep and the cattle and fatten and tend them with anything else in view than the good of their masters and themselves" (Plato, *Republic* 343bc). The force of justice's law repeats the force of might, seeking self-interest and advantage. It works by instrumentality and utility, with the agent's advantage in view like a gunman's. H. L. A. Hart addresses the same point:

A penal statute declaring certain conduct to be an offense and specifying the punishment to which the offender is liable, may appear to be the gunman situation writ large; and the only difference to be the relatively minor one, that in the case of statutes, the orders are addressed generally to a group which customarily obeys such orders. But attractive as this reduction of the complex phenomena of law to this simple element may seem, it has been found, when examined closely, to be a distortion and a source of confusion even in the case of a penal statute where an analysis in these simple terms seems most plausible.[4]

Thrasymachus and Hart address the difficulty that force of law cannot be distinguished from physical coercion, that their identity rests on the advantage of the coercer. Both show, especially the former, the identity of the force of rule and the force of coercion and, if in a different, perhaps more insidious, way, that of the injustice of the authority with which they exercise their force. In this sense, the visibility of the gunman's authority, in direct conflict with the victim, may threaten less harm than legitimate sovereignty, which Hart takes to be the epitome of legitimate authority. Rather than comparing the force of legitimate authority vested in sovereignty and law with physical coercion, as Hart does, perhaps we should compare physical coercion with the force of law, wondering about the coerciveness of legitimation.

Thrasymachus represents Hart's distinction precisely, between legitimate and illegitimate coercion, of the same kind exactly, except for reputation, each a swindle.

> when in addition to the property of the citizens men kidnap and enslave the citizens themselves, instead of these opprobrious names they are pronounced happy and blessed not only by their fellow citizens but by all who hear the story of the man who has committed complete and entire injustice. For it is not the fear of doing but of suffering wrong that calls forth the reproaches of those who revile injustice. (Plato, *Republic* 344bc)

Thrasymachus may not understand that the words "kidnap" and "enslave" belong to law, so that the tyrant who has won the enthusiasm of his country, whether or not benefiting from it personally and institutionally, cannot be spoken of as unjust under law. He understands the comparable force between direct coercion and legitimate authority, even the latter's greater coercion.

The line between reason's coercion and physical coercion remains blurred, as Thrasymachus complains: "And how am I to persuade you? he said. If you are not convinced by what I just now was saying, what more can I do for you? Shall I take the argument and ram it into your head?" (Plato, *Republic* 345bc). Most readers by now have taken sides with Socrates, for Thrasymachus's arguments seem weak under reason's authority. Yet his language echoes the most important truth of any tradition, where a lone voice stands against the multitude. How, if you are not already persuaded of the truth of what I have to say, can I convince you? If reason's force works upon the multitude, it must equally work against it.

In Socrates' words, Thrasymachus must "Persuade us, then, my dear fellow, convince us satisfactorily that we are ill advised in preferring justice to injustice" (Plato, *Republic* 345b). Aside from the fact that nine additional books are required for Socrates to convince his audience of the contrary, the nature of the preference and advantage remains unexamined. Socrates makes claims, along the way, that in their context seem more farfetched than anything Thrasymachus asks us to believe. "Do you not perceive that no one chooses of his own will to hold the office of rule?" (*Republic* 345e–346a). How could we doubt that in our systems of government, in any with which we are acquainted, officials pursue power voluntarily and, in most cases, self-interestedly?

Socrates completes his case with the claim that "Never, then, most worshipful Thrasymachus, can injustice be more profitable than justice" (Plato, *Republic* 354a). Thrasymachus has been tamed by a banquet of words. "A feast furnished by you, Thrasymachus, I said, now that you have become gentle with me and are no longer angry" (*Republic* 354b). Yet Socrates cannot remain content with the discussion, and Glaucon less so.

> Socrates, is it your desire to seem to have persuaded us or really to persuade us that it is without exception better to be just than unjust?
> Really, I said, if the choice rested with me.
> Well, then, you are not doing what you wish. (*Republic* 357b)

The rest of *Republic* takes up this task. And Thrasymachus has told us why he is no longer fearful: "Revel in your discourse, he said, without fear, for I shall not oppose you, so as not to offend your partisans here" (Plato, *Republic* 352b). He may be no less dangerous than he was, but we may no longer fear him, since he will no longer offend the multitude. By accepting the ideas of the many, without offending them, by joining them in community, we become no longer dangerous.

For the greatest danger to the *polis* came not from Thrasymachus but from Socrates, who offended the Athenian majority and was found guilty by them. Thrasymachus represents the force of authority no more (if no less) than Socrates, except that one does so in the shape of a lion, the other in that of a gadfly. We who live by reason cannot help but be deeply offended by Socrates' trial, but, like Nietzsche, we may see Socrates' death as a war of force more than a failure of truth. Christ too died on the cross for offending the majority, also described as a failure of truth. The offense marks Christ's extraordinary if, in Nietzsche's terms, hypocritical power. We need not take up this question here. More to the point, we may grant that Socrates and Christ represent clashes of authority, between Socrates and Thrasymachus, on the one hand, Christ and Pilate, on the other, clashes over truth's authority, over who shall rule with that authority and over which authority shall compose truth.

The difficulty with Thrasymachus's and Hart's reading of the conflict over the force of authority rests with their identification of advantage with a person, so that the benefit for which the ruler rules is his own. That may not always be true or ever germane. Rather, ruling, legitimate and illegitimate, requires authority, and nothing can authorize authority without arbitrary force, whatever the ends of force. Reason cannot authorize itself, because nothing can. Plato's works may be read as repeatedly turning around questions of the authorization of reason's authority, where nothing can provide that authorization. In *Republic* Plato presents us with a narrow interpretation of the stake of authority, defined in terms of advantage and benefit, falling under *technē*, moving us away from injustice.

In *Euthyphro*, injustice appears several times, first in the setting, for Socrates has just returned from attending court to answer his accusers, second in Euthyphro's father's treatment of a violent servant, third in Euthyphro's prosecution of his father for murder. Socrates responds in two ways: "by heaven! Euthyphro, you think that you have such an accurate knowledge of things divine, and what is holy and unholy, that, in circumstances such as you describe, you can accuse your father? You are not afraid that you yourself are doing an unholy deed?" (Plato, *Euthyphro* 4e). Do you know, can you know, can anyone know, what is holy and unholy, pious and impious, virtuous and unvirtuous, to act in complex and difficult circumstances, to bring one's own father to justice, to act ethically at all? The question appears as one of knowledge, leading to Socrates' responses in *Meno*:

> If . . . virtue is some sort of knowledge, clearly it could be taught. (Plato, *Meno* 87c)

> Can you name any other subject, in which the professed teachers are not only not recognized as teachers of others, but are thought to have no understanding of it themselves, and to be no good at the very subject they profess to teach, whereas those who are acknowledged to be the best at it are in two minds whether it can be taught or not? (*Meno*, 96b)

Virtue cannot be transmitted from parents to children, teachers to students, neither invariably nor with assurance.

Shall we accept the assumption that knowledge can be taught? Or shall we interpret the discussion in terms of authority? Virtue possesses no force, although it claims supreme authority. Parents and teachers who possess it can claim no authority over younger people and are respected as having no authority. Despite this, Euthyphro grants to the gods supreme authority over his father's life. "What is pleasing to the gods, and the man that pleases them, are holy; what is hateful to the gods, and the man they hate, unholy" (Plato, *Euthyphro* 7a). Greece possessed many gods, and they might differ over what they find holy and unholy, dividing not over knowledge but authority. Socrates' second response to Euthyphro, "Is what is holy holy because the gods approve it, or do they approve it because it is holy?" (*Euthyphro* 10a), addresses holiness's authority more than knowledge and truth. We may hear the question to address Euthyphro's assurance as to what the gods regard as holy. But this question presupposes too much about the qualities of virtue for us to find it persuasive. Do the gods make the holy holy, or do they find it holy? Why not the former? Because only what possesses goodness of itself can possess authority. Yet Montaigne accepts God's authority, however arbitrary and inscrutable, on the grounds that human authority is more dangerous and opaque. "It is enough for a Christian to believe that all things come from God, to receive them with acknowledgment of his divine and inscrutable wisdom, and therefore to take them in good part, in whatever aspect they may be sent to him."[5] We may read Montaigne to despair of human truth, so that divine commandments, however inscrutable, must take its place. We may read the inscrutability to mark a break between authority and truth, marking the inscrutability of the authority of law, the authority of truth.

If we read Socrates' question to Euthyphro as one of truth, we assume that truth possesses sole legitimate authority. Yet the entire history of philosophy repeatedly suggests that whatever epistemic authority truth possesses, it does not lend that authority to virtue. Either Euthyphro does not know with sufficient certainty the rule of law under which he subjects his father—a certainty we do not on the testimony of many works of literature possess—or whatever Euthyphro may know, whatever the gods may deem holy, we wonder what could possess sufficient authority to justify his prosecution of his father in the case at hand.

On the latter reading, Socrates' question repeats Thrasymachus's representation of law's authority as a vital force. The former represents it less forcefully. In both cases, Socrates replies to questions of authority by establishing his own in the place of the other, overpowering Thrasymachus by words and argument, establishing philosophy as possessing a greater authority, replacing the authority of the gods, however inscrutable, with his own, even as he denies that he possesses authority. We are then led, by being reminded of the opening of the dialogue, to recall that Socrates always refuses authority, even when appearing before the court accusing him of undermining authority. Why should we not accept the testimony of Plato at least to this point, that Socrates' entire life was devoted to challenging authority, that he did so by both establishing his own and repudiating that authority?

Socrates acknowledges authority as his concern in *Euthyphro*: "Where, however, you have reverence, there you have fear as well" (Plato, *Euthyphro* 12c) He speaks of fear of an evil reputation, but that represents a minor concern. We fear injustice, fear that we will violate trust and authority. Similarly, the suggestion that "By this reasoning, holiness would be the science of asking from the gods and giving to them" (*Euthyphro* 14d) fails because it presupposes instrumentality: "But tell me, what advantage could come to the gods from the gifts which they receive from us?" (*Euthyphro* 15a). Whatever authority belongs to holiness, it does not derive from scientific or instrumental knowledge. The authority of the gods and of what they deem holy possesses its own force, can be derived from nothing else, not even *technē*.

Montaigne calls this the "mystic foundation of authority [*fondement mystique de l'autorité*]." "Now laws remain in credit not because they are just, but because they are laws. That is the mystic foundation of their authority; they have no other. And that is a good thing for them."[6] Pascal follows him closely:

> Nothing, according to reason alone, is just in itself; all changes with time. Custom creates the whole of equity, for the simple reason that it is accepted. It is the mystical founda-

tion of its authority; whoever carries it back to first principles destroys it. Nothing is so faulty as those laws which correct faults. He who obeys them because they are just, obeys a justice which is imaginary, and not the essence of law; it is quite self-contained, it is law and nothing more.[7]

Laws possess authority in and of themselves, not as just, not because reason founds them, lends them its authority. One side of this view represents skepticism toward reason, which cannot lend authority to law, which cannot found authority because it possesses none of its own. Justice and virtue possess authority independent of reason. In Hume's famous argument:

> Since morals, therefore, have an influence on the actions and affections, it follows, that they cannot be deriv'd from reason; and that because reason alone, as we have already prov'd, can never have any such influence. Morals excite passions, and produce or prevent actions. Reason of itself is utterly impotent in this particular. The rules of morality, therefore, are not conclusions of our reason.[8]

This argument marks a distinction between "facts" and "values," appearing in extreme form in Kant, where understanding relates to science, reason to morality, that: "Understanding and reason exercise, therefore, two distinct legislations on one and the same territory of experience, without prejudice to each other. The concept of freedom as little disturbs the legislation of nature as the natural concept influences the legislation through the former."[9] At stake for Kant is freedom, the possibility that ethics may be independent of science. At stake for Hume is a skepticism sufficient to disallow reason's authority. In this respect, Hume more directly than Kant addresses authority. Kant takes the authority of law for granted, never addresses the foundation of its authority. The understanding places its judgments under the rule of concepts, under their authority.

Montaigne, Pascal, and Hume challenge reason's authority as the foundation of the force of law. If we hear this challenge, especially in Hume, as a challenge to truth, then skepticism suggests that reason cannot give us any ground for ethical responsibility. When we respond to the skepticism that reason after all gives us whatever truth we require, we leave authority aside, leave aside law's authority. Yet the question posed by Montaigne and Pascal concerns the authority of law, raising the possibility that reason might not be able to confer authority upon law even if reason were truthful and secure. The inadequacy of law's authority may not derive from reason's insufficiency. As Hume suggests, reason may be sufficient in its sphere, but that sphere may not authorize practice. We may consider the possibility that whatever truth reason provides, whatever knowledge it supports, no authority might attach to them. Why must knowledge and truth circulate as forms of authorization?

When Montaigne says that laws possess authority as laws, not as just, we may read him to hold that justice remains obscure, that, as Pascal says, reason has no power to bring us justice. We may read them both instead to hold that the authority that belongs to law cannot be found in reason's truth or justice. Authority possesses a "mystical foundation" because it appears from nowhere, without its own authority, and reason cannot give it authority. The authority of authority cannot spring from reason's authority, represents the "mystical foundation of authority."

This lacuna does not represent a defect in reason, as if something else might give reason authority or as if a better reason might found authority. Hume suggests that reason cannot possess authority in relation to morality, in relation to law. We are considering a reason that can provide truth without authority, separating truth from law, natural law from law's authority, scientific truth from scientific authority. Authority remains unauthorized. Yet it remains. This represents the truth of authority's authority, of the force of law, in Montaigne and Pascal.[10]

Law possesses its own authority because it cannot derive that authority from reason, does not found its authority on justice. We may think of Montaigne, Pascal, and Hume as skeptics. Yet we need not be skeptics about knowledge and truth, not even justice, to suspect authority. We question the authority of law that knowledge, truth, and justice seem to authorize. That authority has no authority. The authorization cannot be authorized. Once we make this distinction, the mystical foundation of law appears in a different light, rings in a different voice.

Hart takes up this question of the authority of law, acknowledging that authority as belonging to law essentially. "The most prominent feature of law at all times and places is that its existence means that certain kinds of human conduct are no longer optional, but in *some* sense obligatory" (Hart, *CL*, p. 6). The language sounds close to Montaigne's: the mysterious obligation of law. Yet Hart finds unacceptable that this authority might be indistinguishable from coercion, from being threatened with a gun. He takes the distinction to rest on a "rule of recognition": "Wherever such a rule of recognition is accepted, both private persons and officials are provided with authoritative criteria for identifying primary rules of obligation" (Hart, *CL*, p. 97), where primary rules define both obligations and sanctions.

Hart formulates the question as if he had Montaigne in mind: "What *can* there be in a rule apart from regular and hence predictable punishment or reproof of those who deviate from the usual patterns of conduct, which distinguishes it from a mere group habit?" (Hart, *CL*, p. 11). He answers that the stability and generality of primary and secondary rules authorize their duress. "In any large group general rules, standards, and principles must be the main instrument of social control, and not particular directions given to each individual separately" (Hart, *CL*, p. 121).[11] The key phrase is "social control." Law is distinguished from individual morality and violence by generality, stability, and repeatability. Yet if these are "added to" violence to make it legislative, we wonder how they can authorize their own authority except as citizens accept that authority as a means of social control. In no way does the violence lessen by the promulgation of general rules. We see this where Hart distinguishes his view from what he opposes, counseling us to "abandon the view that the foundations of a legal system consist in a habit of obedience to a legally unlimited sovereign and substitute for this the conception of an ultimate rule of recognition which provides a system of rules with its criteria of validity, . . . " (Hart, *CL*, p. 107). He promulgates a specific political doctrine, against unlimited and arbitrary sovereignty based on unswerving obedience, in favor of a limited and public system of mutual rules based on mutual criteria of sovereignty. No doubt public, stable, and mutually acceptable criteria of legal force represent superior forms of sovereignty—in most cases. Yet they unavoidably work violence upon some of their members. The clarity and publicity of the obligation to a sovereign in no way weakens its violence. The conditions of a legal system depend on force of law.

> There are therefore two minimum conditions necessary and sufficient for the existence of a legal system. On the one hand those rules of behaviour which are valid according to the system's ultimate criteria of validity must be generally obeyed, and, on the other hand, its rules of recognition specifying the criteria of legal validity and its rules of change and adjudication must be effectively accepted as common public standards of official behaviour by its officials. (Hart, *CL*, p. 113)

We may have our property seized, may be put to death, according to common public standards following rules valid according to "ultimate criteria." Such rules typically fall unequally on members of different races, genders, nationalities, and classes. Moreover, the "ultimacy" of the criteria works another violence, imposes another blindness upon injustice. Universality and publicity represent forms of public legitimacy. We are questioning whether legitimate violence imposes a lesser violence, even less unjust violence, except by its own measure, where its own authority imposes another violence. Even as Hart seeks to escape the violence of the gun, he must acknowledge that the authority of law works by violence, imposing social control. "[T]he life of the law consists to a very large extent in the guidance both of officials and private individuals by determinate rules which, unlike the applications of variable standards, do *not* require from them a fresh judgment from case to case" (Hart, *CL*, p. 132). Hart here calls it "guidance"; elsewhere he calls it "social control." The coercion cannot be denied. Generality represents whatever saves it from illegitimacy. What grants it legitimacy elsewhere is that some accept it. "[A] necessary condition of the existence of coercive power is that some at least must voluntarily co-operate in the system and accept its rules. In this sense it is true that the coercive power of law presupposes its accepted authority" (Hart, *CL*, p. 198). Some people accept the most terrible exercises of power, especially based on race or class. Justice exercises coercive power unjustly, sometimes among the majority.

Like it or not, laws wreak violence, destruction, upon their victims. Like it or not, they possess authority, in both their primary and their secondary forms. Like it or not, they implement control, impose direction upon heterogeneous individuals. We may wonder, following Hart, how stability and generality can authorize human destruction, how the universality of a law can authorize its authority.

We may consider two extreme examples of a justice with neither universality nor stability. When Solomon threatened to cut the baby in two and the real mother protested, we must assume he was prepared to carry out his plan. Otherwise the threat loses all force and becomes a clever trick of fact-finding. Justice was done under the threat of a terrible crime. No one could wish to generalize such an act.

I read a story recently that completed the Solomon threat, wreaking justice in a terrible way. I have no idea whether the story is true. A woman during a war protested that a soldier had stolen soup from her children. After she was warned of the dire penalties for false accusation, she persisted in her accusations. The general then had the soldier cut open, finding evidence in his stomach that what she said was true.

Both stories present us with a violence far beyond what we may find tolerable, revealing the hidden destructiveness in justice, its injustice.

Both present us with a justice greater than human, divine in its retribution, a justice that would triumph at any cost, however unjust. In this scheme of things, archaic injustice reemerges as the violence it bears, marking the destructiveness that belongs to rule. We cannot doubt that even without universality and stability, without repeatability, justice speaks in both these stories—in an intolerable form. We cannot doubt that justice works intolerably, if silently, in modern prisons.

Stanley Fish discusses one side of Hart's attempt to legitimate the authorization of authority in law by appealing to generality and stability, the side relating to law's interpretation. Fish calls our attention to the vanishing gap between interpretation and violence in Hart's discussion and certain juridical views of law. "[I]f it is the business of law to protect the individual from coercion that is random, unpredictable, and arbitrary, then the individual is no less at risk when he is at the mercy of an interpreting court than when he is at the mercy of an armed assailant."[12] Hart seeks to establish legitimacy on general and stable public rules based on the "acknowledgment of reference to the writing or inscription as *authoritative*" (Hart, *CL*, p. 92). Fish argues that interpretation destabilizes every inscription. "[W]hatever is invoked as a constraint on interpretation will turn out upon further examination to have been the product of interpretation, . . . " (Fish, *F*, p. 512).[13] He does not take up authorization, however stable or unstable, the unavoidability of the unfounded nature of the authority whereby law and sovereignty exercise their force. Or rather, he does not take up the injustice of this authority. He claims the inescapability of force in its infinite recession: "The conclusion is inescapable and it is the one I have repeatedly reached: the force of the law is always and already indistinguishable from the forces it would oppose. Or to put the matter another way: *there is always a gun at your head*" (Fish, *F*, pp. 519–20). Put still another way: "[A] mechanism is proposed with the claim that it will keep force—whether in the form of the gunman or the interpreter—at bay; and in each instance force turns out to be the content of the mechanism designed to control it" (Fish, *F*, p. 516).

What of the terrible monstrosity of this force? "Force is simply a (pejorative) name for the thrust or assertion of some point of view, and in a world where the urging of points of view cannot be referred for adjudication to some independent tribunal, force is just another name for what follows naturally from conviction" (Fish, *F*, p. 521). Law inhabits a world of oppression and injustice, of suffering, pain, and death. Fish argues that we can never escape the fear of uncontrollable misery from which Hart wants law to protect us. But Fish then abandons all the sufferings and oppressions that belong to injustice, collapsing them into the urging of points of view and another name for what follows naturally from conviction. He appears to know nothing of violence and suffering as he appears to grasp the force of force: "Force, in short, is already a repository of everything it supposedly threatens—norms, standards, reasons, and, yes, even rules" (Fish, *F*, p. 522). What of the "supposedly"? In this repository, have fear and danger disappeared, along with injustice, collapsed into different points of view? "You may know *in general* that the structure of your convictions is an historical artifact, but that knowledge does not transport you to a place where those convictions are no longer in force" (Fish, *F*, p. 524). Indeed, we can be transported to no place without force, free from injustice, while justice occupies all our time. Yet in this acknowledgment do the ghosts of injustices immemorial continue to haunt us, forcing our convictions to answer to something other than themselves? Although Fish sees with admirable clarity the bonds that tie the force of law to coercion and reason, does he fail to consider the injustices of its mystical foundation?

Derrida joins these questions in "Force of Law," commenting on Benjamin's essay "Critique of Violence"[14] Benjamin addresses revolutionary violence, rejecting the possibility that violence may be thought of as a means to an end. "For what such a system, assuming it to be secure against all doubt, would contain is not a criterion for violence itself as a principle, but, rather, the criterion for cases of its use" (Benjamin, *CV*, p. 277). If we think of cases of its use as fallen into time, then violence itself reflects archaic, immemorial injustice as a standpoint for critique. "For this critique a standpoint outside positive legal philosophy but also outside natural law must be found" (Benjamin, *CV*, p. 279). This leads Benjamin to a point close to Hart and Fish, where their views join at the danger point of authority's lack of authority: "the law's interest in a monopoly of violence vis-à-vis individuals is not explained by the intention of preserving legal ends but, rather, by that of preserving the law itself; that violence, when not in the hands of the law, threatens it not by the ends that it may pursue but by its mere existence outside the law" (Benjamin, *CV*, p. 281). Surely not the mere existence of violence, inside or outside the law, but its authority threatens law's authority, bringing us face to face with the violence of any authority that claims justice, right, that claims to counter injustice. "All violence as a means is either lawmaking or law-preserving. If it lays claim to neither of these predicates, it forfeits all validity" (Benjamin, *CV*, p. 287).

This distinction leads Benjamin to another that for the first time in our entire discussion may enable us to think of the fruitful nature of archaic injustice rather than of how it destroys every nature, the dividedness of injustice before time. Benjamin distinguishes mythic from divine violence. He also speaks of a sphere free from violence, from injustice, an idea with which we cannot agree. "This makes clear that there is a sphere of human agreement that is nonviolent to the extent that it is wholly inaccessible to violence: the proper sphere of 'understanding,' language" (Benjamin, *CV*, p. 289). As Fish and Foucault show, the spheres of understanding, language, and truth prevail as spheres of power, violence, and injustice. The archaic, immemorial nature of injustice haunts the order of time, representing why the political question is truth itself.

The pivotal distinction we find in Benjamin repeats the distinction between law-making and law-preserving violence in archaic language, between mythical and divine violence: "If mythical violence is lawmaking, divine violence is law-destroying; if the former sets boundaries, the latter boundlessly destroys them; if mythical violence brings at once guilt and retribution, divine power only expiates; if the former threatens, the latter strikes; if the former is bloody, the latter is lethal without spilling blood" (Benjamin, *CV*, p. 297).[15] The one speaks Greek, the other Hebrew. Derrida wonders if this discourse should be heard as "more Jewish (or Judaeo-Christian-Islamic) or Greek? More religious, more mythic or more philosophical? . . . And then, the Jew and the Greek, that may not be exactly what Benjamin has in mind for us" (Derrida, *FL*, p. 1035). We hope not, for how could Christians, Jews, and Greeks, together or apart, exhaust the work of injustice? How think of their own injustice except against their outsiders, the Jews within, Africans and Orientals without?

And yet, before Benjamin tells us how to employ archaic violence as criterion, as measure, he shows us that Anaximander's archaic *adikia*, before all time, belonging to the order of time as we seek to pay unending restitution, even in its univocity, divides, here into mythical and divine, or into Christian, Jewish, and Greek, elsewhere dividing again and again. The univocity of injustice inexhaustibly divides it into unending injustices circulating within law, unending injustices circulating in every justice and justification. The archaic, as origin or as no origin, circulates in and before the order of time as inexhaustible deferral.

This tells that injustice immemorial provides no measure, has no essence, divides again and again as every restitution, every debt paid, repeats its violences and oppressions. Fish almost captures this point when he says that "the force of the law is always and already indistinguishable from the forces it would oppose." *"There is always a gun at your head"* (Fish, *F*, pp. 519–20). Yet Fish neglects the terrible monstrosity of these forces that threaten us profoundly. The gun does not disappear, but worse, gets fired again and again, if not at us, then at others. Civilization does not put force and violence away from itself, but contains them within itself by employing them, circulating them. Unlike Benjamin, Fish appears to know nothing of the monopoly on violence the state claims as its sole authority even as individual and institutional violence permeates every level of society.

In the end, Benjamin tells in an authoritative voice what archaic injustice denies can be said at all. "But, all mythical, lawmaking violence, which we may call executive, is pernicious. Pernicious, too, is the law-preserving, administrative violence that serves it. Divine violence, which is the sign and seal but never the means of sacred execution, may be called sovereign violence" (Benjamin, *CV*, p. 300). Mythical, lawmaking violence is pernicious, not in a sense that belongs to law, to measure, or even to violence's justification, but in the immemoriality of its injustice. If Benjamin means to tell us that we must avoid mythical violence but can understand divine violence to be just in its life-giving nature, we must refuse his measure, must refuse any measure that would overcome the dangers of law's force and violence under *technē*. Archaic injustice expresses inexhaustible suspicion of every measure, demanding and imposing unending restitution.

In another way, Derrida makes this point concerning Benjamin's closing sentence, asserting the superiority of divine violence (if the closing sentence does that). For in the closing words, Derrida says, we find Walter Benjamin's authorized signature:

> Not only does it sign, this ultimate address, and very close to the first name of Benjamin, Walter. The also names the signature, the sign and the seal, it names the name and what calls itself *"die waltende."* But who signs? It is God, the Wholly Other, as always, it is the divine violence that always will have preceded but also will have *given* all the first names: *"Die göttliche Gewalt, welche Insignium und Siegel, niemals Mittel Heiliger Vollstreckung ist, mag die waltende Heißen."* (Derrida, *FL*, p. 1037)

We find Benjamin's signature as the divine *Insignium*. In order to proclaim the authority of divine violence, Benjamin must claim two authorizations, one his own, the other God's. Otherwise, these circulate as two, authority under law, law-making, law-preserving, and law-destroying, and the lack of authority of authority, of the force of law, its mystical foundation.

We can find no reason whatever to think that Benjamin took the distinction between mythical and divine violence to found justice, to authorize a measure for just violence. To the contrary, the law-destroying nature of divine violence undermines every measure. Within the founding movement of every violence, seeking its justice and justification, there transpires a reciprocal countermovement against its justness. We are identifying it with archaic injustice. Benjamin shows that we need not, must not, think of it as One, the Same. Yet he speaks of lawmaking and law-preserving as pernicious as if under measure, of law-destroying as sacred under divine sign and seal. Perhaps archaic injustice, mythic or divine, circulates without justice or justification. Perhaps no justice and no authority belong to immemorial injustice. Perhaps when injustice calls for violence, we cannot hope for justification, cannot hope for its justice in any form except under law, precisely at the point where legal justice breaks apart. Archaic injustice works under law in the upheaval of law.

Beyond his discussion of Benjamin, Derrida offers two extreme provocations in "Force of Law." In one he tells us what deconstruction *is*: "deconstruction is justice." In the other, he tells us that while "law (*droit*) is essentially deconstructible" (Derrida, *FL*, p. 943), "justice in itself, if such a thing exists, outside or beyond law, is not deconstructible. No more than deconstruction itself, if such a thing exists. Deconstruction is justice" (Derrida, *FL*, p. 945). Moreover, "the task of a historical and interpretative memory is at the heart of deconstruction, . . . " (Derrida, *FL*, p. 955).

Throughout Derrida's career, readers have wondered whether deconstruction, unending pursuit of the traces of *différance*, had an essence, was the name of a thing or procedure, of a method under law. Readers may have wondered because Derrida refused to tell them explicitly, forcing them to acknowledge, if they granted him authority, that such an authority could not authorize a method of deconstruction. Let us imagine that this withdrawal marks both inexhaustible deferral and suspicion of authority, of the force of law, so that if deconstruction occupied time, history's time, it would have repeatedly to mark refusal of its own authority, endlessly deferring it to another time. All of time, then, would represent the circulation of deconstruction's authority, the economy of its law.

Restitution remains absent in this deauthorization. It remains absent even when we hear that deconstruction is justice while deconstruction is not deconstructible, may be indestructible, while justice—if such a thing exists—belongs outside or beyond law. Does anything exist outside *law*? Does any *thing* exist outside law? Does anything *exist outside*?

Surely Derrida has Anaximander in mind, has something like what Anaximander has in mind, or something like we have in mind as we read Levinas after Anaximander, concerning the age of injustice, before or outside all time, when he speaks of justice outside or beyond law. Surely Derrida remembers, as Heidegger may not, the force of injustice that belongs to time's law. Even so, how can deconstruction *be* justice, and how can justice be *undeconstructible* while law is *essentially deconstructible*? Do we think of archaic injustice as undeconstructible or as given over to the deconstruction of every law? Do we think that archaic injustice evades injustice?

If we are not sure that Derrida has Anaximander in mind, injustice before all law, we cannot doubt that he addresses the mystical foundation of authority, the lack of authorization for authority, even God's authority, the authorization we give whenever we find ourselves in authority. The title of his paper quotes Montaigne and Pascal; in the text he quotes them in full. He begins, however, by noting that he addresses his remarks to his American audience in English as he writes in French, begins by telling them and us that the question that he "must" address is "does deconstruction insure, permit, authorize the possibility of justice?" This question cannot avoid the authority of its authorization.

With what authority can Derrida find the question of deconstruction's authority imposed on him, requiring that he address his audience in English? "This is an obligation, I must *address* myself to you in English" (Derrida, *FL*, p. 921). How can he find himself so obligated, and by what authority? How can deconstruction present itself as so obligated, and by what authority, to authorize the possibility of justice, if not by the mystical authority of immemorial injustice? "The title of this colloquium and the problem that it requires me, as you say transitively in your language, to address, have had me musing for months" (Derrida, *FL*, p. 921). How can the title of a colloquium, with its problematic, "require" anything of Derrida, even if he accepts the invitation? Might he not speak of anything, on anything, say whatever he regards as called for? And if what he regards as called for imposes a requirement, with what authority? Does it repeat authority's authority, a necessity belonging to history's repetitions, or another requirement altogether? And if we accept any necessity, any obligation or requirement, do we grant Habermas's claims concerning the requirements of communication?[16] When we admit the necessity of addresses and claims, if not their obligation, do we admit their authority, admit some authority within them that founds their testability even as nothing founds them?[17]

With what necessity or obligation does Derrida begin in English, address his American audience in English? An instrumental obligation, perhaps, that they will not understand his speech except in English—defeated by the fact that he may not speak or write in English as truthfully, or say the same things in the same ways in English. If we read Derrida as reading Heidegger's German into French, undergoing monstrous changes, then for Derrida to write in English threatens another monstrosity.

Let us suspend this question of language for a moment, returning to the obligation of the question, "Does deconstruction insure, permit, authorize the possibility of justice?" The answer, within the obligation, says that deconstruction does none of these, evades its own authorization, evades any authority, any permissions or assurances, with the monstrous claim that it is justice (if such a thing exists as deconstruction or justice). How can we avoid hearing this monstrous claim, this total authority, as a supreme provocation? If justice rings in the space of authority, together with questions of its own authority, even Authority, then that any reading or writing might emerge at this site of the irruption of injustice—deferring questions of the difference between justice for Derrida and injustice for us—discloses itself as a monstrous irruption into law. The entire discourse unfolds in its monstrosity, one monster after another, that of the obligation to tell the truth, in English, that deconstruction is justice, that justice unfolds outside law.

We have deferred the monstrous obligation to speak English, wondering if it repeated the obligations Habermas and Gadamer[18] address and accept, in Foucault's words, to speak "in the true."[19] The obligation to speak in the true belongs to disciplinary authority. How can Derrida accept such an authority when every attempt to exercise it fails to authorize its truth; when the exercise of that authority reenacts an authorization that brings us face to face with violence, its injustice? How can he respond to such an obligation except by extreme provocation?

The possibility that we may understand as extreme and monstrous provocations Derrida's claims that deconstruction is justice and justice rules outside law brings us to two additional possibilities. One proceeds from the consideration that when Benjamin distinguishes divine from mythical violence, he does not advocate "sacred execution," but presents it as an extreme provocation marking the perniciousness—injustice—of lawmaking violence. The provocation marks the violence of lawmaking and law-preserving as demanding that law be destroyed—though we and Benjamin surely know two things: (1) While individual laws may be abolished, law itself cannot be destroyed. Nor can the obligation to destroy it be justified, for law represents the measure of justification whereby time pays restitution for the violence of its institution. (2) Divine violence cannot offer a measure of acceptable violence, however sacred. The sacredness of divine violence, as Benjamin says, defines no means, no measure, has no measure, marks the injustice of every measure.

The second possibility raised by reading Derrida's understanding of his own necessity as an extreme provocation, promoting other such provocations, suggests that the restitution of justice's law, in all time, paying back for immemorial injustice, repeats and enacts archaic provocation. The archaic injustice that haunts justice's time, the monstrous authority that can have no ultimate authorization, the "mystical" force of law, do not institute another law, another measure, in this sense define no obligations, necessities, or responsibilities, all of which belong to law, but institute (with provocative necessity) the memory of injustice as inescapable provocation, demanding an economy of inexhaustible provocations. This injustice, this divine violence, resists, again and again, any institution of a system of justice whereby injustice can be paid off, including vengeance. The retribution immemorial injustice demands owns no form, and every form belongs to justice, repeats endless injustices. To remember suffering as an obligation to cause others to suffer belongs to law, frequently to bad law, reenacting injustice. To forget suffering as the means whereby we may escape endless vengeance repeats its injustice. We hope to do what Athena did, what mythic violence hopes to do, founding the state by ending violence, preserving the Erinyes circulating among us, furiously and endlessly, reminding us of violences unrepaid. The Erinyes impose upon us a certain obligation, outside law, repeat endless conflict hidden by rules of justice.

We understand Derrida's "obligation" to speak English to address both the endlessly repeated provocations injustice imposes and their institution within language, repudiating what Habermas and Gadamer, and even Derrida,[20] say belongs to language, the universal within it, a human sphere inaccessible to language. "[I]f, at least, I want to make myself understood, it is necessary that I speak your language, I must" (Derrida, *FL*, p. 923). To which we "may" or "must" respond, "Why so necessary?" Does it depend on what "understood" means? For Derrida might speak English for his audience while saying something (in French) that cannot be repeated in English. The *polemos* then may be less the requirement of the conference that he speak English to the audience than of language's authority.[21] Derrida suggests that certain expressions in English have a force absent from French, including "to enforce the law" (*FL*, p. 925). Law's force appears in a certain way in English, perhaps different from, more immediate and direct than, the way it appears in French. "How are we to distinguish between this force of the law, this 'force of law,' as one says in English as well as in French, I believe, and the violence that one always deems unjust?" (Derrida, *FL*, p. 927). It leads Derrida to the subject of his subtitle, the focus of our attention, the "mystical foundation of authority."[22]

We are on the verge of the extreme provocation of the promising side of the mystical foundation of authority, that it cannot authorize itself, that law has no law, meets justice and injustice. We follow several lines of Derrida's thought:

> [1] the origin of authority, the foundation or ground, the position of the law . . . are neither legal nor illegal in their founding movement.
>
> [2] [they] . . . exceed the opposition between founded and unfounded. . . .
>
> [3] The structure I am describing here is a structure in which law (*droit*) is essentially deconstructible, whether because it is founded, constructed on interpretable and transformable textual strata (and that is the history of law (*droit*), its possible and necessary transformation, sometimes its amelioration), or because its ultimate foundation is by definition unfounded. (Derrida, *FL*, p. 943)
>
> [4] it is this deconstructible structure of law (*droit*), or if you prefer of justice as *droit*, that also insures the possibility of deconstruction.
>
> [5] Justice in itself, if such a thing exists, outside or beyond law, is not deconstructible. No more than deconstruction itself, if such a thing exists.
>
> [6] Deconstruction is justice. (Derrida, *FL*, p. 945)

Summarized as follows:

> [7] 1. The deconstructibility of law (*droit*), of legality, legitimacy or legitimation (for example) makes deconstruction possible. 2. The undeconstructibility of justice also makes deconstruction possible, indeed is inseparable from it. 3. The result: deconstruction takes place in the interval that separates the undeconstructibility of justice from the deconstructibility of *droit* (authority, legitimacy, and so on). (Derrida, *FL*, p. 945)[23]

This interval represents the interval of the other, returning us to the obligations of address:

[8] To address oneself to the other in the language of the other is, it seems, the condition of all possible justice, but apparently, in all rigor, it is not only impossible (since I cannot speak the language of the other except to the extent that I appropriate it and assimilate it according to the law of an implicit third) but even excluded by justice as law (*droit*), inasmuch as justice as right (*droit*) seems to imply an element of universality, the appeal to a third party who suspends the unilaterality or singularity of the idioms. (Derrida, *FL*, p. 949)

We return, squinting at Levinas, with apparent inevitability to universality.

Much more appears here that we are obligated to discuss. First, we may consider some issues that emerge from the passages above.

1. The origin of authority, the foundation of law, prevails as neither legal nor illegal in its founding movement. Does this origin represent a foundation? Does a foundation outside law stand under law's authority? Can authority rest on itself if it does not rest on anything else?

Derrida's language sounds founding, aboriginary, even as he speaks against foundations and origins, against laws and regulations, in the authorization of authority. May we hear this unfounding founding to speak of what we have sought to speak of in the immemoriality of injustice, which belongs to law neither legally or illegally?

2. Such an unfounding founding of the origin of authority, perhaps no origin at all, "exceeds" the opposition between founding and unfounding, between foundationalism and antifoundationalism. These oppositions, clearly not one opposition, the same opposition, speak in different places, one of the authorization of law, perhaps of its lack of authority, archaically and immemorially, the other of our time's granting of authority, seeking a foundation or repudiating any foundation. In the language of founding, Derrida tells us that the origin of authority does not belong to a founding movement, within or without. In the language of positions, Derrida tells us that the positing of authority does not take a position. Can we find no other language? Can we circulate in no other economy of truth?

Against these positing, founding movements, Derrida speaks of the origin of authority—he calls it "justice"—as "exceeding" these or any opposing movements. In virtue of this excess, this escape from oppositional movement, justice (if it exists) is undeconstructible. Leaving deconstruction aside for just a moment, we address the excess. For in what way, in what memorable, articulable way, does justice, the origin of authority, exceed law, exceed authority?

This question leads to a double movement, then to several aporias belonging to justice. Deferring each of these circulations, again for just a moment, we understand that justice's excesses mark the limits of law's authority by a different double movement. The force of law exceeds any measure of law's success in two ways: one, that nothing authorizes the authority of law, its "mystical foundation"; the other, that law's authority exceeds what falls under law, where law itself decides, on its own authority, what falls under and over itself, defines its own position. Justice, then, marks law's excessive relation to itself twice, its authority and its territory.

A third, monstrous excess belongs to law, unclearly marked by Derrida. For if justice exceeds any relation between legal and illegal, good and bad, then excessively the territory remains under law. "Which is not to say that they are in themselves unjust, in the sense of 'illegal'" (Derrida, *FL*, p. 943). Or rather, after Anaximander, they are unjust, as all things are unjust, but not in a sense marked by law, for its markings represent unending restitution for injustice. Injustice's excesses belong to law's justice, to its legality and illegality, if still excessive. This marks the monstrous truth belonging to practical judgment, where, perhaps, we find ourselves moving away from Derrida toward Benjamin, far away from Heidegger along with Levinas and Lyotard, listening to Anaximander. To exceed the opposition between founded and unfounded lacks a certain excess of its own, marked by pain and suffering, oppression and destruction. We have marked it as law's unending restitution.

3. Perhaps this difference directly pertains to deconstruction, to the limits given by its construction in time, under law. Law is essentially deconstructible, but justice "in itself" (if such a thing exists) is not. Yet nothing in archaic injustice, immemorial, speaks in any way of its constructibility or deconstructibility. To the contrary, all of time, endlessly, marks restitution for injustice, where that injustice as it (in an enigmatic, monstrous way) "precedes" time, and law's justice circulates repeatedly, constantly, in law and justice. Where, in Derrida and Heidegger, in *Destruktion* and deconstruction, can we find both unending injustice in the greatest acts of justice, and inexhaustible, unending restitution? What does Derrida know of restitution for injustice?

Does deconstruction represent something we do, in time, under law, to law, to *droit*, to any meaning? Does the excess of meaning in any text's iterability mark something deconstructible? Does deconstructibility show something that can be said to belong, as if a quality or property, to something as against anything else? Or does deconstruction exceed any such opposition, between meaning and lack of meaning, one meaning and another, truth and untruth, one side and another, marking its excessiveness? How, if so, can anything, law, construction, be essentially deconstructible as if anything else might not be?

4. Does deconstruction, marking its own excessiveness, also mark its own monstrosity, the monstrous mark of its own injustice? And in this monstrous economy, in the inescapability of injustice and violence, can any achievement be assured, even deconstruction? Do we return with the assurance of the possibility of deconstruction to a founding movement, however unfounded? In this Kantian language, do we face the greatest monstrosity that truth is not assured, can never find assurance, either as deconstruction or as injustice? Injustice immemorial assures us of nothing, not even restitution, not even its possibility. Rather, injustice demands without authority, with nothing to authorize it, the necessity of impossible restitution, endless restitution. The greatest monstrosity of justice's restitution marks its impossibility as we find ourselves obsessively responsible for it. This aporia marks the curse of archaic injustice, expressed in Christianity as original sin, inexhaustibly circulating in finite life without God.

5. If law is not essentially deconstructible because nothing else is essentially undeconstructible, then justice "in itself" is not undeconstructible. Nothing can be deconstructible or undeconstructible, "in itself," as nothing is just or unjust. Or rather, everything can be deconstructed under law, and every law is unjust.

Derrida speaks of justice in itself—if such a thing exists. The in-itself engages us in relation to law's authority in a very different place from immemorial injustice. Perhaps we may regain that place by asking whether such a thing exists. Yet the words "if such a thing exists" (*si quelque chose de tel existe*) (Derrida, *FL*, p. 944) disengage us as they hold their truth at a distance. Is justice some thing (*quelque chose*), and in either case, what could mark its existence? If a thing, and if it exists, how could it be undeconstructible? How can it belong or not belong to time? Can it circulate nevertheless?

More to the point, perhaps, what of the if? What follows the if, existence and thing, sets its limits. Yet this justice in itself, if in proximity to immemorial injustice, marks any limits as unjust. Anaximander's injustice does not exist, either as thing or in time, but unmeasures everything that circulates in time. In this way, it unmeasures the limits of every measure, the injustice of every rule, the violence of every justice, the untruths of every justification. It shows itself as more than anything else unjust, infinitely unmeasurable. It marks the possibility of nothing and the actuality of everything's limits.

6. If deconstruction is justice, then it irrupts at the juncture of its own possibility, ensuring itself. What a monstrous idea, a possibility with

absolute assurance! Rather, if we understand immemoriality as injustice, then deconstruction along with every thought and writing, constructive or destructive, foundational or antifoundational, pays endless restitution for its own and other injustices. If we say that deconstruction is this unending restitution, again we face the possibility that some other form of truth or thought, illegal under law, is not such a restitution, either because it is not unjust or because it knows nothing of injustice, two impossible forms of innocence. We cannot pretend innocence. Does deconstruction's justice offer such a pretense?

Do we pretend innocence in founding the possibility of deconstruction as we do in the cunning of reason? Are deconstruction and justice cunning? Or does injustice's immemoriality speak against any cunning, including its own?

7. The mystical foundation of law's authority represents the impossibility of authorizing, ensuring, the authority of law. Does the assurance of deconstruction's possibility guarantee its authority? Or do we think of archaic injustice as guaranteeing nothing, not even its own authority, of circulating where authority possesses no authorization, guaranteeing the possibility of nothing in particular, nothing at all? Every authority, every authorization, every guarantee, repeats injustice, possesses no authority for its authority, cannot be authorized or guaranteed. Nothing guarantees the possibility of deconstruction, of justice, of any achievement, of any authorization or de-authorization. Nothing guarantees necessity, guarantees obligation. We are obsessed with infinite responsibilities without guarantees.

This interval, between deconstructibility and undeconstructibility, may be reinterpreted as the interval between the justice of law and the injustice of justice, between every lawful authority and the impossibility of its authorization, the absence of its authority. Even here, however, we find something missing. This interval, marked by the absence of every assurance and guarantee, marks both injustice and restitution. Where, in deconstruction, do we find restitution? Where, out of deconstruction, can we gain restitution?

8. To address oneself to the other in the language of the other; justice as right seems to imply an element of universality. The universality of justice's law belongs to it intrinsically against the possibility that universality represents the irruption of something mystical in justice's authority. The universality of law either represents its stability or repeats the imponderability of its authority. Nothing, not even universality, frees us from the monstrosity of law's authority.

Against the universality of law, which we have interpreted as marking the immemoriality of the injustice of its authority as a foundation for law's authority, the natural opposition marks the particularity, the uniqueness, of the other. To speak to the other in the language of the other, where every language echoes repetition. This disappearance of the other as a unique individual, this deauthorization and untruthfulness of individuality, has belonged to philosophic and scientific discourse, as well as law, from Aristotle to Hegel. No doubt, under law's universality, individuals suffer monstrous and repeated injustices. What, however, of this truth's injustice? What can we give up in this narrative of the privilege of the voice of the other?

We have addressed this question in the light of Levinas, the privilege of the other and the other's language. Derrida addresses it in ways that remain for consideration. Before we take them up, there remain questions of universality. Shall we grant to language the privileging of universality, the impossibility of de-universalization? Does this universality mark language's injustice, to abandon the particular in universality's authority, or can we speak against this injustice, against the opposition of universal and particular, as we grant the importance of responsibility before and for the other? Can we grant de-authorization in the authority of language's universality, as we consider the universality of natural law to speak of the lack of authority of authority?

Against the universality of language we recognize the particularity of the other's language, so that when we try to speak to the other, we address the other in the other's language. Language here marks the particular, both in the sense that German differs from French as well as English, as Derrida points out repeatedly, and in the idiosyncracies of the other's language. Repeatability does not represent universality, but imposes a different authority. The universality of law, if within its *technē*, its instrumentality, differs from the universality of language, its language or any language. We learn these things from Fish and Derrida.

Derrida's claim that deconstruction is justice is followed by several others. One speaks directly to the privilege of language.

> It is unjust to judge someone who does not understand the language in which the law is inscribed or the judgment pronounced, etc. . . . This injustice supposes that the other, the victim of the language's injustice, is capable of a language in general, is man as a speaking animal, in the sense that we, men, give to this word language. Moreover, there was a time, not long ago and not yet over, in which "we, men" meant "we adult white male Europeans, carnivorous and capable of sacrifice." (Derrida, *FL*, p. 951)[24]

Derrida remains among the few who acknowledge the importance of animal victimization to the constitution of Western subjectivity and law. Lyotard's own understanding of animals as victims is based on precisely the premises Derrida asks us to reexamine, the privilege of language. "[T]he animal is deprived of the possibility of bearing witness according to the human rules for establishing damages, and as a consequence, every damage is like a wrong and turns it into a victim *ipso facto*" (Lyotard, *The Differend*, p. 28). Is it because animals cannot speak, cannot bear witness, that they are exemplary victims? Do we repeat, if by negation, the privilege of language whereby animals may be victimized, in calling them victims *because* they lack language? Derrida shows, in Heidegger, the repetition of this privilege even in one concerned to question traditional forms of Western privilege.

To what do we owe our authority but the claim of authority, finally, that we can speak of questioning, worlding, truthing, in a voice of truthful authority? The authority belongs to language, in Heidegger to the German beyond the Greek language.[25] All turns around where *Geist* meets *Geschlecht* in the most high. "As always, the profound and the haughty are allied in the most high: the highest of what guides the spiritual guides of *die hohe Schule* and the depth of the forces of earth and blood."[26] Earth and blood take us to violent sacrifice, typically Spirit's sacrifice of itself—but this is Hegel! A sacrifice without scars. Are there scars in Heidegger? Are there always scars? Do the scars have scars? Does the pure cut leave scars in Derrida? Do these scars antedate the order of time against which the Laws and Reason of Spirit seek to prevail? Do we, are we willing to, hear the violence in sacrifice as a suffering for which all time is not long enough? Were the murder of Jews, the enslavement of Africans, the subjection of women, the repulsion of sexualities, necessary sacrifices, wounds that history can heal? Could there pass enough time to pay restitution for the truth of this violence? Could the greatest danger of nostalgia and utopia represent that they would render their due once and for all, without unending memory of the debt that can never be paid?

This claim of the most high: does it repeat *Geschlecht*, always violent, oppressive, in the Voice of the Master?[27] "The Master is bound to recognize that His Culture is not as homogeneous, as monolithic as He believed it to be. He discovers, with much reluctance, He is just an other among others."[28] How does this reluctant discovery pertain to truth? Are we, in our heterogeneity, to give up the political question as one of truth, to understand the political question as an other?

We recall the possibility that animal sacrifice in Greece marked a respect we no longer understand. "By expressing their ambivalence and remorse concerning even an animal killing, by humanizing the animal and showing a regard for its 'will,' the sacrificers put away from themselves the worst possibility: that they will kill human beings, and kill without pity, becoming themselves bestial."[29] Nussbaum assumes without question that killing human beings is worse than killing animals. We wonder whether an economy of animal sacrifice, violence toward animals, might show instead that animal sacrifice repeats without measure or law what it hopes to achieve, the injustice of human life delimited by injustice toward animals over whom human beings exercise dominion. This authority, founded on and justifying violence, possesses no authority, certainly no authority founded on reason, law, language, or hands, no authority founded on any gift, not even God's gift to humanity of dominion over animals. On this reading, it marks the unauthorized authority of humanity.

To claim that animal sacrifice expresses respect toward animals represents supreme hypocrisy. Nussbaum does not say this, but she may be read as doing so. Rather, animal sacrifice represents the limits of injustice toward humans, avoiding that injustice by killing animals, at least, here, in an ethico-political, not an instrumental way. At least, then, animal sacrifice in Greece as described here belonged to injustice, if at the expense of another injustice. There prevailed no restitution toward animals. Nussbaum's view confirms what Derrida suggests, that we define the limits of our relationship to humanity, ethical and political, by animal sacrifice.

If we acknowledge the inescapability of injustice, circulating everywhere, endlessly demanding restitution, then the killing of animals represents an enduring monstrosity, even killing by other animals, for which we may understand nature as well as human society to incur an endless, boundless debt. All of nature pays restitution for the losses of the past—pays without measure. Human life, under law and measure, cannot avoid paying for the same debt within memory and demanding a measure. We may not be able to avoid punishing criminals, putting some to death, causing deaths by accident, living surrounded by pain and suffering. We may not be able to avoid any of these things, but we may diminish them, care for them, mourn. As we find ourselves incapable of avoiding them, memory of our injustices makes us human. Respect, charity, toward others, human or otherwise, including every natural creature, imposes an unmeasurable debt for which human life seeks endlessly for measures to live by, in the shadow of this sublime responsibility. Charity, responsibility, valor represent the force of archaic, immemorial injustice imposing upon us unending restitution.

Derrida brings these concerns before us, though we may wish he had pursued them further. He leaves them aside "for the moment," though we may regard them as present in mythical and divine violence. Instead, he pursues a variety of themes closely related to Anaximander's immemorial injustice, always in the language of justice. Justice corresponds to a double movement:

> 1. The sense of a responsibility without limits, and so necessarily excessive, incalculable, before memory; and so the task of recalling the history, the origin and subsequent direction, thus the limits, of concepts of justice, the law and *droit*, of values, norms, prescriptions that have been imposed and sedimented there, from then on remaining more or less readable or presupposed. (Derrida, FL, p. 953)

> 2. This responsibility toward memory is a responsibility before the very concept of responsibility that regulates the justice and appropriateness (*justesse*) of our behavior, of our theoretical, practical, ethico-political decisions. (Derrida, FL, p. 955)

These represent the immemoriality of injustice except for the theme of restitution, of which Derrida speaks in a different context.[30]

1. The responsibility without limits imposed by immemorial injustice opens a historically familiar space, both in our recollection of God's commandments and in the universality of law that replaces them. How does a responsibility without limits differ from conformity to law without limits, from Abraham's obedience to God without limits? Kierkegaard shows us the inescapable aporias within such an obedience without limit.[31] He does not show how such an obedience may pay unending restitution for whatever falls into time so that the obedience, the justice, always circulates as temptation, injustice. Abraham's greatness expresses temptation, his obedience transgression, his justice injustice. *This* injustice does not belong to the laws of temptation, transgression, or justice. But it haunts them everywhere. The ghost that haunts them, everywhere and forever, forever prevents them, prevents any historical memory, from fulfilling, meeting, injustice's demands. This impossibility, however, cannot be located, can be located no more than excess. Does Derrida perhaps locate the point of excess too precisely? "Consequently, never to yield on this point, constantly to maintain an interrogation of the origin, grounds and limits of our conceptual, theoretical or normative apparatus surrounding justice . . . " (Derrida, FL, p. 955). Constantly to maintain vigilance toward the apparatus, but not toward justice's injustice?— "knowing that this justice always addresses itself to singularity, to the sin-

gularity of the other, despite or even because it pretends to universality" (Derrida, *FL*, p. 955). Singular idioms and singular others: does this singularity repeat a certain privilege, of language and of universality, where the singular echoes in the harmony of the universal? What of the group, the kind, the neighborhood, the locale? What of a proximity that is neither absolutely singular nor absolutely universal, but absolutely not absolute at all?

2. In this refusal of absoluteness, within its absolution, do we find another privileging of the rule? The responsibility toward memory irrupts "before"—*devant*—the regulation, what rules (*règle*), over justice, authorizing our ethico-political decisions. In this situating of critique, of injustice, alongside the rule, together with decision, do we subject injustice to justice's measure in time, under law? Can we tell the difference, an excessive difference, between justice under law (*droit*) and another justice, excessive justice? What difference can we hear between *loi* and *droit*, if they both circulate in time, except through another *in*justice that does not look to any justice, to any measure? "Justice is an experience of the impossible" (Derrida, *FL*, p. 947). It marks the impossible but unmistakable experience of suffering and oppression.

We return to Levinas and the absolute singularity of the other where, however singular the idioms, we must impossibly address ourselves to the other in the language of the other. What necessity? What impossibility? What singularity? The disappropriation of the appropriation of the address, of language, of the universality of language in relation to the singularity of the other? The impossibility of the singular other, the singularity whose impossibility belongs neither to universality nor to humanity, the unthinkability of any singular in relation to other singulars? The absolute singularity of the other specifies an other—perhaps a subject, perhaps human, even God. "Levinas speaks of an infinite right: in what he calls 'Jewish Humanism,' whose basis is not 'the concept of man,' but rather the other; *l'étendue du droit d'autrui [est] un droit pratiquement infini.*"[32] The impossibility of this other, the impossibility of our address to the other, lies in the impossibility of any specification, even as Derrida specifies the other's singularity. Justice demands specification, however universal, demands that we know who has standing before the bar. Injustice makes no such demand, stands wherever it may be demanded, where not demanded, has nothing to do with standing or demanding, nothing to do with the specification of being as individual, singular, refuses any authority, even that of the singular or universal, even that of its own immemoriality. The impossibility of injustice differs in all these ways from the impossibility of justice.

The aporia of injustice echoes that it is nothing, cannot be measured or thought, has no standing, except in time, under law, where injustice undermines every such authority. Injustice defeats itself, repudiates its own authority.

Is justice different from truth, demanding its time, that its time be now? If a moment never arrives when we can say that justice is here, can we say that truth has arrived? *Arrive-t-il?* If the deferral history imposes on truth and justice is always undecidable, do we find this undecidable everywhere as we seek to regulate it? If justice will not wait, will truth wait? Can we say that truth belongs to deferral while the good demands implementation, or does the truth of truth repeat the aporia?

We add another aporia to Derrida's three,[33] taking truth's and justice's madness, monstrosity, seriously. It is not that we do not know how to achieve justice within a regulation that must be deregulated to be just, how to achieve justice immediately when truth defers itself, how we are to decide the undecidable without the possibility of escape from its undecidability. All of these follow Kierkegaard in presenting justice as something beyond intelligibility even as our finiteness prevents us from achieving that intelligibility. The madness that haunts us prevails as justice's monstrosity, its monstrous madness. "Left to itself, the incalculable and giving idea of justice is always very close to the bad, even to the worst for it can always be reappropriated by the most perverse calculation. It's always possible" (Derrida, *FL*, p. 971). Taking one step further: *Justice is unjust*; the greatest acts of goodness promote oppression and suffering. They actually do so, in living history. Injustice comes before justice because acts of justice fail, fail to be just. Critique is inescapable, not in what we cannot and do not know, but in what we cannot help but know: that we and our friends are unjust. Nothing can save us from that injustice, nothing in or out of time. No idols can save us.

VIII

IDOLATRY'S AUTHORITY

Götterdämmerung! *Götzen-Dämmerung*![1] The Twilight of the Gods—do they still march, at dusk? The dusk of the idols—is it already March? Does the owl still fly? Do we have time for Nietzsche? Does he still stride? Will he cease to march? And what of his abominable views of women? What of his germanness, still German, still germane? What of his gait? What could it mean to end philosophy with Nietzsche? To end philosophy after Nietzsche, forgetting Nietzsche? To end Western philosophy without repeating Western philosophy's theme of the end? To forget injustice?

God died yesterday or today. We broke the idols long ago, when God ordered their destruction. We think of God with feet of clay. We search for a hammer to destroy, once and for all, the idols' feet of clay, leaving God in authority. An exercise in futility? What matter that we reflect on authority's disruption, from within, if without a certain humility, overcome by Nietzsche? Perhaps not all humility belongs to Christianity, self-denying, denying its will to power. May we shatter the idols, as the day of Western power ends, with a different humility, a different authority?

To philosophize with a hammer, shattering the feet, the heads of clay. Surely the heads materialize obdurately in stone, their heads of stone—but mine and yours? Are they flesh, full of care? And what of their hearts? Does God care? Can we care without God?

Nietzsche places us between the death of God and the dusk of the idols, the death of Truth and the shadows of Falsehood. Nietzsche echoes in the place of danger in which the hammer strikes but does not

191

destroy. And why not? "For once to pose questions here with a *hammer*, and, perhaps, to hear as a reply that famous hollow sound which speaks of bloated entrails—what a delight for one who has ears even behind his ears, . . . " (Nietzsche, *TI*, p. 465). Before the echo in the ears, echoing of and to their ears, before another repetition of authority, what of the hammer? What blow do we strike as we march to war?

> Perhaps a new war, too? And are new idols sounded out? This little essay is a great declaration of war; and regarding the sounding out of idols, this time they are not just idols of the age, but eternal idols, which are here touched with a hammer as with a tuning fork; there are altogether no older, no more convinced, no more puffed-up idols—and none more hollow. (Nietzsche, *TI*, p. 466)

We go to war again carrying a hammer, to sound the idols, to make them ring their flat hollow tone, their empty thud. These do not echo idols of the age—but eternal, still hollow, none older. Yet do we know of idols older than the age, not to say any age, eternal? What kind of eternity can remain for any gods, even God, in our age, our sophisticated, puffed-up age that thinks that it has disposed of every idol? Have Nietzsche and Heidegger disposed of all the idols, hammered them into oblivion, into dust, and in that achievement completed the revaluation of all values, once and for all? What of their humility? What of ours? What hammer might shatter the hammer's new authority?

How does the revaluation of all values shatter the authority of the gods, or does it again present an angry God who would destroy his competitors? Why does Nietzsche speak of idols, false gods, rather than of the twilight of the greatest gods, the dusk of Dionysus or Apollo?

On 30 September 1888, the first book of the Revaluation of All Values was completed (Nietzsche, *TI*, p. 466). How can we say that God is dead? God is dead! Long live Nietzsche! Long live Heidegger! Long live a united Germany!

> The Germans—once they were called the people of thinkers: do they think at all today? The Germans are now bored with the spirit, the Germans now mistrust the spirit; politics swallows up all serious concern for really spiritual matters. *Deutschland, Deutschland über alles*—I fear that was the end of German philosophy. (Nietzsche, *TI*, p. 506)

Idolatry's Authority 193

Give up all idols, all idols for all values, all values for all humanity, all humanity for all time! Give up, with a hammer! Lie down, before the idols of the age, lay down the hammer! There resound only idols of the age, no eternal idols. God is dead, spirit bores us, leaving room for new idols of the age, this age and no other. In the twilight of the eternal idols, the unending twilight of our giving God up into nihilism, however accomplished, what have we left but new idols, one puny idol after another, marching in succession; marking the succession of time? The idols mark the march of time: Plato, Aristotle, Aquinas, etc. Alexander, Caesar, Charlemagne, Hitler, etc. Slaves, serfs, proles, women, etc. Kant, Hegel, Nietzsche, Heidegger, etc. The Germans etc. Locke, Jefferson, Lincoln, Reagan, etc. The Americans etc. Now the Chinese, Japanese, Africans, Latinos, etc., and the others, etc. All idols. Always idols. All steeped in idolatry. Etc. etc. The idolatry of etcetera.

Do we remember the Terror, the mark of new idolatries, as another idol? Do we remember The Holocaust, the New Terror, as another idolatry? Do we remember one holocaust, one terror, one idolatry, after another, as if history were filled with hammers breaking the feet of one idol after another, building the Pantheon with the shards, ensconcing those cleansed and refreshed old idols in their new places?

Where we take our hammers in hand to break the feet of clay, to draw the curtain of the gods over the sun into twilight, in the hammering text we find the following:

> Man has created woman—out of what? Out of a rib of his god—of his "ideal." (Nietzsche, *TI*, p. 468)

> *Among women*: "Truth? Oh, you don't know truth. Is it not an attempt to assassinate all our *pudeurs*?" (Nietzsche, *TI*, p. 468)

> The perfect woman perpetrates literature as she perpetrates a small sin: as an experiment, in passing, looking around to see if anybody notices it—and to make sure that somebody does. (Nietzsche, *TI*, p. 469)

Man is the god; woman the ideal. Man perpetrates War; women perpetrate a small sin, an experiment. What if the twilight of the gods represented an experiment? Did you notice it? What if you did not? Did you notice the quotation marks? And what if women in their experiment revalued the highest values? "Women are considered profound. Why?

Because one never fathoms their depths. Women aren't even shallow" (Nietzsche, *TI*, p. 470). Without the gods the depths disappear, leaving everything shallow, as it was, with shallow gods, the march of the idols, Man the God. Instead of weeping at tragedy, we laugh.

Nietzsche laughs at tragedy, laughs at the highest values, laughs at the German spirit. "Can an *ass* be tragic? To perish under a burden one can neither bear nor throw off? The ease of the philosopher" (Nietzsche, *TI*, p. 468). Remember the Greeks! And what of that other god, Dionysus? What of his feet of clay? What of the ancient religion Nietzsche calls "tragedy"? Consider the possibility that tragedy represents another idol—call it Greek! The idol of the ideal, the highest, the tragic loss of the highest. Heidegger calls it German. The new idol of German destiny as the call of philosophy.

Take the hammer, laughing, and break Heidegger's feet of clay, Smash Nietzsche's nose! Will they forgive you? Will we forgive you? Smash their ears! Zarathustra asks his heart if he must smash their ears with his hammer. "There they stand, there they laugh. They do not understand me; I am not the mouth for these ears. Must one smash their ears before they learn to listen with their eyes?"[2] Must one smash the idols to bring about the twilight? What if it became too dark to see the idols for the gods?

Praise Zarathustra, for he destroys the idols without becoming another idol. How does he do it? How does he do it surrounded by monstrous idols on every hand? "With heroes and honorable men it would surround itself, the new idol! It likes to bask in the sunshine of good consciences—the cold monster!" "Escape from the bad smell! Escape from the idolatry of the superfluous!" (Nietzsche, *Z*, pp 161–62). Can we escape from the idolatry of the escape, the dream of the hero, the tyranny of the hammer?

> In order effectively, practically to transform what one decries (tympanizes), must one still be heard and understood within it, henceforth subjecting oneself to the law of the inner hammer? In relaying the inner hammer, one risks permitting the noisiest discourse to participate in the most serene, least disturbed, best served economy of philosophical irony. Which is to say, and examples of this metaphysical drumming are not lacking today, that in taking this risk, one risks nothing.[3]

One narrative of the hammer tells that if we destroy the idols' feet of clay, we will live among the gods. The hammer belongs to Thor. And yet,

Götterdämmerung! Another narrative tells that we risk nothing in wielding the hammer, for in drumming we remain within the temple, preserve the economy of drumming, the sovereignty of reason. And yet, Samson! We bring the temple down upon ourselves. And Hobbes! The twilight of the gods without a dawn. May we hear another alternative, philosophizing with a hammer without idolatry toward philosophy's limit, inner or outer?

Perhaps, after Gianni Vattimo,

> precisely the notion of foundation, and of thought both as foundation and means of access to a foundation, is radically interrogated by Nietzsche and Heidegger. Both philosophers find themselves obliged, on the one hand to take up a critical distance from Western thought insofar as it is foundational; on the other hand, however, they find themselves unable to criticize Western thought in the name of another, and truer, foundation. It is this that rightly allows us to consider them to be the philosophers of postmodernity. The "post-" in the term "postmodern" indicates in fact a taking leave of modernity.[4]

God represents the foundation—or do we find the notion of foundation idolatrous, with the true God around the corner of our postmodernity? And what of Nietzsche's and Heidegger's "radical" challenge, not just another challenge, interesting, pleasant, uplifting, but "radical"? Do we mark another idolatry, another god, closer to what Nietzsche describes as an idol of the age—except that this "radical" discourse, rather traditionally, if in a different voice, breaks with its age, perhaps with every age in the language of time? This language of an age, of departing from modernity, seems to speak without immemoriality, forgetting the age of immemorial injustice, especially its own injustice. Does this forgetfulness of injustice represent another idolatry? The memory of archaic justice, whether Being's or The Other's, even Justice's Own, takes leave of God in the name of another idol, in the name of Man.

When God dies, Who remains but Man?

Let us forswear anthropology!

Does the age of injustice drum forth other idols?

Let us take leave from, give up, mark the twilight of every foundation, divine or idyllic. Let us forget that every foundation, however idolatrous, marks the idyll of our forgetfulness with a hammer. As we take leave, do we give up foundations idyllically, idolatrously? If not, why would we do so, except in the name of truth—or in the name of Truth, another idol?

How idolatrous can it be to "radically" destroy every foundation, including the foundations of modernity, without building another foundation? The twilight of the foundations marks what? Not the dawn of another foundation. Perhaps the unending night, or dusk, of no foundation. And why take this as radical except in the appearance of other gods? Why praise radicality? And when, except at dusk?

And these gods, what languages do they speak? Do they speak English, Russian, Greek; Latin, Bantu, Javanese? They speak German, always German, not even French—in this radical challenge. The language of foundations speaks German—after the Greek. The language of radical departure from foundations speaks German—after our destiny. What idolatry marks our new destiny? With what *Götzen* do we mark the sovereignty of our *Geschick*, mark the advent of the radical?

And Ross! (Ross who?) What of Ross? (What Ross?) Does he—do I?—speak German, French, English? (American!) Does he speak Woman, Gay, Lesbian? (Man!) Does he speak Euro, Western, African, Asian, Latino? (American!) Colored, multi? (How many multi?) Pre- or post-? All these idols! Will they never die? Will the end of modernity mark their end?

Modernity represents the movement of thought as radical. If all foundations rest on God, then in the twilight we seek a radicality without foundations as if without God. What then but idols, but idolatry? Let us bring the metaphysical tradition to a close and end philosophy with the beginning of thinking—in the name of what new idols? Whose subjection and what abjection? Have we forgotten our ancient subjection in the abjection of our new idolatry? Let us call it "Anthropological"! *"I teach you the overman.* Man is something that shall be overcome. What have you done to overcome him?" (Nietzsche, *Z*, p. 124). Indeed Anthropological, however radical and highest, especially and highest. In the overcoming of the subject, do we hear the whispers of other subjects, mine and yours, engaged in battle? Yours are Kant and Hegel; Vattimo's are Nietzsche and Heidegger—writing after Foucault and Derrida. Mine are French. My heroes! My idols! Those terrible French, always yearning to be German.

My idols are Whitehead and Dewey. I must be extinguished.

Can we live without heroes unless we ourselves are heroes, others' heroes? Zarathustra comes down from the mountain. He does not come up from the mines or cross the prairie. Christ lived in the desert, and that was very hard. How much harder to live in the city's core! How hard to live without heroes!

We have come round, or down, again to monsters, this time idols: our monstrous idols; our idolatry of monsters. Think what Nietzsche does with monstrosity, how different—yet the same.

> The anthropologists among the criminologists tell us that the typical criminal is ugly: *monstrum in fronte, monstrum in animo*. . . . A foreigner who knew about faces once passed through Athens and told Socrates to his face that he *was* a *monstrum*—that he harbored in himself all the bad vices and appetites. And Socrates merely answered: "You know me, sir!" (Nietzsche, *TI*, p. 475)

As Alcibiades says, in a voice of love, another idolatry. And Heidegger made himself a Nazi. Socrates and Heidegger were monsters, loved as monsters, hated as monsters. If they, our idols, show themselves as monstrous, do we yearn for the same?

What if the twilight of the gods were the *Walpurgisnacht* of other idols? What if *Götterdämmerung* left us with nothing but idolatry? Would that compose the new religion? What represents the difference between true and false gods, God and Heidegger, the economy of difference? Can we still think of Heidegger as a man rather than a Man? Can we think of any member of the Pantheon as a human being, Plato or Aristotle, Heraclitus or Parmenides, Shakespeare or Eliot, Heidegger, Irigaray, or Lispector? What philosophy, what memory, but idolatry?

A bit more from Nietzsche, a bit more unsavory (remembering his monstrous remarks about women):

> In origin, Socrates belonged to the lowest class: Socrates was plebs. We know, we can still see for ourselves, how ugly he was. But ugliness, in itself an object, is among the Greeks almost a refutation. Was Socrates a Greek at all? (Nietzsche, *TI*, p. 474)

> Is the irony of Socrates an expression of revolt? Of plebeian *ressentiment*? . . . Does he *avenge* himself on the noble people whom he fascinates? (Nietzsche, *TI*, p. 476)

Does Nietzsche? And what of this nobility, another monstrous idol? Another stupid idol?

If Germans are stupid,[5] Jews are ugly. Perhaps Socrates was a Jew, all monsters Jews (Lyotard calls them "jews"). In naming them as monsters— Greek monsters—do we mark our own monstrosity? Not I: I am a Jew! What a monstrous thought! Have you no shame?

We cry out that Jews were slaughtered under false gods, under Greek/Christian/German rule. Derrida, a French/Algerian/Jew replies that these are Judeo/Greek/Christian gods. And what of German, French gods? What of "/"? Leave out the English and Americans despite—or because of—the honor of their democratic traditions, another idol. *Toujours la gloire!* What is *your* destiny? All this geophilosophy!

How can the end of modernity be told in one language, the German language, at a particular moment, destiny's moment? How can the end of modernity have a destiny? How can Vattimo tell the end of modernity in Italian in a German voice—not to mention, after the Holocaust? And the Holocaust—has that become another idol?

We will never forget Egypt!

We will never forget Germany!

We will never forgive!

And what of our injustices?

Nietzsche again: "Any distinction between a 'true' and an 'apparent' world . . . is only a suggestion of decadence, a symptom of the *decline of life*" (Nietzsche, *TI*, p. 484). Only the highest! To be Dionysian at the highest, to affirm the terrible, the questionable, the real—but never the ordinary, for that never stands high. Do we make Dionysus the new idol, a dangerous and terrible idol, always masked? At least we know we worship masks! And with what masks? "All that is good is instinct—and hence easy, necessary, free. Laboriousness is an object; the god is typically different from the hero. (In my language: light feet are the first attribute of divinity.)" (Nietzsche, *TI*, p. 494). Others—not you and I—have heavy, ugly feet!

Without Nietzsche and Heidegger—and the others, Adorno and Benjamin, Derrida, Foucault, Irigaray, Trinh Minh-ha, and Levinas, Kant and Hegel, Wittgenstein, Dewey, even Hobbes—we might not have challenged the Enlightenment consensus on Rationality—in a certain way. Possibly in no way. We owe an immense debt, immmeasurable. We owe an immeasurable debt to Heidegger and Nietzsche. But one was a Nazi, the other mad. And Spinoza said monstrous things about women.[6]

Monstrous!

I wish to live in a world without monsters. I wish to live among the gods, lightly, without idolatry—except that they rule as monsters, and never go away.

What can save us from idolatry, I toward Spinoza, Whitehead, and Dewey, you toward Heidegger and Nietzsche, still others toward women, Africans? How do we take up our identities except in idolatrous form, reawakening the Subject?

Identity is idolatry! Our identity is idolatry! Are we ready to take on, take over, that challenge? Nietzsche said it explicitly, yet we find it impossible to hear: "What alone can be our doctrine? That no one gives man his qualities—neither God, nor society, nor his parents and ancestors, nor he himself" (Nietzsche, *TI*, p. 500). Nor he himself, nor any other person, not even Nietzsche and Heidegger, no subject, no identity. What then do we do when we write of the "radical challenge" brought about by Nietzsche and Heidegger marking the end of everything else, everything traditional and foundational, except to affirm that "we postmoderns" in this radical challenge will be made, have been made, have been given our qualities, by these two Germans? Not even others, countless others. Not even remembering our mothers and sisters or our ancestors' slaves. Not even remembering our limits, smashing them with a hammer.

Perhaps we do not confront foundations as much as limits. Perhaps we do not face our foundations and limits as much as our unlimits. Perhaps we find idols everywhere excessively marking our limits. And then we find our unlimits. Let us give them a name: *Dionysus*! The new ancient god is dead, died long ago when that other God was sovereign. His name is Apollo, another monstrosity.

Remember Hecuba, her monstrosity marked by bestiality; remember when K. dies "like a dog." Humanity finds its limits marked by animals, their irrationality and our carnivorousness. We husband animals for our use, domesticate and devour them, subject them, enslave them. Perhaps we could not be human if we did not do these things. Perhaps we define our identities as human by doing these things. Here again, Nietzsche has something to say:

> To call the taming of an animal its "improvement" sounds almost like a joke to our ears. Whoever knows what goes on in menageries doubts that the beasts are "improved" there. They are weakened, they are made less harmful, and through the depressive effect of fear, through pain, through wounds, and through hunger they become sickly beasts. (Nietzsche, *TI*, p. 502)

Does he speak of animals or humans? When we improve our zoos as animal habitats, do we "improve," "tame," or "domesticate" any less? Animals appear frightful, not because they can kill us. Few can. Few do. Animals persevere as frightful because we perceive our monstrosity in their eyes, repeat their idolatry.

And so we farm them, use them, eat them. We respond to their monstrosity by becoming monsters, worse monsters than they could be, justify our monstrosity by their monstrosity, all in the name of Reason.

The monstrosity of Reason. In this respect, like many others, Nietzsche may tell the truth by telling it backward: "The morality of *breeding* and the morality of *taming* are, in the means they use, entirely worthy of each other: we may proclaim it as the supreme principle that, to *make* morality, one must have the unconditional will to its opposite" (Nietzsche, *TI*, p. 505). The breeding and taming belong to monsters on both sides, the monstrosity of animals, the marketing of monsters who must be tamed, and the monstrosity of tamers and their authority. Authority rules monstrously. As our monstrosity, it marks our subjection. This represents the abject truth Nietzsche marks. Animals mark the limits of our divinity by idolatry. "Thou shalt not bow down thyselves to them, nor serve them: for I the LORD thy God *am* a jealous God, . . . " (Exodus 20). In the service of a jealous, monstrous God! How monstrous the golden calf! How monstrous the rage of God at Dionysus, at representing everything we feel! Represent! But do not bow down, repent. Do not accept representation's authority, any authority, even God's monstrous authority. The monstrosity of the highest authority.

Remember the highest where Nietzsche challenges modernity:

> *Critique of modernity.* Our institutions are no good any more: on that there is universal agreement. . . .
> Witness *modern marriage*. All rationality has clearly vanished from modern marriage; . . . The rationality of marriage—that lay in the husband's sole juridical responsibility, which gave marriage a center of gravity, while today it limps on both legs. (Nietzsche, *TI*, pp. 543–44)

Authority again, mated with reason. Reason gives to its marriage with authority its center of gravity—or would reason be helpless without authority? As for authority, what need has it for reason, as Nietzsche says? Marriage requires authority, sole and absolute authority, regardless of reason.

Perhaps our reason limps today because its marriage with authority favors neither. "[W]hen society cannot affirm itself as a whole, down to the most distant generations, then marriage has altogether no meaning. Modern marriage has lost its meaning—consequently one abolishes it" (Nietzsche, *TI*, p. 544). Authority circulating down to the most distant generations, virtually forever. What incredible authority! What god could possess it? Or does our question represent idolatry, the forceful idolatry of authority?

Nietzsche authorizes us to philosophize with a hammer as if we might shatter the ancient idols—replacing them with idols of the age, with Nietzsche himself, or Heidegger, with the greatest authors. The authority of the age. We remember Anaximander marking the immemoriality of authority, the age of its injustice, the ageless authority of justice and authority, of authorization.

The author, then, what of the author?

When Foucault asks about the author, "What matter who's speaking?,"[7] he does not repudiate the author but questions the function of "the author" in relation to a plurality of egos, of subjects.[8] We hope to distinguish the human being who wrote the *Iliad*, who lived and died at a particular time (if any did), from the "author-function" circulating in relation to the unity of discourse, to classes and positions, to authority. We hope to do so both in cases where we know the author and in cases where the author presents a historical problem. We hope, through the author-function, to establish the authority of the text, to read the text within its governing discourse, through an act of authorization. Foucault does not say, but perhaps implies, that the "author-function" idolizes the author.

Perhaps he does not say it because in a certain way, at least here, the idols disappear: "We can easily imagine a culture where discourse would circulate without any need for an author. Discourses, whatever their status, form, or value, and regardless of our manner of handling them, would unfold in a pervasive anonymity" (Foucault, "What Is an Author?" p. 138). Do we imagine a discourse without authority, a reading/writing, a text, a work, without authorization? Or do we imagine an authorization without an author?[9]

We need not imagine a culture where discourse would circulate without an author. We belong to, find ourselves on the verge of, such a culture, the computer/information technology culture, where messages circulate over subsidized networks either unsigned or if signed effectively anonymous; the advertising/marketing culture, where the most influential messages circulate freely, unsigned; in Eastern Europe and Latin America, where a signature risked imprisonment and death but texts and messages circulated nevertheless.

The last two examples represent forms of contemporary authority. Where the author disappears, new authorities arise. More likely, in reverse, the author disappears when other forms of authority circulate that do not require an author for their authorization: the anonymity of democracy; the government of leaks. No one knows this better than Foucault. Why pretend that this "imagined culture" dissociates itself from authority and injustice when it dissociates itself from the author?

The first, computer/information technology, represents our dream of circulation without force, of texts without authors, of an economy of exchange without loss. Let us ignore the subsidization of such networks by corporate and government beneficence, institutions unknown for their self-sacrifice. Let us ignore the cost of the technology within which such an economy functions, ignore the restriction of this freedom of information to an elite. Let us ignore the continued circulation of authority in both the state and its challengers around authors who sign their names from prison. Or rather, let us ignore each of these separately to mark in their conjunction the truth that with the dispersion of the author's name into the anonymity of authority, a new régime of authority emerges, repeatedly marked by Foucault. "In short this power is exercised rather than possessed; it is not the 'privilege,' acquired or preserved, of the dominant class, but the overall effect of its strategic positions—an effect that is manifested and sometimes extended by the position of those who are dominated..." (Foucault, *Discipline and Punish*, pp. 26–27). The dispersion of the author, of the author's authorizing authority, Dispersion of the Subject, represents Another Authority, presents other idols, authorizes a new idolatry.

This authorization and idolatry concern Derrida repeatedly, but especially in "Restitutions,"[10] where the shoes, the owner of the shoes, Van Gogh or an unknown peasant woman, raise questions of attribution. For Heidegger and Meyer Schapiro secretly correspond over "a well-known painting by Van Gogh,"[11] that famous artist; two famous, well-known authors corresponding on a well-known painting by a famous artist; described by another acclaimed philosopher as "a famous picture by Van Gogh" (Derrida, *R*, p. 281). Do we still circulate around questions of authorization, the fetish of the author? For Derrida continues, concerning this great discourse: "Through everything just announced, it can be seen to communicate (without its 'author' 's knowing it?) with the question of fetishism, ..." (Derrida, *R*, p. 267). Fetishism of the shoes, vaginal symbols; fetishism of the author, symbol of the authority of the subject, the sovereign authority of the famous subject. Fetishism of the renowned author: "The hearing having begun thus, he writes to Professor Heidegger (that's what he calls him when speaking of the colleague and correspondent, and simply Heidegger for the famous thinker, author of *The Origin of the Work of Art*): ..." (Derrida, *R*, p. 276). Would there have taken place a correspondence between the two famous thinkers, Heidegger and Schapiro, without celebrated Van Gogh? Would we have a *Truth in Painting*?

The fetish of idolatry. The economy of truth.

And this correspondence: what does it address but the authority with which Heidegger attributes the shoes to a peasant woman, questions of attribution and possession, authorization? Behind it all, we hear Heidegger's authority. "Is it a matter of rendering justice to Heidegger, of restituting what is his due, his truth, the possibility of his own gait and progress?" (Derrida, *R*, p. 301). Schapiro gets it "wrong": "Thus Schapiro is mistaken about the primary function of the pictorial reference. He also gets wrong a Heideggerian argument which should ruin in advance his own restitution of the shoes to Van Gogh: . . . " (Derrida, *R*, p. 312). Right and wrong, as if Derrida's discourse were not a putting to work of truth. As if Schapiro's could not be, even when mistaken. As if Heidegger's discourse were not captive to the same authority. As if the authority were not pathetic.[12] "Why and by what right does Heidegger, talking about the 'famous picture,' authorize himself to say 'peasants' shoes'?" (Derrida, *R*, p. 305). The question of authority as a question of the subject authorizing himself, excluding other subjects' truths. "[I]s it enough for Heidegger to be wrong to make Schapiro right?" (Derrida, *R*, p. 359). As if the question of truth required wrong and right. As if the question of authority required right and wrong.

Perhaps not "I OWE YOU TRUTH IN PAINTING AND I WILL TELL IT TO YOU," but "I OWE YOU AUTHORITY IN TRUTH AND I WILL PAY IT BACK TO YOU" always and everywhere.

Yet, in *Truth in Painting*, Derrida presents the authority of truth with a "limp": "Yes, let us suppose for example two (laced) right shoes or two left shoes. They no longer form a pair, but the whole thing squints (*louche*) or limps, I don't know, in strange, worrying, perhaps threatening and slightly diabolical fashion" (Derrida, *R*, p. 265). Let us suppose that truth owes nothing to a subject. "But what," as well-known Irigaray suggests, "if the 'object' started to speak?"[13] What if the diabolical threat were a snare. "The 'subject' sidles up to the truth, squints at it, obliquely, in an attempt to gain possession of what truth can no longer say" (Irigaray, *SOW*, p. 136). "Whatever proof you claim to have in hand, the signatory of a picture cannot be identified with the nameable owner of an essentially detachable object represented in the picture" (Derrida, *R*, p. 279). Why whatever proof? Why proof in the picture, about the picture, beside the picture? Why a truth demanding proof? What truth, what fascination, has proof? Does it give reason's compensation? "I did not say, like Heidegger, *they are* peasant shoes, but against him: *nothing proves that they are peasant shoes* . . . ; and I did not say, like Schapiro, they are the shoes of a city dweller and even of Van Gogh, but against him: nothing proves or can prove that 'they are the shoes of the artist, . . . '" (Derrida, *R*, p. 364). With what *pointure* do we measure what nothing can prove? Why restore the restitution of truth through proof to an owner? What kind of pay requires proof?

We remember philosophizing with a hammer as if we might bring down the temple of the gods by shattering their feet of clay, at least, like Samson, uprooting the pillars of our civilization—gloriously to die, at least to limp and squint. We remember that even here we hear the famous subject, still the male subject, still seeking possession, subjecting himself to old idols, circulating as another idol.

We return to the interminable project at a certain point of modernity's postmodernity of escaping from the idols: "Under what conditions, then, could one *mark*, for a philosopheme in general, a *limit*, a margin that it could not infinitely reappropriate, *conceive* as its own, in advance engendering and interning the process of its expropriation (Hegel again, always), proceeding to its inversion by itself?" (Derrida, *T*, p. xv). By squinting, limping? By an unveiling of the limits of the mark, the pregnancy of the conception? By surprise, obliquely? (Derrida, *T*, p. xi). Or do they all idolatrously repeat our subjection under the abjection of their authority?

Even in Derrida, we see other possibilities marked by "always Hegel," as if we had to grant that Hegel did what he said he did, brought philosophy to an end, at twilight, where Spirit gave up all other idols and became its own white Western God. Hegel always. Known in advance. The "in advance" circulates Hegel. Why does Derrida accept this advance even as he wishes to acknowledge the impossibility of marking, for philosophy or for the West, a limit that cannot be reappropriated, that does not become another god? Why give up in advance? Why give up before or name the idols in advance, as if they always ruled? What of new idols within our idolatry? Beware the idolatry of the hammer! Beware the idolatry of the printing press as our culture ceases to live in print!

> In terms of the manual printing press, then, there is not one tympan but several. (Derrida, *T*, p. xxvi)

> Will the multiplicity of these tympanums permit themselves to be analyzed? Will be led back, at the exit of the labyrinths, toward some *topos* or commonplace named *tympanum*?
> It may be about this multiplicity that philosophy, being situated, inscribed, and included within it, has never been able to reason. (Derrida, *T*, p. xxvii)

Toward some common place around which we congregate as subjects, philosophers, worshiping ancient idols? And if we refuse, if we can refuse to worship, can we refuse to worship the "never been able"? The limits of reason? "Will it be said, then, that what resists here is the unthought, the suppressed, the repressed of philosophy?" (Derrida, *T*, p. xxviii). Power without resistance, authority without obstruction, justice without injustice—all impossible. And yet, the task, another task, this truth authorizes another task, a work, yet to be inscribed, with another authority. "In order no longer to be taken in, as one so often is today, by the confused equivalence of these three notions, a conceptual elaboration must introduce into them a new play of opposition, of articulation, of difference" (Derrida, *T*, p. xxviii). As if every "new play" that broke old idols with a hammer did not restore us to idolatry.

As "always," Hegel said it in advance:

> In this way the gods are formed by human imagination, and they originate in a finite fashion, being produced by the poet, by the muse. They have this finitude essentially in themselves, because so far as the content is concerned they are finite, and in virtue of their individuality have no connection with each other. They are not discovered by the human mind as they are in their essentially existent rational content, but in so far as they are *gods*.[14]

Hegel speaks of the Greek gods embodied in sensible form. We, after Nietzsche, speak of our gods embodied in historical form, rejecting the idolatry of Spirit, of Reason's God, for another idolatry reminiscent of ancient Greece.

We hope to remember our idolatry.

Gianni Vattimo seems to believe that modernity ends—more precisely, *la fine della modernità* arrives—spoken in German.[15] We remember what Nietzsche says about the Germans,[16] except perhaps for Heidegger and Nietzsche himself, restoring us to the highest. "What the 'higher schools' in Germany really achieve is a brutal training, designed to prepare huge numbers of young men, with as little loss of time as possible, to become usable, abusable, in government service" (Nietzsche, *TI*, p. 510). If Vattimo can speak of the *post-histoire*, the "end of history," only in German, not even Italian, I will speak in American English about the French end of Italian Vattimo, as I take French Derrida to do, always: the end of Heidegger as the beginning of another thought, perhaps in French, or English, certainly not German, and certainly not forgetting that Heidegger and Nietzsche wrote German; the end of a thought that may repeat Heidegger, Kant and Hegel, the Greeks, without acknowledging its false gods. How can we forget that the effort to obliterate the jews was German as we grant that the effort to remember the forgotten was German? And whose remembrance now? "The Heidegger affair is a 'French' affair."[17] What other philosophy can we think except geophilosophy, once German, later French or American?

I hope to geophilosophize German gods.

Vattimo recalls the end of modernity along two German axes: one defined by Nietzsche and Heidegger; the other represented by *Geschick* and *Verwindung*. We may hear the questions Vattimo poses for us concerning the end of history as repetitions of the conjunction, the identities, along and between these two axes, the conjunction of Nietzsche with Heidegger, excluding everything French and English, everything non-Western, reappropriating the non-Western; the conjunction of *Geschick* and *Verwindung*, remembering the endless contaminations of the former, of German destiny, of Our Destiny, Western, German destiny, at the point of Our *Verwindung*, Our Western *Verwindung*, defined by Vattimo as "an overcoming which is in reality a recognition of belonging, a healing of an illness, and an assumption of responsibility" (Vattimo, *EM*, p. 40). *Geschick* meets, joins, repeats *Verwindung*, repeating National Socialism's contaminated destiny, perhaps the greatest *Verwindung* of all. What represents the meaning of *Verwindung*?

Verwindung appears in "Der Satz der Identität," in *Identity and Difference*, in relation to the *Ge-Stell*:

> Denn im Er-eignis spricht die Möglichkeit an, daß es das bloße Walten des Ge-Stells in ein anfänglicheres Ereignen verwindet. Eine solche Verwindung des Ge-Stells aus dem Er-eignis in dieses brächte die ereignishafte, also niemals vom Menschen allein machbare, Zurücknahme der technischen Welt as ihrer Herrschaft zur Dienstschaft innerhalb des Bereiches, durch den der Mensch eigentlicher in das Er-eignis reicht,[18]

translated by Joan Stambaugh into English:

> For in the event of appropriation the possibility arises that it may overcome the mere dominance of the frame to turn it into a more original appropriating. Such a transformation of the frame into the event of appropriation, by virtue of that event, would bring the appropriate recovery—appropriate, hence never to be produced by man alone—of the world of technology from its dominance back to servitude in the realm by which man reaches more truly into the event of appropriation. (Heidegger, *ID*, p. 37)

Verwindet becomes overcoming; *Verwindung* becomes transformation. The word appropriate appears twice in English. Does it echo in German except as *Verwendung*, except as a necessity repeated twice, in *Brauchen* and *Haften*? Stambaugh absorbs, in English, the appropriate into *Er-eignis*'s appropriation. Vattimo absorbs the entire panoply of overcoming, belonging, healing, and responsibility, dispersed throughout in this passage, into *Verwindung*. And what, we ask, of its injustice? What of the injustice of its authority?

We remember what happens to the proper when it passes into French from German, from *Ereignis* to *le propre*, where the distortions of the subject's ownership passes into the subject's proprieties, the meeting place of the appearance of a certain subject and the rules of its recovery. We remember the force of the distortions of both the *Ge-Stell* and its *Verwindung*.

What if our *Verwindung* were an overcoming, an over and beyond, a moving elsewhere, from the *Ge-Stell* to somewhere else, profoundly, intrinsically, distorted, masked?

What if our *Verwindung* were a proper appropriation, an event, in which history's eventfulness appeared "more truly," more authentically, in a repetition without recovery?

What if *Verwindung* were our destiny?

What if destiny belonged to the *Ge-Stell*, toward which we hope for a *Verwindung*?

What if the meeting place, the belonging-together, the *Zussamengehörigkeit* of Nietzsche and Heidegger, of *Geschick* and *Verwindung*, of each pair and of both pairs together, the belonging-together of belonging-together, marked a point of exclusion, another unjust exclusion, however authentic or appropriate, however truthful? Would this be idolatry? Can we hear *Geschick* as a *Verwindung*, after Germany's monstrosity, without contamination? Nietzsche wrote of that contamination before the emergence of the monstrous geophilosophical possibility for us today that:

a. Nietzsche and Heidegger represent Germany's destiny at Buchenwald and Auschwitz, but perhaps not in the same way *our* destiny.
b. Our *Verwindung* belongs to the *Ge-Stell* as completely as it belongs to its (and our) recovery, monstrously distorted.
c. This distortion represents what saves us from another idolatry, which we cannot remember, cannot keep in mind, before the force of the idols.

We retrace the moments in which the new idols appear in the *Verwindung* of modernity: "if Nietzsche's and Heidegger's philosophical intuitions are to appear once and for all irreducible to the kind of *Kulturkritik* that permeates all early twentieth-century philosophy and culture, they may do so only in relation to those things that are revealed by post-modern reflection on the new conditions of existence in the late industrial world" (Vattimo, *EM*, p. 1). Once and for all and forever; irreducible finally to their own century, as if we might once and for all and forever control the future; and "only" in relation to the finally and completely new conditions. All of this seeks to control the future as completely, more completely—a true *Verwindung*—than any view of progress. Vattimo repeatedly restates this *Verwindung*, again and again, we might say, "completely" idolatrously, as: "a first 'flashing up of the *Ereignis*'" (Vattimo, *EM*, pp. 20, 46, 160, 161). In Stambaugh's translation: "In the frame, we glimpse a first, oppressing flash of the appropriation" (*Ein ersten, bedrängendes Aufblitzen des Ereignisses erblicken wir im Ge-Stell*) (Heidegger, ID, pp. 38, 103). What happened to the *bedrängendes*, the oppression, plague? What of the catastrophe? Doesn't destiny present a history of catastrophe as a history without catastrophe?

Vattimo "does not treat post-modernity as the 'end of history' in this catastrophic sense" of the end of humanity" (Vattimo, *EM*, p. 5). Does he treat history as catastrophic in any sense? He reads Benjamin's sense of catastrophe without redemption:

> Walter Benjamin, in his "Theses on the Philosophy of History," discusses the "history of the victors"; only from their point of view does the historical process appear to be a unitary one which can be described as rational and consequential. The vanquished cannot see it in the same light, primarily because their own affairs and struggles have been violently cancelled from the collective memory. (Vattimo, *EM*, p. 9)

Benjamin's words, in English, are:

> The nature of this sadness stands out more clearly if one asks with whom the adherents of historicism actually empathize. The answer is inevitable; with the victor. And all rulers are the heirs of those who conquered before them. Hence, empathy with the victor invariably benefits the rulers. Historical materialists know what that means. Whoever has emerged victorious participates to this day in the triumphal procession in which the present rulers step over those who are lying prostrate.[19]

Sadness. Lying prostrate. Catastrophe. The Messiah comes, redemptively, as another catastrophe, the Antichrist. Nietzsche said it before, in Foucault's striking reading: "Humanity does not gradually progress from combat to combat until it arrives at universal reciprocity, where the rule of law finally replaces warfare; humanity installs each of its violences in a system of rules and thus proceeds from domination to domination."[20] That embodies catastrophe and redemption![21]

What price where *Geschick* meets *Verwindung*? What price indeed! What catastrophe? What accounts for the price of taking leave of a catastrophic history in which the vanquished do not see in a different light, but have been canceled, trampled, do not see at all? What pays off their restitution? What offers their redemption?

"What legitimates post-modernist theories and makes them worthy of discussion is the fact that their claim of a radical 'break' with modernity does not seem unfounded as long as these observations on the post-historical character of contemporary existence are valid" (Vattimo, *EM*, pp. 10–11). Breaking with the end of history, the end of domination, of violence, oppression? What of the radicality of the break, the break in extreme radicality? Can this be free from idolatry for the new? "These all indicate that late modernity is the place where, perhaps, a different possibility of existence for man emerges" (Vattimo, *EM*, p. 11). Perhaps only a new idolatry of the perhaps and only. "An accomplished nihilism is today our only chance . . . " (Vattimo, *EM*, p. 20). Our only chance. The first and only, radical new beginning. Nietzsche and Heidegger, our new idols, "the philosophers of the 'radical' crisis of humanism" (Vattimo, *EM*, p. 39). "If the liquidation of the subject at the level of social existence may be given a meaning that is not merely a destructive one, this may be achieved through the 'critique of the subject' that the radical theories of the crisis of humanism—especially Nietzsche's and Heidegger's—have developed" (Vattimo, *EM*, pp. 45–46). Not merely destructive, but. . . . The radical theories of Nietzsche and Heidegger—and who else? The idolatry in radical onlyness. "The condition of encountering radical cultural alterity represents the basis of the notion of ethnographic hermeneutics, . . . " (Vattimo, *EM*, p. 153).

Vattimo touches on perhaps a truly radical point of alterity in a quotation from Guardieri: "those who have lamented the deaths of cultures have neither known how to see, nor wanted to see, that these same cultures—which are as obsessed as we are with the myth of abundance—have nevertheless produced their own specific way of entering into the Western universe."[22] Multiculturalism, the death of cultures, the end of history, the challenge to the canon, patriarchy and antipatriarchy, *all belong to the West*! How monstrous, shattering our post-historical destiny, played out again on the battlefield of domination and violence! To which Vattimo says, "what we see today is an ensemble of contemporaneous 'swerves' of the primitive, . . . " (Guardieri, "Les Sociétés primitives aujourd'hui," p. 60; Vattimo, *EM*, p. 158). "Cultural anthropology is aware that in our world it must deal with the marginality of the primitive, and of every culture that is other" (Vattimo, *EM*, p. 159). And what of "the primitive," still primitive (in translation), except as itself a residue of "Third-Worldliness," still Western? So long as "the primitive" and marginality remain Western. Another Western privilege, domination and superiority. Always Western authority.

Let us return with catastrophe to where *Geschick* in its catastrophic contamination meets *Verwindung*. "To listen to the call of the *Ge-Stell* as a 'first flashing up of the *Ereignis*' thus means to allow oneself to live radically the crisis of humanism. . . . The leaving behind of humanism and metaphysics is not an overcoming, but rather a *Verwindung*; . . . " (Vattimo, *EM*, p. 46). A radical crisis, a *Verwindung*, but not a catastrophe, where the *Verwindung* and the destiny retell one catastrophe after another.

> This unveiling and disclosing is at once the final moment, the culmination, and the beginning of the crisis of metaphysics and humanism. Such a culminating moment is not the result of an historical necessity nor of a process guided by some sort of objective dialectic; rather, it is *Gabe*, the giving and the gift of Being, whose destiny exists only as a sending-forth, a mission, and an announcement. For these reasons, in essence, the crisis of humanism is not an overcoming but a *Verwindung*, a call for humanity to heal itself of humanism, to yield itself up and resign itself to humanism as something for which humanity is destined. (Vattimo, *EM*, pp. 40–41)

Despite the beauty of this healing, yielding, and resignation, we may shudder before the domination and violence of its culmination and finality, the Westernness of its humanity, especially the propriety of this call to the event of appropriation, as if it might be the only call of destiny. Even in and for our time: our Western destiny.

Verwindung and *Geschick* circle round each other.

> In this epoch thought stands in a position of *Verwindung* in regard to metaphysics. Metaphysics is not abandoned like an

old, worn-out garment, for it still constitutes our "humanity" in *geschicklich* terms; we yield to it, we heal ourselves from it, we are resigned to it as something that is destined to us. (Vattimo, *EM*, p. 52)

Always We; and destined for Us. The utmost refusal of plurality, heterogeneity, fragmentation. We and Us find a new idol, arising in the twilight, resigning us to idols even in the dusk. "[I]t is something to which we must yield, from which we must heal ourselves, and to which we must resign ourselves" (Vattimo, *EM*, pp. 59–60). Always Must, again our Destiny, within our *Verwindung*. The necessity of another God within the death of God: our destiny, to which we must be resigned in our greatest abhorrence.

The event of Being as destiny resists alienation and utopia, two idols of "our" tradition, only to fall under new idols as the destiny of idolatry. In this emergence of new idols as our destiny, we pass from twilight to a new morning. Vattimo is explicit about the mourning:

> This last implication of "the philosophy of morning" and of the *verwindend* "essence" of thought is especially pertinent, though it entails many problems related to the question of the possibility of a "philosophy of history." Like the death of God in *The Gay Science*, the *Verwindung* too is an "event" whose consequences we have just begun to comprehend. (Vattimo, *EM*, p. 180)

And what if the *Verwindung* has already fallen into catastrophe? What of redemption as catastrophe, National Socialism as redemption?

What of the new Messiah? *Deutschland über alles.*

What of the New Science? Reason over God's Truth.

What hammer can we bring to science's authority?

IX

SCIENCE'S SPELL

Aristotle opens his *Metaphysics* with the words, "All men by nature desire to know [*eidenai*]" (*Metaphysics* 980). Let us set aside for the moment the authority of such a claim by nature, where what exists by nature "has *within itself* a principle of motion and of stationariness" or rest (Aristotle, *Physics* 192b), the authority of a nature that rests or moves within itself rather than from without, things whose "attributes . . . belong to them in virtue of what they are" (Aristotle, *Physics* 192b). In Aristotle, after Plato, knowledge, *epistēmē*, belongs from the first to desire (*orexis*), to what exceeds the very form in which it moves from itself. Human beings, men and women, Greeks and strangers, desire to know, may desire to know beyond any natural limits, any limits of science, may impose their knowledge upon themselves and others from the excesses of desire, all by nature.

Aristotle's example of what human beings by nature desire to know comes not from science but from "the delight we take in our senses [which] are loved for themselves; and above all others the sense of sight" (*Metaphysics* 980). Let us set aside the proximity between knowledge and vision (*eidenai* again) as another excessive irruption of desire, postpone our wonder at why the delight we take in vision belongs to *epistēmē* rather than to beauty, why Aristotle repeatedly gives the sense of sight priority. We may yet be struck by the remoteness of this delight, this desire, in sight, from any science, struck by the possibility that the necessity and law of science may fulfill the desire to know no better than any sense, sight or touch.

Human beings desire to know, but do they by nature desire to

213

know by science, by law and necessity? Or does their desire to know belong to that preexistence spoken of in *Posterior Analytics*, knowledge before all knowledge, requisite to knowledge, supporting and undermining the authority of every knowledge, swept over again and again by desire? "All instruction given or received by way of argument proceeds from pre-existent knowledge" (Aristotle, *Posterior Analytics* 71a). By what necessity? "We suppose ourselves to possess unqualified scientific knowledge of a thing . . . when we think that we know the cause on which the fact depends, . . . and, further, that the fact could not be other than it is" (*Posterior Analytics* 71a). This necessity, under cause and law, circulates repeatedly.[1] Scientific knowledge presents itself in laws and causes, in what occurs by necessity, leaving aside for the moment knowledge's necessity.

For Aristotle qualifies the necessity twice, once by the impossibility of proving necessity to one who refuses it: "For just as the geometer has nothing more to say to one who denies the principles of his science—this being a question for a different science or for one common to all—so a man investigating *principles* cannot argue with one who denies their existence" (*Physics* 185a). By those who deny the existence of principles, Aristotle indicates that he has in mind those who claim the oneness of Being, but the impossibility of proving principle or law as such remains. If science investigates conditions and principles, requires laws, then there persists a form of thought about laws and principles, and it cannot remain science.

The second qualification of necessity adds chance and spontaneity, cause and repetition. "[T]here is a third class of events . . . which all say are 'by chance'—it is plain that there is such a thing as chance and spontaneity; . . . " (Aristotle, *Physics* 196a). What comes to pass by necessity and law comes to pass always, or for the most part. But in nature, things also come to pass and move variably. These do not compose the object of science, but Aristotle never claims that they do not compose the object of knowledge. To the contrary, in the passages in *Nicomachean Ethics* on practical wisdom, *phronēsis*, the theme of necessity and invariability reappears as knowledge, together with *phronēsis* and intuition.[2]

Four forms of reason, wisdom, or knowledge pertain to things variable and invariable, with different spheres of relevance, without ranking, without hierarchy, each free from deception, free from error. The necessity of science, of *epistēmē*, belongs to things, to nature, by means of principles and laws, even here not quite always, universally, but for the most part. Science gives us knowledge through demonstration of that which is necessary and either invariable or for the most part. But nature is filled with spontaneity and chance, and those things that are variable require a different knowledge, *phronēsis*, while philosophic wisdom pertains both to virtue and to Being. Moreover, scientific knowledge would be impossible without intuition or induction. How, we wonder, can a knowledge of variable things not itself be variable?

Aristotle speaks of these many forms of knowledge as he speaks of many causes and many substances—four throughout. In the case of substance, though there are "several senses in which a thing may be said to 'be'" (Aristotle, *Metaphysics* 1028a), one is primary in all ways, "first in every sense" (*Metaphysics* 1028a). In the case of causes, though they closely resemble the senses of being, none is primary. In the case of knowledge, none of the four forms seems to be primary, though Aristotle does not refuse the question of authority among them. "But again it is not *supreme* over philosophic wisdom, i.e. over the superior part of us, any more than the art of medicine is over health; . . . . Further, to maintain its supremacy would be like saying that the art of politics rules the gods because it issues orders about all the affairs of the state" (Aristotle, *Nicomachean Ethics*, 1145a). The argument suggests that supremacy does not pertain to the arts and virtues but to us. Moreover, Aristotle returns in the next section from the necessity and completeness of philosophic wisdom to the most part.[3] He speaks of the most authoritative but arrives at a knowledge that seems to possess no authority except that of the greater number.

What of science's authority? In the passages we have considered so far, authority rules in the name of authoritativeness, as if we rank opinions according to their authorities rather than their truths, and in the name of necessity, pertaining to nature rather than to science, though three of the four forms of knowledge do not represent science and do not give us necessity. (Intuitive knowledge may mark an exception.). It cannot be said that Aristotle disdains questions of authority, since he speaks of supremacy and authoritativeness, but it appears peripheral in these passages. In an important passage in *Metaphysics,* however, authority emerges in full force. "[F]or the wise man must not be ordered but most order, and he must not obey another, but the less wise must obey [*peithesthai*] him" (*Metaphysics* 982a). He continues: "Such and so many are the notions, then, which we have about Wisdom and the wise." Shall we read this as Aristotle's agreement with the many or as representing the popular view of wisdom? Shall we read *peithesthai* as obedience or persuasion? Aristotle discusses each of the above characteristics of knowledge again,[4] concluding, "And the science which knows to what end each thing must be done is the most authoritative (*kuriōs*) of the sciences, and more authoritative than any ancillary science; and this end is the good of that thing, and in general the supreme good in the whole of nature" (*Metaphysics* 982a). He tells us explicitly that authority belongs to science, commanding obedience. Even so, nature acts variably, by chance and spontaneity, and for the most part; moreover, no science of sciences may circulate in general, no science of the whole of nature. He claims that such a science does exist, of being *qua* being, but never replies to Plato's critique of such a science. A science of sciences knows nothing, has no object.[5] We question why science—or any knowledge—possesses authority, why it must possess authority, whether knowledge and truth can be imagined without authority.

This question returns us to Plato, to a reading of *Phaedrus* in relation to epistemic authority. As in so many dialogues, in *Charmides*, *Meno*, and *Euthyphro*, in *Phaedrus* Plato concerns himself with excessive authority, interpretable in part as authority without knowledge and truth, but where even knowledge's authority rules excessively, appearing in *Republic* where the state dissolves. For in *Republic* the philosopher-king both represents shadows on the wall of the Cave and, as in the myth of metals, creates them, both returns to the Cave bearing the mysterious light of the Good and can foster and preserve the state only by knowing the proper cycles of human breeding, regulating the future, however vainly.[6] We may read this relation to the future as Plato's acknowledgment of temporal corruption or as acknowledging the importance of an empirical knowledge that does not belong to the Good, that cannot be derived from the Sun, that remains within the Cave, that cannot be allowed to pass away as we acknowledge that it remains unknown, obscure expression of the intermediate forms of enigmatic and unknown futures, of the children of our children—all in the voice of propriety.

This relation between knowledge and its children's children, toward the future, echoes throughout *Phaedrus*. Yet before we undertake to read the dialogue in detail, we may briefly note the form in which science's authority appeared at the birth of the Enlightenment.

Modernity appeared, in Descartes and after, in relation to authority, especially epistemic authority, divided around the claim to authority. "There remains but one course for the recovery of a sound and healthy condition—namely, that the entire work of the understanding be commenced afresh, and the mind itself be from the very outset not left to take its own course, but guided at every step; and the business be done as if by machinery."[7] The repudiation of all prior authority as doubtful and uncertain, diseased, joins with the establishment of a new mechanical foundation for epistemic authority, in the eye of reason itself. Locke's

Essay begins with the repudiation of all self-authorization in the famous if excessive image of a void, a figure that denies any possibility of its own authority: "Let us then suppose the mind to be, as we say, white paper, void of all characters, without any ideas:—How comes it to be furnished?"[8] How indeed, except as it does, providing whatever ideas by means of which we think, as if without founding authority? Hume's skepticism, too, presents itself in relation to authority, together with dogmatism subverting any claim to authority:

> Reason first appears in possession of the throne, prescribing laws, and imposing maxims, with an absolute say and authority. Her enemy, therefore, is oblig'd to take shelter under her protection, and by making use of rational arguments to prove the fallaciousness and imbecility of reason, produces, in a manner, a patent under her hand and seal. This patent has at first an authority proportion'd to the present and immediate authority of reason, from which it is deriv'd. But as it is supposed to be contradictory to reason, it gradually diminishes the force of that governing power, and its own at the same time; till at last they both vanish away into nothing by a regular and just diminution.[9]

This arresting image of reason's disruption, from within, of the authority it claims to possess, also from within, of any possible authority, represents one side of classical empiricism, the undermining of any authority before experience, where experience can at best be for the most part, cannot give us necessity, therefore cannot achieve Aristotle's sense of science, coupled with general prescriptive rules of causation, just sixteen pages earlier, that take on remarkable authority: "Since therefore 'tis possible for all objects to become causes or effects to each other, it may be proper to fix some general rules by which we may know when they really are so" (Hume, *Treatise*, p. 173). If they really are so, do they carry reality's authority, especially if we remember that their authority belongs to custom and habit, constant conjunction, always for the most part and never always? The rules move from generally to always, slipping from the limits of reason in causal inference to universal general authority: "There must be a constant union betwixt the cause and effect.... The same cause always produces the same effect, and the same effect never arises but from the same cause" (Hume, *Treatise*, p. 173). Hume slips from a skepticism toward constancy and uniformity that seems designed to disperse epistemic authority to a reliance on the Same unmatched in philosophy, establishing supreme authority. "It is experience only which gives authority to human testimony, and it is the same experience which assures us of the laws of nature."[10]

Modern science arose in this Janus-like posture in relation to authority, where the authority of the church was repudiated so that science might assert its own authority, but where the form of the repudiation repudiated science's claims to authority. The one exception may be Locke, whose epistemology comes close to a truth without authority, where we may know what we know from experience, however implausibly an experience without memory, without history, therefore without prior authority. If we cannot pursue Locke's line very far, it is because we recognize the hold of authority on us, that we are always subjected to authority, so that no image of a void, free from that hold, can represent our epistemic condition. Hume comes closer to our expectations, where reason always claims authority, science's authority, even as what we know of science's insatiable demand for evidence must undermine every authority, especially its own. Modern science grants the aporia that its own inordinate authority rests upon repudiation of every authority.

How shall we respond to this aporia? However strangely, we return to *Phaedrus*, reading it as a work on science's authority.

Socrates meets Phaedrus at the edge of the city. Phaedrus has just left Lysias, son of Cephalus, reminding us of *Republic* suggesting its kinship with *Phaedrus* around the themes of knowledge, virtue, desire, and the state. Yet where *Republic* takes place in a group of at least seven, concerning public virtue, public twice, *Phaedrus* presents a dialogue with only two characters, outside the city walls, suggesting intimacy and privacy. Socrates and Phaedrus repeatedly speak of each other as "my love" (or "friend," *philia*), with intimate forms of address.

Neglecting the distinction between *erōs* and *philia*, Nancy speaks of love at the edge of the community in a way deeply indebted to *Phaedrus*: "For the community, lovers are on its limit, they are outside and inside, and at this limit they have no meaning without the community and without the communication of writing: this is where they assume their senseless meaning. Reciprocally, it is the community that presents to them, in their very love, their singularities, their births, and their deaths."[11] This strange, senseless reciprocity of intimacy and community, marked by writing, represents our relation to Plato and his writing.

Cephalus (*Kephalon*) refers to the head; the name *Phaedrus* expresses radiance, beauty, light; *Lysias* (*lysis*) suggests advantage. The question always returns to Socrates, what *Sōkrates* means. Here, in the dialogue *Phaedrus*, that question touches us with especial force, matched perhaps only by *Symposium*, in Socrates's speech representing Diotima teaching him the philosophy of love (Plato, *Symposium* 201d), repeating that he knows nothing and never from himself, in Alcibiades' speech describing him as "satyr" and "silenus" (*Symposium* 215bd), and at the close, where

> all the others had either gone home or fallen asleep, except Agathon and Aristophanes and Socrates, who were still awake and drinking out of an enormous bowl which they kept passing round from left to right. . . . Socrates was forcing them to admit that the same man might be capable of writing both comedy and tragedy—that the tragic poet might be a comedian as well. (*Symposium* 223d)

Socrates remains impervious to alcohol, remains philosophical under all circumstances; *Symposium* moves from love's advantage to its divinity to Socrates' divinity to poetry, where Socrates and poetry appear both as supreme objects of love and its supreme activities, at a point where disciplinary boundaries between tragedy and comedy break down, possibly where the quarrel of old between poetry and philosophy disappears (Plato, *Republic* 607b). But *Symposium* and *Republic* tell other stories.

Phaedrus, "off for a walk outside the wall" (Plato, *Phaedrus* 227a), has just left Lysias, who, in Socrates' words, "was giving the company a feast of eloquence" (*Phaedrus* 227b). At the prospect of hearing Lysias's speech, Socrates describes his desire as "above all business" (*Phaedrus* 227c). The speech, then, which concerns love (*erōs*) (*Phaedrus* 227c), appears framed for us by Socrates' and Phaedrus's love of discourse, a theme repeated throughout the dialogue, emphasizing their eagerness to hear, to participate in, to partake of speaking and writing, of knowledge, philosophy. "However, I'm so eager to hear about it that I vow I won't leave you even if you extend your walk as far as Megara, up to the walls and back again as recommended by Heraclitus" (*Phaedrus* 227d).

To this point—less than one page of the opening of the dialogue—we have been presented with the themes of love (*erōs* and *philia*) and desire, writing and speaking—philosophy—and the walls of the city, the limits of politics and law, of human society. At this point, several other themes unfold, repeated throughout the dialogue. Phaedrus asks, "Do you expect an amateur like me to repeat by heart, without disgracing its author, the work of the ablest writer of our day, which it took him weeks to compose at his leisure?" (*Phaedrus* 228a). Phaedrus is an "amateur" (*idiōtēs*),[12] an idea repeated throughout the dialogues, for Socrates repeatedly denies that he represents a professional at truth, claims himself a private person. Despite so much of the tradition's reading of the dialogues, including Nietzsche, as developing the idea of philosophy as a propositional, public discourse, a *technē*, Socrates never claims to possess it even when he seems to be defending it. When Phaedrus asks him whether he has heard anything better than Lysias's speech, he denies that a better speech originates within himself. "I am of course well aware it can't be anything originating in my own mind, for I know my own ignorance, so I suppose it can only be that it has been poured into me, through my ears, as into a vessel, from some external source, though in my stupid fashion I have actually forgotten how, and from whom I heard it" (*Phaedrus* 235d). Always ignorant, Socrates represents the consummate amateur at knowledge, suggesting that the professional at truth—Sophist or scientist—betrays the honor of truth. Socrates' most important truths always come from others: Sappho, Diotima, poets of old. This remarkable figure of memory and displacement belongs to storytelling, always told after having been heard from others, always an unacknowledged departure. Writing preserves that figure's truth but seems to evoke a counterfigure: I can show you how my truth differs from that other, provided it is present in writing. This figure inaugurates the themes of memory and repetition.

And so, Phaedrus and Socrates, the private lovers of truth, contrast with Lysias the public speechwriter. Phaedrus's amateurishness compels him to memorize Lysias's speech, as if he could not make so fine a speech himself, as if Lysias's authority as a public writer resides in Phaedrus's memory, in his ability to repeat that speech exactly, as if knowledge, truth, memory, history, might represent exact repetitions, might circulate as perfect public imitations, of an original, rather than a living memory of a truth whose currency lies in its mobile vitality. We remember, if for a moment, book 10 of *Republic* again, framed as a critique of *mimēsis*: "The creator of the phantom, the imitator, we say, knows nothing of the reality but only the appearance. Is that not so?" (Plato, *Republic* 601c). We also remember Socrates, who always imitates and thereby knows the reality.

What, we may ask, marks memory if not repetition? What marks knowledge if not repetition of our teachers? What marks science if not public circulation? Could this represent the question at the heart of *Phaedrus* and *Republic*, if they had a heart?

Socrates replies that Phaedrus (a) listened like a true "lover of discourses" to the speech again and again; (b) obtained a copy of the speech and pored over it the whole morning (Plato, *Phaedrus* 228bc); (c) has the speech under his cloak (*Phaedrus* 228e). A true lover of discourse appears as a deceiver, for love pretends, in its excessiveness, to be more attractive than it may be, takes on, in its excesses, more than it can control, gives itself over to passion. Desire and love appear in the form of excess. The striking form of this excess here appears as a consuming passion for discourse, for truth. Socrates' love for Phaedrus and his love for discourse belong together, inseparably, joined with the power of one person over another, teacher or storyteller. "A hungry animal can be driven by dangling a carrot or a bit of green stuff in front of it, similarly if you proffer me volumes of speeches I don't doubt you can cart me all round Attica, and anywhere else you please" (*Phaedrus* 230e). Need we remember that Socrates would not leave Athens for exile, that his truth required him to stay, even to his death? Can we read any Platonic dialogue without remembering Athens's injustice to Socrates? Knowledge, country, power, and desire circulate around each other so tightly here that we cannot begin to disentangle them.

Where shall we place ourselves to pursue philosophy's truth? Outside the walls of the city, away from the crowds, the clamor of business and utility, under a tree. "There's some shade, and a little breeze, and grass to sit down on, or lie down if we like" (*Phaedrus* 229b). Let us lie down together, you and I, far from the crowds, "a delightful resting place, with this tall, spreading plane, and a lovely shade from the high branches of the *agnos*. . . . In fact, my dear Phaedrus, you have been the stranger's perfect guide" (*Phaedrus* 230bc). A stranger to whom or what, we ask? Not to Phaedrus, certainly, for they are in an intimate spot together, intimately joined in a moment of *erōs* and *philia*. Perhaps, as Phaedrus says, a stranger to nature: "Anyone would take you, as you say, for a stranger being shown the country by a guide instead of a native—never leaving town to cross the frontier nor even, I believe, so much as setting foot outside the walls" (*Phaedrus* 230d). What kind of strangeness, we ask? Socrates' reply, that he is "a lover of learning, and trees and open country won't teach me anything, whereas men in the town do" (*Phaedrus* 230e), leads to the dialogue's second reference to Pharmakeia.[13] We passed over the first, near the beginning, where Phaedrus asks whether he and Socrates are close to where Boreas seized Orithyia (Ōreithyian) from the river Ilissus, and whether Socrates believes the story. Socrates replies,

> I should be quite in the fashion if I disbelieved it, as the men of science [*sophoi*] do. I might proceed to give a scientific account of how the maiden, while at play with Pharmacia [*Pharmakeia*], was blown by a gust of Boreas down from the

rocks hard by, and having thus met her death was said to have been seized by Boreas, though it may have happened on the Areopagus, according to another version of the occurrence. (*Phaedrus* 229cd)

We find the story of Orithyia and its scientific understanding linked or joined by Pharmacia. What Socrates says here about knowledge may strike us as remarkable given a traditional reading of how Plato resolves the quarrel between poetry and philosophy:

> For my part, Phaedrus, I regard such theories as no doubt attractive, but as the invention of clever, industrious people who are not exactly to be envied, for the simple reason that they must then go on and tell us the real truth about the appearance of centaurs and the Chimera, not to mention a whole host of such creatures, Gorgons and Pegasuses and countless other remarkable monsters of legend flocking in on them. If our skeptic, with his somewhat crude science, means to reduce every one of them to the standard of probability, he'll need a deal of time for it. I myself have certainly no time for the business. (*Phaedrus* 229de)

Socrates associates *sophia* here with cleverness and industry, measure and probability. He has no time for the business: "and I'll tell you why, my friend. I can't as yet 'know myself'; as the inscription at Delphi enjoins, and so long as that ignorance remains it seems to me ridiculous to inquire into extraneous matters" (*Phaedrus* 230). This represents a famous Socratic rule, that one's first business is to know oneself (*gnōnai hemautōn*). It returns us, enigmatically, to our opening question, who is Socrates?, given that we are told who Cephalus, Lysias, and Phaedrus are by their names, but seem to spend forever seeking Socrates—and ourselves.

Let us assume either that we will find Socrates later, in *Phaedrus* or in *Symposium,* throughout the dialogues, or that we will never find him, but that the search for him, for his and our self-knowledge, frames the dialogues. The undertaking, for the present and perhaps beyond, occupies our field of vision. Socrates' story of Pharmacia must strike us as strange in its double juxtapositions, of Orithyia with Pharmacia and of mythology with science and philosophy.

Socrates says of science (*epistēmē*) that it is clever and industrious, gives probability, where magic falls before us. And we have here no minor magic, no potion or medicine, but the divinity of nature, in all her glory, the beginning of the world. For the story of Orithyia appears doubled in Greek, once the story of the king of Athens, Erechtheus, who defeated Eleusis, calling up the Eleusinian mysteries, whose daughter Orithyia was carried off and raped by the north wind, Boreas, who then marries her and keeps her by his side;[14] the second the story of Eurynome, the goddess of creation, whose union with Boreas brings order out of chaos (Graves, *Greek Myths*, p. 27). The story of Orithyia and Boreas represents *poiēsis*, bringing forth from nonbeing, order from disorder, in the play of magic as menace and mystery, in the play of Pharmakeia, where the *pharmakon* brings together all at once, in its strangeness, a variety of answers to our question of strangeness: *pharmakon* as medicine, drug, madness, remedy, poison, potion, agent, dye, pigment, color; *pharmakos* as sacrifice, scapegoat;[15] *pharmakeus* as wizard. Desire circulates as poison and cure, madness and remedy, menace and magic, in the colors of the rainbow.[16]

Phaedrus traditionally concerns desire and writing. Yet in the juxtaposition of *pharmakeia* and *sophia*, the latter falls on the side of probability and measure where *pharmakeia* evokes the gods of chaos and primeval disorder from which order sprang. Where shall we place Socrates' self-knowledge? With science or Boreas? With philosophy or magic?[17]

Socrates and Phaedrus arrive, upon the termination of this speech, at their delightful resting place, with a lovely shade and stream, a beautiful, intimate spot where two lovers of discourse may carry on their private activities. Shall we ask if they are lovers? Shall we take them to be engaged in love, as they say they are? "Anyhow, now that we've got here I propose for the time being to lie down, and you can choose whatever posture you think most convenient for reading, and proceed" (Plato, *Phaedrus* 230d). An intimate spot for erotic play with Pharmakeia: "Yet you seem to discovered a recipe [*pharmakon*] for getting me out" (*Phaedrus* 230d). They proceed with Lysias's speech. We begin: "You know how I am situated, and I have told you that I think it to our advantage that this should happen" (*Phaedrus* 230e). A pretty dull beginning for a speech on love, especially for two lovers of knowledge (*philomathēs*) (*Phaedrus* 230d); perhaps appropriate for a speech on advantage, on business, on the business of love, making a business of love. For Lysias makes love his business.

Choose the nonlover for your lover and reap the advantages of good business; reap the benefits of good economic judgment, gain good measure. "Lovers [*herastēs*], when their craving is at an end, repent of such benefits as they have conferred [*poiēsōsis*], ... " (*Phaedrus* 231ab). "Again, lovers weigh up profit and loss accruing to their account by reason of their passion, ... " (231b).[18] All benefits, advantages, profits, losses, accounts, measures, proprieties; all love measured by accounting principles, goodness, justice, as benefit, advantage, *technē*. How can such a love be a god (*Phaedrus* 242e)?

Lysias's speech, as his name indicates, presents love without desire, *erōs* without passion, repenting *poiēsis*, entirely under benefit, advantage, or utility. Socrates' reply, to Phaedrus's question concerning its excellence (*Phaedrus* 234d), repeatedly emphasizes what it lacks, delight, ecstasy, and worship: Bacchus. "I was thrilled by it. And it was you, Phaedrus, that made me feel as I did. I watched your apparent delight in the words as you read. And as I'm sure that you understand such matters better than I do, I took my one cue from you, and therefore joined in the ecstasy [*sunebakkheusa*] of my right worshipful companion" (*Phaedrus* 234d). Phaedrus takes these remarks as a joke, especially the suggestion that he understands such matters better than Socrates. But Socrates' words can be taken as serious, not only on love, the subject of Lysias's speech, but on writing and truth: they belong so profoundly to desire, to passion and ecstasy, that we can understand the words pertaining to them only in relation to ourselves and others, intimately. Lysias's speech fails because it lacks *erōs*, passion, not just in emphasizing benefits and goods, utility, but in its public anonymity, totally without the intimate, personal relation Socrates bears to Phaedrus, the relation he calls *sunebakkheusa*, Bacchic frenzy, divine madness.

If we read Lysias's speech as utilitarian, then in *Phaedrus* Plato presents a blistering critique of a utilitarian *erōs*, thereby a powerful critique of a utilitarian ethics, though a rights-based ethics fares little better, since it falls under rule and measure, if not under advantage, still without madness. Lysias's final words above, in the voice of the nonlover, express the claim we may take *Phaedrus* to lay to rest, that "the proper course, surely, is to show favor not to the most importunate but to those most able to make us a return" (*Phaedrus* 233e). This proper return, benefit or advantage, belongs to *technē*, lacking madness, without *pharmakeia*, *mania*, or *poiēsis*.

How then does Phaedrus understand the excellence of this speech? "The outstanding feature of the discourse is just this, that it has not overlooked any important aspect of the subject, so making it impossible for anyone else to outdo what he has said with a fuller or more satisfactory oration" (*Phaedrus* 235b).

Erōs appears in Lysias's speech as *technē*, lacking passion, madness, and magic, contained rather than divine, exhaustive rather than inexhaustible. This exhaustion appears in two different ways, one again within *technē*, presenting to us and Socrates the challenge to show what Lysias has overlooked, leading to Socrates' first speech. The second way relates inexhaustibility to *pharmakeia* and *mania*, to unlimit. For how, we may ask, can Eros be divine if always limited by rule? We may compare Pausanias's speech in *Symposium* based on the distinction between good and bad, beneficial and disadvantageous, high and low forms of love.[19] "Now it is the object of the Athenian law to make a firm distinction between the lover who should be encouraged and the lover who should be shunned" (Plato, *Symposium* 184). As Foucault puts it: *"The insistence of the rule. Power is essentially what dictates its law to sex. Which means first of all that sex is placed by power in a binary system: licit and illicit, permitted and forbidden"* (Foucault, *History of Sexuality*, p. 83). Diotima replies that Love represents

> A very powerful spirit, Socrates, and spirits, you know, are halfway between god and man.
>
> . . . .
>
> They are the envoys and interpreters that ply between heaven and earth, flying upward without worship and our prayers, and descending with the heavenly answer and commandments. (Plato, *Symposium* 202e)

Nothing heavenly, nothing spiritual, inhabits Lysias's view of love.

Here the theme of inexhaustibility relates on one side to exhaustion, to *technē*'s perfectibility, where the idea of epistemic authority encourages recurrent claims that by the end of this or that century, science will know everything important about the physical universe, human nature, art, a theme of death, the end of metaphysics, modernity, or scientific progress. This idea of death belongs to *technē*, to perfectibility, where the measure of science's truth rests in the thought of its completion, where the measure of art's achievement suggests its culmination. Advantage, utility, benefit, under measure, suggest measurable fulfillment, so that we may account for all the items in circulation, calculate full satisfaction. *Erōs*, desire, magic, and the divine have no such measures, permit no such achievements. The industriousness of scientists, evoked above, speaks to the same sense of closure, of perfectibility under rule, as Lysias's utilitarian advantage. The idea of human rights, also under rule, fares little better.

Love's excessiveness irrupts here in relation to exhaustion and perfectibility, as form, as if fulfillment of love and truth might be possible, thinkable or unthinkable. The perfectibility of *erōs* may be distinguished from its representativity; yet throughout *Phaedrus* the representation of writing and discourse, of representation, circulates intimately with magic and madness, as if knowledge and truth with their representations—*mimēsis*, storytelling, narration; dialogue and philosophy—all share *mania* and *pharmakeia*.

We return to the remarkable figure of repetition and memory that emerges in Socrates' response to Phaedrus's characterization of Lysias's speech as exhaustive, not that Socrates can come up with something new and different, but that he remembers something better, though he cannot quite say where or what (Plato, *Phaedrus* 235d). This story does not fool Phaedrus, who mocks the idea that Socrates' ideas come from elsewhere. He leaves untouched, however, the circulation of repetition and memory in relation to perfectibility. Scientists and Lysias repeat without passion, without divine inspiration, represent benefits, categories, distinctions, classifications. Love, truth, knowledge represent a different repetition, an enigmatic, mysterious, impassioned memory, closer to *pharmakeia* and *mania* than *lysis*.

Madness appears briefly in Lysias's speech as an affliction (*nosos* rather than *mania*): "Why, the man himself admits that he is not sound, but sick [*nosos*], that he is aware of his folly, but cannot control himself" (*Phaedrus* 231d). It appears again (as *nosos*) in preface to Socrates' first speech, mimicking Lysias, in Phaedrus's words: "I will allow you to take for granted that the lover is less sane [*nosein*] than the nonlover, ... " (*Phaedrus* 236b). Why, we ask, does Phaedrus permit Socrates this one assumption, rather than love's fickleness, for example? Perhaps because love deeply belongs to madness, mimicking malady, illness, while we know of constant, faithful lovers. Perhaps we mark here a foreshadowing of Socrates' second speech, where love's madness belongs to it profoundly. But not yet.

Socrates' first, mimetic, speech is preceded by several important figures, most of which we have seen before. For he pretends to hesitate before challenging Phaedrus's "darling Lysias." Phaedrus responds, "We are by ourselves in a lonely place, and I am stronger and younger than you, for all which reasons 'mistake not thou my bidding' and please don't make me use force to open your lips" (*Phaedrus* 236d). Phaedrus's desire is irresistible, overwhelming, to the point of force. Socrates replies with a figure repeating the theme of the amateur (*idiōtēs*), displacing it from Phaedrus to himself, repeating in a slightly modified voice the arguments he used before to persuade Phaedrus to tell him Lysias's speech. "But, my dear good Phaedrus, it will be courting ridicule for an amateur [*idiōtēs*] like me to improve on the same theme as an accomplished writer" (*Phae-*

drus 236d). In both cases, the amateur—Phaedrus or Socrates—is favorably compared with the professional, the scientist, speechmaker, or Sophist. In both cases, the desire for discourse, for truth, is unsurpassable. "[H]ow could I possibly do without such entertainment?" (*Phaedrus* 236e).

Socrates precedes his remarks responding to Phaedrus's disclaimer that he did not know the speech by heart by saying: "I know my Phaedrus. Yes indeed, I'm as sure of him as of my own identity [*hemautoū*]" (*Phaedrus* 228b). We have read the question of Socrates' identity as central to the dialogue. It returns here in force: "Beware. Do not deliberately compel me to utter the words, 'Don't I know my Socrates? If not, I've forgotten my own identity [*hemautoū*],' . . . " (*Phaedrus* 236c). Socrates' and Phaedrus's identities share an insatiable, unsurpassable desire for discourse, for philosophy and truth. The inscription at Delphi to know thyself joins discourse and truth with prophecy in relation to inexhaustible desire and inexhaustible force. We come to know something of who and what Socrates is here, as we do from Alcibiades' speech in *Symposium*—first, that he is infinitely moved by desire, by love of discourse, knowledge, and truth; second, that this movement, this inspiration, underlies the power of his influence, the force of his persuasiveness; third, that this movement from within, love of wisdom, works together with Phaedrus's like desire in an intimately erotic, private relation.

Socrates begins his imitation (but not emulation) of Lysias's speech with two striking differences: a paean to the Muses, and the assumption that the nonlover is a lover pretending to be a nonlover: "Come, then, ye clear-voiced Muses, whether it be from the nature of your song, or from the musical people of Liguria that ye came to be so styled, 'assist the tale I tell' under compulsion by my good friend here, . . . " (*Phaedrus* 237). The Muses' song reminds us of another moment we passed over without remark, that in the place where Phaedrus and Socrates lie, in private, away from the city, the cicadas sing (*Phaedrus* 230c). They sing again, at a striking point of the dialogue (*Phaedrus* 259ad), to which we will return.

Socrates begins his first speech:

> Well then, once upon a time there was a very handsome boy, or rather young man, who had a host of lovers, and once of them was wily, and had persuaded the boy that he was not in love with him, though really he was, quite as much as the others. And on one occasion, in pressing his suit he actually sought to convince him that he ought to favor a nonlover rather than a lover. (*Phaedrus* 237b)

For Lysias's speech betrays itself in two striking ways: once in its form, despite Phaedrus's praise of its completeness, for it has no life, no inner vitality, presents a disorderly list of advantages and benefits, betraying its own assumption of order; the second its lifelessness without desire. How can we understand the nonlover to pursue the boy without desire and desire's deceit? We must assume, if we are to consider such a speech, that it possesses at least two divinities within it, moving it, one the inspiration of its desire, moved by love, the other the inspiration of its Muses, moved by creative spirit. Lysias's speech lacks both these elements.

Who is this boy, this beloved, around which the narrative spins? In *Meno*, a boy appears. Shall we doubt his presence here? Let us wait. "[I]f anyone means to deliberate successfully about anything, there is one thing we must do at the outset. He must know what it is he is deliberating about; . . . " (*Phaedrus* 237c). Socrates interrupts himself to praise the eloquence of his speech in striking words: "Well, Phaedrus my friend, do you think, as I do, that I am divinely inspired?" "For truly there seems to be a divine presence in this spot, so that you must not be surprised if, as my speech proceeds, I become as one possessed; . . . " (*Phaedrus* 238cd). Divine possession belongs to discourse and truth. Perhaps, despite Socrates' claims, we may find it lacking in this instance.

Present are two closely related themes of identity: Socrates' identity, related to the Delphic inscription; and Eros's identity, the immediate topic of concern. We remember from Alcibiades that we should regard Socrates as the supreme object of our desire, however ugly he may be, in his *aretē* and his ignorance. He concludes: "[The boy] should have known that the wrong choice must mean surrendering himself to a faithless, peevish, jealous, and offensive captor, to one who would ruin his property, ruin his physique, and above all ruin his spiritual development, which is assuredly and ever will be of supreme value in the sight of gods and men alike" (*Phaedrus* 241c).

We thought with Phaedrus that this was half the story, and that Socrates "would have an equal amount to say about the nonlover, enumerating his good points and show that he should be the favored suitor. Why is it, Socrates, that instead of that you break off?" (*Phaedrus* 241d). Socrates instead makes recompense for his blasphemous injustice. He acknowledges his sin in words akin to Anaximander's: "The fact is, you know, Phaedrus, the mind itself has a kind of divining power, for I felt disturbed some while ago as I was delivering that speech, and had a misgiving lest I might, in the words of Ibycus, 'By sinning in the sight of God win high renown from man'" (*Phaedrus* 242d). Can we take for granted that "the mind itself has a kind of divining power" concerning injustice even where we doubt that we can recognize justice, doubt that justice can be given any but proximate form? Socrates suggests we can.

The blasphemy is clear: "If Love is, as he is indeed, a god or a divine being, he cannot be an evil thing; yet this pair of speeches treated him as evil" (*Phaedrus* 242e). The sin that calls for purification (*Phaedrus* 243) rests on the assumption, stated explicitly by Phaedrus, of madness's evil.

> in reality, the greatest blessings come by way of madness [*manian*] indeed of madness that is heaven sent. . . . No, it was because they held madness [*manias*] to be a valuable gift, when due to divine dispensation, that they named that art as they did, though the men of today, having no sense of values, have put in an extra letter, making it not *manic* but *mantic* [*mantikēn*]. (*Phaedrus* 244ac)

We are on the verge of the high ecstatic point of the dialogue, Socrates' speech on the divinity of love, less than halfway through the dialogue—though, as in *Meno*, the climax of the dialogue divides it in two, forcing us to wonder at what follows, what could follow, such sublime ecstasy. Yet we are not ready to embark on this reading without a certain gathering of forces.

First, within our reading, we find ourselves at a point of fifteen English pages out of forty-nine into the dialogue (seventeen Greek pages of fifty-two) with an enormous cluster of themes before us. Let us hazard the hypothesis that by now we have encountered all the themes of the dialogue, a striking range, that the rest of the dialogue works them through. We list them here, largely in the order of the dialogue:

desire
   appetite
   love
Pharmakeia
the city, politics, power, law
   public, private
intimacy
nature
memory
repetition
writing
truth and deception
science

technē
storytelling, narration
citizens, strangers
recipes, rules
magic
mastery
   amateur
measure
advantage, benefit
goodness, justice
   injustice
menace, danger
perfectibility
madness
prophecy
divine inspiration
poiēsis

We may reduce this list to more manageable proportions.

   desire
   power
      public, private
   knowledge, science
      truth, writing, and representation
   memory
   magic
   madness
   menace
   nature
   technē, *poiēsis*, Pharmakeia
   justice, goodness
      injustice

What may we make of this list? An answer would represent our interpretation of the dialogue, an interpretation beyond our reading so far. At this point we may consider the following, to which we will return upon the culmination of our reading. Derrida suggests, in "Plato's Pharmacy," that writing and the *pharmakon* always appear together in *Phaedrus*, that we are to read the dialogue as presenting writing in the ambiguity of the *pharmakon*. We may consider that this proximity of writing with magic as medicine and poison circulates with truth, desire, and power as well, along with the others. The interpretation to which we will return holds that the longer and shorter lists represent inexhaustible mirrors of representation, that desire, power, truth, and representation circulate together with magic and madness in the general economy of nature and *poiēsis*.

Our second gathering of forces before we throw ourselves into the climax of the dialogue belongs to the dialogue itself. For Socrates opens his second speech with a remarkable figure: "Where is that boy I was talking to? He must listen to me once more, and not rush off to yield to his nonlover before he hears what I have to say" (*Phaedrus* 243e). The boy, we remember, was the speaker's beloved, Socrates' beloved, where Socrates pretended to be a nonlover, but now no longer, now speaks openly to his beloved of love. But to whom was Socrates speaking? Phaedrus responds: "Here he is, quite close beside you, whenever you want him" (*Phaedrus* 243e). Can we imagine a more erotic response? Socrates and Phaedrus lie alone together, in a private spot far from the city, engaged in highly charged, erotic activities, pervaded by love and desire, punctuated by references to how well they know each other, love each other, to the intimacy of their friendship. Can we take the entire dialogue as an intimate dialogue of love, of activities in private places, sexual, erotic, and more, posing for us the question of what activities belong in private, what activities belong to love? Can we suppose that the entire dialogue represents an intimate, erotic coupling, unlike *Symposium* for example, which takes place in public? Can we read the dialogue so that the discourse it provides on discourses tells us something of truth, of self-knowledge, and of love?

And so to the climax of the dialogue, in relation to which all the preceding may be foreplay, and what follows . . . —but let us not anticipate. The boy—who else but Phaedrus?—is close beside Socrates, whenever he wants him—wants him, not merely needs him.

Socrates' second, climactic and erotic speech moves as follows:

> "False is the tale" that when a lover is at hand favor ought rather to be accorded to one who does not love, on the ground that the former is mad [*mainētai*]. (*Phaedrus* 244)

> in reality, the greatest blessings come by way of madness, [*manion*] indeed of madness [*manias*] that is heaven-sent. (*Phaedrus* 244b)

> the men of old who gave things their names . . . held madness to be a valuable gift, when due to divine dispensation. (*Phaedrus* 244c)

We remember that the gods blessed Socrates' first speech, coming from the Muses, divinely inspired (*Phaedrus* 238c). We may also remember that *Ion*, whose gift as rhapsode suggests *technē*, receives Socrates' dispensation as a gift from the gods (Plato, *Ion* 542b). We wonder whether such a divine gift may belong to knowledge, if not to *epistēmē* or *sophia*, to science, may belong to *pharmakeia* and *poiēsis*, to a greater and madder truth, reshaping the old quarrel between philosophy and poetry into a distinction between a knowledge free from madness, under *technē*, appearing in *Phaedrus* as *lysis*, and a truth from the gods, filled with madness, prophecy, and *pharmakeia*.

Three forms of divine madness represent superior perfection, prophecy, purification, and *poiēsis*.[20] These represent a madness far superior, far beyond, closer to the gods than sanity, measure, benefit, or calculation.

Could there be too much sanity in *Republic*, too little madness, excess, especially in the truth of human *aretē*, divided into one excellence for each man or class rather than multifarious and complex? That may be told as another story.[21] Our story here is told in *Phaedrus*. Socrates tells of the immortality of the soul and, thereby, of all things, animate and inanimate, under her care, guided by the wings of *erōs*, of desire, tells of the divinity of a living being, the divinity of a human soul.[22] What we are told moves strangely from the gods to human beings.

> For the souls that are called immortal, so soon as they are at the summit, come forth and stand upon the back of the world, and straightway the revolving heaven carries them round, and they look upon the regions without. (Plato, *Phaedrus*, 247c)

> Such is the life of the gods. (*Phaedrus* 248a)

> For only the soul that has beheld truth may enter into this our human form . . . and such understanding is a recollection [*anamnēsis*] of those things which our souls beheld aforetime as they journeyed with their god, looking down upon the things which now we suppose to be, and gazing up to that which truly is.
>
> Therefore is it meet and right that the soul of the philosopher alone should recover her wings, for she, so far as may be, is ever near in memory to those things a god's nearness whereunto makes him truly god. Wherefore if a man makes

right use of such means of remembrance [*hypomnēmasin*], and ever approaches to the full vision of the perfect mysteries, he and he alone becomes truly perfect. (*Phaedrus* 249cd)

"All soul is immortal" (*Phaedrus* 245c), but only divine souls can behold true being (*Phaedrus* 247cd). Even so, philosophers can recollect their memory of true being, overcoming their forgetfulness and confusion. Even so, lovers are aroused by beholding beauty, and their wings begin to grow, called by others "demented" (*Phaedrus* 249e). Every human soul has had contemplation of true being (*Phaedrus* 250). We move from the gods to philosophers to lovers to every human being, as if the disclaimers proclaim themselves through overcoming and forgetfulness.

These dialectical movements circle around remembering true being, reminded of it by beauty, a memory within forgetfulness, an awakening from *lēthe*. We may be reminded of *Meno*, also a dialogue circling round recollection and forgetfulness, with a similar structure, an opening onto a central question of virtue—what it is and whether it can be taught— reaching a displaced climax around the nature of recollection in the slave-boy exchange, followed by a divergence. *Phaedrus* turns around the wings of desire, framed in relation to memory and forgetting. *Meno* turns around recollection, framed in relation to virtue. We may be reminded also of the themes of memory and repetition throughout *Phaedrus* contrasting science and writing with philosophy, while here and in *Meno*, philosophy's truth presents itself in the form of memory.

If we are reminded of *Meno*, we may remember Meno's description of Socrates as *pharmakeus*:

> Socrates, even before I met you they told me that in plain truth you are a perplexed man yourself and reduce others to perplexity. At this moment I feel you are exercising magic and witchcraft upon me and positively laying me under your spell until I am just a mass of helplessness. If I may be flippant, I think that not only in outward appearance but in other respects as well you are exactly like the flat sting ray that one meets in the sea. Whenever anyone comes into contact with it, it numbs him, and that is the sort of thing that you seem to be doing to me now. (Plato, *Meno* 80)

Perplexed himself, Socrates bewitches others in the service of truth. Shall we entertain the possibility that this perplexity, helplessness, numbness, along with madness, belong to truth, that the recollection, *mnemosynē*, of which Socrates speaks, represents delusion, that truth irrupts in the proximity of illusion, numbness, madness, untruth?

We have come to the most erotic moment in *Phaedrus*, giving a different meaning to the possibility that Socrates' speech represents the climax of the dialogue. We take immortal souls to stand upon the spine of the world, moving far from philosophy, to souls moved by beauty, moved by sexual desire and lust. The memory that stirs us is divine (240d) in an extraordinary image of a sexual climax.

> Next, with the passing of the shudder, a strange sweating and fever seizes him. For by reason of the stream of beauty entering in through his eyes there comes a warmth, whereby his soul's plumage is fostered, and with that warmth the roots of the wings are melted, which for long had been so hardened and closed up that nothing could grow; then as the nourishment is poured in, the stump of the wing swells and hastens to grow from the root over the whole substance of the soul, ... Meanwhile she throbs with ferment in every part (*Phaedrus* 251a–c).[23]

In the frame of divine love for true being, before its Christianization, we are presented with a passionate account of the desire, the yearning, the bodily fluids, the pent-up tension, the orgasmic release of the sexual act. Leaving aside whether such an account pertains more to men than women, we cannot help but take this account as material, embodied, a strange figure in relation to an otherworldly reading of desire.

What shall we make of such a portrayal? That the experience of the soul beholding immortal and divine beauty contains a pleasure superior in every way, yet similar in form, to sexual intercourse? That a sexual orgasm's extraordinary power points to something beyond material embodiment? That the excesses of desire, found in mad obsessions of lovers and in the overwhelming pleasures of sexual encounters, speak of something beyond limits, of a surpassing of the limits of limits, of limits' authority, whose excesses belong, as Socrates says, to *mania*, prophecy, purification, *poiēsis*, and love, bodily love? Here, desire names excess, the desire lacking in Lysias's speech but also lacking in science, in *sophia*, lacking in *Republic* except in relation to the philosopher, whose love of *sophia* knows no bounds. *Phaedrus* asks us to imagine, in the teeth of the traditional reading of the dialogues, that the limits of *technē*, under calculation and measure, fail because those limits know no excesses, madness or desire, circulate too far from their limits. Sexual love places us at our limits, not just at the moment of orgasm, but in beholding another being who for us transcends any possibility of remaining within our limits. If not, if we have never known the madness of love—told by every narrative tradition—we remain within love's advantage, seeking our's and others' benefits, not an unknown or empty life, but a life contained by rule. The Montagues and Capulets fall before the dreams and deaths of Romeo and Juliet.

To ask a question we will ask again, why doesn't Socrates' speech end here, and why doesn't the dialogue end with it? What answer can we give but that we have not yet reached the climax, the truth, are still within the foreplay even in this shuddering and sweating, flooding and streaming. The excesses and madnesses of desire belong to the rest of our themes, listed above, and we have not traced them except in relation to beauty, to sexual love. We have barely begun to explore the play of Pharmakeia.

In any case, in a figure Socrates frequently repeats as if to displace the force of his authority, he tells us that Eros is named by the celestials Pteros, after his wings, that is, after his heavenliness and excessiveness, but "you may believe that or not, as you please; . . . " (Plato, *Phaedrus* 252c), as if we may believe any of the rest, as we please. The story turns from the heavens and the beauty of their lure to how the charioteer and his steeds may remember their divinity. We repeat the story already told, in a different voice. Repeatedly, throughout the dialogues, and throughout each dialogue, we repeat a story we may have already heard, in a different voice as if it were another story.

For now we turn from the heavens to the earth, from the back of the world to the charioteer with his steeds, once again displacing the claim that only the immortal or divine soul, or if not that, only the philosopher's soul, or if not that, only the true lover of beauty, can know true desire, now any of us finite lovers, divided into three, as if love itself were divine, belying every preceding only.[24]

We return to highly erotic language: "Now when the driver beholds the person of the beloved, and causes a sensation of warmth to suffuse the whole soul, he begins to experience a tickling or pricking of desire, . . . " (*Phaedrus* 254). This time, however, it is in service to restraint, however coercive, against "a monstrous and forbidden act" (*Phaedrus* 254b). "[T]he driver . . . jerks back the bit in the mouth of the wanton horse with an ever stronger pull, bespatters his railing tongue and his jaws with blood, and forcing him down on legs and haunches delivers him over to anguish" (*Phaedrus* 254e)[25] Despite the menacing images of sexual violence present throughout this entire scene, the result is humility and peace. "And so it happens time and again, until the evil steed casts off his wantonness; humbled in the end, he obeys the counsel of his driver, and when he sees the fair beloved is like to die of fear. Wherefore at long last the soul of the lover follows after the beloved with reverence and awe" (*Phaedrus* 254e). Restraint wins over wantonness, leading to the philosophic life, an image of peace within sexual desire, enchantment in menace, *pharmakeia* again; but also desire's excess within peaceful reverence. For the wanton steed, however restrained, still yearns for the forbidden act.[26] As before, the philosophical life, returning to true being, a life free from sexual fulfillment, attains the highest goal. Except that before, we saw that the greatest of erotic pleasures stemmed from the fourth kind of madness. Here, again, even if a little careless, these lovers have their share of immortality, "for it is ordained that all such as have taken the first steps on the celestial highway shall no more return to the dark pathways beneath the earth, but shall walk together in a life of shining bliss, and be furnished in due time with like plumage the one to the other, because of their love" (*Phaedrus* 256de). Even here, however wanton, true lovers gain their wings and walk in shining bliss. For Eros is a god, in whatever form, Apollinian or Dionysian. He offers excess on every hand, that of being and immortality; that of beauty and the good; that of bodily love. Excess, madness, magic, *poiēsis*, all belong to Eros. Perhaps they belong to truth.

And so, with fiery incandescence, the climax comes to a close. We have risen on mad and fiery passion to heavenly heights, before true being. What could follow such exalted speech? What further madness calls? We find ourselves but two-thirds through the dialogue.

One madness, one obsession, that does not appear in this paean to love marks the love of men and women, parents of their children. Children have not yet appeared in name, though they appear later and are implied in reference to Pharmakeia. Heterosexual love shows itself in disguised form. To this point in the dialogue, we work within homoerotic (but not women's) love, man and man, man and boy, Socrates and Phaedrus. If we read the dialogue as an act of love, as we must, however tentatively, the act has come to consummation. What now? What greater pleasure than the act of love? What fulfillment? Does love end with an orgasm? How could we imagine that it might? What of the children? What of their future?

We imagine our two lovers continuing their act, their feast of love, begun in a private, intimate place, a feast of discourse, of philosophy and truth. How might they continue? They cannot achieve a greater climax than Socrates' speech. But love does not end, may not even begin, with an erotic climax, but begins in foreplay and ends in afterplay, in the intimacy to which the sexual act gives rise. Love moves within the scene of intimacy.

Even so, the drab discourse to which Phaedrus and Socrates fall after shedding their wings seems too dull for *erōs*, though we note one accomplishment, that Socrates replaces Lysias as Phaedrus's lover: "It makes me afraid that I shall find Lysias cutting a poor figure, if he proves to be willing to compete with another speech of his own" (*Phaedrus* 257c). Socrates appears a better lover, sexually and truthfully. For truth circles around him, in the background of every dialogue, the Athenian court that found him guilty, repeated in a striking reference to Egypt (*Phaedrus* 274–75).

Be that as it may, we again face the point of writing speeches, as if Lysias might be just a "speech writer," a shameful state of being (*Phaedrus* 257c). Socrates responds: "Then the conclusion is obvious, that there is nothing shameful in the mere writing of speeches" (*Phaedrus* 258d). What then shall we take as shameful? Socrates goes on to make a distinction that circles back to the very beginning of the dialogue, reminding us of our earlier reading of Pausanias's speech in *Symposium*: "Then what is the nature of good writing and bad? Is it incumbent on us, Phaedrus, to examine Lysias on this point, . . . " (*Phaedrus* 258e). Phaedrus responds: "Is it incumbent! Why, life itself would hardly be worth living save for pleasures like this. . . . " (*Phaedrus* 258e).

Writing represents itself as free from shamefulness and as giving rise to the highest of pleasures. Writing, with discourse and truth, join together here with love, with sexual pleasure, the highest pleasure. Even so, we remember Pausanias's speech distinguishing two gods of love, one base and vulgar, the other heavenly. "No one, I think will deny that there are two goddesses of that name—one, the elder, sprung from no mother's womb but from the heavens themselves, we call the Uranian, the heavenly Aphrodite, while the younger, daughter of Zeus and Dione, we call Pandemus, the earthly Aphrodite" (*Symposium* 180e). No one will deny it but Socrates in *Phaedrus* (as well as in *Symposium* where "love was neither beautiful nor good" [201e]), presenting a different refusal of the opposition of good and bad love. We also remember Socrates' disdain for science, which opens the dialogue: "the invention of clever, industrious people who are not exactly to be envied, . . . " (*Phaedrus* 229d). We may take as common to both Pausanias's speech on love, divided into good and bad, and clever, industrious scientists, a concern with distinction and opposition, with good and bad, right and wrong, true and false, high and low. Must Socrates and Phaedrus distinguish good writing from bad? Could such distinction represent the highest good? Possibly after Pausanias, in the mode of science, *technē*. For another possibility marks the question as ruining the madness to whose heights we have soared, shattering our wings, loading us down with forgetfulness. How can we read the question of distinguishing good writing from bad, making precise distinctions at all, except as raising questions of *technē* without *erōs* or *mania*?

Socrates' response to Phaedrus reminds us of the cicadas, a figure distant from *technē*. "The story is that once upon a time these creatures were men—men of an age before there were any Muses—and that when the latter came into the world, and music made its appearance, some of the people of those days were so thrilled with pleasure that they went on singing, and quite forget to eat and drink until they actually died without noticing" (*Phaedrus* 259c). This extraordinary tale of excess, madness unto death, appears in relation to love and the Muses. Shall we disdain the possibility that this figure of Bacchic excess, musical madness, arises here to offset the figure of good and bad, of *technē* and *epistēmē*, with which we are surrounded? Socrates continues that the cicadas, "to which the Muses have granted the boon of needing no sustenance right from their birth, but of singing from the very first, without food or drink, until the day of the death, after which they go and report to the Muses how they severally are paid honor among mankind, and by whom" (*Phaedrus* 259c). Socrates represents this sickness, madness, unto death, desire's passion beyond all limits, as a boon, joined with the image of the Muses' honor, of art, *poiēsis*, beyond all regulation, rendering misleading the passages in *Republic* and *Ion* concerning art as a *technē*. We remember that in *Republic* the poets are permitted to return to the *polis* upon giving a poetic defense.[27] The Myth of Er directly follows, one of the greatest stories of life beyond death. We have considered the possibility that Ion's rhapsodic greatness comes from the gods as another *poiētic* madness. In both cases, the good as *technē* receives supplementation if not supplanting as *poiēsis*, much closer to divine enchantment.

In *Phaedrus* analogously, we are exploring the possibility that the long discussion late in the dialogue (259–74) of the rules and forms of good and bad writing presents them as belonging to *technē*, not the gods, as repeating Socrates' earlier rejection of science as lacking love, madness, magic, or divinity, as lacking what the cicadas possess to an extreme, a yearning, a love, for music beyond all measure. We are exploring the possibility that the afterglow of love's desire repeats the foreplay with the overwhelming difference, at least for the two lovers in their private spot, that Socrates has overcome his public rival, his speechmaking rival who lacks divine inspiration and makes speeches praising the advantage of sanity over divine madness, of advantage over excess. We wonder how the Socrates who disdained science at the beginning of the dialogue, who rejects Lysias's division of love into good and bad, who agrees that there is nothing shameful in the mere writing of speeches, can propose methods for producing good and bad writing without repudiating the measures and calculations he rejected earlier as lacking divine madness, how the Socrates who revels incessantly in the magical attraction of writing and speaking can repudiate writing itself. If he does both, and he says he does, how can we read his doing so?

Socrates presents his question as a proposal: "the subject we proposed for inquiry just now was the nature of good and bad speaking and writing; so we are to inquire into that" (*Phaedrus* 259e). We may be reminded of Lysias's and Socrates' first speeches, concerned with good and bad love. We may also be reminded of the similar moment in *Meno*, after its climax, the slaveboy scene, where Socrates similarly proposes an inquiry into whether virtue can be taught while openly acknowledging that it is not his preference. "If I were your master as well as my own, Meno, we should not have inquired whether or not virtue can be taught until we had first asked the main question—what it is" (Plato, *Meno* 86d). Socrates is Meno's teacher, not his master; Phaedrus's lover, not his master. Mastery belongs to *technē*.

So do good and bad speaking and writing. We have returned to *technē*, to Lysias and science. What of the possibility that this entire discussion from where we find ourselves (Plato, *Phaedrus* 260) to the story of Theuth (Plato, *Phaedrus* 274) belongs to *technē*, repeats the themes of advantage, benefit, calculation, and measure? If we can consider such an interpretation, we must note how it proceeds and the points of interruption. In dialogic order, with minor repetitions: "there is nothing shameful in the mere writing of speeches" (*Phaedrus* 248d). Shall we keep this point firmly in mind as we proceed through what appear to be entirely opposite suggestions? "[W]hen . . . music made its appearance, some of the people of those days were so thrilled with pleasure that they went on singing, and quite forgot to eat and drink until they actually died without noticing it" (*Phaedrus* 259c). Can we ignore this fantastic image of an excess of love and desire far beyond any ordinary life, as if the gods and Muses, being and beauty, impose on us passions beyond any limits?

By way of contrast, consider good and bad speechmaking as a *technē*. "[T]he subject we proposed for inquiry just now was the nature of good and bad speaking and writing, so we are to inquire into that" (*Phaedrus* 259d). Such a good and bad belong to *technē*, suggesting an art of truth remote from *erōs* and *poiēsis*. As absurd as may appear, since we have taken Lysias's speech as a *technē*, shall we in this return to that speech remember Socrates' claim that such a *technē* lacks *erōs*? Have we come to understand *erōs*'s truth as a *technē*? "But what about the words 'just' and 'good'? Don't we diverge, and dispute not only with one another but with our own selves?" (*Phaedrus* 263). Love, justice, goodness—*erōs, dikē, agathon*—all appear as terms that we dispute about not only with one another but within ourselves. How then, what meaning can we give to knowing the truth of such terms except within their dispute? Socrates does not mean simply "for the moment," until the philosopher or scientist settles once and for all what love, justice, and goodness mean, for the contestedness belongs to the terms.[28] What kind of justice echoes here but one in intimate proximity to and with injustice, with Socrates' trial and death, forever remembering Socrates' death? What kind of truth, of knowledge, pertains to such contested terms, to such broken, contested, disrupted terms, except a broken, contested truth, a knowledge—always repudiated, denied—closer to madness than to *technē*?

In what way closer? "Any discourse ought to be constructed like a living creature, with its own body, as it were; it must not lack either head or feet; it must have a middle and extremities so composed as to suit each other and the whole work" (*Phaedrus* 264c). Socrates presents a perfect image of rhetorical perfection, lacking but one thing: life. This image represents a corpse. For we remember what a living creature possesses, not head or feet, suitable extremities, but an immortal soul (*psychē*).[29] The entire dialogue calls up the question of what composes *psychē*, what makes a living creature of a corpse, brings the wings of *erōs* to truth, makes a vital, truthful presence of writing and speech, of language? Socrates answers, divine madness (*Phaedrus* 265). It speaks in a voice of play (*paidia*; related to *paideia*) (*Phaedrus* 265c) and contrasts with two procedures whose "significance" (*dynamin*) may be seized in a "scientific fashion" (*technē*) (*Phaedrus* 265d).

> The first is that in which we bring a dispersed plurality under a single form, seeing it all together. (*Phaedrus* 265d)

> The reverse of the other, whereby we are enabled to divide into forms, following the objective articulation; we are not to attempt to hack off parts like a clumsy butcher, but to take example from our two recent speeches. The single general form which the postulated was irrationality; next, on the analogy of a single natural body with its pairs of like-named members, right arm or leg, as we say, and left, they conceived of madness as a single objective form existing in human beings. (*Phaedrus* 266)

And so on. Now, Socrates has not followed this procedure in *Phaedrus*; the great, climactic speech on divine madness and love bears no relation to this taxonomic method; the speeches that do are Lysias's and Pausanias's, representations of *technē*. Such a method lacks irrationality, madness, love, and inspiration. Where, we ask, can we find the gods?

For the moment no matter. The method described appears elsewhere in the dialogues, in *Sophist* and *Statesman* especially, but also in *Philebus* with the difference we have noted.[30] "[W]e may let each one of all these intermediate forms pass away into the unlimited and cease bothering about them" (Plato, *Philebus* 16e). What of these intermediate forms together with the one and its unlimit? Can we take them to appear as art and measure, *technē* and *sophia*, then let them pass away into the unlimited and cease bothering about them? Do they possess *erōs*, *mania*? Where can love and madness arise before us except as disputed terms among the other disputed terms, of goodness and justice, unendingly disputed terms, immemorial injustice?

Socrates continues: "Believe me, Phaedrus, I am myself a lover of these divisions and collections, that I may gain the power to speak and to think, and whenever I deem another man able to discern an objective unity and plurality, I follow 'in his footsteps where he leadeth as a god'" (Plato, *Phaedrus* 266b). First, he is a lover, carried away by madness; second, he follows those who can discern unity and plurality as if they were gods, recalling *Philebus* leading us to ask what becomes of the passing away—God alone knows; and third, the god whose footsteps leadeth is Calypso, and he who is led is Odysseus, one deceiver led by a goddess described as a god, expecting deceit. What image of unbroken, objective truth appears here? What madness? For Odysseus's star turns repeatedly on madness.

All this concerns the art of rhetoric (*logōn technēs*), an art without love's madness, an art made intelligible only through such a madness—Socrates' love of these divisions and collections. Language without love lacks truth even as art.

What follows (preceded by Socrates' remark that he sees several "holes in the fabric" [*Phaedrus* 268]) brings us back to madness (*mainein*), the *pharmakon*, and magic:

> Suppose someone . . . said, "I know how to apply such treatment to a patient's body as will induce warmth [*thermainein*] or coolness, as I choose; . . . ." What do you imagine they would have to say to that?

> They would ask him, of course, whether he also knew which patients ought to be given the various treatments, and when, and for how long.
> Then what if he said, "Oh, no, but I expect my pupils to manage what you refer to by themselves"?
> I expect they would say, "the man is mad [*mainetai*]; he thinks he has made himself a doctor by picking up something out of a book, or coming across some common drug [*pharmakiois*] or other, without any real knowledge [*technē*] of medicine" (*Phaedrus* 268c)

The man is mad, like the lover of true being and beauty, like Socrates himself; without any real knowledge of medicine, as Socrates repeatedly describes himself, expecting his pupils to learn by themselves, not to be taught by him, as virtue, in *Meno* can be learned, acquired, but cannot be taught as a *technē*.[31]

To think that medicine can be known but not taught separates knowledge from its *technē*. We can take Socrates to suggest in *Meno* that while virtue may be knowledge, statesmen do not possess it, or we can take him to suggest that it requires a knowledge that cannot be taught, that cannot then be a guide to public life, that it is closer to gadfly than *technē*, closer to magic, to *pharmakeia*, than to *sophia*, science. The doctor claims *epistamenos* but expects his pupils to learn by themselves. What if he claimed ignorance but yearned, like his students, for wisdom, *sophia*, yearned for a knowledge whose recipes were closer to *pharmakeia* than to *epistēmē*?

Or to *poiēsis*. For Socrates continues with two analogies, one to tragedy, the other to music, with a difference:

> Now suppose someone went up to Sophocles or Euripides and said he knew how to compose lengthy dramatic speeches about a trifling matter, and quite short ones about a matter of moment, that he could write pathetic passages when he chose, or again passages of intimidation and menace, and so forth, and that he considered that by teaching these accomplishments he could turn a pupil into a tragic poet [*poiēsin*]. (*Phaedrus* 268d)

What recipe, knowledge, or *technē* marks the difference between writing dramatically and *poiēsis*? The physician can cure where necessary; the poet can write, tragically or comically. What more can we expect—save *erōs* and *pharmakeia*? Moreover, the physician denies that he can teach his pupils what he knows; the hypothetical poet claims that by teaching what he knows, he teaches *poiēsis*.

The musical analogy continues these ambiguities:

> My good sir, it is true that one who proposes to become a master of harmony must know the things you speak of, but it is perfectly possible for one who has got as far as yourself to have not the slightest real knowledge of harmony. You are acquainted with what has to be learned before studying harmony, but of harmony itself you know nothing. (*Phaedrus* 268e)

What kind of knowledge? Lysias's or Socrates'? *Technē* or *poiēsis*? Where can we find true being, *erōs*, divine madness? And the cicadas, do they sing the madness of music rather than its art, its science, its passion and inspiration? What in the world could knowledge of harmony tell us that would make us a musician? And how could we learn it?

Socrates' exemplar of one who knows speeches and writing is not Sophocles or Euripides, but Pericles, returning us to public life (*Phaedrus* 269e), the most finished exponent of the art itself (*auton technē*), possessing knowledge (*epistēmēn*). Shall we forget at this point, where Pericles appears superior to Lysias and Thrasymachus, Socrates' experience with public life? Shall we forget divine madness in *erōs*, *poiēsis*, and *pharmakeia* in pursuing philosophy as a *technē*?

> there is a nature that we have to determine, the nature [*physis*] of body in the one, and of soul in the other, if we mean to be scientific [*technē*] . . . when we apply medicine [*pharmaka*] and diet to induce health and strength, or words and rules of conduct to implant such convictions and virtues as we desire. (*Phaedrus* 270b)

Technē on the one hand, implanting virtue; *pharmakeia* and *mania* on the other. Does *psychē*'s nature belong to *technē* or to *erōs* and *poiēsis*?

We began *Phaedrus* with Lysias's speech representing *technē*, contrasted with Socrates' two speeches, one still representing *technē*, with a difference, representing a lover acting as a nonlover, for a nonlover cannot pursue advantage, through *technē*, without *erōs* or *orexis*. The second speech moves from *technē* to *mania*, then to *poiēsis*. Shall we continue our reading by assuming that the circulation of *technē* and *poiēsis* around each other remains to haunt us, that the climactic speech represents

Socrates' triumph as a lover over Lysias, but there remains *technē*, always remains the circulation of *technē*. For throughout the final third of the dialogue, Phaedrus forgets *erōs*, lapses back into *technē*, as if he does not remember the distinction between *technē* and *poiēsis*.

Socrates gives us, in the final third of the dialogue, as firm a contrast between *technē* and *poiēsis* as we may find where we cannot give that contrast over to *poiēsis*, where *technē* continues to haunt *poiēsis*. The cicadas and Muses, the setting of the dialogue in nature, *physis*, work against any *technē*. But *technē* continues to circulate, irresistibly. Indeed, Socrates tells how to be as scientific (*technikos*) as possible about writing. "[W]hen he is competent to say what type of man is susceptible to what kind of discourse; . . . and when, on top of all this, he has further grasped the right occasions for speaking and for keeping quiet, . . . then and not till then has he well and truly achieved the art (*Phaedrus* 271d–72b). Of whom shall we read this as a description? Of Socrates and his claims for medicine (*pharmakeia*), lacking magic, ambiguity, self-knowledge, *erōs*? Or of Lysias, of discourse as *technē*? If we are not sure, Socrates tells us that "one mustn't believe all one is told" (*Phaedrus* 272), while Phaedrus comments, "still it does seem a considerable business" (*Phaedrus* 272b), leading Socrates to suggest "that makes it necessary to thoroughly overhaul all our arguments, and see whether there is some easier and shorter way of arriving at the art; . . . " (*Phaedrus* 272c). The primary argument has been given several times, most of all in the climactic, erotic center of the dialogue, that this art of discourse, writing and speech, of truth belongs to *erōs, mania, pharmakeia*. The secondary argument suggests how difficult even Phaedrus may find it to accept magic and madness as the nature of truth, how impossible we may find it to separate magic and madness in truth from *technē*. This argument presents the cumbersomeness and technicality of a *technē* of discourse as too difficult in its technical ways to represent the truth of truth, which is difficult in another way, in the ways that magic and madness are difficult, not technically but aporetically.

What could represent this easier way? Why, to avoid truth altogether, and to settle for plausibility. "[T]here is . . . absolutely no need for the budding orator to concern himself with the truth about what is just or good conduct, nor indeed about who are just and good men whether by nature or education" (*Phaedrus* 272d). Have we forgotten that "just" and "good" appear as contested terms that we have not settled even in ourselves, may never have settled in ourselves? "Whatever you say, you simply must pursue this probability they talk of, and can say good-by to the truth forever" (*Phaedrus* 272e). Shall we hear this as an alternative to the art of discourse, or as its extremity?[32] Can truth, can philosophy, be divided into good and bad, proper and improper, any better than love or beauty? Do all lovers, of beauty and truth, yearn beyond measure, madly, for true being? Did we agree that there is nothing wrong with writing?

What do we know at this point about discourse, about knowledge and truth, except that it has nothing wrong with it? "Now do you know how we may best please God, in practice and in theory, in this matter of words?" (*Phaedrus* 274b). Phaedrus does not know. Does Socrates within his ignorance? And if not, what shall we take the preceding discussion to tell except to give us no answer? Socrates has no answer, but he has a story: "I can tell you the tradition that has come down from our forefathers, but they alone know the truth of it" (*Phaedrus* 274c). And so we commence the story of Theuth on writing, of whose truth our forefathers alone knew.

> when it came to writing Theuth said, "Here, O king, is a branch of learning that will make the people of Egypt wiser and improve their memories; my discovery provides a recipe [*pharmakon*] for memory and wisdom [*sophias*]." But the king answered and said, " . . . If men learn this, it will implant forgetfulness [*lēthēn*] in their souls; . . . What you have discovered is a recipe [*pharmakon*] not for memory [*mnēmēs*], but for reminder [*hypomnēseōs*]." (*Phaedrus* 275)

Pharmakon, lēthē, alētheia, hypomnēmasin, recollection and reminder, come together in this passage—shall we say inseparably?[33] Can we truly tell the difference between remedy and poison, reminder and recollection, *hypomnēseōs* and *hypomnēmasin*? Can we tell the difference where the gods disagree, where Ammon and Theuth, Zeus and Hermes, disagree? May we read *Euthyphro* against its pieties, as if we might know what the gods disagree about, as if instead virtue and truth were what the gods disagree about, so that even they cannot tell, so that we may not be able to tell, by *technē*, at best by *poiēsis*, except that *poiēsis* cannot tell except as *pharmakon*? And how, we ask again, can writing of itself be bad (if that question can be asked in proximity to Orithyia's rape and Eros's madness)?

What is the answer? Derrida replies:

> But Theuth, it should be noted, spoke not another word. The great god's sentence went unanswered.

. . . .

> After closing the pharmacy, Plato went to retire, ...
> (Derrida, *PP*, p. 169)

Can we, can Plato, close the pharmacy? Do we wish to do so?

Preceding Socrates' famous answer we find a brief exchange: "It is easy for you, Socrates, to make up tales from Egypt or anywhere else you fancy" (Plato, *Phaedrus* 275b). "For you [Phaedrus] apparently it makes a difference who the speaker is, and what country he comes from; you don't merely ask whether what he says is true or false" (*Phaedrus* 275c). Does this idea of truth belong to divine madness, to *erōs*, or does it belong to *technē*?

The conventional reading of this passage takes it to express the famous Platonic position that truth and falsity have nothing to do with speaker or context, to be history- and context-free. Yet Socrates constantly makes up tales from elsewhere, from Egypt and Atlantis, as if that matters, as if we are to think it matters, though Phaedrus accepts the rebuke—and much, much more: "I deserve your rebuke, and I agree that the man of Thebes is right in what he said about writing" (*Phaedrus* 275c). He accepts the rebuke and Ammon's or Thamos's truth, without argument, lacking any argument, against the claim in 258d that there is nothing wrong about writing as such, and even more, against the climactic story's tale of recollection (*hypomnēmasin*) (249c). What argument might overcome these powerful movements? "[A]nyone [*technēn*] who leaves behind him a written manual, . . . must be exceedingly simple-minded; . . . if he imagines that written words can do anything more than remind [*hypomnēsai*] one who knows [*eidota*] that which the writing is concerned with" (Plato, *Phaedrus* 275e). Recollection again, reminding us of the erotic climax.

The famous answer, then:

> You know, Phaedrus, that's the strange thing about writing, which makes it truly analogous to painting. The painter's products stand before as if they were alive, but if you question them, they maintain a most majestic silence. It is the same with written words: they seem to talk to you as though they were intelligent, but if you ask them anything about what they say, from a desire to be instructed, they go on telling you just the same thing forever. And once a thing is put in writing the composition, whatever it may be, drifts all over the place, getting into the hands not only of those who understand it, but

equally of those who have no business with it; it doesn't know how to address the right people, and not address the wrong. And when it is ill-treated and unfairly abused it always needs its parent to come to its help, being unable to defend or help itself. (*Phaedrus* 275de)[34]

Phaedrus's response implies a warning: "Once again you are perfectly right" (Plato, *Phaedrus* 276). Can Socrates ever be perfectly right, can anyone, but within *technē*? His response speaks of "another sort of discourse . . . of unquestioned legitimacy" (Plato, *Phaedrus* 276). Images of parents and their illegitimate and legitimate children present themselves as repetitions of desire, of *erōs*. Writing's faults appear as three:

1. Written works repeat themselves forever.
2. Written works wander all over the place (always different).
3. Written works need their parent to defend them.

(1) and (2) cancel each other. The infinite repetitions of writing and memory repeat themselves as always different; every wandering represents a repetition. (1) and (2) may be linked with (3) in the form we have repeated again and again, the death of writing circulating without its parent, without recollection, a death that belongs to knowledge, science, and *technē* no less than writing: the death of truth, the death of the madness and *erōs* of truth. For the living truth

> is written in the soul of the learner, that can defend itself, and knows to whom it should speak and to whom it should say nothing. (Plato, *Phaedrus* 276)
>
> You mean no dead discourse, but the living speech, the original of which the written discourse may fairly be called a kind of image. (*Phaedrus* 276b)

Still written, but alive, pulsing in the immortal *psychē* as *erōs, mania, pharmakeia*, pulsing in private rather than in dead publicity. We do not escape writing to speech, writing repetitively to thought, for thought repeats memory, recollection, being, repeats itself forever, always differently, as writing must do so as not to be *technē*, representing the inexhaustible circulation of judgment we call "semasis."

What then does a living and truthful spirit do with knowledge? Again two images appear:

> For serious purposes wouldn't he behave like a scientific [*technē*] farmer, sow [*speiras*] his seeds in suitable soil, and be well content if they came to maturity within eight months? (*Phaedrus* 276b)
>
> And are we to maintain that he who has knowledge [*epistēmas*] of what is just, honorable, and good has less sense than the farmer in dealing with his seeds? (*Phaedrus* 276c)
>
> Then it won't be with serious [*spoudē*] intent that he "writes them in water." . . . (*Phaedrus* 276c)

We note the pun between *speiras*, "to sow," and *spoudē*, "seriously" but also "hastily."[35] Writing's seriousness belongs to *technē*, sowing its seeds in suitable soil, content if they come to maturity in time. Instead, that thought that belongs to the soul's passionate madness writes "by way of pastime, collecting a store of refreshment both for his own memory [*hypomnēmata*], against the day 'when age oblivion [*lēthēs*] comes'" (*Phaedrus* 276d). And here we find justice: "How far superior to the other sort is the recreation [*paidian*] that a man finds in words, when he discourses about justice and the other topics you speak of" (*Phaedrus* 276e). Justice, goodness, love, and madness all belong to *paideia*, to children, legitimate and illegitimate, to desire.

Three points remain concerning the art (*technē*) of writing. "First, you must know the truth about the subject that you speak or write about; that is to say, you must be able to isolate it in definition, and having so defined it you must next understand how to divide it into kinds, until you reach the limit of division; . . . " (Plato, *Phaedrus* 277b). Contrasted with a different relation to writing, away from *technē*, restoring us to public life.[36]

Phaedrus begins erotically, ecstatically circling around the themes we have listed in order of their appearance:

desire
   appetite
   love
Pharmakeia
the city, politics, power, law
   public, private
intimacy
nature
memory

repetition
writing
truth and deception
science
technē
storytelling, narration
citizens, strangers
recipes, rules
magic
mastery
   amateur
measure
advantage, benefit
goodness, justice
   injustice
menace, danger
perfectibility
madness
prophecy
divine inspiration
poiēsis

We shortened this list to the following, all appearing in the first fifteen pages.

desire
power
knowledge, science, writing, truth
memory, history
magic
madness
menace
nature
technē, poiēsis, Pharmakeia
goodness, justice, injustice

What then follows? What of the rest of the dialogue? What of science and its authority?

We have read *Phaedrus* in two ways, one erotically, ecstatically, soaring with the wings of desire, consummated passionately in an act of love. Socrates and Phaedrus, in a private, intimate place, far from the crowds, perform a supreme act of love. And what, we ask, represents such love, represents intimacy? What passionate fulfillment of beauty and desire? Talk, speech, philosophy; *pharmakeia, mania, erōs, poiēsis*. The ecstatic, erotic moment of love, the climax of the dialogue, follows a foreplay of technique, of *technē*, a mechanical analogue of love represented by Lysias, indistinguishable from the absence of love. Socrates gives us passionate, erotic love fulfilled in a supreme climax, soaring on the wings of desire. What, the dialogue asks, and answers, represents the wings of desire, the life of the soul? What but *pharmakeia, mania, erōs, poiēsis*, circulating together? And what, we ask, follows the climax of love, with its mad yearning for beauty and its recollection of true being? What, but truth, but knowledge?

What truth, what knowledge? The first half of *Phaedrus* represents the movement of love from *technē* to *pharmakeia, mania,* and *erōs*: shall we take the second half to return us to *technē*? The philosopher-king returns from the light of the sun to the cave, still in the full blinding flame of desire, and Socrates returns from Diotima to death in the city. What we remember of injustice belongs to Socrates and his city more than to true being. The claims of the *polis* cannot be denied, the claims of law, authority, and power. They cannot be denied because they represent the authority of life, the corporeality of love's fulfillment, the embodiment of desire. Immortal souls stand on the spine of the world. Philosophers shed and regain their wings. But human beings have other lives than philosophy. Lovers fulfill their dreams of erotic passion and regain their wings, walking together in a life of shining bliss—and thereafter.

The truth, the knowledge *Phaedrus* tells, reveals the wings of living truth in the animate soul as against dead science, dead *technē*, dead art, dead writing, dead memory, dead repetition, perhaps even dead gods. All dead! What gives them life, lifts their wings? What madness animates the wings of their desire? What economy?

That question climaxes our first reading: what brings to knowledge, truth, and writing the living truth they require? The erotic climax constitutes fulfillment in the form of truth, the living recollection of a living truth, constituted by desire, by love's madness. The final third of the dialogue represents a return from the spine of the world to forgetfulness of that truth except for its living pulsation, the desire that moves it. We return to *technē* because we cannot live without it, because we circulate within it, but we hope to remember its injustices, remember how easily it falls dead, remember the deadness of the art of writing, remember the fancifulness of writing as we write, remember the deadness of *technē* and the lack of seriousness of *poiēsis* as we pursue *technē* and *poiēsis*, as if a certain skepticism as to our own ignorance and lack of seriousness might represent whatever seriousness we can attain. We read the end of *Phaedrus* as the loss and remembrance of the wings of love, a falling back from *poiēsis* to *technē*, remembering love and being as *pharmakon*, *poiēsis* as *pharmakon*, as we read the return of the philosopher from the sun in *Republic* as a conflicted, erotic act rather than as restoration of order.

In this way, the intimacy of erotic union, between Socrates and Phaedrus, consummates itself as truth, a truth questioning its own veracity, concerned with its madness and untruth.[37] The wings of desire lift us up erotically to forgetfulness and recollection, to repetition and memory, each falling dead before our eyes, each regaining its immortal wings.

The second reading gives us a different, but not incompatible answer to the same question. What constitutes the wings of desire, the life of truth? We recollect our shorter list, shortened further:

desire
power
truth
memory
magic
madness
menace
nature
technē
poiēsis
Pharmakeia
injustice

May these represent mirrors of each other, infinite, inexhaustible, circulating, broken mirrors of repetitions and differences, limit and unlimit? Here the ambiguous figure of Pharmakeia mirrors knowledge and goodness, signaling the ambiguous general economy of desire's excesses as magic, madness, and *poiēsis*. If desire, power, truth, and *poiēsis* represent unending mirrors of each other, as the first part of *Phaedrus* suggests, then each falls under the spell of Pharmakeia, of that ambiguity in which we cannot tell decisively, cannot tell with *technē*, by rule or law, the difference between good and bad. Under Pharmakeia's spell we cannot distinguish by rule or law good and bad love or desire, good and bad power, justice and injustice, good and bad writing, truth, or representation, true and false science, all mad, all divided by madness. Nor can we tell with either *technē* or *poiēsis*, by rule, by law, cannot tell at all, the inexhaustible and inescapable differences between *technē* and *poiēsis*. *Technē*'s death gives forth *poiēsis*'s truth; *poiēsis*'s *pharmakon* marks *technē*'s injustice. All circulate as life and death. All circulate ambiguously in the economy of life and death, the inexhaustibility of living truth and death.

After we soar to the heavens on mad wings of desire, we fall back into *technē* and law, into law's authority and unending injustice, but not altogether, not as if we had never known, never been disturbed by, the madness of truth, but remember madness and injustice as *erōs* and *pharmakeia*, within *poiēsis*, where *poiēsis* represents *technē*'s injustice. We remember injustice as *hypomnēmasis* and *hypokeimenon*. We remember *pharmakeia* as *technē*, law, as law's and justice's *pharmakeia*, as science's spell. We remember them as injustice and inexhaustibility, as inexhaustible injustice.

What, on such a reading, can we say of science's authority? That its public law represents the death of living truth—an inevitable death? That its rules and laws represent the death of god—an inevitable death? That its accountability represents the death of memory as reminder? We cannot distinguish memory from reminder, as we cannot distinguish life and death, by *technē*, by rule and law, by any repeatable distinction. But not by giving up any thought of difference. Rather, these forms of death, the forms we cannot escape, the forms we live by, represent unending injustice—in justice. We find ourselves endlessly circulating before injustice in justice.

What kind of science might circulate unending injustice as its truth? We take up the obligation to represent our circulation of inexhaustible mirrors as science, not away from science, where *technē* joins *poiēsis* and where *poiēsis* falls back into *technē* for its truth. Our mirrors of desire, power, and knowledge mirror memory, magic, and madness on the one hand, *technē*, *poiēsis*, and *physis* on another, justice and goodness on a third—the three or more hands (or gifts, or spells) of Pharmakeia, all unfolding injustice's danger. We seek science's authority, as we have sought authority here and there, as a juncture of *technē* and *poiēsis*. We seek to absorb, however disruptively and uncomfortably, science, justice, goodness, and law into *technē*, to absorb desire, power, memory, magic, and madness into *poiēsis*, with injustice's danger the point where they meet and fall apart. The figure of this menacing injustice we preserve as Pharmakeia. We may divide this figure by another proximity, in *Phaedrus* between *pharmakeus* and *pharmakos*, between subject as producer, under *technē* and *poiēsis*, however mad or inspired, dangerous or unjust, and subject fallen under oppression, bearer of the injustices of the world, circulating with them throughout history.

X

WITCHES' SCIENCE

In the West, science and magic circulate together, pairing off repeatedly in opposition: science-magic; reason-superstition; truth-untruth; demonstration-ritual; progress-stasis; enlightenment-witchcraft. We have returned Pharmakeia to circulation to disturb the march of these antitheses, disturbing science's idolatry with her witchery, disturbing the hold of *technē* on *poiēsis* in the name of Eurynome, disturbing the complacency of *poiēsis* in the monstrosity of Boreas. In Pharmakeia's circulation, *technē* gives itself to *poiēsis*, magically and superstitiously, then returns. Under the sign of Pharmakeia, science subjects itself to witchcraft even as the circulation of *poiēsis* returns to *technē*.

The movement goes from *Phaedrus* to *The Phenomenology of Spirit*, retracing the themes above save one, that of science as *pharmakon*, of Pharmakeia as witch. We remember that science in Hegel may never arrive on the scene, but comes forth in its circulation.[1] Even so, Hegel can speak of reaching its completeness; and although Spirit's arrival marks its ultimate sacrifice, ambiguously, the ambiguity of arrival and sacrifice, Spirit lacks enchantment. What if Spirit represented enchantment? We might then speak of Absolute Spirit in the voice of Pharmakeia. Or we may speak of Pharmakeia as losing her madness, her sorcery, in Spirit.

Instead, let us pass by Hegel in his memories of Greece to question modern science's authority and law, pass away from Socrates as *pharmakeus* and *pharmakos*, wizard and sacrifice, as embodiment of desire's and truth's excesses, as if that embodiment belonged to one whose unending project, however dangerously and enigmatically, were to know himself, as

253

if self-knowledge, again in Hegel as well as Plato, represented a Subject in Whose Mind Knowledge was written to be recollected, rather than representing the immortal soul present everywhere in nature, in animate and inanimate things, as madness and desire, a Socrates of *erōs* and *mania*.

Let us turn to that side of modern science that circulates its lawfulness in the form of collectivity and anonymity, *technē*'s publicity. Even speaking of a side of science presses us against the possibility that no account of its authority, Hegelian or Humean, can be given authority. In Lyotard's words:

> With modern science . . . It is recognized that the conditions of truth, in other words, the rules of the game of science, are immanent in that game, that they can only be established within the bonds of a debate that is already scientific in nature, and that there is no other proof that the rules are good than the consensus extended to them by the experts.[2]

The possibility of science's autonomy here presupposes epistemic authority. Yet we may imagine the autonomy of science, the self-grounding of scientists' activities, as truth without authority, that is, as self-justification without subjection. What, after Hegel, is called the "problem of reflection" rests on authority, on more than authority, on Reason's superior, overriding authority.

Lyotard tells two "metanarratives" of legitimation, belying the possibility that science might establish its own legitimation—though we may grant that it establishes its own truth: "humanity as the hero of liberty" (Lyotard, *PC*, p. 31); and "philosophy must restore unity to learning" (Lyotard, *PC*, p. 33). Metanarratives authorize and legitimate. We contrast such authorization, if we can, with the possibility of a discourse of truth without authority, lacking authorization, knowing nothing of legitimation, thereby nothing of law and rules. The contrast presents us with a science without authority, even expert, epistemic authority, but with yearning and desire, *erōs, mania*, and *pharmakeia*. What in Lyotard represents Pharmakeia? Certainly neither *savoir* nor *connaissance*: "Knowledge [*savoir*] in general cannot be reduced to science, nor even to learning [*connaissance*]" (Lyotard, *PC*, p. 18). The French language can speak of knowledge divided in opposition, yet cannot capture science's menace and magic. Possibly nothing in Lyotard remembers Pharmakeia. One enters *technē*'s world in opposition.

What of a science without legitimation, without authority? "A science that has not legitimated itself is not a true science; if the discourse that was meant to legitimate it seems to belong to a prescientific form of narrative, like a 'vulgar' narrative, it is demoted to the lowest rank, that of an ideology or instrument of power" (Lyotard, *PC*, p. 38). Lyotard approaches Pharmakeia from a pagan direction:

> when I speak of paganism, I am not using a concept. It is a name, neither better nor worse than others, for the denomination of a situation in which one judges without criteria. And one judges not only in matters of truth, but also in matters of beauty (of aesthetic efficacy) and in matters of justice, that is, of politics and ethics, and all without criteria. That's what I mean by paganism.[3]

Deciding without criteria, judgment or *phronēsis*, *poiēsis* but not *technē*, has a long and powerful history, alongside the history of science, perhaps deciding without authority, thereafter taking on authority. Yet the language of paganism, if equated with postmodernity, speaks of judgment without criteria as if that might become ordinary, routine, at least can be read as such, might circulate without danger and injustice, though Lyotard seems to acknowledge both injustice and danger: "in the stories of Greek and Roman mythology . . . there is ruse, ... Ruse is an activity bound up with the will to power, because the will to power, if the word is to have a meaning, is carried out without criteria" (Lyotard and Thébaud, *JG*, p. 16). Without criteria, but not without danger; justice without criteria, weighed down incessantly by injustice. What, we ask, represents the danger of paganism's injustices—what but the return of criteria within the absence of criteria, the return from *poiēsis* to *technē*, disrupting *technē*'s criteria; what but sorcery within the freedom from rules, the threat of the *pharmakon* to destroy not only rules but itself, destroy truth; what but love's madness as the untruth of truth, the injustice of justice?

What in *Phaedrus* legitimates, what could legitimate, Socrates' truth? What of the possibility that truth demands and receives no legitimation, no authorization, not even in Socrates' voice? What serves as Socrates' metanarrative in *Phaedrus* and how does it pertain to truth's authority? The great speech in which immortal souls stand on the spine of the world subverts its own authority again and again, from immortal souls to the philosopher, from the philosopher to the lover of beauty, from lovers of beauty to ordinary lovers. What legitimates recollection, when recollection cannot be distinguished from reminder? What legitimates the soul's truth when that truth bears its writing on itself? What does the Delphic oracle authorize as self-knowledge except *mania* and *pharmakeia*? What of the authority of Orithyia when, playing with Pharmacia, menaced by Boreas at the creation of the world, sexually assaulted, she gives birth to the world as an act of injustice? What if that represented the menace, the danger, of truth and its authority, the danger that truth might have no authority, but still be truth? What if that represented injustice's danger without the possibility of vengeance?

We wonder at the possibility of a mad, erotic science whose authority vests in *pharmakeia*. We wonder whether science might always, from the beginning, claim its unjust authority by wizardry or witchcraft.[4]

Phaedrus moves away from science as *technē* in the form of self-knowledge, with *erōs* and *philia, mania* and *pharmakeia*. We may hear this rejection as falling upon the self, withdrawing from the public, economic world into private, solitary authority. We may hear it instead to suggest that the withdrawal represents an erotic act between two lovers, that truth belongs to *erōs*, to desire. Here truth belongs less to a subject than to an activity, less to a public, collective activity than to a private but not solitary activity, not solitary at all, but private, together in proximity with love, with charity, circulating under *pharmakeia*'s multifarious heterogeneity.

Without *pharmakeia*, Arendt tells us of the fading of the distinction between private and public.[5] Yet also without slavery, as if slavery did not break apart the distinction between public and private, as if women's restriction to the home did not represent the hold of the public over the private. *Phaedrus*'s private realm of *erōs* does not include the circulation of women or slaves. Yet we can hear *pharmakeia*'s illusions in Arendt's account of freedom:

> The distinctive trait of the household sphere was that in it men lived together because they were driven by their wants and needs. . . .
>
> The realm of the *polis*, on the contrary, was the sphere of freedom; and if there was a relationship between these two spheres, it was a matter of course that the mastering of the necessities of life in the household was the condition for freedom of the *polis*. (Arendt, *HC*, p. 29)

Except for women and slaves, who were either excluded from the realm of freedom or occupied it as witches, *pharmakidos*. We find the realm of freedom in *Phaedrus* in private, where Socrates and Phaedrus play with Pharmakeia. Even so, we may see, in Arendt's understanding of the private, something hidden from most readings of *Republic* organized on the principle of the division of labor: "division of labor is precisely what happens to the laboring activity under conditions of the public realm and what could never have happened in the privacy of the household" (Arendt, *HC*, p. 44). May we read this division of labor and virtue, grounding the organization of Plato's *Republic* as an act of sorcery, brought about by Socrates the greatest *pharmakeus*, making us all sorcerer's apprentices, bringing us before the danger that we cannot distinguish by *technē* between the public and private realms, between science's objectivity and love's magical madness, between restricted and general economy?

Arendt acknowledges this madness as perversity: "Each time we talk about things that can be experienced only in privacy or intimacy, we bring them out into a sphere where they will assume a kind of reality which, their intensity notwithstanding, they never could have had before" (Arendt, *HC*, p. 46). What if truth perversely belonged together with love's madness and intimacy but, when spoken, circulated in public? What if truth belonged to *poiēsis* in private, but circulated with *technē* in public, circulated with Pharmakeia in Boreas's danger? What if we understand that women, like Pharmakeia and Socrates, are witches, that they present to public science the threat that science has no truth but Pharmakeia's, erotic madness and poisonous law? What if the distinction between public and private, even in science, parallels the distinction between *technē* and *poiēsis*, circulating in the form of ambiguities and dangers?

What in modern science represents *pharmakeia*, menace and propaedeutic? What in modern science represents authority's menace and danger? What in modern science respects *technē* as a *pharmakon*? As we speak of the dispersion of the subject-agent into collectives and data banks, do we remember Pharmakeia? Or do they represent another menace and magic?

Let us not leave the individual subject too quickly, as if magic might be performed collectively and comfortably in public. We remember that Socrates and Phaedrus leave the city; we remember Socrates' death in the city. Let us return to the authorization of science as an activity of a knowing subject. We remember Michael Polanyi, reminding us of the importance of the agent where we have no rules, as if science were *poiēsis* rather than *technē*: "An art which cannot be specified in detail cannot be transmitted by prescription, since no prescription for it exists. It can be passed on only by example from master to apprentice."[6] It circulates by example. Polanyi moves against the universality and objectivity of science on one side, challenging its anonymity and impersonality as if science needed no human beings.

It is by his assimilation of the framework of science that the scientist makes sense of experience. This making sense of experience is a skilful act which impresses the personal participation of the scientist on the resultant knowledge. (Polanyi, *PK*, p. 60)

Every act of personal assimilation by which we make a thing form an extension of ourselves through our subsidiary awareness of it, is a commitment of ourselves, a manner of disposing of ourselves. (*PK*, p. 61)

In an extraordinary understanding of this commitment to the unknown and unthinkable in science, to science as *pharmakos* and *pharmakeus*, Polanyi approaches inexhaustibility. "To hold a natural law to be true is to believe that its presence may reveal itself in yet unknown and perhaps yet unthinkable consequences; it is to believe that natural laws are features of a reality which as such will continue to bear consequences inexhaustibly."[7] Perhaps this inexhaustible reality does not come close enough to madness, unreason. Perhaps this inexhaustible reality, mirroring the inexhaustibility of science and truth, of law, remains within *poiēsis* against *technē*, a *technē* of rules, but still the superior authority of science's *poiēsis*, circulates in the illusion of *technē*'s superiority and authority. For, "to learn by example is to submit to authority. You follow your master because you trust his manner of doing things even when you cannot analyse and account in detail for its effectiveness" (Polanyi, *PK*, p. 53). Or does Phaedrus follow Socrates because of love, *erōs* and *philia*, follow him not in spite of but because he knows Socrates as *pharmakeus* and *pharmakos*, deceptive wizard, magical producer, sacrificial loss, because of death?

Why does Polanyi submit us to authority, falling back from *poiēsis* to *technē* under authority, to a certain authority, a good authority with a good master, rather than opposing oppressive authority? Why does the truth of science require, impose, such authority? "When I speak of science I acknowledge both its tradition and its organized authority, and I deny that anyone who wholly rejects these can be said to be a scientist, or have any proper understanding and appreciation of science" (Polanyi, *PK*, p. 164). Can we reject science's authority but affirm the circulation of its tradition—including its authoritarianism, misrepresentations, and injustices? Can we repudiate science's tortured history and lament its authority, its inescapable but always excessive propriety? Must we blind ourselves to the injustices of science's authority and its tradition in order to call ourselves "scientist"? What authority can science have but collective administrative authority, an authority we might not allow an art that reveals itself in "yet unknown and perhaps yet unthinkable" works?

> this group of persons—the scientists—administer jointly the advancement and dissemination of science. They do so through the control of university premises, academic appointments, research grants, scientific journals and the awarding of academic degrees which qualify their recipients as teachers, technical or medical practitioners, and opens to them the possibility of academic appointment. . . . The cultivation of science by society relies on the public acceptance of these decisions as to what science is and who are scientists. (Polanyi, *PK*, pp. 216–17)

What but political authority, in the sphere of science, granted by society to authorize scientists to exercise authority over science, thereby over society? Not persuasion, of a truth we may or may not wish to accept, but an authority vested in an authorized class of masters. "The recognition granted in a free society to the independent growth of science, art and morality, involves a dedication of society to the fostering of a specific tradition of thought, transmitted and cultivated by a particular group of authoritative specialists, perpetuating themselves by co-option" (Polanyi, *PK*, p. 244). A free society depends on both the autonomy of science and its cultivation, authorizing a group of specialists perpetuating themselves.

What danger can justify such circulation of authority without the slightest sense of danger? Polanyi equates fanaticism and skepticism, universal doubt and totalitarianism, claims to acknowledge danger.

> Modern fanaticism [Marxism and Nazism] is rooted in an extreme scepticism which can only be strengthened, not shaken, by further doses of universal doubt. (Polanyi, *PK*, p. 298)[8]

> The attempt made in this book to stabilize knowledge against scepticism, by including its hazardous character in the conditions of knowledge, may find its equivalent, then, in an allegiance to a manifestly imperfect society, based on the acknowledgment that our duty lies in the service of ideals which we cannot possibly achieve. (*PK*, p. 245)

To present the danger, to forestall any evasion of its danger, we ask about the injustice of this imperfection, of the possibility that the ideals we serve may bring about destruction and oppression. What of the injustices, the destructions and oppressions of science and its truths? What of the consequences for the environment and human beings, the injustices of Reason and the injustices perpetrated upon Unreason? What of the danger that science may kill, may maim, may blunt poetic imagination? What of the danger that science's circulation may destroy *poiēsis* with the cut of *technē*?

> in spite of the hazards involved, I am called upon to search for the truth and state my findings. To accept commitment as the framework within which we may believe something to be true, is to circumscribe the hazards of belief. It is to establish the conception of competence which authorizes a fiduciary choice made and timed, to the best of the acting person's ability, as a deliberate and yet necessary choice. (Polanyi, *PK*, p. 315)

Authority again, circumscribing the hazards of commitment, as if the commitment claimed authority without authorization and circumscribed the limits of belief without danger, without *technē*'s danger, as if science might be neither *pharmakeus* nor *pharmakos*, where the latter's death serves as the magical opening within which truth emerges. Can science accept its death as its truth? Can science accept its death as Western truth? "I shall regard the entire culture of a modern, highly articulate community as a form of superior knowledge.... My own appreciation of any 'superior knowledge' within a foreign culture is subject, of course, to my acknowledgment of the superior knowledge of my own culture, and this will have to be allowed for" (Polanyi, *PK*, p. 375). Or does the superior knowledge of any culture belong to *technē*, especially the colonial thrust of the superior knowledge of My Culture over and within a foreign culture, as if that culture's knowledge presupposes my superior authority? The claim of such an authority returns from *poiēsis* to *technē*, to *technē*'s measure, leaving behind as a festering germ of skepticism both *poiēsis*'s unmeasurable truth and the hazard of a truth without authority. We wonder if the uncontrollable dread of skepticism and relativism represents fear of Pharmakeia's witchery. We wonder if Pharmakeia represents disruption of any restricted economy of truth, circulating by exchange and measure, an economy of scientific truth, demanding its authority. We wonder if Pharmakeia marks truth's general economy.

Truth demands authority and submission. "When referring to such superior knowledge we are not laying down standards for judging the persons to whom we attribute this knowledge; we are submitting, on the contrary, to the standards laid down by them for our own guidance"

(Polanyi, *PK*, p. 376). Skepticism presents so great a danger, of a truth without authority, that even within our own commitments to truth, we throw ourselves down before others, submitting to their superior authority as our truth. Remembering Hobbes, we must fear anarchy as the greatest danger, giving ourselves over to authority, fearing skepticism more, as we acknowledge the birth of science against authority. "Once these opponents were defeated, however, the slogan remained and came to imply that the pursuit of science required the repudiation of *all* authority and *all* tradition. It became very misleading at this point, since, as we shall see, the pursuit of science certainly does not and cannot repudiate all authority and tradition."[9]

Science cannot escape tradition and authority; perhaps nothing can. We may not be able to repudiate them, but we may be suspicious, must be suspicious of submission to authority, subjection as tradition. And why such submission, why such subjection, as if truth without authority represented a greater danger than falsehood? What of the danger of authority? What of the injustices of trust? "[W]e must accept the authority of those from whom we would learn, and trust them; and also we must accept science as a valid system of thought, we must believe in science" (Thomson, *TAST*, p. 27). Would we speak of trust and authority if we fully accepted the rational powers of science both to convince and to set limits to its powers? Do we find ourselves forever circulating within the economy defined by Aristotle as *peithō*, the goddess of persuasion and obedience? Can we think of science with the authority only of its truths? "The authority of the scientific interpretation of the world rests on its own intrinsic powers to convince us out of itself of its truth. There is no higher authority to which we can go to judge or prove the scientific interpretation of the world and its ultimate beliefs" (Thomson, *TAST*, p. 39). Science becomes the highest authority in the absence of any higher authority. God refuses to die. The idols march.[10] Even where we recoil before the self-imposed powers of science, we fall under its authority. To appeal to perhaps a greater authority than Polanyi:

> the authority of persons is based ultimately, not on the subjection and abdication of reason, but on recognition and knowledge—knowledge, namely, that the other is superior to oneself in judgment and insight and that for this reason his judgment takes precedence, ie it has priority over one's own.[11]
>
> Thus the recognition of authority is always connected with the idea that what authority states is not irrational and arbi-

trary, but can be seen, in principle, to be true. This is the essence of the authority claimed by the teacher, the superior, the expert. The prejudices that they implant are legitimised by the person himself. (Gadamer, *Truth and Method*, p. 249)

The truth shall be known. What has this to do with authority? What has this to do with personal authority? Socrates denies at every opportunity that he knows anything, that he wishes to be granted authority, as if the authority of knowledge granted a superiority abhorrent to his role as teacher. He stands before us as a teacher without mastery, without superiority, at least artful or technical superiority, belongs to no restricted economy of truth. Though he must frequently demonstrate that he possesses such an authority, he repeatedly repudiates it; moreover, he fails to forestall his death. As against the authority of teacher, superior, expert, Socrates claims the authority of *pharmakeus* and *pharmakos*, claims to teach as one who must die, one who must fail, one whose superiority, like Christ's, remains a sacrifice within its history. Nietzsche can revile both Socrates and Christ because of their sacrifice, because of the masks they wore, because they remain *pharmakon*s for us as artful medicine, to be taken in proper, measured doses. But they remain masked, Dionysian, magical and menacing. For them to circulate artfully belies their truth.

Reading Gadamer again: "At any rate understanding in the human sciences shares one fundamental condition with the continuity of traditions, namely, that it lets itself be addressed by tradition" (Gadamer, *Truth and Method*, p. 251). Science in general, not just the human sciences, lets itself be addressed by tradition suspicious of authority, of authority's oppressions, injustices, and illusions. Alternatively, science lets itself address and be addressed by the oppressions, injustices, and *pharmakon*s of authority, suspicious of tradition, of the oppressive continuity of tradition. We may call this suspicion, today, "genealogy." "Let us give the term *genealogy* to the union of erudite knowledge and local memories which allows us to establish a historical knowledge of struggles and to make use of this knowledge tactically today."[12] Perhaps the difference between hermeneutics and genealogy marks the *pharmakon*, repeating the difference between *technē* and *poiēsis*. For Gadamer seems to agree with Foucault on the subjugation inherent in science's authority. "[T]he successes of modern sciences rest on the fact that other possibilities for questioning are concealed by abstraction."[13] Yet where Foucault seeks insurrection, Gadamer reinstates authority. "[T]here is something else to which we are witness, and which we might describe as an *insurrection of subjugated knowledges*" (Foucault, "Two Lectures," p. 81)[14] "Only a hermeneutical inquiry would legitimate the meaning of these facts and thus the consequences that follow from them" (Gadamer, *PH*, p. 11). Like Polanyi, Gadamer cannot give up authority and legitimacy. We fear the excessive powers authorized to science, excessive powers masking other authorities, respond with continuing suspicion and insurrection, in myriad forms. Consider another understanding from Foucault on the side of science:

> 1. Ideology is not exclusive of scientificity. . . .
>
> . . . .
>
> 3. By correcting itself, by rectifying its errors, by clarifying its formulations, discourse does not necessarily undo its relations with ideology.[15]

Gadamer represents hermeneutics as insurrection in a voice that does not know its own injustices, does not know its own dangers, dares not think of sacrificing itself, dares not face its own limits. "The phenomenon of understanding, then, shows the universality of human linguisticality as a limitless medium that carries *everything* within it . . . because everything (in the world and out of it) is included in the realm of 'understandings' and understandability in which we move" (*PH*, p. 25). Everything, without limit, circulating.

Shall we call this limitlessness, this everything, of language—"German"? Shall we call it—*"Geschlecht"*? We have seen that Heidegger calls it "the gift," at the same time reinscribing language's authority as the mark of The Human in the hand. The gift—of language, speech, or thinking—is not given to animals or machines, but only to "us." To which Lyotard responds, as Derrida never quite brings himself to say, and as we say to set it aside, but primarily to set Heidegger's and Gadamer's German aside in a contaminated relation to authority: "The Heidegger affair is a 'French' affair. One can detest this designation, and I detest it for the geophilosophy it contains and propagates, and which, among others, comes to us (again) through Heidegger, from the present (and probably irremediable) darkening of the universalism of the Enlightenment."[16] Lyotard speaks of "the jews" as what (or who) circulate for us before memory as a signifier of what we find ourselves forever forgetting. This forgetting, for us, belongs to injustice immemorially. We forget, in our justice and law, what we must never forget, our and their injustices.

Why so detest geophilosophy? For its resistances to truth's circulation? For its affirmation of local authority?

The injustice, which we constantly forget and must recall, that so haunts Plato's writings, that haunts *Phaedrus* as *hypomnēmasin*, circulates for us here as the injustice that disappears in science's law, in the reality of science's truth. Let us follow Lyotard's lead for the moment by pursuing the French away from the German, the French fear of authority away from the German respect for authority, the remembrance the French probably wish they could forget, of The Terror, of living and circulating the injustice of the Enlightenment, from Gadamer, for example, to Bachelard where this hidden appears once more, remembering Polanyi. "The belief in reality is essentially the conviction . . . that what is real but hidden has more content than what is given and obvious."[17] This more content of the real but hidden circulates as inexhaustible, dangerously, obliviously inexhaustible; we add that what is given and obvious also circulates inexhaustibly. We may hear as perhaps more French, more unsafe and unjust, another of Bachelard's remarks on reality, moving from a safe to a more menacing sense of reality. "Don't different thoughts of one and the same mind have different co-efficients of reality?"[18] We add a variant to this question: don't different thoughts of reality, don't different realities and different truths of different realities, have different injustices, have inescapable injustices, shifting our allegiances as much as the coefficients of reality?

What coefficients might we forget?

Compare what the witches say, speaking of "professional wisdom": "It seems to us that because there is only one reality, there can be only one real truth and that science describes those facts. Our teachers and our texts affirm this authority of scientific specialists."[19] How does such a single reality work with Polanyi's inexhaustible reality? How can we find ourselves subjected to epistemic authority surrounded by inexhaustibility, remembered and forgotten? How, except through the *pharmakon*, working as *pharmakeus, pharmakos,* and *pharmakis,* sacrificial, dangerous wizard-witches, performing inexhaustible magic and illusion, can we find science's truth, science's spell? How, except where truth itself collapses the distinction between *poiēsis* and *technē*, collapsing the distinction between science and art, science and magic? Can we think of science's inexhaustibility without subjecting ourselves to its illusions and untruths, truth and untruth, without dismantling its authority, without falling under its spell?

Let us speak of science's reason without Pharmakeia. "We believe scientific methods are rational because we believe that they require, and get, criticism of a most far-reaching sort. Science is supposed to be distinguished from religion, metaphysics, and superstition *because* its methods require criticism, test, falsifiability" (Addelson, *IT*, p. 62). Yet if we grant the rationality of science's authority, as critical without superstition, what represents the limits of its self-criticism? Have we imposed an absolute barrier at its limits, marked as objectivity and rationality? Can we recognize the power struggle over these limits?

Some do: "a crucial way in which a discipline maintains its status as 'science' is by manipulating the historical record so that it appears to be the inevitable outcome of the course of inquiry up to that point."[20] We may, against Foucault, and without insurrection, call these "ideologies," "designed to prevent criticism and revision" (Fuller, *SE*, p. 34). Our response to ideology here lacks insurrection, lacks injustice. First, social epistemology defines its project as managerial, entirely under *technē*, without menace or magic:

> The fundamental question of the field of study I call social epistemology is: *How should the pursuit of knowledge be organized, given that under normal circumstances knowledge is pursued by many human beings, each working on a more or less well-defined body of knowledge and each equipped with roughly the same imperfect cognitive capacities, albeit with varying degrees of access to one another's activities?* (Fuller, *SE*, p. 3)

Imperfection and multiplicity lack inexhaustibility, fail to acknowledge authority's oppressions under *technē*'s rule. "[T]he *Authoritarian Theory of Knowledge* . . . in a nutshell . . . says that the rationality of thinking for oneself diminishes as society's knowledge gathering activities expand to the point of requiring a division of cognitive labor into autonomous expertises" (Fuller, *SE*, p. 278). The claim and argument circulate in *technē* with no hint of *poiēsis* or *pharmakon*, love or beauty, sorcery's spell.

The argument continues in technical form: "To what extent is expertise relevant to the sorts of goals which normally cause us to seek knowledge?" (Fuller, *SE*, p. 279). Suppose the answer, after Lysias, were that we seek knowledge to confer benefit and advantage upon ourselves, and that experts represent the most reliable source of such advantages— because they are not mad, insane. Have we forgotten desire? Have we achieved something without truth and goodness because those are contested, always contested, always mirrors of Pharmakeia? What of the possibility that the very role of experts hides from us and themselves the ambiguities of Pharmakeia, repudiating *pharmakeus* and *pharmakos*, thereby becoming, in the form of scientific expertise, wizards and deceivers, promulgating overweening authority far beyond any legitimate or possible authority; becoming wizards awaiting sacrifice while constantly protesting against their sacrifice, against their injustices?

Here we may grant the exceptional role taken up by feminist critiques of science, by the witches, beyond social epistemology within its frame of reference, since those who speak have been excluded. "I will use the notion of cognitive authority to argue that making scientific activity more rational requires that criticizing and testing social arrangements in science be as much a part of scientific method as criticizing and testing theories and experiments" (Addelson, *IT*, p. 65). First the critique of cognitive authority belongs to science's rationality, belongs to its authority—with what consequences for science and reason?

> prestige hierarchies, power within and without the scientific professions, and the social positions of researchers themselves affect which group can exercise cognitive authority. Thus these features of social arrangements play a major role in determining . . . what counts as a legitimate scientific problem and solution. In the end, they affect how we all understand the nature of our world and our selves. (Addelson, *IT*, p. 65)

Feminist social epistemology tells that what we know of the world and reason depends on the social configurations of authority and practice, that the very form of objectivity in science masks rule and oppression, masks injustice in the form of truth. This tale intimately relates to Foucault's claim that "'Truth' is linked in a circular relation with systems of power which produce and sustain it, and to effects of power which it induces and which extend it. A 'régime' of truth"[21] Science does not lack objectivity, but objectivity circulates in a régime of power and authority, presenting us with a certain view of the world. What science knows of the world reflects an organizing hierarchy of authority, an *unexamined* authority. "It is the *unexamined* exercise of cognitive authority within our present social arrangements that is most to be feared. Illegitimate politicization and rampant irrationality find their most fruitful soil when our activities are mystified and protected from criticism" (Addelson, *IT*, p. 80).

In a moment of hesitation, Addelson seems to suggest that a more self-critical scientific rationality, a social scientific rationality, might save reason from its blindness. Of course, greater self-criticism will protect us from oversights—under *technē*. Self-criticism could do nothing if blindness were endemic, if science were *pharmakeus*, anarchical, as Addelson suggests ethics may be: "The solution is to admit that morality takes place *in media res*, not making judgments in one's private conscience. Anarchist ethics [without law or rule] is for people out in the world working together" (Addelson, *IT*, p. 152). If we assimilate this view of ethics to science, anarchical science, without rule or law, then *in media res* means in the witchery of lived, historical practices, where authority may be proposed and achieved but imposes itself upon us always exceeding any achievement. We find science assimilated to *praxis* in excessive anarchical ambiguity, where objectivity means subjugation.

This subjugation rules in private, in sexual and erotic subjugation, where women and children experience the full public force of Objectivity, the Force of Law, not of course alone, for men experience objectivity's public subjugations also, men of color, of different backgrounds, and "white" men of "the same" background, the pervasiveness of injustice. Yet feminist witches present to science and the public realm the challenge that public freedom in its nature subjugates and oppresses in private. That marks the heinous truth of slavery and colonialism, something classical Marxism knows but seems unable to say given its emphasis on the public, the proletariat, even in Engels's famous paper on the family, that the private realm represents where the experience of oppression falls most harshly and most silently—realms of gender and sexuality, repeated in domestications of class and race. Socrates and Phaedrus meet in private, meet erotically, in an event of truth, where the entire happening, private, erotic, and truthful, replays Orithyia's rape, madness and magic, sorcery and disruption, within the space between *poiēsis* and *technē*, a space filled with *pharmakeia*, with *erōs* and *philia*, with sexuality and gender, where female children and women circulate as repetitive objects of injustice.[22]

Listen to Pharmakeia speaking in Arendt's voice: "The only efficient way to guarantee the darkness of what needs to be hidden against the light of publicity is private property, a privately owned place to hide in" (Arendt, *HC*, p. 63). A privately owned place in which to commit atrocities, predominantly against women and children, but in other worlds against slaves and household servants, even against one's own factory workers. Arendt's wonderful account of the public "realm of freedom" needs to be tempered by the injustices of the private realm of *erōs*:

> the reality of the public realm relies on the simultaneous presence of innumerable perspectives and aspects in which the common world presents itself and for which no common measurement or denominator can ever be devised. (Arendt, *HC*, p. 52)

> Being seen and being heard by others derive their significance from the fact that everybody sees and hears from a different position. (p. 52)

> The end of the common world has come when it is seen only under one aspect and is permitted to present itself in only one perspective. (p. 53)

The heterogeneity of the common world may appear under such masks as to obscure the subjugation of the private realm, of women and children. The heterogeneity presents itself as another injustice, another authoritarian injustice.[23]

The threat of feminist criticism of science presents the possibility that science's practices subjugate women. The next step extends that critique from the West to its non-Western others, suggesting that science's hegemony subjugates non-Western forms of knowledge at the same time that it subjugates non-Western peoples and ways of life. This critique does not belie science's effectiveness or expertise, does not ask us to repudiate science, but calls upon us to acknowledge the injustices of its techniques, the dangers of the most "enlightened" forms of knowledge, menaces that haunt various economies of knowledge, instrumental and technical, anarchical or social.

How far-reaching is this critique, for the moment feminist critique? Does it belong to *technē*, does it direct itself at "bad" science or at science's rationality? Does it seek improvement of science or does it hope to transform the way in which we think of science?

> What, one may ask (and, as feminists know, many have), has feminism to say about—what *could* feminism have to say about—physics (or chemistry, mathematics, or logic)? Physics, after all, seems pure of any content that would (or could) be affected by sex-gender and politics.
>
> There are two short answers to the question. The most obvious is *we simply don't know yet.*[24]

We don't know. Could we ever know, satisfactorily and truthfully, and what would such knowledge tell? What happens to the *pharmakon*, to *pharmakeus* and *pharmakos*, when we achieve such knowledge? And why would we wish to do so? "[W]ould it be *good news* if it turned out that only physics, mathematics, logic, chemistry, or whatever, show no evidence of our experiences of politics and sex/gender? Are we willing to say 'if physics is all right, so is science'? . . . Does it save science?" (Nelson, *WK*, p. 250). Perhaps these women are witches, feminist women, Lynn Nelson and Kathryn Addelson, as Socrates was *pharmakeus* and as so many women were *pharmakidos*, burned as witches. Perhaps, as Socrates may have begun an epoch of magic that made a *pharmakos* of magic, of the *pharmakon*, in the name of Reason, issues of sexual difference and gender may, with other differences, historical and cultural differences, open another epoch of knowledge and science, may lay another spell on truth, a spell that questions the sorcerer's authority over his apprentice except as authority's sorcery, a sorcery of masks and difference, remembering that "we are difference, that our reason is the difference of discourses, our history the difference of times, our selves the differences of masks" (Foucault, *Archaeology of Knowledge*, p. 131)

Asked about the masked, irrational element in his analysis of politics and truth, the *pharmakon*, whether it destroys any rational politics, Foucault responded with the following question: "Are we all not too familiar with the kind of politics which answers in terms of thought or consciousness, in terms of pure ideality or psychological traits, when one speaks to it of a practice, of its conditions, of its rules, of its historical transformations?"[25] We hope to bring to light the subjugated and hidden injustices of Truth and Justice. We hope thereby to embark upon another politics, not one that would reinstate Reason's Truth, another justice, as if without injustice, without Dionysus, without masks, as if any authority might be without masked injustice. We hope to "save science" as we "save politics"—if anything could destroy them—as truthful and good, promulgating authority, yet profoundly suspicious of the ever-present, inescapable, menacing injustice of their excessive authority, suspicious of their hold on what exceeds them. We hope to save science under science's spell, belonging to the inexhaustible gods.

In a striking figure commemorating a famous image in Kant, Nelson calls science to our attention as an edifice. "For Descartes, the 'edifice of science' was an inverted pyramid, secured by 'certain truth' at its base, and growing, by cumulative and certain steps, themselves inexorably determined (without failures of our wills) by a logic inherent to inquiry, and evidence that announced itself" (Nelson, WK, p. 309). Against this edifice, she speaks, like Addelson, of another rationality. "[W]e cannot reasonably maintain the view that politics and sex/gender have nothing to do with science—either good science or bad" (Nelson, WK, pp. 311–12). The good and bad science take us back to *technē*, though Nelson rejects such a return in her discussion of physics, rejects the view that "feminist criticism is properly directed only at bad science" (Nelson, WK, p. 249). To the contrary, the two questions she asks of such criticism, whether we know with certainty that physics and chemistry cannot be divided by sexual and gender difference, and whether it would be better if they were not, circulate as witches' questions, where we may never know in the sense that the questions break down the hierarchy, the edifice of science, in which the edifice's injustices come to the fore. Sandra Harding speaks of this breakdown as instability: "we can learn how to . . . find in the instability itself the desired theoretical reflection of certain aspects of the political reality in which we live and think; to use these instabilities as a resource for our thinking and practices. No 'normal science' for us!"[26]

We remind ourselves of Kant's own edifice and plan, reading the alternative not as tragic but as magic:

> We have found, indeed, that although we had contemplated building a tower which should reach to the heavens, the supply of materials suffices only for a dwelling-house just sufficiently commodious for our business on the level of experience, and just sufficiently high to allow of our overlooking it. The bold undertaking that we had designed is thus bound to fail through a lack of material.[27]

At this extraordinary point in the First *Critique* Kant suggests that we may fail to reach the heavens, the supersensible, due to lack of material rather than to the project's aporia. Kant's continuation returns us to Nelson's figure of witchcraft: "not to mention the babel of tongues, which inevitably gives rise to disputes among the workers in regard to the plan to be followed, and which must end by scattering them over all the world, leaving each to erect a separate building for himself, according to his own design" (Kant, *Critique of Pure Reason*, p. 573). Locality, relativity, individuality, subjectivity all enter this figure. But so does authority, for we remember one god's response to a comparable edifice:

> And the Lord came down to see the city and the tower, which the children of men builded. And the Lord said, Behold, the people *is* one, and they have all one language; and this they begin to do; and now nothing will be restrained from them, which they have imagined to do. (Genesis 1.5–6)

There can be no one language and no one edifice of reason or sovereignty, not because human beings are many, divided and fragmentary, but because language, meaning, reason, and truth circulate as divided and fragmentary, inexhaustible, magical and excessive. If we understand science's truth to belong to *technē*, it belongs as *poiēsis*'s displacement, through magic and deceit, through masks, as *pharmakon*, *pharmakeus*, *pharmakis*, and *pharmakos*. The witches lead us, not to a better science, rid of its technical defects, rid of blindness to its social and human biases, but to a science scattered over the world, divided and broken, mischievously dispersed, by witches and demons, monkeys and squirrels, scattered upon the ground.

If authority's injustice inescapably falls upon us, we receive it by disputing its sovereignty, the sovereignty of its domination, scattering its authority everywhere. "[T]he relationships we have explored indicate that a different science and a different society will come about together, if at all. A different science will not be *the result* or by-product of a different kind of society, but part and parcel of any such society coming to be" (Nelson, *WK*, p. 316). A different science and a different society, both weighed down by the broken edifice of sovereign authority, seeking to scatter authority everywhere, seeking to tear down the impotent tower representing truth's might.

We ask again, perhaps with greater irony, would it be good news that science might be objective, that politics might be by rule? What goodness of rules except by *technē*, except by another rule? What better science might take up the witches' critique—better or another injustice? What *technē* except one magically transformed by *poiēsis*, transformed into a *pharmakon*, where we cannot tell, decisively by rule, the difference between good and bad science, because they play on the field of contested truths, where we cannot tell even in ourselves, for ourselves, the truth? This sets the limit to relativism, finally, that it gives itself a nonrelativistic, unmagical, un-self-deceived economy of truth.

What if all knowledge, especially science, circulated with desire and magic as *pharmakon*? Would that make science more or less dangerous? Would it make truth more or less fearsome? What if, as the witches say, science judged by taste, a recipe, a *pharmakon*, a witches' brew? What kind of society, what kind of politics, knows the responsibility of truth's danger, of its witchcraft? Surely not one that would deny its truth, deny the immense, irretrievable danger of denying its truth. Rather, after Socrates in *Phaedrus* again, we take responsibility, take up the debt, for Pharmakeia as she plays on the dangerous shores between *technē* and *poiēsis* in the name of art, between poetry and philosophy, first by insisting on the *erōs* that gives life to knowledge, poetry or science, then on the *technē* that gives justice to *poiēsis*, that returns from poetry's wandering to the desperate needs of the *polis*.

Pharmakeia's play belongs to mischief, magic and enchantment, first giving life to *technē*, as if *technē* were always dead, then giving mischief to mischief, to *poiēsis*, expressing the mischief of her play, refusing it privilege as if *technē*. It follows for science that, like Socrates, we fall away from *technē* into *poiēsis* as truth's spell, the *erōs* and *philia* whose madness speaks and acts against the dangers of *technē*'s deadness, urges us to rise up against the oppressions of its injustices, thereafter recognizing another injustice, another danger, belonging to *poiēsis*, that it wanders forever, bringing us to the collapse of the Tower of Babel.

And this Tower, with its ruin, does it collapse the edifice of public building, *poiēsis* or *technē*, collapse the economy of public science? Does this science's objectivity free it from injustice as the very edifice of objectivity imposed injustices on the witches, who fought back again and again, calling for us to remember the rape of Orithyia as immemorial injustice as we remember her founding of the world as *poiēsis* where we hope to remember science's law? Orithyia's rape forces us to know the truth of nature and its sciences as another rape, unending, immemorial rape, where that rape, its destruction and sacrifice, circulates with sorcery and witchcraft, as if nothing were innocent, certainly not science or *technē*, nor *poiēsis*, as if even innocence were unjust, circulating *technē*'s justice as science and law together with *poiēsis*'s injustice and rule.

With the *pharmakon* we return to think of science's authority in the shadow of its injustices without giving up its truth, without repudiating its authority, like Socrates acknowledging the limits of that authority as a moment of enchantment.

Consider when Dewey refuses science the authority of the *logos*, granting it but local authority derived from local activities: "all logical forms (with their characteristic properties) arise within the operation of inquiry and are concerned with control of inquiry so that it may yield warranted assertions."[28] What kind of warrant?—proximate, local warrant, belonging to a situation, derived from ongoing practices. "The problem reduced to its lowest terms is whether inquiry can develop in its own ongoing course the logical standards and forms to which *further* inquiry shall submit" (Dewey, *Logic*, p. 5). Such a self-origination represents modernity, and Dewey in this sense is modern, characterized by a hypothetical rather than dogmatic temperament.

Why, we ask, should further inquiry submit to the standards of past inquiry, continuing to circulate within one economy? Why should science build an edifice upon the foundation of past investigations, rather than allowing for the coexistence of many dispersed and heterodox, subjugated knowledges? Why must the language of science, in so nonauthoritarian a philosopher as Dewey, speak in a voice of authority and subjection?

Dewey tells of the inescapable locality of inquiry and logic, throws us into history, tells that further inquiry has no standards and forms but the ones that have emerged, historically and locally, from past inquiry, in a language without injustice and danger, without Pharmakeia. Like Lyotard, he represents inquiry as without criteria but circulating in time, as pagan in Lyotard's sense, a pagan science, yet as if we might tolerate science's paganism only because without danger, without injustice.[29] The progressive, operational, hypothetical, natural, and social characteristics of logic and inquiry mark their locality, mark a locality entailing a certain inexhaustibility, but perhaps not the menacing, painful inexhaustibility of injustice, not Pharmakeia's pain. For the autonomy of logic seems, in a representation of modernity's reflexivity, to counter the disruptive economy of the others. "Logic as inquiry into inquiry is, if you please, a circular process; it does not depend upon anything extraneous to inquiry" (Dewey, *Logic*, p. 20). Dewey explains what he means by autonomy, as if the circle might be closed without danger.[30] Dewey approaches the abyss and recoils, a mark of his temperament: "The mystery of time is thus the mystery of real individuals. It is a mystery because it is a mystery that anything which exists is just what it is" (Dewey, "Time and Individuality," p. 240). May we add the abysmal mystery of abyssal injustice, add that the uncertainty, indeterminacy, and contingency of individuality pertain to judgment and truth, to creativity and novelty, so that we cannot regulate, control by rule, and cannot regulate our own failures, as we cannot avoid regulation? To succeed is to fail. To judge is to fail. To fail is to run the risk of not knowing one has failed. The madness of the *pharmakon* is that, in practice, we cannot tell truth from untruth, liberation from oppression, except locally, requiring another mad judgment without criteria. Untruth and truth, injustice in justice, circulate together. All the dangers that make us turn to *technē* to save us circulate within it, within science, as we return from the uselessness of *poiēsis* to bring *pharmakeia* into *technē*.

That is what we may hear in Dewey, though it appears to echo there in silence. *"Inquiry is the controlled or directed transformation of an indeterminate situation into one that is so determinate in its constituent distinctions and relations as to convert the elements of the original situation into a unified whole"* (Dewey, *Logic*, pp. 104–5). Dewey offers the apotheosis of a local *technē*, a compelling view of a *technē* without authority, or with but hypothetical authority. Yet the language continues to resonate within the circle of *technē* without *poiēsis*, away from the abyss: control, direction, determinateness, unification. If we read each of these terms as mad, dangerous, and magical, filled with Pharmakeia's witchcraft and ambiguities, the possibility of inquiry's profound injustices comes to the fore—a possibility unimagined by Dewey.[31]

The possibility emerges of a science without method or criteria, not a science safe without regulation and rule, not a science authoritative in spite of the absence of rule, but a science whose technicalities place it in profound danger. The witches tell that women, among countless others, have fallen under science's oppressions, that science's anonymity marks profound injustice, that the very truth of science, physics' as well as anthropology's truth, perpetrates injustice, injustice upon women and men, injustice upon truth and knowledge: the subjugation of knowledges, the oppression of reason. The one thing missing in Dewey represents what is hypothetical and multifarious in time, individuality, and experience as meeting at a point of injustice in justice and truth. The subjugation of justice as injustice; the subjugation of truth as untruth, the movement of Pharmakeia.[32] May we hear the injustice of intelligence's *technē* echoing in this helpful? "[T]he choice is not between throwing away rules previously developed and sticking obstinately by them. The intelligent alternative is to revise, adapt, expand and alter them. The problem is one of continuous, vital readaptation" (Dewey, *Human Nature and Conduct*, pp. 239–40). The danger circulates as continuous improvement, however local and hypothetical, as if every better might not present a supreme danger, illusion. Locality's danger as inexhaustibility circulates as intelligence's injustice.[33]

Whitehead understands the clash of differences among individuals as evil.[34] We pursue this theme of evil into the injustice of science's authority, encountering another authority. "The doctrine of necessity in universality means that there is an essence to the universe which forbids relationships beyond itself, as a violation of its rationality. Speculative philosophy seeks that essence."[35] Necessity repeats authority twice, first as closure of the universe around its rationality, second as philosophy's necessity. Reason's closure leads to God in a certain way, spoken of in a voice far from witches and wizards. "God is the ultimate limitation, and His existence is the ultimate irrationality. . . . No reason can be given for the nature of God, because that nature is the ground of rationality."[36] Even as Whitehead revised his account of God, supplementing his primordial nature, unconditioned by any temporal conditions, by his consequent nature, dependent on the temporal world, he kept this ultimate irrationality at the limits of reason, defining rationality, never imagining the evil of an arbitrary order to the universe or of a rationality that demands such an order. We may imagine bewitching both the consequent nature of God, responding to the individuality of events, and the primordial nature of God, at each moment an order responsive to the individuality of events, another adaptation.[37] Evil and injustice may remain unthought even here, remain unthought as in Dewey, unless we take the temporality and adaptability of God in response to the world to represent monstrosity and injustice, unless we think with Pharmakeia of the "necessary goodness" (Whitehead, *PR*, p. 345), "wisdom" (*PR*, p. 346), and "tenderness" (*PR*, p. 346) of God, of their monstrous deceit.

How might we think of such monstrosity in relation to science? First, reason represents both truth and untruth, however enigmatically: "In its turn every philosophy will suffer a deposition. But the bundle of philosophic systems expresses a variety of general truths about the universe, awaiting coordination and assignment of their various spheres of validity" (Whitehead, *PR*, p. 7). We add science to philosophy and conflict and heterogeneity to the variety of general truths. "If science is not to degenerate into a medley of *ad hoc* hypotheses, it must become philosophical and must enter upon a thorough criticism of its own foundations" (Whitehead, *SMW*, p. 24). We may hear this as founding or disruption. We confront science's *technē* with *poiēsis*. "I hold that the ultimate appeal is to naïve experience and that is why I lay such stress on the evidence of poetry" (Whitehead, *PR*, p. 125). "It should be the task of the philosophical schools of this century to bring together the two streams into an expression of the world-picture derived from science, and thereby end the divorce of science from the affirmations of our aesthetic and ethical experiences" (Whitehead, *SMW*, p. 218). We add, after Heidegger's critique of the Age of the World-Picture, the evils of concrete experience and the injustices of the marriage between poetry and science. "Wherever we have the world picture, an essential decision takes place regarding what is, in its entirety. The being of whatever is, is sought and found in the representedness of the latter."[38] This recognition belongs to philosophy, which "can exclude nothing."[39] The critique of science against its divorce from experience saves it against the dogmatism of its *technē*. "Religion should connect the rational generality[40] of philosophy with the emotions and purposes springing out of existence in a particular society, in a particular epoch, and conditioned by particular antecedents. . . . " (Whitehead, *PR*, p. 15)

Speaking of Wordsworth and Shelley, Whitehead asks: "Is it not possible that the standardised concepts of science are only valid within narrow limitations, perhaps too narrow for science itself?" (Whitehead, *SMW*, p. 118). Perhaps we find science always too narrow for science itself. Perhaps *technē* must fail its own projects unless it gives itself over to a *poiēsis* that destroys it, or threatens it while promoting it. For "Beauty is a wider, and more fundamental, notion than Truth"[41] reflecting the injustice and transitoriness of the rule of law. "Thus a system of 'laws' determining reproduction in some portion of the universe gradually rises into dominance; it has its stage of endurance, and passes out of existence with the decay of the society from which it emanates" (Whitehead, *PR*, p. 91); "there is disorder in the sense that the laws are not perfectly obeyed, and that the reproduction is mingled with instances of failure" (ibid.). If this language echoes obedience, the authority vested in natural laws doubly rules incompletely. We remember evil. And we remember time.

> Modern science has imposed on humanity the necessity for wandering. Its progressive thought and its progressive technology make the transition through time, from generation to generation, a true migration into uncharted seas of adventure. The very benefit of wandering is that it is dangerous and needs skill to avert evils. We must expect, therefore, that the future will disclose dangers. It is the business of the future to be dangerous; and it is among the merits of science that it equips the future for its duties. (Whitehead, *SMW*, p. 291)

It is the business of the future to be dangerous; science equips the future for its duties—and its dangers. "I put forward as a general definition of civilization, that a civilized society is exhibiting the five qualities of Truth, Beauty, Adventure, Art, Peace" (Whitehead, *Adventures of Ideas*, p. 353). If we add that civilization here includes every society, every tribe, every adventure; that these are not human only, but that human beings disclose them in nature, we approach valor's injustice in justice. Peace treasures practice in the circulation of injustice, treasures practice—truth, beauty, adventure, and art—as justice's restitution for immemorial injustice. Truth, beauty, adventure, art, and peace represent the play of Pharmakeia, her monstrous, dangerous, joyful play.

Danger represents the business of the future, and science, within the future, belongs to that danger. Whitehead speaks of science equipping the future, as *technē*, but he also speaks of it as imposing wandering, threatening danger. Science belongs to danger, represents monstrosity, as and because it equips us to meet danger. Science, *technē*, belongs to the future as *poiēsis*, brings about the future in its monstrosity, brings forth that future as *technē*, brings *poiēsis* back upon *technē* as its life, its *erōs*, its madness and danger, its evils and injustices.

What, then, but a wandering science, from *technē* to *poiēsis* to elsewhere and back again, circulating in the magic of Pharmakeia, in the excesses of *mania*, so mad, so excessive, so magically deceptive and masked, that *technē* cannot hold the line against *poiēsis*, that *poiēsis* falls back into *technē* for its efficacy, falls away from monstrosity into subjection, into authority, whose injustice returns us to wandering? What but a dangerous, monstrous science? What but a monstrous economy of *technē* and *poiēsis* to represent the dangerous plenitude of nature, the circulation of order and disorder?

What but reason's limits?

> The thesis that I am developing conceives "proof," in the strict sense of that term, as a feeble second-rate procedure. Whenever the word "proof" has been uttered, the next notion to enter the mind is "half-heartedness." Unless proof has produced self-evidence and thereby rendered itself unnecessary, it has issued in a second-rate state of mind. (Whitehead, *Modes of Thought*, p. 66)

We interpret this self-evidence as kin to Socrates' self-knowledge, cousins of *poiēsis* and *technē* but married to Pharmakeia. By the authority of what law, if not Pharmakeia's law, if not an arbitrary law with arbitrary authority that grounds the faith in reason, the faith in *technē*, an arbitrary authority borrowed from *poiēsis* assigned to *technē*? Pharmakeia again!

Where does *pharmakeia*, where do magic and madness, fall upon us who live in modern times, with modern technology? Shall we hear the call of the *Gestell* as falling on one side or the other of *poiēsis* and *technē*? How can we avoid reading Heidegger as privileging *poiēsis*, as if it might free itself from *technē*, as if it might be supreme over *technē*?

With Pharmakeia by our side, we may question Heidegger about the *Gestell*, especially the destiny of the *Gestell*, its *Geschick*, question Heidegger's questioning of modern technology and science. We remember Vattimo's rendering of *Verwindung* as destiny, yielding, and overcoming.[42] This destiny seems to give privilege to history, to our fallenness into time as *Geschick*, to which we must somehow resign ourselves, as if that falling and resignation were not themselves ekstatic, away from themselves, put away by Pharmakeia.

In "The Origin of the Work of Art," Heidegger asks about the possibility of art still inaugurating, still founding, another historical epoch, or whether in the *Gestell*, as Hegel suggests, such a possibility comes to an end. "The question remains: is art still an essential and necessary way in which that truth happens which is decisive for our historical existence, or is art no longer of this character?"[43] We recoil from the privilege granted to art, turning to other happenings of truth, only to find science denied. "[S]cience is not an original happening of truth, but always the cultivation of a domain of truth already opened, specifically by apprehending and confirming that which shows itself to be possibly and necessarily correct within that field" (Heidegger, "Origin of the Work of Art," pp. 61–62)[44] We ask two questions of this refusal of science: (1) With what privilege, with what authority, can we speak of science's failing except *technē*'s authority, without *poiēsis*, a science without *poiēsis*, and what of Pharmakeia, what of the illusions, the masks, that divide *technē* from *poiēsis*? (2) Can we speak of being caught within the *Gestell*, marked by modern technology, by *technē*, without speaking of, accepting, our destiny, without granting a certain privilege to "our" destiny, without authorizing both *Geschick* and *Geist*?

And if we, beside Pharmakeia, release the love and madness that break up the barrier between *poiēsis* and *technē*, a barrier whose very authority and strength undermines its own authority, *alētheia*'s authority, what possibility remains of refusing science truth as we refuse it authority? With what masks do we repudiate science in the *Gestell*? What kind of science? With what truth's authority?

We hope to think of modern technology and science through thinking of the essence of *technē*. We come to *poiēsis*: "Technology is therefore no mere means. Technology is a way of revealing. If we give heed to this, then another whole realm for the essence of technology will open itself up to us. It is the realm of revealing, i.e., of truth."[45] *"Technē* belongs to bringing-forth, to *poiēsis*; it is something poetic" (Heidegger, *QT*, p. 294). Heidegger, like Phaedrus (but not *Phaedrus*), understands *technē* in proximity to *poiēsis*, a thinking that "strikes us as strange" (ibid.), but not perhaps a mad, erotic strangeness, filled with witchcraft. For "the revealing that holds sway throughout modern technology does not unfold into a bringing-forth in the sense of *poiēsis*" (*QT*, p. 296). How, we may ask, can modern technology avoid *poiēsis*? And from what point of view might we imagine that it could except that of a *technē* without *poiēsis*, Lysias's *technē*? "Everywhere everything is ordered to stand by, to be immediately on hand, indeed to stand there just so that it may be on call for a further ordering. Whatever is ordered about in this way has its own standing. We call it the standing-reserve [*Bestand*]" (Heidegger, *QT*, p. 298). We call the claim of this standing-reserve *"Gestell"* [enframing]: "Enframing means the gathering together of that setting-upon that sets upon man, i.e., challenges him forth, to reveal the real, in the mode of ordering, as standing-reserve" (Heidegger, *QT*, p. 302). In a language, a voice, of essence that goes back to the forgetfulness with which this enframing sets itself upon the earth, Heidegger remembers its forgetfulness at the same time that this enframing forgets the *pharmakon* disturbing the space between *poiēsis* and *technē*. The between, the ambiguity between, *poiēsis* and *technē* circulates as an oblivion in the setting forth of standing-reserve, except for the absence, the forgetfulness and exclusion, madness and magic, of what cannot be accepted within the privilege of the *Geschick* of *Geist*.

The proximity of *technē* with *poiēsis* falls away into *technē*, a doubled and triple *technē*, where the instrumentality of things repeats itself as the advantage of things over their disadvantage, ordering against their disordering, *technē* against *poiēsis*, a proximity at war, repeated in Heidegger. For the proximity lacks madness, lacks the madness of *erōs*, derived from the gods as sorcery and magic, lacks the ambiguity of the mad economy of science's truth and *technē*'s advantage, goodness and justice ambiguously undermined by *pharmakeia*'s injustice, truth's untruth. "Modern science's way of representing pursues and entraps nature as a calculable coherence of forces.... sets nature up to exhibit itself as a coherence of forces calculable in advance, ..." (Heidegger, *QT*, pp. 302–3). Shall we give this in advance, this temporality, over to *technē*, or shall we reaffirm its *ekstasis*, its mobility and deceptiveness, in this way of thinking of modern science? Do we hear in this thought of modern science a thought *away* from modern science's *technē* or its repetition? Have we allowed ourself to recognize the *poiēsis* in science's *technē*, thereby magically destroying this view of science? Shall we listen to the in advance as immemoriality or as destiny, as a *Geschick* of *Geist* or as its disruption?

We hope to question the coherence of this view of calculation from the standpoint of *pharmakeia*'s *poiēsis*, especially as physics, *physis*'s truth. This disruption of physics as *pharmakeia* belongs together with the disruption of technology, not as instrumental projection, domination over time, but as filled with time's danger, menace. This menace, this menace of *poiēsis* in the play of *pharmakeia*, rings against instrumentality, calculation, and measure—an against that plays its own games with *pharmakeia*.

Can such a play be heard in Heidegger? "Hence physics, in its retreat from the kind of representation that turns only to objects, which has been the sole standard until recently, will never be able to renounce this one thing: that nature reports itself in some way or other that is identifiable through calculation and that it remains orderable as a system of information" (Heidegger, *QT*, p. 304). Will never renounce; will always remain orderable. Who can speak in such a voice but one who calculates and measures, who renounces *erōs*? Who can speak in such a voice but one who relinquishes *poiēsis* to *technē* without a return? "The essence of technology, as a destining of revealing, is the danger. The transformed meaning of the word 'enframing' will perhaps become somewhat more familiar to us now if we think enframing in the sense of destining and danger" (Heidegger, *QT*, p. 309). Here Heidegger does not warn us of a danger from which he will save us, but tells us of a danger that belongs to the *Gestell* as mysterious enframing. We add that *pharmakeia* represents the danger, circulates it as mysterious and magical, as madness and destruction, also as healing. But destiny! How can we give ourselves to danger's destiny without giving up too much of its magic? What might represent the upsurgence of the saving power if not technology and science, *poiēsis* and *technē*, the dance of Pharmakeia?

XI

JUSTICE'S INJUSTICE

If the history of philosophy, Western philosophy, lies in the shadow of Plato,[1] the Platonic dialogues lie in the shadow of Socrates, his trial and death. The Western tradition circulates under three memorable injustices, oblivious to countless others: one to Socrates; the second to Christ, repeated today, after Nietzsche, as we again kill God; the third, proclaiming the superior truth of Western justice, the rule of law. These injustices mark the inescapability of our subjection to injustice—and to justice. We remember Socrates, but we forget our own injustices, our countless injustices, forget that we belong to Athens even where not European, Western.

Listen to an aboriginal story:

MUSA WO

There was a fellow long ago who married many wives. They were all giving birth to these children. One woman remained pregnant for forty years. So the man drove her from town.

She had only one machete and she cut the bush with it. Then she built a small hut there. She was there for one full year. One day she went to cut wood in order to cook and eat cassava. Then the child in her stomach said, "Mother, don't split the wood. Drop the machete on your knee."

So this woman dropped the machete on her knee, and a boy jumped out. He was completely grown, and he had a beard. She asked, "Hey, child, what's your name?"

Things went on like that. Then a fellow chief had his daughter initiated in the Sande Society and gave her to him. The night she arrived and joined the man in his house, the Troublemaker came again. He said, "I've just had your future divined. It is said that you should sacrifice a Sande initiate. They say that will prolong your life."

"Aah," he said, "but how will we do it?"

He said, "They say that once you have killed her you should bury her in your own house. You should set a red bucket at the head of her grave." So the Troublemaker provoked this and they killed the child.

That very night he walked back to visit the girl's father. He told him, "Your child whom you recently initiated into Sande—the one you gave to this man—this very night, just after they had lain together, he killed her! He buried her in the house and set a red bucket at the head of the grave. She's there. She died there."

I've heard that little story, and I've told it.[2]

Summarizing Musa Wo's features in Western form:

> He is a deposed royal aspirant. He is miraculous in birth and abilities, and full of righteous indignation and plans of revenge, both for the sake of his wronged mother and in pursuit of his rightful place in the succession. But in achieving these ends he becomes an amoral monster, an unrestrained psychopath who murders his own creations. He is Hero and Trickster. (Consentino, "Midnight Charter," p. 28)

This figure, Musa Wo, recalls the figure of the *pharmakon* (*pharmakeus* if not *pharmakos*) in the form of unending injustices. With this figure, we subject ourselves to the project we have undertaken, to bring this magical and immemorial injustice back to *technē*, as virtue and truth, as *aretē*, to speak of ethics and politics in the circulation of life and death, as charity, sacrifice, and valor. Musa Wo joins *pharmakeus* and *pharmakos*, *poiēsis* and *technē*, witchcraft and science, at a point of sacrifice where these conjunctions represent a certain repetition, identity, a disruption of the Same, to tell of charity and valor, good and evil without rules, witches and destruction disrupting *technē*'s economy.

Listen to another story:

> In the old days, if someone fired a gun all you would see was water coming out of the gun. People could collect the bullets with their right or left hand. In those days, you could cut someone with a cutlass and the cutlass would break into pieces. In the old days, things happened which were fearful and wonderful.
>
> An Akuropon elder[3]

And another, in a Western voice:

> When a man accedes to the kingship, he and his subjects know that he has one year within which to live up to the challenge of his office and bewitch three close relatives. One relative may be anyone in his matriclan; another relative must be someone in his immediate uterine family (often a sibling); and the third relative must be either his own child . . . or his sister's child. There are similar requirements for newly installed queens and male and female village chiefs. My informant assured me that the rule is carried out in every case.[4]

Bewitching means killing, killing members of one's family where kinship means everything. And it cannot end. Sovereign power in Beng and other African societies rests on the closest proximity to catastrophic injustice.

> The Highest Beng officials make use of the power of witchcraft; indeed, the legitimacy of their rule depends on their obligatory (though circumscribed) practice of witchcraft. But other witches, who do not hold political office, are reviled and were at one time killed. Witchcraft for the Beng does represent the height of immorality, but it is not only practiced by immoral people, for all that. Kings as well as witches use this power, but witches use it unrestrictedly for their own benefit, whereas kings use it only for the political "good." (Gottlieb, "Witches, Kings," p. 264)

Can we hear in this proximity of sovereign power with utmost evil both immemorial injustice and the menace of danger, in a way unknown to the West after the Greeks? (Yet remember *Macbeth*.) Can we hear injustice in justice, still justice?[5] Framing the place of witchcraft the Beng relate the Earth to sacrifice:

> If one is desirous of obtaining something (either material or social), one can offer a sacrifice to the Earth, called *dolë ló*, to request it. In this case, one is obliged to offer a second sacrifice to the Earth, called *tō bolë*, three years later to thank the Earth (whether or not the Earth in fact granted the request). If the petitioner neglects to thank the Earth three years later with the second sacrifice, some one else in the petitioner's matriclan will be killed by the Earth. (Gottlieb, "Witches, Kings," p. 258)

Sacrifice returns us to restitution for immemorial and unknown injustices. "One may ask why the Earth does not simply kill the delinquent petitioner directly as a punishment. In this case, the Earth would not obtain the required sacrifice (*tō bolë*) and thus would only succeed in gaining punishment but not, as it were, restitution" (Gottlieb, "Witches, Kings," p. 258).

We may find in this repetition of sacrifice a perpetuation of injustice, a repetition of injustices toward others without the saving grace of *technē*'s justice. We hope to institute upon this law of sacrifice another law of protection against the perpetuation of death as sacrifice, against the Greek perpetuation of death as vengeance. We hope that Athena, in some bright form, possibly not a Greek or Western form, may descend upon the Beng society and transform the witches' blood sacrifices into protective law. But the Beng remember, as we have trouble remembering, that political power rests on danger, that the Erinyes walk furiously among us. We may ask the Beng to remember the ambiguities of sacrifice. They remember what we forget, the monstrosities of the sacrifices of power. They continue to mourn the danger of mourning.

Witches and kings meet here in closest proximity. What we hope to remember, the greatest danger for us to forget, lies within the ambiguity, the masks, the truths, of Pharmakeia, as if we may accept, may wear, these masks without danger, as if we might not care about the danger of her injustices as she reminds us, tells us the truth, of the danger of other injustices. Justice tells us that we must remember the catastrophes, yet never acquiesce in catastrophe as the identity of history, never accept slavery as a moment in the advance of history, never let any sense of advance, as progress, culmination, even circulation, weaken our sense of past and future injustices.

To read sacrifice into Pharmakeia's or Musa Wo's play as a truth without danger, to believe that "to live is to sacrifice and to be sacrificed" represents a generic truth, expresses sacrifice without charity, without valor, without utmost danger. We add the inexhaustibility of the sacrifice, the loss of something beyond imagination or representation, a loss belonging to archaic injustice. We question the masks, the ambiguities, of injustice and truth. We question the monstrosity of danger.

Others have questioned these ambiguities. "What does it mean to acknowledge the ambiguous character of social achievements in the very practice of authority? Why is it a good thing to do? And what implications does it carry for the form of public life?"[6] Such questions follows *technē* while we struggle with Pharmakeia's *poiēsis*, with madness, mischief, and magic, with idolatry, subjection, and monstrosity, as signatures of authority. We struggle with Pharmakeia's masks obscuring the questions we bring to every mask. Such an ambiguity, derived from *erōs* and *mania*, takes us on a journey far from *technē* even as it returns. As our journey passes through the magical abysses of truth, we wonder at our own *poiēsis* and *technē*, wonder at how to distinguish our truth from untruth, reason from unreason, where we know how authoritarian and dangerous such a distinction may be.

Beware of *technē*'s, law's, authority! Beware of authority's truth!

> We need to begin by drawing a distinction between epistemic and epistemocratic authority. Epistemic authority is that which is ascribed to the possessor of specialized knowledge, skills, or expertise.... epistemocratic authority attempts to assimilate political authority to the nonpolitical epistemic authority of the technician or expert.[7]

Pharmakeia and Musa Wo tell us to beware of the expert authority with which one might authorize such a distinction, to beware of the laws of *technē* that would impose such a cut. May not every authority, every truthful authority, blur the distinction between epistemic and epistemocratic authority, blur the rent between good and bad, beneficial and dangerous authority, forgetting madness and magic? Do we fall into authority's subjection and monstrosity, surrounded by idolatry, by Pharmakeia's masks, wherever we exercise authority, truth's or virtue's authority? Beware of any authority, especially truth's authority, that would offer a model of virtuous authority! Beware especially of science's law! Beware of law's authority, of the demand of instrumental, technical Law to inscribe reason's authority where reason knows no law!

Beware of these warnings as another authority, *poiēsis*'s authority over *technē*, Pharmakeia's authority over law! Witchcraft does not protect us from *technē*. Nothing could, nor can we desire that anything should. Sorcery circulates with *technē* and with *poiēsis*. Magic, *pharmakon*, power, desire, and truth represent different names for the juncture between *technē* and *poiēsis*, justice and injustice, law and memory, within authority, for the otherwise of authority, that we hope to remember as we circulate under law. Beware of the warning, the pain of warning! Beware of heights!

What does immemorial injustice in the circulation of Pharmakeia, the monstrous masks and sacrifices of authority's injustices, give us as the materiality, the *technē*, of *praxis*?

> Politics . . . is the threat of the differend. It is not a genre, it is the multiplicity of genres, the diversity of ends, and par excellence the question of linkage. (Lyotard, *The Differend*, p. 138)
>
>   Politics always gives rise to misunderstandings because it takes place as a genre. . . . At the same time, though, politics is not a genre, it bears witness to the nothingness which opens up with each occurring phrase and on the occasion of which the differend between genres of discourse is born. (Ibid., p. 141)

Praxis, politics, is not a genre but takes place as a genre, materializes into *technē*. Politics both works as *technē* and bears witness to the differend, to heterogeneity and difference as injustice, in their monstrosity. Politics circulates in this space of heterogeneity and arbitrariness, the *poiēsis* of becoming, time, becoming *technē*, requiring *technē*'s heterogeneity and multiplicity. Politics threatens us twice, the injustice of its or any *technē*, even restitution, and the monstrosity of injustice circulating in time as justice. Politics fulfills us twice, the justice of its *technē*, the valor of its injustices. Valor represents the juncture of *technē* and *poiēsis* as injustice in justice.

Injustice circulates in time as justice, works as *technē*. Justice's *technē* represents the work of injustice, whatever work it can undertake, in time, endless time. Justice works out the endless debt, the inexhaustible restitution, given by the call of injustice, the unauthorized authority of the demand for justice. *Poiēsis* here does not represent poetry in particular, literature or art, even music, disciplinary forms of *technē*'s measures. *Poiēsis* represents time's diachrony, the discontinuities, breaks, abysses, the obsessive work of bringing nonbeing into being. This bringing forth, this general economy, inflicts a call, a demand, an obligation, imposed as the Good, circulating in time as endless restitution, law and justice, for immemorial injustice. We are called to remember injustice, inexhaustibly, remember injustices we may have totally forgotten, remember injustices that may never have taken place. This memory represents the inescapability of injustice, the irresistibility of the call of the Forgotten, the monstrosity of our subjection to the debt of injustice. It represents the work of justice, authority's economy.

What hope derives this memory from monstrosity, subjection, and idolatry, from madness, magic, and witchcraft? Listen again to the witches. "Pluralistic authority is intolerably unsystematic to some, and to others it is politically fearful. But we have good reasons to bear conflict, diversity, and ambiguity here at the heart of the political concept traditionally associated with unity, clarity, and assent. Clutter and confusion can become elements in a defense of pluralistic authority from a peculiarly personal point of view."[8] Witches thrive on clutter and confusion, disordered heterogeneities subverting the clarity of authority. Even here we beware of a clutter that masks a hidden authority, for example the tumult of the market, the hidden authorities of wealth and power, that do not shine in the light. Even here we beware of unjust authority, but we acknowledge injustice overtly, overtly acknowledge the catastrophes of chaos and confusion, rather than taking unity, clarity, and assent as unambiguous, undangerous norms. Even so, we beware of writing normatively against normative authority, beware of writing under rules, without confusion, beware of normalizing economy.

Foucault suggests that before classical representation something extraordinary spoke the Same.

> The whole volume of the world, all the adjacencies of "convenience," all the echoes of emulation, all the linkages of analogy, are supported, maintained, and doubled by this space governed by sympathy and antipathy, which are endlessly drawing things together and holding them apart. By means of this interplay, the world remains identical; resemblances continue to be what they are, and to resemble one another. The same remains the same, riveted onto itself.[9]

Listen to another voice, Pharmakeia's other voice, working in our time.

> When we put in the new water line, we found out that there had been an old water line that we were following. I used the functioning of my understanding of the Hebrew names for God to run the water line from our home to the Carriage House and it was a collaborative endeavor involving a stone mason who called to me as I was talking with Jerry about getting water to the other buildings on our property, the stone mason asked me to "turn on the water." We figured out the

best way to run the water logically and ended up digging along the old water line while putting down a new water line. It takes "two to make the things all right, it takes two to make it out of sight" is playing on the radio. (A bird is chirping near by. A bird is the only animal that you cannot cut in half in Scripture. A bird flies in the heavens.)[10]

Signs circulate everywhere, teeming in inexhaustible profusion. Signs show up everywhere, at any time. Anything may resemble, signify, anything else, by multiple affinities and conjunctions. Such a profusion, confusion, of signs and representations gives us magic, works as magic, *poiēsis*, plays with Pharmakeia. This play represents, signs and shows, without the brutal, authoritative cuts of reason, without cutting away with absolute authority, what does not fit our measures. This teeming profusion of signatures without authorization undermines authority's authority, yet does not destroy authority. We must run a water line; we hope to make it the best we can. Pharmakeia gives us another best, disrupts the authoritarian hold of *technē* by *poiēsis*'s authority, grants a pluralistic, entangled authority. Conflict, diversity, and ambiguity; clutter and confusion; a peculiarly personal pluralistic authority; could they circulate with unity, clarity, and assent as we remember their injustice?

Listen to the witches. "[S]ociolinguists recently have argued that female patterns of speech reveal a different expressiveness than do male patterns. Rhythms, nuance, emphasis, and assertiveness, in tone and syntax, appear to vary with gender. Nevertheless, we define the masculine mode of self-assured, self-assertive, unqualified declarativeness as the model of authoritative speech."[11] Shall we imagine that privileging masculine norms as authoritativeness, authorizing norms of masculine authority, represents the sole danger, that if we grant the witches' voices we will tune in to a better authority? Or do such voices warn us of the dangers of every authority and every norm, including their own dangers, warn us of the menaces of benignity and goodness and of monstrosity, witchcraft, and subjection?

> Compassion has the potential for humanizing authority. If women do not speak authoritatively, perhaps their hesitancy reveals the ambiguity, and the choices, behind all rule systems. By reminding us of this ambiguity, the voice and gesture of compassion shocks us into a memory of what has been hidden by the ordered discourse of authority. (Jones, "On Authority," pp. 165–66)

By reminding us of compassion's ambiguities, the voice of compassion reminds us of the injustices of authority and justice, inescapable masks, displaying the work of Pharmakeia in her ambiguity of suffering and truth, truth and suffering, played out to the end of the world.

A *praxis* without utopia. The monstrosity of every authority. The injustice of truth.

Shall we call this humane? Can any authority authorize humanity?

We may wish to recollect, as we approach the close of our narrative of injustice, the thought that the political question is truth itself. What might this mean to us now that we have remembered the witches? For the moment we reply with two further questions. In what ways does injustice belong to truth? In what ways does truth belong to power? Foucault answers the second: "Truth is a thing of this world; it is produced only by virtue of multiple forms of constraint. And it induces regular effects of power. Each society has its régime of truth, its 'general politics' of truth; . . . ."[12] Truth is made by power; among the effects of a régime it constructs its truth.

The first question calls us under the aegis of truth and power to account for the truth of power and truth, especially, here, for the truth of truth. What of the truth and what of the politics of what Foucault tells us when he says that the political question is truth itself? In the language of injustice, calling us to account, may we speak of the politics, the power and injustice, of the political question and its truth? Truth, even our truth, even the truth of the political question, circulates in a particular régime, but cannot be held fast within that régime, because of resistance or contingency, because of injustice, because of magic, all figures of the *pharmakon*, of the otherwise, inexhaustibility and excess, where ethics and politics belong. Power gives rise to and circulates together with resistance, necessity to contingency, justice to injustice, *technē* to *poiēsis* and Pharmakeia. To each, dividing their opposition, belong monstrosity and subjection.

We seek a monstrosity that would remember its own monstrosity, the monstrosity of monstrosity, canceling oppression, subjugation, suffering, but not canceling injustice or its monstrosity, not the monstrosity and subjection of authority, of every authority, even magical authority. "Humanity does not gradually progress from combat to combat until it arrives at universal reciprocity, where the rule of law finally replaces warfare; humanity installs each of its violences in a system of rules and thus proceeds from domination to domination."[13] As we hope to relinquish war we vow to remember the violences and dominations of peace. We hope to remember that the lines we hope to draw between war and peace, one authority and another, continue to pay restitution for unending injustices.

Catharine MacKinnon suggests that the lines we, men or women, hope to draw between sexual intercourse and rape, *erōs* and sexual violence, do not exist "under conditions of male domination."[14]

> The point of defining rape as "violence not sex" or "violence against women" has been to separate sexuality from gender in order to affirm sex (heterosexuality) while rejecting violence (rape). The problem remains what it has always been: telling the difference. (MacKinnon, *FMMS*, p. 619)

> Instead of asking, what is the violation of rape, what if we ask, what is the nonviolation of intercourse? (*FMMS*, p. 619)

> Rape is only an injury from women's point of view. It is only a crime from the male point of view, explicitly including that of the accused. (*FMMS*, p. 625)

What if we accepted MacKinnon's understanding of law if not of desire? What if she represented the poverty of the law, certainly of the Law, before the *pharmakon* of sexual desire, before the ambiguity of Pharmakeia's truth, rape as power, founding world or state, under conditions of male domination or any political conditions whatever? What if sexuality, with its hold on sex, owed its existence to a monstrous and immemorial injustice, to unending male injustice, so that the lawful distinction between rape and sexual love, between the cruelest violence between men and women and the most caring act of intimacy, disappeared? What if politicality, the state, with its hold on life under its dominion, imposing subjection, owed its existence to a monstrous and immemorial and unjust authority, so that no measure existed, no line could be drawn, between just and unjust authority? And still we draw the lines, again and again.[15]

What if the best were worst—not "close to" the worst, as Derrida says, requiring us to calculate?[16] Incalculable justice, incalculable deconstruction, if such a thing exists, forces us to calculate. What if we cannot calculate the difference between injustice and justice, but must still calculate, finding no distinction under *technē* between justice and injustice, best and worst, but must represent the absence of any such distinction as we calculate? What if the very best became the very worst, still the very best? What of Orithyia's rape?

What if we accepted MacKinnon's suggestion that no measure of justice or law can be authorized without injustice, without repeating men's injustice against women, distinguishing sexual intimacy from rape, *erōs* from violence, repeating male domination, extending this understanding to law and authority, but refused, with her, to draw another line, equally obscure and unjust, between male domination and *erōs*, between good and bad law, under *technē*? What if we granted her along with other women the role of witches, the role they have always played, as they played with Pharmakeia, as they were seized together with Pharmakeia, as they have always been subjected to male domination and sexual violence—but remembered male witches and the shedding of racial blood? What if the dream that women might define the crime of rape belonged to *poiēsis* while the law that brought that crime to justice belonged, always belonged and always will belong, to *technē*'s economy, to Law? What if no line could be drawn between *technē* and *poiēsis*, if Pharmakeia's *poiēsis* defined no measure? What if rape represented a terrible crime against women while its definition remained obscure? What of the injustice of our complacency?

What if the distinction that cannot be drawn between rape and intimacy repeated the distinction that cannot be drawn between male domination and love, the line that cannot be traced between *poiēsis* and *technē*, Pharmakeia's line? What if we cannot draw these lines because such a line repeats the excesses of desire, places us otherwise, with justice's injustices, yet cannot abandon the attempt to draw them? What if we cannot draw these lines within *technē* but must continue to represent and define them, still within *technē* but called by an injustice that belongs to *poiēsis*, not to *technē*. Here, the circulation of sexuality, within desire, expresses desire's excessiveness, breaking apart every authority, especially the authority of law and *technē*. What if we could establish no distinction under law except one that repeated another injustice, another male-dominating injustice, an always-present, inescapable injustice toward women?

We refuse to imagine a female-dominating injustice as we refuse to accept a male-dominating injustice.

How can we acknowledge, give way before, repay the immemorial injustices of men toward women, adults toward children, injustices older than every other injustice, older than the injustices of the West toward the non-West, older than the immense age of slavery? How can we accept the injustices of men toward women without giving way to a dream of utopian, contained desire that would repeat the injustice of male desire?

Don't women want to be screwed, even as they are unjustly screwed? Don't women want to be wanted, even if it sometimes means rape? Don't women participate in the injustice? How much does that diminish the injustice?

Let us imagine that some women do not want to be screwed by men, wanted by men, if it means rape—or ever! Does that repeat justice or injustice?

Sexual intercourse cannot be broken away from sexual violence, from rape, except in terms of moments in sexual desire that have no acceptable lines of demarcation: penetration and consent. When does penetration become violence, acceptable or unacceptable violence? When does unspoken consent become coercion? In what silent space? Do these questions pertain only to male-dominated societies or do they represent the ambiguities of the *pharmakon*, circulating in magic and witchcraft? Acknowledging the excesses of sexual desire, the excessiveness that exceeds all excessiveness, makes it impossible to contain that desire under law. Violence, domination, oppression belong to desire as inexhaustible excesses circulating inexhaustibly otherwise. This otherwise belongs to things as well as men and women in the form of unending, inescapable injustices.

Such a recognition fails to diminish any injustice, does not level injustice into justice, does not justify sexual or any other violence, but imposes unending debts without culmination, without restoration. We seek unending restitution as violence against violence, the domination of domination, struggling against desire's desire to exceed itself, against desire's inexhaustibility as another injustice, against the complacency of perpetual violence, and against the darkness of unending struggle. The threat the witches offer, that MacKinnon offers, represents the impossibility of holding the limits of law tightly against the excesses of its authority. Pharmakeia's gender threatens to disrupt the strongest and most familiar laws that bind us to life and death, to the future, organized around sexuality, where public and private meet, in sexual violence, in the indistinguishability of sexual crimes from sexual love, the heinousness of intimate oppressions where we hope to be safe. This meeting of public and private, violence and intimacy, circulates in gender's economy.

The promise Pharmakeia offers represents the possibility that the unlimitedness of law's authority represents, achieves justice, the best (and worst) justice we can achieve, attained at no particular moment but stretched endlessly through time in the ambiguity of its fulfillment. Fulfillment as deferral! Injustice in justice! In this way we resist the hesitations in the three aporias of justice Derrida describes.[17] Justice's restitution in law represents law's injustice. The archaic marks not justice but injustice. The urgency of justice represents both the injustice of deferral and justice's restitution. The inversion takes the undecidability and urgency of *praxis*, the responsibility of Western injustice, the endless restitution, as justice, as the very best we can achieve—and worst. The best in the worst; injustice in justice; justice in injustice, the play, the rape, of Orithyia with Pharmakeia.

MacKinnon takes up rape and pornography, two acts that mimetically repeat private acts of intimacy in the monstrosity of public demonstration. Abortion inhabits a similar space of desire and power, that our time seems to take to represent its injustice. Why has abortion become the most polarized issue of our time, in the United States, along with the right to die and environmental disaster, with the rights of animals in human society and the deaths of animals together with their habitats? What of the inescapability of our *Geschlecht*? What of our memories of monstrosity? What of witches—in German, *Hexe*; in Mende, Musa Wo (the Muses again)?

We list several parallels:

1. Like rape, abortion represents where sexuality circulates in public, where the distinction between public and private, society and individuality, power and desire, fragments, marking the monstrosities of democracy.
2. Where sexuality becomes sex, desire meets *technē*, meets the future's relation to life and death. Abortion represents a place where desire and intimacy fall entirely under *technē*, law's authority, as if thereby to control their dangers, instituting *technē*'s dangers, as if private relationships might be given over entirely to *technē*'s measures.
3. Where individual deaths become routine, death on the world stage grows in importance, of those human beings and works that represent to us our tradition and thereby our future (whoever "we" may be). The death of what has never been alive takes on remarkable importance, as if humanity's entire future were at stake in each woman's decision to have a child. We hear the secret terrors of *Lysistrata* reappearing, denying to men their last control over their reproductive destiny.
4. As always, in the West, we reply to sacrifice and loss by Law. We insist that human beings have no right to choose their death without the sanction of law as we insist that other living creatures be sacrificed to our comfort. We insist that the state has the right to keep people alive who want to die even as it fosters institutions that cause the deaths of many who hope to live, refusing them care.
5. What if we granted every woman unquestioned authority over her reproductive future, and every woman chose to have no children, chose abortion? What if "my" woman chose abortion rather than bearing "my child"? What if a woman chose abortion rather than bearing a child engendered by violence?

6. What if we granted every human being unquestioned authority over that person's life and death, and every human being chose to die? What if that represented the answer to immemorial injustice, to choose to die against the slings and arrows of sacrifice and loss? What must we do against such a nihilism, facing such a repudiation of Law, instead of a nihilism without consequences?
7. What of the death of humanity? What of the inevitability of the death of humanity? What of the injustices we offer to the future as we grant it authority over us, that we may seek to avoid by denying the future authority? What of deaths we cannot mourn?
8. What of the death of our planet, of the environmental disasters we wreak upon it as sacrifices to our presence? What of the fact that those who live affluently, who enjoy the fruits of long-lasting injustices, have the most to say about those whose survival demands destruction of the rain forest and the creatures that live there?
9. What of the inescapable truth that those who profit most from catastrophic injustices demand the greatest sacrifices in restitution—from others, seldom from themselves?
10. What restitution? In particular, what restitution for unending injustices toward animals, unending injustices of animals toward each other and unending injustices of human beings toward animals in the name of *Geschlecht*? How can we take animals as all the same, even the Same, under reason's law, even Reason's Law, where we refuse, must refuse, where we hope in the name of injustice to refuse the same to human beings? We remember, hope to remember, unending injustices toward human beings, in slavery, concentration camps, and murder, of prisoners captured in war, especially women, the fruits of war, then Africans sold into slavery, always Jews, but also Armenians and Greeks. We do not hope to remember, simply forget, unending injustices toward animals, who as Animal, all appear the same, indifferently, the same by species, the same as individuals, for they do not remember, do not reason—like Us.

Law demands that we inscribe a line sharply cleaving sexual violence from sexual love, rape from intimacy, life from death, the promise of the future from its sacrifices and injustices, justice from injustice. And we cannot live without law, though we may hope to escape from Law. We cannot live without *technē*'s law, without the lines, the inscriptions, that circulate *technē*'s measures, not even without their authority, though we may hope to escape from Measure and Authority. We cannot live without *technē*, but we may hope to live within *technē*'s economy, under its *poiēsis*, where we take all living, dying, coming to be and passing away, to repeat immemorial injustice, represented by Pharmakeia, as poison and cure, as catastrophe and promise, reason and unreason, inseparably. We inscribe the lines, the measures, demanded by *technē*'s law under the gaze of Pharmakeia, where every line falls under arbitrary, unjust, immemorial, painful authority, every inscription authorizes both *pharmakeus* and *pharmakos*, where we who make the law offer it up as sacrifice as we cannot live without it.

And still, remembering Pharmakeia, *pharmakeus, pharmakis*, and *pharmakos*, magic and sacrifice, we hope for goodness, hoping not to forget goodness' injustice but hoping to know injustice's *jouissance*. Must we give happiness over to *technē*, or can happiness circulate together with injustice?

Can we grant the space between rape and embodied love, between sexual violence and abuse and sexual intimacy, to contain no lines dividing it, no laws defining it, except those that circulate under immemorial injustice, under Pharmakeia's threat of pain and injustice, without instituting the greatest injustice of all, that we take sexual injustice as the norm, even the Law? Can we enter Pharmakeia's magical space, threatening and terrifying space, without opposing her authority to Reason's Authority, so that we glorify unreason, sorcery, even madness?

Does that represent the greatest injustice of all, as if Orithyia's rape were nothing?

Do the witches, light and dark, Greek, German, English, or non-Western, threaten the authority of reason without which we may have no truth at all? Or can we, in becoming wizards and witches ourselves, dark and light, north and south, subvert the authority of reason and law, science and measure, under *technē*, subvert *technē*'s perfectibility under Law, without giving up reason's truth, without giving way to misery?

Witches and sorcerers have always congregated with animals, as if the ambiguities of their magic fell into Pharmakeia's magical spaces. Where we cannot tell the difference, any difference that matters, between human beings and animals, where animals walk the earth in mystery and magic, there reason collapses into mad monstrosity, love's madness—for we human beings love animals, have always loved animals, as animals have loved us—and the truth of the essence of human beings dissolves into the magical essences of animals. Animals represent *poiēsis*, never *technē*, impossibly *technē*, represent *poiēsis*'s gift to Pharmakeia as we subject them repeatedly to *technē*, to our instrumentality. In this way, injustice toward animals marks the ever-present, inescapable circulation of immemorial injustice. In irony, but not simply irony, we may call the difference between animals and human beings, call our injustice toward animals and justice toward human beings, the *ethical difference* of which our law is oblivious, an oblivion essential to its *technē*. This oblivion represents our abjection toward the authority of the subjection, the abjection in our subjection, lorded over animals as the price of Adam's sin. We rule over animals as the mark of sin, immemorial injustice.

Technē's message to Pharmakeia tells that even bad-tasting medicine, harmful medicine, can be good for us, can be measured as better against its poisonous dangers. We have, in our play with Pharmakeia, refused *technē*'s authority, refused the measure of reason's perfection. We struggle against immemorial injustice and the darkness of its authority to take up reason's claim to a critical suspicion of every authority, of divine authority, a suspicion that kills God, without taking up another authority. Can we grant reason its truth as both *technē*'s and *pharmakeia*'s truth, refusing oblivion toward its injustices?

Can we understand the meaning of restitution for immemorial injustices, of restitution within the continuing play of injustices? Can we understand *technē* as restitution for the unending injustices of *poiēsis*?

Following our reading of *Phaedrus* we may extend the repetitions of our injustices as we have disclosed them here and elsewhere[18] in the form of a long, perhaps strange, list, lacking order, possessing no law but its own, most entries appearing somewhere in our discussions, not without repetition:

    injustice, restitution, debt
        law
        order, disorder
        measure, rule
    locality, inexhaustibility, ergonality
    power, desire, representation
    truth, knowledge
    time, memory, history
        mourning
        teleology, end
        destiny
        older, younger
    power, politics
    desire
    ethics, responsibility, guilt
    charity, sacrifice, valor
    West, non-West
        canon
        rule

Master, mastery
German, French, Western, non-Western
   Geschlecht
   Hitler
   Jews
   concentration camps
   holocaust
   catastrophe
   mourning
language, writing, speech
technē, poiēsis
nature, *physis*
   state of nature
   natural law
monstrosity
   animals
subjection, abjection
   subjugation
violence, domination, oppression
   Geschlecht
   force
   blood
   sexual violence
   penetration
   slavery
race, class, ethnicity
authority, law
writing, speaking, language
community, agreement, difference, common world
sex, sexuality, sexual difference, gender
danger, peril, menace
right, wrong
work, *ergon*
norm, normality, normativity
reason, truth, *logos*
peace, war
equality, difference, Same
technē
   measure, technology, calculation, law
   instrumentality
   exchange

    economy
    circulation
science, knowledge, truth
private, public
    person
    property
    propriety
    community
humanity, humanism
    subject, subjection, abjection
modernity
    postmodernity, posthistory, postcoloniality
liberation, terror
sovereignty
labor, work
force, necessity, obligation, responsibility
vengeance
high, highest
Spirit
heresy, aporia
Other, other
    subaltern
    animal
    machine
witches
    familiars
virtue
excess
beauty
art, nature, *poiēsis*
music, song
    spirit
    gods, divine
righteousness, law
reality, simulation
limit, unlimit
masks, Dionysus
visibility, Apollo, law
perfection, perfectibility, *technē*
superior, inferior
legitimation, law

rights, utility
individuality, community
loi, droit
Geschlecht
erōs, philia
body
   hand
   gift
   language
freedom, liberation
   reason, truth
culture
plurality
   heterogeneity
   adaptability
   danger
body, extension
demonic, monstrosity
judgment
value
totality, referent, reality
wrong, tort, damage
madness
sublime, unrepresentable
   colossal, monstrous
Erinyes, Eumenides, Muses, Musa Wo
coercion, force of law
   mystic foundation of authority
mythos, poiēsis
   mythical violence
   divine violence
deconstruction
   justice
animals
   carnivorousness
repetition, memory, time
victim
idolatry
   gods
   witches, wizards
     pharmakon

Verwindung
redemption, catastrophe, mourning
   Messiah
   destiny

We remember our lists from *Phaedrus,* first the longer:

desire
   appetite
   love
Pharmakeia
the city, politics, power, law
   public, private
intimacy
nature
memory
repetition
writing
truth and deception
science
technē
storytelling, narration
citizens, strangers
recipes, rules
magic
mastery
   amateur
measure
advantage, benefit
goodness, justice
   injustice
menace, danger
perfectibility
madness
prophecy
divine inspiration
poiēsis

Then the shorter:

desire
power
truth

memory
magic
madness
menace
nature
technē, poiēsis, Pharmakeia
injustice

Our reading of *Phaedrus* followed the suggestion that these ten moments of justice circulating within injustice mirror each other, nature's *mimēsis*, represent the univocities, inexhaustible unisons and resonances, harmonies and disharmonies, stillnesses and polyphonies, of ingredients in time, nature's general economy.[19] Desire, power, knowledge, and memory mirror each other as Pharmakeia, magic, madness, and danger, the goodness and justice of nature's *poiēsis*, falling into time as restitution, endlessly repeating restitution for immemorial injustice, echoing injustice, debt, restitution. Justice as injustice! Injustice in justice, restitution! These represent the incomprehensibility of the circulation of truth as untruth, justice and law as injustice and unmeasure, the rule of *technē* under, subjected to, sacrificed to, *poiēsis*'s injustice. Here desire as excess, exceeding itself, exceeding any control, any law, any rule of reason, mirrors knowledge's truth, the play of power, all together defining goodness and justice as endless restitution, the immemoriality of time, past, present, and future as restitution for injustice, remembering injustice, remembering injustice's oblivion as another trace of injustice.

Restitution represents the good, under *technē*'s law, as refusing *technē*'s authority, refusing Law's authority as we cannot act without authority. If we call this refusal skepticism, we install its authority over all other authorities, as if it rules together with the Law. If we call it relativism, we install it at the center where it displaces all other centers as if ruling the center under its Law. We have chosen, instead, after Plato, after Africa yet within a Western subjection of Africa, to call it "Pharmakeia's Music":[20] magic's mimetic madness as justice and truth; as power and desire; remembering *technē* before *poiēsis*, subjection to a *poiēsis* that cannot rule without, except for, *technē*. Restitution here as *poiēsis* belongs to *technē* under, after, or within the musical play of Pharmakeia, whose magic and madness, Dionysus's mad and magical masks, obscures every rational law, every truthful law, with the madness of desire and power—obscures and displaces, but does not replace them.

We accept the authority of law and truth, science's law, as Pharmakeia's threat to obscure every authority with unending, inexhaustible suspicion. We accept authority but refuse it authorization. We impose Pharmakeia's authority within the obscurity of her suffering, repeating the madness of desire as mimetic figures of power and truth, of science. Here *poiēsis* as *mimēsis* represents the magic whose aporias found a justice of immemorial injustice, a truth of untruth, a science without authority, undermined by witches' lack of authority. A *poiēsis* of traces and uncertainties. A *mimēsis* subject to distrust. A *technē* of wonder; a law suspicious of Law; an economy of immemorial injustice and restitution.

With this representation of restitution, we return to our Master list.[21] We think of restitution as a movement against The Master's Authority, against authority within authority—for The Master's Culture threatens to become the Only Culture as we mark, perhaps without reluctance, its heterogeneity. We mark its heterogeneity in blood.

Can we reduce our longer list to something smaller, more measured, economical?

justice, injustice, law
nature, *physis*
   locality, inexhaustibility, ergonality
   power, desire, representation
   knowledge, truth, language
canon
   West, non-West
mastery
   subjection, abjection, monstrosity
   slavery
   animal sacrifice and possession
time, memory, history
technē, *poiēsis*
economy, measure, circulation
public, private
violence, domination
   blood
   force
   sexual violence
   danger

We may think of these as mirrors of each other and authority, representations of authority, authorizations and displacements of authority, reflections of Pharmakeia. We may think of them as Pharmakeia's *mimēsis*, her play with Dionysus, her bewitchment by the Erinyes, leading to Orithyia's rape. Let us think of this danger with the greatest possible suspicion of the authority of any rule of law as imposing another excessive violence, of the danger of rule without authority. Never shall the Erinyes become Eumenides! Authority represents something we cannot live without but cannot accept without hatred and suspicion. The violence of authority requires that we refuse to authorize authority. Our responsibility, our debt, to injustice circulates as suspicion of every authority. The call of injustice imposes authority but refuses it authorization. We call this call and refusal, ethics or politics. It circulates as nature's general economy. It echoes Pharmakeia's musical play.

The form of our suspicion of *technē*'s authority appears as *poiēsis*, but we maintain profound suspicion of a *poiēsis* that knows nothing of suspicion, that knows nothing of its own injustices as it marks others' injustices. We maintain a profound suspicion as well of a suffocating suspicion that refuses justice's *poiēsis*. The form of our suspicion, perhaps in German, appears as *Geschlecht*, marking every appearance of *erōs* and *philia*, every sexual subjection, however intimate, however private, marking the most private recesses of our embodiment with colossal public monstrosity.

Authority and necessity meet in the Rule of Law. They fall apart into catastrophic monstrosity where we remember others' sacrifices with unassuageable pain, remember with our pain others' sacrifices, remember in our painful memories of unrepresentable sacrifices, terrible losses beyond recall.

We think of injustice circulating with justice under the rule of law, mirroring power, desire, and representation as nature's excesses, where *poiēsis* and *technē* meet and divide each other, threaten each other with the other's danger, repeating the themes of blood, life and death, sexual violence and sexual intimacy, threaten and fulfill each other. We may think of these under the sign of Pharmakeia, who represents for us the beginning of the world as a rape, the possibility that the beginning, the end, every moment of the world falls under the law of sexual violence, not because of male domination, not only because of male domination, but in the ambiguities, the uncertainties, the collapse of law's authority at every point of the institution of its authority. We may think of them under the mark of Musa Wo, whose authority renders the destructive mischief of any authority, depends on the dangers of authority, calling to our attention our oblivion toward the terror of authority—a terror never absent from Hobbes, never absent from any sovereign authority, however legitimated, however justified, however rational.

Can we live with such terror, such enthusiasm, at the collapse of authority, at least the collapse of Authority? How can we live without them?

How can we laugh with them? What peace do they bring? What *jouissance*?

We mark the regions between ethics and politics within the spaces between private and public, spaces we have represented as nothing except what power allows, repetitions of the ambiguities of power. With Arendt, we take the public to represent collective spaces of appearance, of difference and heterogeneity. Away from Arendt, we take this public to exercise authority over the spaces of intimacy, letting them unfold where power chooses, controlling and mastering them otherwise. It follows that the heterogeneity of the public world falls monstrously into the spaces it defines between its heterogeneity and the homogeneities of families and individual worlds, selves and persons, *erōs* and *philia*, effectively no spaces at all, no spaces of difference at all, except that no public can exercise power without it, can circulate without its otherwise, without its magic.

Can that mark Musa Wo's lesson for us?

The spaces between ethics and politics repeat the differences represented by the "-" in *ethics-politics*, a univocity of the same except for differences owned by power, disrupted and exceeded by desire, inexhaustibly exceeding themselves, repeating immemorial injustices as the law, the justice, of ethics-politics. This impossible difference of the "-" (or "/") represents another excess, a dangerous, threatening, monstrous excess, where ethics and politics circulate in unjust restitution for immemorial injustice, repeating injustice in their restitution.

How may we think of, how may we practice, restitution for immemorial injustices? We have given several answers, acknowledging yet refusing other answers, especially refusing: (1) an ethics of exchange and substitution, *technē* without *poiēsis*; (2) an ethics given monstrously through the gift of language, repeating the monstrosity of *Geschlecht*; (3) the abjection of the subject, thrown down under the authority of the Other, repeating *Geschlecht*'s monstrosity.

Our answers have followed other trajectories: subjection, abjection, and monstrosity; justice and law as restitution for immemorial injustice; the play of Pharmakeia and Musa Wo as the magic and madness of reason's truth, the circulation together of *technē* and *poiēsis*; the reflections of power, desire, and representation, echoing locality, inexhaustibility, and ergonality;[22] all in the general economy of injustice. The "-" of *ethics-politics*, for us, falls into these monstrous spaces of aporia between subjection and abjection, Law and law, justice and injustice, *technē* and *poiēsis*, spaces defined in Greek by Pharmakeia, by Dionysian masks, but circulating against the authority of the "forever Greek" Western economy in the voice of Musa Wo.

We represent the lack of authority of authority, refuse to authorize authority, any and every authority, as we find ourselves gripped by authority, unable to work without authority, unable to enter ethics-politics except through the circulation of authority. This refusal of authority's authority, of a Law of Law, of reason's authority over itself, repeats the mysteries and magic of inexhaustible local places, circulating the inexhaustibility of inexhaustible places in nature's economy, without the force of limits that might legislate an indomitable Law of Limits. Mystery and magic here represent the monstrous and exhilarating play of the world into which our ethics-politics falls.

We represent this play of the world as Pharmakeia, playing at the edges of the *polis* with the Furies, where law collapses. We remember inescapable and immemorial injustices, represent the violence of Orithyia's abduction as the economy of charity, sacrifice, and valor. And we remember that even this representation, especially this representation, threatens us with its *pharmakon* within, warning us of the monstrosity of the sacrifice, of the *pharmakos*, that we cannot take Socrates' death or Orithyia's rape in vain, lightly, under the necessity of the law. If we follow Nietzsche's narrative of the birth of reason with Socrates, we must remember, as Nietzsche seems to forget, the monstrous death of Socrates and the unending monstrosity of sexual violence as *Geschlecht*, as human *aretē*.

Reason arises in a monstrous event of unreason, madness, founds itself on its own madness, perpetuates its madness, madly denies that madness to itself. Reason makes unending restitution for the madness of its perpetration in seeking to promulgate and foster Socrates' virtue, Greek *aretē*. The restitution reason forgets strives toward the madness that circulates within it, the insanity of law's authority, as if authority could ever possess rational authority.

We associate restitution with justice and law, under *technē*; we subject *technē*'s law to *poiēsis* as the play of Pharmakeia, the mythic remnants of the Erinyes haunting every event, chanting songs of fear and injustice. We associate *poiēsis* with the Muses, especially with *mousika* and Musa Wo, the play of music representing *poiēsis*, understanding the circulation of the Erinyes as indistinguishable from the play of *Mousikos*, a repetition of *pharmakon* as *pharmakos*, injustice and destruction. We represent the difference between *technē* and *poiēsis* as the difference between the Furies and the Muses, between Musa Wo and the Mousēs, no difference at all, where each repeats the madness, frenzy, of the authorization that founds the authority of the state, founds the ethical-political. This "-" repeats the monstrosity, the monstrous danger, of Pharmakeia. This "-" repeats the monstrosity, the Erinyes, circulating in music's *mimēsis*, without innocence.

Restitution here circulates within the walls of the city, under law, falling into the play of Pharmakeia, where the Furies walk, haunting every institution of law. We may call this force, this authorization, of law, restitution for injustice, provided that we listen to Orithyia's scream of pain, to the Erinyes' fury, that every restitution institutes injustice. We may call this echo of the Erinyes a furious suspicion of justice's law provided that we listen to the play of Pharmakeia's magic, sorcery and witchcraft, listen to the silent voices of the creatures surrounding her and us, from within their own injustice, telling us of the *jouissance* of her play.

What do those who are not slaves owe the victims of slavery? What restitution? Shall their children's children be given work when there is not enough work for others, for the slaveholders' children's children, men and women? What does the world owe the survivors of the Holocaust, including Jews who never lived in Europe? What do those who are not Jews owe to the Jews whose relatives were murdered in concentration camps, in gas chambers? What do the children of the children of slaves owe? Surely not denial of gas chambers. Surely not denial of death, a monstrous injustice, repudiating any possibility of restitution. And what of the jews?

What do I, a Jew, owe to the children of slaves? Shall I remember their oppression? How could I forget? Shall I remember the murder of countless Jews, shall I remember it as my oppression, demanding restitution, even if none of my relatives were killed in a concentration camp, but were killed in Eastern European pogroms? Again, what restitution? And what of the Armenians? And women, still killed today for their dowries, killed for too small a dowry, killed because they are women, because there are too many women, because they are not men? And children?

What do female children of countlessly oppressed women; what do Jews, men and women, of countlessly mistreated Jews; what do Armenians; owe to the children and grandchildren of Islamic, Greek, American slaves? Can we say in general, under law, what we owe, what is owed, what may be, must be, rendered in restitution except within the rule of law? And why think of law in general, repeating reason's hold? Why think of general economy except as disturbing reason's hold? Can we remember Solomon's wisdom as a justice without repetition, without generality?

If we give privilege to the grandchildren of slaves over others who have suffered oppression, even over others who have suffered the oppressions of wealth and privilege, do we repeat the injustices of privilege? If we give privilege to women's liberation over others who have suffered slavery but not the endless sufferings, the unending subordination of women, do we repeat the injustices of privilege? Under what law—certainly no Law, and without Reason—can we give priority to black men over white women, to black women's blackness over white women's womanness, what law of justice, as if these different oppressions could be measured against each other?

Under what law can we grant privilege to women who suffer sexual violence under consensual conditions, mixed with alcohol or stigma, over those who suffer under nonconsensual conditions? Under what law can men be imprisoned for possessing pornographic materials, for purchasing pornographic materials, for sexual intercourse and sexual yearnings, when surrounded by manufactured sexualities?

Under what law can we punish German children and their children for the sins of their parents, punish Polish children for the sins of their parents, hold Russian children innocent of the sins of their parents? Under what law? With what innocence?

What if endless debates over democracy and autocracy, freedom of speech and freedom of press, positive and negative liberties,[23] circulated in the economies of unending oppression, of subjugation by gender and blood? Would we give up democracy, give up its freedoms in restitution to its continuing oppressions? Or do we remember the victims of other régimes, remember that every régime that would institute oppression destroys individual freedoms, freedom of expression? Can we bring to the terrible dangers of democracy another danger, beyond all danger, a heterogeneity in democracy that shatters every rule of *technē*, including freedom's rule? Can our restitution to democracy's injustice circulate within an unbroken commitment to freedom, negative and positive, in speech and writing, an unbroken commitment representing broken authority, refusing all these freedoms another authority?

No restitution can take place without injustice, no justice without injustice. No restitution can circulate without subjection, no law without abjection. But we cannot stop seeking restitution, even if it requires endless time, inexhaustible restitution, endless deferral of injustice, repeating countless injustices, more and other injustices, subjecting us to further monstrosities. This endlessness marks the general economy of injustice.

If we take Marx's critique of modern capitalism to possess scientific authority, under another law, we bring ourselves before a conflict of laws, each seeking to become the Law. If instead we take Marx's critique of ideology to represent the irruption of injustice within modern reason's law, science's law, a critique that knows injustice where it finds it, including the injustice of a capitalism that has triumphed over every alternative, at that point, where capitalism identifies with *technē*, with instrumentality and teleology, where capitalism circulates as the *Geschlecht* of human fulfillment, the gift of humanity, then socialism offers not another technique of human fulfillment under law (or Law), but whispers injustice as the unspeakable secret of community.

Here the names of Marx and Freud share the secret possibility of a hidden injustice, the one in ideology, the other in repression, two forms of oblivion in which desire's excesses hide their most terrifying forms, at the destruction of truth, hidden in the name of authority. Here marxism's and psychoanalysis's scientificity does not represent restitution, for they repeat injustice, but expresses the magical, ambiguous, self-canceling representation of their powers and desires. Here the magical ambiguity of justice's injustice, the play of Pharmakeia with Musa Wo, the Furies with the Muses, tell us of endless restitution.

The contradictions of capitalist economy will bring it down as it grows to forestall every threat. The contradictions belong to capitalism, that is, to reason, enlightenment, and law, including the law of the market and the economy of wealth. The contradictions belong to reason, but no child of reason, of the gods or humanity, will replace its contradictions. To the contrary, if reason cannot escape from madness, either its own or the madnesses that circumscribe it, then no divine madness, of Eros or Pharmakeia, can escape from reason or unreason. *Poiēsis* has nothing to offer against *technē*, nothing against, but madness, magic, within, uplifting *technē* beyond its instrumentality and teleology to the magic within, a sorcery that inexhaustibly represents injustices, new and old.

Catharine MacKinnon asks us to remember that for every man falsely accused of rape countless women have been raped without legal restitution. We cannot reply to these countless injustices, cannot render their victims restitution, by punishing an innocent or guilty man. We cannot offer restitution against historical injustice by another injustice or even an act of justice. Nor can we measure against the countless injustices borne by women the injustices borne by men, especially in a world that is unjust for all, for men and women as well as children. We cannot measure as if Reason offers us a Law of Restitution.

We offer restitution without a Law of Restitution. We bring restitution under *technē*, under law, without Law's Authority, undermining that Authority by the threat of *poiēsis*, undermining *poiēsis*'s authority by remembering Musa Wo's fury, the Erinyes's fury at Pharmakeia, who does not, cannot determine, under law, Restitution's Law.

Injustice circulates in the inexhaustibility of events and things, exceeding every law, every restitution, every *technē*. Injustice repeats the inexhaustibility exceeding every law, the silent break of *technē*'s law. Injustice represents the otherwise of inexhaustibility that breaks the hold of being's law.

Within this excess and inexhaustibility, we reply with charity, restitution for law's injustices. Yet we cannot apply a law to charity without rendering another injustice. Charity's injustice repeats inexhaustibility without authority, circulates as sacrifice. The circulation of inexhaustibility with locality, sacrifice with charity, in the name of injustice, the economy of time as sacrifice, as memory and loss, befalls us as valor. Valor represents the otherwise of the good that circulates between charity's inexhaustibility and sacrifice's locality, the otherwise that refuses their hold upon us as another injustice.

Reason has nothing to say to sacrifice's despair at its own injustice. Reason has nothing to say that it has not already said, in bringing sacrifice under law, under *technē*. Yet reason remains reason for all that, under law, and *technē* resolves itself into the sorcery and fears of *poiēsis*, marked by Pharmakeia, only to return to itself as valor, where valor marks the juncture of charity and sacrifice, reason and madness, justice and injustice, the place where they meet otherwise.

In a terrifying identity, Derrida says that "Deconstruction is justice." He hopes to inscribe a justice immemorially before law, before *technē*, the Erinyes' law. Instead, we memorialize the Erinyes as the forces of injustice, walking the city's streets shrieking new cries of guilt. Suppose deconstruction circulated not as justice, immemorially, but injustice. Suppose deconstruction spoke at the installation of every authority in its ethical-political voice, inhabiting the space of the "-"? Suppose deconstruction, as critique, sought to bring *technē*'s law back to injustice by remembering the threat of the Mousēs and Erinyes, together with Pharmakeia, echoing the witchcraft of Musa Wo. What of such deconstruction?

Suppose injustice could be brought to an end only at the end of the world—another injustice! Suppose law's authority and justice's restitution enacted endless immemorial injustices, endless memories of sacrifices and losses, irreplaceable deaths, unforgettable sufferings and pains, inexhaustible injustices and losses! What restitution may we enact in the shadows of sacrifice and charity? What restitution can light the candle but one enacted in the shadows of charity and sacrifice?

What but injustice's injustice, older and younger than itself, in the form of law, *technē*'s measure, older and younger in the togetherness of justice and injustice, *poiēsis* and *technē*?

We come, after Anaximander, in our time, after his time, belonging to an immemorial history, a memory of injustice, seeking restitution, knowing that all of time fails to endure long enough for restitution, but that every moment renders restitution. On the side of *poiēsis*, we remember that every event or work, following Arendt, establishes a public space of difference, of community, wreaking injustice. The public space of appearance, of being together, rests on inexhaustible sacrifices and losses. On the side of *technē*, of law, we recall that every event, every instrument, renders restitution for injustice, inexhaustibly renders restitution for inexhaustible sacrifices and losses.

We add, where *poiēsis* meets *technē*, that we cannot distinguish, cannot separate by rule or law, justice from its injustices, restitution from domination and oppression. This lack of distinction, lack of distinctiveness, of justice, inseparable from loss, from death, life inseparable from death, renders justice's restitution in the form of law. Law achieves its goal, its authority, under reason's madness, by enacting and repeating injustice as it achieves justice, renders restitution by distinction. This restitution renders the circulation of *poiēsis* and *technē* as a play of Pharmakeia, poison and cure, catastrophe and healing, witches and sovereigns. In this restitution, in this healing that abjectly preserves its subjection, wounds never close, or when they close leave scars, leave endless scars—still restitution, still joy.

And now, as we conclude our restitution to Anaximander, rendering restitution for Anaximander as we repeat the authority of the West in recalling its injustices, we find ourselves returning to Hegel to ask whether we find ourselves in our memories of injustices, in our inescapable memories of endless injustices for which we hope and seek to find restitution, always reenacting injustice, whether we find ourselves in our unhappy consciousness.[24] After Bloch, do we remember vengeance in Greece as the inescapable circulation of the Furies, our original sin for which we must pay endless retribution, vengeance after vengeance after vengeance? Or does such an economy circulate too great an injustice for us to bear? And with what measure? After Freud, do we remember our original, immemorial injustice as the load we bear against which civilization wars in vain?

If all are immemorially guilty, can we find any more guilty than others except under *technē*'s law? By what measure would we find any more guilty or all equally guilty as if guilt belonged first of all and always to *technē*? What of witches' guilt, Orithyia's guilt, as victim and as mother of the world? How would we measure the sins of the mother of the world? How would we measure the sins of the children of the Holocaust?

In refusing to let reason's absolute authority, absolute law, heal the wounds of fate, do we repeat the endless cacophony of violence and domination as another injustice imposed on injustice? And if we agree that two injustices do not make one justice, what of this endless injustice? What happy restitution?

Levinas denies that the ethical face to face, complete responsibility before the Other, requires happiness to seal its fate.[25] Happiness does not belong to the ethical-political, but belongs to *technē*, to instrumentality and teleology. Yet our ethical-political, the "-" that divides and joins them, also joins *technē* to *poiēsis, technē-poiēsis*, joins injustice with justice. The restitution that repeatedly collapses into another injustice institutes justice. Law institutes justice as *technē* under the magical inspiration of the Mousēs, in the play of *mousika*, exceeding the rule of law as Pharmakeia. If this movement reversed, if we let it reverse in our thought of restitution, then the juncture of injustice with *poiēsis*, endlessly repeating justice's injustices, would pay endless restitution for every injustice. In this sense, injustice's restitution renders justice. In this sense, *technē*'s law belongs to the good, in the play of witchcraft, sorcery, and magic, in their ambiguities, in the economy of their sacrifices and losses, in the spaces between humanity and animality, where the witches play, where we shed and drink sacrificial blood as the greatest enactment of injustice—and justice.

Abandon hope, ye who enter time. Abandon hope that justice may be cleaved from injustice, under law.

Abandon hope, ye who live in time, that injustice belongs to human beings, to their subjection, as if things, animals and things, creatures and things, natural things, mechanical things, did not abjectly fall under subjection, into domination. To divide justice from injustice according to humanity reinstitutes the immemorial injustice of *Geschlecht*.

Abandon hope, ye who live in justice, of measuring happiness under law. Happiness belongs to unending restitution. We hope to pay restitution not as sorrow, guilt, shame, or vengeance, but as happiness without measure.

If human beings have the right to life, liberty, and the pursuit of happiness, so does every animal and every thing. After Spinoza, nature's justice represents the right of each thing to pursue and to desire its own way, however magical, to pursue whatever freedom is possible within its necessity. Yet human beings cannot live with these rights except in conflict, within injustice, calling for repeated restitution. Natural creatures cannot live within their magic except among the conflicts of injustice. *La réalité comporte le différend*; injustice composes nature; restitution composes nature's economy.

Nature's justice falls into time as law and *technē*, reason's truth. Yet we presuppose in this falling something older circulating, perhaps not older than time, but archaic, immemorial, nature's movement and relations, the relevance of things to one another as injustice. Locality in nature, nature's inexhaustibility, represents nature's necessity, its hold on itself as law, but also law's slippage, the slip of its hold on truth and reason, given as natural law, a slippage as injustice. Nature's relevance to and within itself, natural things moving and being moved, undergoing and instituting, in time, marks injustice, an archaic injustice whose immemoriality resists the authority of time. Injustice does not lend its authority to all time, to any time, but resists, displaces, any law of time, including its own truth in time, displaces and resists authority, its own authority, as injustice, as restitution, as nature's economy.

Injustice belongs to nature as relevance, natural things in relation to each other. Injustice belongs to nature as inexhaustibility, natural things exceeding each other's powers. Injustice repeats the aboriginality of nature, fulfilled in time as *technē* and *poiēsis*, realized as truth and law, as justice.

The sins of justice's law blind us to the call for restitution, as if we owed nothing to others, as if we might be happy without debt. We grant this call to Levinas, the debt and responsibility to the Other, except that we refuse to define its limits, so that it falls upon us everywhere, monstrously falls upon us everywhere even toward those we cannot grant reciprocity as subjects. This call of *praxis*, what we call ethical-political, echoes charity, with two further resonances, the inexhaustibility of charity and the sacrifices charity demands. Immemorial injustice repeats the claim of inexhaustibility upon us. Restitution replies with *technē*'s justice, with inexhaustible *technē* joining the inexhaustibility of *poiēsis* in the "-," the economy, of valor.

Valor represents the juncture of *technē* and *poiēsis* as *praxis*, of ethics and politics as the "-" where justice meets injustice in justice; of restitution with injustice; of charity and sacrifice under law.

How can we remember immemorial authority, the excesses of every legal authority, except in the form of endless suspicion and restitution? And because this suspicion and restitution enact another unjust authority, impose other wounds, can we avoid taking justice's injustice as always both older and younger than itself? We remember, in our memories of archaic injustices, that injustice is also younger, along with its justices.

We remember our subjection to every must, every necessity, including the authority of the we, the force of community and proximity. This suspicion of necessity's force, within reason and community, renders justice's law in the economy of its injustices.

We remember our suspicion of the we and the many, of consensus and multiplicity, remember to be suspicious of diversity's authority.

We remember the mother of the world as victim of monstrous injustice, remember the monstrosity of goodness.

Do our wounds overcome us? Can injustice bring peace?

> The Adventure of the Universe starts with the dream and reaps tragic Beauty. This is the secret of the union of Zest with Peace:—That the suffering attains its end in a Harmony of Harmonies. The immediate experience of this Final Fact, with its union of Youth and Tragedy, is the sense of Peace. In this way the World receives its persuasion towards such perfections as are possible for its diverse individual occasions. (Whitehead, *Adventures of Ideas*, p. 381)

Against the dream of the end we dream of inexhaustible restitution. Against the tragedy of injustice we remember Musa Wo. Against the teleology of perfection we pursue the impossibility of a "harmony of all perfections" (Whitehead, *Adventures of Ideas*, p. 356) as justice, as peace. We seek peace not as perfection but as injustice's justice, without measure, injustice in justice, as authority's lack of authority, still authority.

With this return to authority's lack of authority we reinstitute the monsters of injustice in the economy of lawful representation, reason's truth, remembering the monstrosities of truth as immemorial injustices.

An ethics-politics of monstrous injustice, of injustice's monstrosities.

An ethics-politics of monstrous injustices within nature's locality and inexhaustibility, as charity, sacrifice, and valor.

The inexhaustible injustices of inexhaustible valor.

The inexhaustible play of the Erinyes, together with Pharmakeia, the endless dance of restitution for immemorial injustices.

Tell me the story of Pharmakeia.

    justice, injustice, law
    nature, *physis*
       locality, inexhaustibility, ergonality
       power, desire, representation
       knowledge, truth, language
    canon
       West, non-West
    mastery
       subjection, abjection, monstrosity
       slavery
       animal sacrifice and possession
    time, memory, history
    technē, poiēsis
    economy, measure, circulation
    public, private

> violence, domination
>> blood
>> force
>> sexual violence
>> danger

Tell me the story of the monstrosity of goodness, the abjection of the subject, endlessly subjected to excessive authority, the unjust restitution, as justice, for endless injustice.

> justice, injustice, law
> nature
> power, desire, representation
> time, memory, history
> *technē, poiēsis*
> violence, domination
> the good

Tell me the story again of Pharmakeia. Beware of Musa Wo.

NOTES

Chapter I. Injustice's Debt

1. Whoever "we" may represent, however homogeneous or multifarious, repetitions of injustice. How can we write or think without a "we"?

2. "Into those things from which existing things have their coming into being, their passing away, too, takes place, according to what must be; for they make reparation to one another for their injustice according to the ordinance of time, as he puts it in somewhat poetical language" (Simplicius, *Phys.*, 24, 18 [DK 12 B 1]. Quoted from John Manley Robinson, *An Introduction to Early Greek Philosophy* [*EGP*] [Boston: Houghton Mifflin, 1968], p. 34. All Greek fragments are quoted from this edition unless otherwise indicated. We translate *tisis* as restitution, remembering the injustice of punishment.)

"[W]ar is universal and justice is strife" is from Heraclitus, 5.19, in Robinson, *EGP*, p. 92 (DK 22 B 102).

3. I distinguish law from Law, authority from Authority, after Foucault's distinction between power and Power. See n.30, this chapter.

4. Martin Heidegger, "The Anaximander Fragment" (*AF*), in *Early Greek Thinking*, trans. D. F. Krell and F. A. Capuzzi (New York: Harper & Row, 1984). Derrida reminds us that Heidegger's relation to the Greeks did not remain fixed: "Twenty years later, Heidegger will have to suggest, in short, that the Greek language has no word to say—nor therefore, to translate—*Geist*: at least a certain *Geistlichkeit*, if not the *Geistigkeit* of *Geist*.... The *Geist* of this *Geistlichkeit* could be thought only in *our language*" (Jacques Derrida, *Of Spirit* [*OS*], trans. G. Bennington and R. Bowlby [Chicago: University of Chicago Press, 1987], pp. 70–71). The Greeks may have been too close to Being, as "we" may be perhaps too far from it, if "our language" speaks German. And what, we wonder, of the proximity of other languages, French or English, to immemorial injustice?

"The Anaximander Fragment" was written after that twenty years, after Heidegger's rethinking of the relation of the Greeks to Being and after his disastrous collision with "the highest" German spirit.

5. The Anaximander fragment, from Heidegger, *AF*, p. 29: "kata to chreōn didonai gar auta dikēn kai tisin allēlois tēs adikias," canonically translated into German as "in das hinein geschicht auch ihr Vergehen nach der Schuldigkeit; denn sei zahlen einander gerechte Strafe und Buße für ihre Ungerechtigkeit nach der Zeit Anordnung."

6. "As it reveals itself in beings, Being withdraws" (Heidegger, *AF*, p. 26).

7. Jean-François Lyotard, *Heidegger and "the jews"* (*HJ*), trans. A. Michel and M. Roberts (Minneapolis: University of Minnesota Press, 1990), p. 4.

8. Emmanuel Levinas, *Otherwise than Being or beyond Essence* (*OB*), trans. A. Lingis (The Hague: Martinus Nijhoff, 1981), p. 3.

9. The word *proper* does not sound in the French of "dans le sentir de la responsabilité" (Emmanuel Levinas, *Autrement qu'être ou au-delà de l'essence* [The Hague: Martinus Nijhoff, 1978], p. 136), but echoes in the *soi-même* of *l'ipséité*, another, vulnerable identity: "The unjustifiable identity of ipseity is expressed in terms such as ego, I, oneself, and, this work aims to show throughout, starting with the soul, sensibility, vulnerability, maternity and materiality, which describe responsibility for others" (Levinas, *OB*, p. 106).

10. In *Der Spiegel*, quoted by Derrida: "I am speaking of the special relationship, inside the German language, with the language of the Greeks and their thought. It is something which the French are always confirming for me today. When they begin to think they speak German: they say definitely that they would not manage it in their language" (Derrida, *OS*, p. 69).

11. Close to Levinas, Lyotard writes of the hold of Being's essence on Heidegger's thought of destiny, making him forget the Forgotten: "remaining anchored in the thought of Being, in the 'Western' prejudice that the Other is Being, it has nothing to say about a thought in which the Other is the Law.... Freedom is owed not to the Law but to being. And by this misprision, Heidegger's thought reveals itself, quite despite itself, as, in its turn, the hostage of the Law. This is its real 'fault'" (Lyotard, *HJ*, p. 89). In Levinas's words: "Heidegger tries to conceive subjectivity in function of Being, of which it expresses an 'epoque': . . . Every overcoming as well as every revaluing of Being in the subject would still be a case of Being's essence." "Our inquiry concerned with the *otherwise than being* catches sight, in the very hypostasis of a subject, its subjectification, of an ex-ception, a null-site on the hither side of the negativity which is always speculatively recuperable, an *outside* of the absolute which can no longer be stated in terms of being" (Levinas, *OB*, pp. 17–18). Do we hear, beyond Levinas if not Lyotard, the otherwise beyond subjectivity, especially the Western Subject, toward nature's others?

12. "Why always say of painting that it renders, that it restitutes?" (Jacques Derrida, "Restitutions" [*R*], in *The Truth in Painting*, trans. G. Bennington and I. McLeod [Chicago: University of Chicago Press, 1987], p. 258). Why always say of truth that it restores us to an absent presence, to a proper place; of Van Gogh's painting of two shoes: "to discharge a more or less ghostly debt, restitute the shoes, render them to their rightful owner; if it's a matter of knowing from where they *return*, . . . "? (Derrida, *R*, p. 258). See chap. 8, pp. 202–203.

13. "—And yet. Who said—I can't remember—'there are no ghosts in Van Gogh's pictures'? Well, we've got a ghost story on our hands here all right" (Derrida, *R*, p. 257).

14. Plato, *Parmenides*, in *Plato: The Collected Dialogues*, ed. E. Hamilton and A. Cairns (Princeton, N.J.: Princeton University Press, Bollingen Series, 1969), 128e. All quotations from Plato are from this edition, except where otherwise noted.

15. See my *Locality and Practical Judgment: Charity and Sacrifice* (New York: Fordham University Press), forthcoming, and *The Ring of Representation* (*RR*) (Albany: State University of New York Press, 1992). The latter, especially, composes the theme of nature's *ergonality*, work, as representation, resonating as a triangle of locality, inexhaustibility, and ergonality. We represent things as local, limited, but represent every limit as limited, local, leading beyond itself inexhaustibly. Locality and inexhaustibility work through power, desire, and representation, reverberating through pairs of sonant categories: locale-ingredient, unison-resonance, belonging-departing, stillness-polyphony. The theme of our work here sounds the injustices within the triangle of power, desire, and representation. Together with the injustices in things, in local, inexhaustible things and their work, charity expresses inexhaustibility, sacrifice expresses locality, valor expresses work. Charity represents our immeasurable responsibility; sacrifice represents inescapable injustice; valor represents the work we do in the conjunction of injustice and responsibility.

We echo the categories of ergonality, the fragmentation and dispersion of identity, the disruption of its authority, expressing archaic injustice:

> A *locus*, located and locating, in spheres of relevance: a *locale* of its *ingredients*; an ingredient of other locales.
> An ingredient, one among many other ingredients in a locale: as one, a *unison* with many *resonances*, the other ingredients relevant to it in that locale.
> A unison including many other unisons: a *superaltern unison* located in a *superaltern locale*.
> An ingredient with a superaltern unison in a superaltern locale *belongs* there, otherwise it *departs*. Every ingredient belongs to and departs from any of its locations in *harmony* and *disharmony*.
> An ingredient together with other alternatives ingredient in a locale: such an ingredient works there in *polyphony*, otherwise in *still-*

ness, lacking possibilities. Every ingredient echoes stilly and polyphonically in any of its locations. (Ross, *RR*, p. 13)

Charity represents responsibility together with injustice.
Sacrifice represents the injustice of responsibility.
Valor represents immemorial injustice as restitution.

16. "The wounds of the spirit [*Geist*] heal and leave no scars behind" (G. W. F. Hegel, *Phenomenology of Mind* (*PM*), trans. J. Baillie [London: Allen & Unwin, 1964], p. 676). These lines precede the final chapter on Absolute Knowledge, emphasizing sacrifice. "Knowledge is aware not only of itself, but also of the negative of itself, or its limit. Knowing its limit means knowing how to sacrifice itself" (*PM*, p. 806). Even here, the question of scars remains: Anaximander's *adikias*. The sacrifice is our own.

17. Alfred North Whitehead, *Process and Reality*, corr. ed., ed. D. R. Griffin and D. W. Sherburne (New York: Free Press, 1978), p. 340.

18. G. W. F. Leibniz, "On the Ultimate Origin of Things," in *Leibniz Selections*, ed. P. Wiener (New York: Scribners, 1951), p. 351.

19. Hannah Arendt, *The Human Condition* (Chicago: University of Chicago Press, 1958), p. 52.

20. Jean-Luc Nancy, *The Inoperative Community* (translation of *La communauté désoeuvrée*), trans. P. Connor, L. Garbus, M. Holland, and S. Sawhney (Minneapolis: University of Minnesota Press, 1991).

21. Michel Foucault, "Theatrum Philosophicum," in *Language, Countermemory, Practice* (Ithaca, N.Y.: Cornell University Press, 1977), p. 192.

22. Derrida speaks in "Violence and Metaphysics," after Levinas, of the violence of light, suggesting that "Light is only one example of . . . 'several' fundamental 'metaphors,' but what an example! Who will ever dominate it, who will ever pronounce its meaning without first being pronounced by it? What language will ever escape it? How, for example, will the metaphysics of the face as the *epiphany* of the other free itself of light?" (in Derrida, *Writing and Difference*, trans. A. Bass [Chicago: University of Chicago Press, 1978], p. 92). Never mind the authority required to dominate light, even to hope to escape from its authority. See also Luce Irigaray, *The Speculum of the Other Woman*, ed. G. C. Gill (Ithaca: Cornell University Press, 1985).

23. "With the notion of the sublime . . . Kant will always get the better of Hegel. The *Erhabene* persists, not over and beyond, but right in the heart of the *Aufgehobenen*" (Jean-François Lyotard, *The Differend* [Minneapolis: University of Minnesota Press, 1988], p. 77).

24. "I would like to call a *differend* [*différend*] the case where the plaintiff is divested of the means to argue and becomes for that reason a victim" (Lyotard, *The Differend*, p. 9)

25. See n.15, this chapter.

26. Ludwig Wittgenstein, *Tractatus Logico-Philosophicus*, trans. D. F. Pears and B. F. McGuinness (London: Routledge & Kegan Paul, 1961), p. 151: "What we cannot speak about we must consign to silence."

27. I call the play, the circulation, of judgment upon judgment "semasis" (see Ross, *RR*, chap. 2).

28. Trinh T. Minh-ha, *Woman, Native, Other: Writing Postcoloniality and Feminism* (Bloomington: Indiana University Press, 1989), p. 101.

29. Michel Foucault, "Truth and Power," in *Power/Knowledge*, trans. and ed. C. Gordon (New York: Pantheon, 1980), p. 131.

30. Michel Foucault, *The History of Sexuality*, vol. 1, trans. R. Hurley (New York: Vintage, 1980), p. 95. Following Foucault, I distinguish Power under law from power everywhere (*pouvoir* from « le » *pouvoir*), Law from law, Humanity from humanity. The subtitle of the French edition, untranslated, is *la volonté de savoir*.

31. Years ago, I pursued a notion of responsibility akin to Levinas's, close to archaic injustice, distinguishing between *pervasive responsibility* and *complete responsibility*, the former a condition of humanity, the latter within the moral life:

> The notion of pervasive responsibility is derived from the fundamental interrogative posture a moral agent bears toward the world he lives in, and the unavoidable obligation he has to *respond* to the questions that arise by *seeking* answers. Pervasive responsibility is the precondition of obtaining answers. It is the attitude of *being obliged to respond*, of standing before events interrogatively and accountably for the actions we undertake or omit. . . .
>
> However, there is another conception of responsibility, in which we go beyond the affirmation of a moral commitment of perpetual interrogation and response, to the awareness of the methods needed for the resolution of moral conflicts. . . .
>
> There is required a second notion of responsibility, according to which some men are responsible for what they do while others are not. I shall call this *personal* or *complete responsibility*. (Stephen David Ross, *The Nature of Moral Responsibility* [Detroit: Wayne State University Press, 1973], pp. 235, 236)

I have not changed my view of a responsibility more pervasive than personal responsibility, but I believe I have gained a different sense of its truth. It now appears as charity, joined with sacrifice as valor.

I no longer speak of human beings as "men."

The notion of pervasive responsibility bears affinities with Levinas, as quoted here. Alphonso Lingis, Levinas's translator, describes his and Heidegger's views of responsibility, emphasizing their affinities: "Responsibility is a bond. It is a bond with an imperative order, a command. All subjective movements are under an order; subjectivity is this subjection. This bond does not only determine a being to act, but is constitutive of subjectivity as such, determines it to be" (Lingis, Translator's Introduction, in Levinas, *OB*, p. xiii). Lingis goes on to distinguish this responsibility before Being in Heidegger from Levinas's relation to the other: "But—and this is the most distinctive and original feature of Levinas's ethical philosophy—the locus where this imperative is articulated is the other who faces—the face of the other. . . . Responsibility is in fact a relationship with the other, in his very alterity. Then a relationship with alterity as such is constitutive of subjectivity" (p. xiii). If archaic injustice disappears in Heidegger, vanishing into the oblivion of Being's authority, it appears in Levinas in relation to the other's subjectivity, constituting my subjectivity. If we hesitate to grant Being privilege over beings, even belonging with them, hesitate at such an injustice, we may hesitate to grant the injustice of limiting responsibility for injustice to the subject-other, as if *things* bore neither responsibility nor injustice.

We struggle with the authority of the subject: "The problem of transcendence and of God and the problem of subjectivity irreducible to essence, irreducible to essential immanence, go together" (Levinas, *OB*, p. 17). We add in this language injustice irreducible to subjectivity, even as God.

32. Ari Shavit, "On Gaza Beach," *New York Review of Books*, 18 July 1991, p. 4, speaking of Israeli guards in Palestinian internment camps.

33. "My relationship with the other as neighbor gives meaning to my relations with all the others. . . . This means concretely or empirically that justice is not a legality regulating human masses, from which a technique of social equilibrium is drawn, harmonizing antagonistic forces. . . . Justice is impossible without the one that renders it finding himself in proximity" (Levinas, *OB*, p. 159).

Chapter II. Authority's Rule

1   Richard T. de George, *The Nature and Limits of Authority* (Kansas: University Press of Kansas, 1985), p. 1.

2. Ibid., p. 14.

3. Ibid., p. 17.

4. E. M. Adams, "The Philosophical Grounds of the Present Crisis of Authority," in *Authority: A Philosophical Analysis*, ed. R. Baine Harris (University, Ala.: University of Alabama Press, 1976), p. 3. Adams's article was written in 1969, at a moment at which there appeared to many to be a crisis of authority. At a moment, perhaps not always.

5. Cicero, *Laws* I, VI; reprinted in *The Great Legal Philosophers* (*GLP*), ed. Clarence Morris (Philadelphia: University of Pennsylvania Press, 1971), p. 44.

6. Cicero, *Laws*, III, III; in Morris, *GLP*, p. 53.

7. Ronald Dworkin, *Law's Empire* (Cambridge: Harvard University Press, 1986), p. vii. An unabashed affirmation of the supreme authority of law *at its best*. See also chap. 11, n.15.

8. Jacques Derrida, "Force of Law: the 'Mystical Foundation of Authority,'" *Cardozo Law Review* 11 (1991): 919; Walter Benjamin, "Critique of Violence," in *Reflections*, ed. P. Dementz (New York: Harcourt Brace Jovanovich, 1986), p. 293.

9. Franz Kafka, *The Trial*, trans. W. Muir and E. Muir (New York: Modern Library, 1956), p. 269.

10. "Law without force is an empty name, a thing without reality, for it is force, in realizing the norms of law, that makes law what it is and ought to be" (Rudolf von Ihering, *Law as a Means to an End*, trans. I. Husik [Boston Book Co., 1913]; reprinted in Morris, *GLP*, p. 406). "[I]n societies like ours the command of the public force is intrusted to the judges in certain cases, and the whole power of the state will be put forth, if necessary, to carry out their judgments and decrees" (Oliver Wendell Holmes, Jr., "The Path of the Law," *Harvard Law Review* 10 (26 March 1897): 457; reprinted in Morris, *GLP*, p. 421). "Laws proper, or properly so-called, are commands; laws which are not commands, are laws improper or improperly so called" (John Austin, *Lectures on Jurisprudence* [London: John Murray, Ltd., 1875]; reprinted in Morris, *GLP*, p. 336).

11. Two examples: "Thou shalt have no other gods before me" (Exodus 20.3); "And thou shalt make it a perfume" (Exodus 31.34–35).

12. Michel Foucault, *Madness and Civilization* (New York: Random House, 1965), p. v. See here, chap. 6, pp. 139–46.

13. Thomas Hobbes, *Leviathan* (*L*) (Indianapolis: Bobbs-Merrill, 1958). All references to *Leviathan* are to this edition.

14. "It is necessary to understand that war is universal and justice is strife, and that all things take place in accordance with strife and necessity." "War is the father and king of all" (Heraclitus, Fragments 5.22 and 5.24, in Robinson, *EGP*, p. 93 [DK 22 B 80 and DK 22 B 53]).

Derrida appears to have something like this in mind when he says that justice is oldest of all, after Heraclitus, and that *dikē* is strife, war, *adikia*: justice is injustice. (Derrida, "Force of Law," p. 927.)

15. For a detailed discussion of representation in Hobbes, see my *The Ring of Representation*, chap. 3.

16. See ibid., chaps. 4 and 6.

17. See the detailed discussion of the exchange between Socrates and Thrasymachus in chap. 7, pp. 159–67.

18. John Rawls, *A Theory of Justice* (Cambridge: Belknap Press of Harvard University, 1971).

19. John Locke, *An Essay Concerning the True Original, Extent, and End of Civil Government* (*T*), in *The English Philosophers from Bacon to Mill*, ed. E. A. Burtt (New York: Modern Library, 1939), chap. 1, p. 404.

20. See chap. 2, n.8.

21. Foucault, *The Order of Things* (New York: Vintage, 1973), p. 257.

Chapter III. Law's Injustice

1. We are pursuing Whitehead's sense that evil lies in the nature of finite things, not just in their *archai*. If health (or justice) "is the proportionate mixture of the qualities" (Alcmaeon, DK 24 B 4), it presupposes a conflict at the very heart of their proportion. We question whether restitution may be proportionate, under measure and law, which are not themselves unjust, or whether their own justice and proportion retain the conflict from which they arise.

We are pursuing the triangle of locality, inexhaustibility, and ergonality as injustice; the triangle of power, desire, and representation as restitution.

2. Heraclitus, fragment 5.22, in Robinson, *EGP*, p. 93 (DK 22 B 80). In Derrida's reading of Heidegger reading Heraclitus, justice *is* injustice: "and for example for Heraclitus, *Dikē*—justice, *droit*, trial, penalty or punishment, vengeance, and so forth—is *Eris* (conflict, *Streit*, discord, *polemos, Kampf*), that is, it is *adikia*, injustice as well" (Derrida, "Force of Law," p. 927).

3. "The meaning of Peace is most clearly understood by considering it in its relation to the tragic issues which are essential in the nature of things. Peace is the understanding of tragedy, and at the same time its preservation" (Alfred North Whitehead, *Adventures of Ideas* [New York: Macmillan, 1933], p. 368).

4. Hesiod, *Works and Days*, 175–80, in Robinson, *EGP*, 1.16, p. 18.

5. See Benjamin, "Critique of Violence," and see discussions here, pp. 172–75.

6. Hesiod, *Works and Days*, 216–18, in Robinson, *EGP*, 1.18, p. 20.

7. Aeschylus, *Eumenides* (*E*), trans. E. D. A. Morshead, in *The Complete Greek Drama*, ed. W. J. Oates and E. O'Neill, Jr. (New York: Random House, 1938), p. 287.

8. But more and more root out the impious,
For as a gardener fosters what he sows,
So foster I this race, whom righteousness
Doth rend from sorrow.
(Aeschylus, *E*, p. 303)

9. Herodotus, *Histories*, 7.10, in Robinson, *EGP*, 2.38, p. 37. Robinson calls this, after Emerson, a law of compensation as balance and proportion. We wonder whether it may rather represent the law of excess in every compensation, for which history must pay unending restitution.

10. Heraclitus, 5.19, in Robinson, *EGP* [DK 22 B 102].

11. Ibid., 5.29 [DK 22 B 60].

12. Ibid., 5.33 [DK 22 B 50].

13. Parmenides, 6.10, in Robinson, *EGP*, p. 113 (DK 28 B 8).

14. Ibid.

15. "The institution of slavery in antiquity, though not in later times, was not a device for cheap labor or an instrument of exploitation for profit but rather the attempt to exclude labor from the conditions of man's life" (Arendt, *The Human Condition*, p. 94).

16. German students.
The National Socialist revolution rings in the total collapse of our German existence [*Dasein*].

. . . .

The Führer himself, and he alone, is the German reality of today, and of the future, and of its law. Learn to know always more deeply. Starting now each thing demands decision and every action, responsibility.
Heil Hitler! Rector Martin Heidegger. (Martin Heidegger, "Deutsche Studenten," *Freiburger Studentenzeitung* 15 [8th semester], no. 1, Nov 3, 1933, 1; quoted in Victor Farias, *Heidegger and Nazism*, ed. J. Margolis and T. Rockmore, trans. G. R. Ricci, [Philadelphia: Temple University Press, 1989], pp. 118–19)

17. It appears in German as *Geist* and as *Geschlecht*. See Derrida's critique of Heidegger (Jacques Derrida, "*Geschlecht* II: Heidegger's Hand," in *Deconstruction and Philosophy*, ed. J. Sallis [Chicago: University of Chicago Press, 1987]) and *Of Spirit*. See here, chap. 6, pp. 149–52.

18. See chap. 1, p. 3.

19. Whitehead, *Process and Reality*, p. 39.

20. The play of repetition and difference as tradition belongs to some non-Western traditions in a masked way. V. S. Naipaul speaks of the hold of repetition on writing in Java.

> I met a young man who wanted above everything else to be a poet and to live the life of the mind. . . . The mother was a person of culture and elegance; that should be stressed. She was elegant in visage and dress and speech; her manners were like art; they were Javanese court manners.
>
> So I asked the young man . . . "But isn't your mother secretly proud that you are a poet?" He said in English . . . "She wouldn't have even a sense of what being a poet is."
>
> . . . It would be rejected as a impossibility, because for the poet's mother the epics of her country—and to her they would have been like sacred texts—already existed, had already been written. They had only to be learned or consulted.
>
> For the mother, all poetry had already been written. (V. S. Naipaul, "Our Universal Civilization," *New York Review of Books*, 31 January 1981, p. 22)

21. "Viewed from a sufficient distance, all systems of philosophy are seen to be personal, temperamental, accidental, and premature. . . . In a word, they are human heresies" (George Santayana, "Philosophical Heresy," *Obiter Scripta*, ed. J. Buchler and B. Schwartz [New York: Scribners, 1936], p. 94). See my *Metaphysical Aporia and Philosophical Heresy* (Albany: State University of New York Press, 1990) for a detailed discussion of aporia and heresy in the tradition, reworking Santayana's ideas. The themes of injustice and restitution quite transform these ideas in relation to the tradition, precisely what we are exploring here.

22. As I have in my own way in *Metaphysical Aporia*.

23. Some traditions do not welcome heresy as enthusiastically as the West. See n.20, this chapter.

24. See Martin Bernal, *Black Athena: The Afroasiatic Roots of Classical Civilization* (New Brunswick, N.J.: Rutgers University Press, 1987).

25. Some examples are in *Phaedrus* where both Theuth and Ammon come from Egypt, later represented by the Greeks as Hermes and Zeus (*Phaedrus* 274de); in *Timaeus*, where the Egyptian goddess Neith is later called "Athena" by the Greeks (*Timaeus* 22); and *Critias*, reaffirming that the story of Atlantis originated in Egypt (*Critias* 113a).

26. Gayatri Spivak, "Can the Subaltern Speak?" (*CSS*) in *Marxism and the Interpretation of Culture*, ed. Cary Nelson (Urbana: University of Illinois Press,

1988), p. 291. See my *The Ring of Representation*, chaps. 3 and 10, for additional discussions of her critique.

27. She expresses our concern with the Greeks directly, doubled in relation to origins: "This paper is committed to the notion that . . . a nostalgia for lost origins can be detrimental to the exploration of social realities within the critique of imperialism" (Spivak, *CSS*, p. 291).

28. Ibid., p. 294. See also, "If, in the context of colonial production, the subaltern has no history and cannot speak, the subaltern as female is even more in shadow" (ibid., p. 287). "On the other side of the international division of labor, the subject of exploitation cannot know and speak the text of female exploitation, even if the absurdity of the nonrepresenting intellectual making space for her to speak is achieved. The woman is doubly in shadow" (ibid., p. 288).

29. Trinh Minh-ha, *Woman, Native, Other*, pp. 98–99.

30. The passage continues: "and there is a double, or more than double, glut of occupation in the life we have rightly described as concerned with the practice of every virtue of body and mind. . . . every free citizen will need an ordered disposition of all his hours; he must begin with it at daybreak, and follow it without any intermission until the succeeding dawn and sunrise. . . . In fact, that any citizen whatsoever should spend the whole of any night in unbroken sleep, and not let all his servants see him always awake and astir before anyone else in the house, must be unanimously pronounced a disgrace and an act unworthy of a free man, whether such a regulation should be regarded as law or as custom" (Plato, *Laws* 807de).

31. With the conclusion: "Then laws seem to be written copies of scientific truth in the various departments of life they cover, copies based as far as possible on the instructions received from those who really possess the scientific truth on these matters" (Plato, *Statesman* 300d).

32. It seems the easiest task to pass a rule regulating sexual conduct: "To see that the thing can be done, and how it can be done, is perfectly easy" (Plato, *Laws* 839c). "I say it is the law's simple duty to go straight on its way and tell our citizens that it is not for them to behave worse than birds and many other creatures which flock together in large bodies" (Plato, *Laws*, 840d). Except it shows itself to be supremely difficult. "But if, alas, they should be corrupted . . . " (Plato, *Laws* 840e). And this difficulty remains in all questions of rule and law. "[I]f we are ready, as they say, to stake the whole future of our polity on a throw of triple six or triple ace, why, so we must, and I, for one, will take my share in the risk. . . . But the hazard we run, mind you, is no slight one; there are not many others to be compared with it." "The dream on which we touched a while ago in our talk, when we painted our picture of the partnership of the mind and the head, will have found its fulfillment in real and working fact, if and when we have

seen our men scrupulously selected, duly educated, settled at the end of the process in the nation's central fortress and established there as guardians whose likes we have never seen in our whole lives for perfection as protectors" (Plato, *Laws* 969). We have never seen the like in our whole lives, but we will take a chance on it, as on a throw of the dice, although it represents the greatest hazard ever seen. One alternative holds that "we shall have to abandon the foundation of your city . . . " (Plato, *Laws* 969c). Does this alternative remain the only alternative for us, with the proviso that we cannot avoid the city, thereby cannot avoid injustice? We live under a system of law, of rule, always at great risk of injustice, where justice remains the unending activity of rectifying injustice, where rectification and restitution have no measure, arrive at no achievement, define what virtuous life may achieve, unending struggle with authority under law.

33. "[I]n no circumstance must one do wrong" (Plato, *Crito* 49b). "So one ought not to return a wrong or an injury to any person, whatever the provocation is" (Plato, *Crito* 49d).

34. *Minos*, from *The Works of Plato*, vol. 4, trans. T. Taylor (New York: Garland, 1984), p. 179. *Minos* is currently regarded as spurious. It has not always been so regarded, and may be thought genuine again.

35. Ibid., p. 182.

36. Ibid., p. 186.

37. The first appearance turns around the complex relationships among the young Socrates, Zeno, and Parmenides and to themselves. "That is where you are mistaken, Socrates; you imagine it was inspired, not by a youthful eagerness for controversy, but by the more dispassionate aims of an older man, . . . " (Plato, *Parmenides* 136e).

38. See also: "Therefore, at all times the one both is and is becoming older and younger than itself" (Plato, *Parmenides* 152e). "In this way the others will be younger than the one, the one older than the others" (Plato, *Parmenides* 153b). "Therefore, the one, if it *is* so, is not becoming, either older or younger than the others which *are* so" (Plato, *Parmenides* 154c).

39. Form and law present what belongs to things and their obligations—in time. To the idea of an *archē* we respond twice in Parmenides' words: "Only a man of exceptional gifts will be able to see that a form, or essence just by itself, does exist in each case, and it will require someone still more remarkable to discover it and to instruct another who has thoroughly examined all these difficulties" (Plato, *Parmenides* 135b). "But on the other hand . . . if . . . a man refuses to admit that forms of things exist or to distinguish a definite form in every case, he will have nothing on which to fix his thought, so long as he will allow that each thing has a character which is always the same, and in so doing he will completely destroy the significance of all discourse" (Plato, *Parmenides* 135c).

We respond twice in time, in relation to form and law. Discourse's law requires forms that only someone of exceptional gifts can discern. Law's requirements impose immense difficulties, repeatedly placing us at the edge of an abyss. Justice remains unknown and obscure; yet without it we possess neither wisdom nor virtue.

In the age of injustice, justice unfolds as nothing, nothing without injustice. The thought of justice without injustice, like being without nonbeing, appears too soon (Plato, *Parmenides* 135d), always too soon, representing why no end may come to the undertaking of truth and justice. The no end here plays against the alternative that without a form we "will completely destroy the significance of all discourse." The no end refers to the age of injustice and untruth before time, outside law, not evil and falsity in time, by law.

40. Discussed at length in the reading of *Phaedrus* in chap. 9.

41. All references to Aristotle, except as indicated, are from *The Basic Works of Aristotle*, ed. Richard McKeon (New York: Random House, 1941).

42. See also: "Scientific knowledge is judgment about things that are universal and necessary, and the conclusions of demonstration, and all scientific knowledge, follow from first principles. . . . This being so, the first principle from which what is scientifically known follows cannot be an object of scientific knowledge, of art, or of practical wisdom; . . ." (Aristotle, *Nicomachean Ethics* 1141a).

43. Chap. 9 takes up this possibility in detail.

44. Aristotle, *Magna Moralia*, from *The Complete Works of Aristotle*, ed. Jonathan Barnes (Princeton: Princeton University Press, 1984), 1195a.

45. Benedict de Spinoza, *A Political Treatise*, trans. R. H. M. Elwes (New York: Dover, 1951), p. 386.

46. Ibid., p. 387.

47. Benedict de Spinoza, *Ethics*, ed. James Gutmann (New York: Hafner, 1949), I, Appendix.

48. Levinas rejects Spinoza's *conatus* as interest in being where the otherwise than being bears a passivity beyond all passivity. Yet we may read Spinoza's *conatus* to express an endeavor, a desire, beyond all desires, representing an essence beyond all essence, otherwise than essence. "Each thing, in so far as it is in itself, endeavors to persevere in its being" (Spinoza, *Ethics*, III, Prop. 6). "The effort by which each thing endeavors to persevere in its own being is nothing but the actual essence of the thing itself" (Spinoza, *Ethics*, III, Prop. 7).

49. We remember the univocity of being. See Foucault, "Theatrum Philosophicum," and chap. 1, p. 8.

50. I discuss this in my *Metaphysical Aporia*, pp. 71–76.

51. Even so, in *Timaeus*, men who fail *aretē* in one life become women in the next (Plato, *Timaeus* 42bc).

52. "The story is that once upon a time these creatures were men—men of an age before there were any Muses—and that when the latter came into the world, and music made its appearance, some of the people of those days were so thrilled with pleasure that they went on singing, and quite forget to eat and drink until they actually died without noticing" (Plato, *Phaedrus* 259c). See the discussion in chap. 9, p. 238.

53. In Cixous, Kristeva, and Irigaray especially, where she speaks of the "feminine" rather than women: "The feminine cannot signify itself in any proper meaning, proper name, or concept, not even that of woman" (Irigaray, *This Sex Which Is Not One*, trans. C. Porter [Ithaca, N.Y.: Cornell University Press, 1985], p. 156). "[W]hat I want, in fact, is not to create a theory of woman, but to secure a place for the feminine within sexual difference" (Irigaray, *This Sex*, p. 159).

We may also rewrite Lyotard's comment on "the jews": How could this thought, a thought so devoted to remembering that a forgetting (of Being) takes place in all thought, in all art, in all "representation" of the world, how could it possibly have ignored the thought of sexual difference or gender, which, in a certain sense, thinks, tries to think, nothing but that very fact? How could this thought forget and ignore "Women" to the point of suppressing and foreclosing to the very end the horrifying (and inane) attempt at silencing, at making us forget forever what, for men, reminds us, ever since the beginning, that "there is" the Forgotten?

54. Baron de Montesquieu, *The Spirit of the Laws*, in Morris, *GLP*, p. 161.

55. Leibniz, "On the Ultimate Origin of Things" (*OUOT*), in *Leibniz Selections*, p. 351.

56. Leibniz, "On Destiny or Mutual Dependence," in *Leibniz Selections*, p. 572.

57. Jean-Jacques Rousseau, *The Social Contract* (*SC*), trans. G. D. H. Cole (New York: Dutton, 1950), p. 15.

58. Jeremy Bentham, *An Introduction to the Principles of Morals and Legislation* (*PML*), in Morris, *GLP*, p. 263.

59. Levinas calls it the assembling of beings whose "essence is interest" (Levinas, *OB*, p. 4). The assembling of which Bentham speaks destroys interest by composition.

60. "Of an action that is conformable to the principle of utility one may always say . . . that it is right it should be done" (Bentham, *PML*, p. 263).

61. John Stuart Mill, *Utilitarianism* (U), in *The English Philosophers from Bacon to Mill*, ed. E. A. Burtt (New York: Modern Library, 1939), p. 900.

62. "THE SCIENCE OF RIGHT has for its object the Principles of all the Laws which it is possible to promulgate by external legislation. . . . theoretical knowledge of Right and law in Principle, as distinguished from positive Laws and empirical cases, belongs to the pure SCIENCE OF RIGHT" (Immanuel Kant, "Kant's Philosophy of Law [An Exposition of the Fundamental Principles of Jurisprudence as the Science of Right]" [*SR*], in Morris, *GLP*, p. 241).

63. See my *Metaphysical Aporia*, chap. 8, for a discussion of aporia in Kant.

64. Immanuel Kant, *Critique of Practical Reason*, from *Kant's Critique of Practical Reason and Other Works on the Theory of Ethics*, trans. T. K. Abbott (London: Longman's, Green, 1954), p. 146: "[T]he concept of a causality free from empirical conditions, although empty (*i.e.* without any appropriate intuition), is yet theoretically possible and refers to an indeterminate object; but in compensation significance is given to it in the moral law, and consequently in a practical sense."

65. "It founds upon the principle of the possibility of an external Compulsion, such as may co-exist with the freedom of everyone according to universal Laws. . . . this compulsion is quite consistent with the Freedom of all, . . . " (Kant, *SR*, p. 243). It represents an authority whose universality does not abridge freedom. Hobbes shows himself more honest than this: the unabridged liberty marks the excesses of authority within itself. The consistency has no measure.

66. G. W. F. Hegel, *Hegel's Philosophy of Right* (*PR*), trans. T. M. Knox (London: Oxford University Press, 1967), p. 7.

67. We leave aside questions of the state, for example in war: "War has the higher significance that by its agency, as I have remarked elsewhere, 'the ethical health of peoples is preserved in their indifference to the stabilization of finite institutions; . . .'" (Hegel, *PR*, p. 210). War reflects the contingency of state sovereignty, together with its plurality. "The nation state is mind in its substantive rationality and immediate actuality and is therefore the absolute power on earth. It follows that every state is sovereign and autonomous against its neighbors" (Hegel, *PR*, p. 212). War's higher significance marks the limits of absolute authority. Authority knows no limit, in that sense cannot authorize itself. Does it follow, by analogy, that reason, truth, law, and desire, which depend for their efficacy on authority, possess no authorization?

68. "As a person, I am myself an *immediate* individual; if we give further precision to this expression, it means in the first instance that I am alive in this bodily organism which is my external existence, universal in content and undivided, the real pre-condition of every further determined mode of existence. But, all the same, as person, I possess my life and my body, like other things, only in so far as my will is in them" (Hegel, *PR*, p. 43).

69. See chap. 9.

70. "An animal cannot maim or destroy itself, but a man can" (Hegel, *PR*, p. 43). "An animal too has impulses, desires, inclinations, but has no will and must obey its impulse if nothing external deters it" (Hegel, *PR*, p. 229).

71. "Apes, too, have organs that can grasp, but they do not have hands. The hand is infinitely different from all the grasping organs—paws, claws, or fangs—different by an abyss of essence" (Martin Heidegger, "What Calls for Thinking?" *Basic Writings*, ed. David Farrell Krell [New York: Harper & Row, 1977] p. 357). Derrida says of this line: "Here in effect occurs a sentence that at bottom seems to me Heidegger's most significant, symptomatic, and seriously dogmatic" (Derrida, "*Geschlecht* II, p. 173). See chap. 6 for a detailed discussion of *Geschlecht*.

72. This archaic injustice of property appears in Hegel as inexhaustible plenitude. "The finitude of the subjective will in the immediacy of acting consists directly in this, that its action *presupposes* an external object with a complex environment" (Hegel, *PR*, p. 79). Complexity reflects the immeasurability of authority as if no individual, no event, can belong determinately to anyone, to any authority. "Hence, in the case of a complex event . . . it is open to the abstract Understanding to choose which of an endless number of factors it will maintain to be responsible for it" (Hegel, *PR*, p. 79). "[E]thical life is the concept of freedom developed into the existing world and the nature of self-consciousness" (Hegel, *PR*, p. 105). This existing world represents a complex environment permeated by indeterminacies of efficacy, responsibility, and authority. The absoluteness of sovereignty in the state belongs to the externalization, belongs to its complexity, realized in kinds.

The authority of the state, its absolute sovereignty, rests on its dispersion into distinctions of class and kind. Ethics in Hegel reflects class distinctions, class authority: "A man actualizes himself only in becoming something definite, i.e. something specifically particularized; this means restricting himself exclusively to one of the particular spheres of need" (Hegel, *PR*, p. 133). This expresses a traditionally Platonic view of self-realization, following *Republic* except that virtue for both belies the univocity of civic role. The absolute power of the sovereign, realized in the state, contrasts with the complexity of the environment and the finitude of action, resolved into distinctions of virtue and class.

73. John Dewey, *Philosophy and Civilization* (New York: Minton, Balch, 1931), p. 3.

74. John Dewey, *Human Nature and Conduct* (New York: Modern Library, 1930), p. 238.

75. John Dewey, "Context and Thought," in *Experience, Nature, and Freedom*, ed. R. Bernstein (Indianapolis: Bobbs-Merrill, 1960), p. 107.

76. John Dewey, *Experience and Nature* (New York: Dover, 1958), p. 4.

Chapter IV. Economy's Measure

1. G. W. F. Leibniz, "Whether the Essence of a Body consists in Extension," in *Leibniz Selections*, ed. p. Wiener (New York: Scribners, 1951), p. 101.

2. George Berkeley, *Principles of Human Knowledge* (*PK*), in *The English Philosophers from Bacon to Mill*, ed. E. A. Burtt (New York: Modern Library, 1939), p. 525.

3. G. W. F. Leibniz, "On Substance as Active Force Rather than Mere Extension," in *Leibniz Selections*, p. 158.

4. G. W. F. Leibniz, *The Monadology*, in *Leibniz Selections*, p. 533.

5. "Each portion of matter is not only divisible *ad infinitum*, as the ancients recognized, but also each part is actually endlessly subdivided into parts, of which each has some motion of its own: otherwise it would be impossible for each portion of matter to express the whole universe." "Whence we see that there is a world of creatures, of living beings, of animals, of entelechies, of souls, in the smallest particle of matter" (Leibniz, *Monadology*, p. 547).

6. Alfred North Whitehead, *Process and Reality* (*PR*), corr. ed., ed. D. R. Griffin and D. W. Sherburne (New York: Free Press, 1978), p. 65.

7. "This extensive continuum expresses the solidarity of all possible standpoints throughout the whole process of the world. It is not a fact prior to the world; it is the first determination of order—that is, of real potentiality—arising out of the general character of the world. In its full generality beyond the present epoch, it does not involve shapes, dimensions, or measurability; these are additional determinations of real potentiality arising from our cosmic epoch" (Whitehead, *PR*, p. 66).

8. See also: "Extension is the most general scheme of real potentiality, providing the background for all other organic relations" (Whitehead, *PR*, p. 67). "Every actual entity in its relationship to other actual entities is in this sense somewhere in the continuum, and arises out of the data provided by this standpoint" (Whitehead, *PR*, p. 67).

9. Alfred North Whitehead, *Science and the Modern World* (New York: Macmillan, 1925), pp. 249–50.

10. "[W]hat is metaphysically indeterminate has nevertheless to be categorically determinate" (Whitehead, *Science and the Modern World*, p. 250).

11. Michel Foucault, "Nietzsche, Genealogy, History," in *Language, Countermemory, Practice* (Ithaca, N.Y.: Cornell University Press, 1977), p. 151.

12. Jean-François Lyotard, *The Postmodern Condition: A Report on Knowl-*

edge, trans. G. Bennington and B. Massimi (Minneapolis: University of Minnesota Press, 1984), pp. xxiii–xxiv.

13. Jean-François Lyotard, *The Differend* (*D*) (Minneapolis: University of Minnesota Press, 1988), p. xi.

14. Martin Heidegger, "The Origin of the Work of Art," in *Poetry, Language, Thought*, trans. A. Hofstadter (New York: Harper & Row, 1971), p. 62.

15. In *Science and the Modern World*, these appear as "abstractive hierarchies" (*SMW*, p. 234).

16. Michel Foucault, "Truth and Power," in *Power/Knowledge*, p. 131. See also: "In societies like ours, the 'political economy' of truth is characterised by five important traits. 'Truth' is centred on the form of scientific discourse and the institutions which produce it; it is subject to constant economic and political incitement . . . " (ibid.). "Let us consider the stratagems by which we were induced to apply all our skills to discovering its [sex's] secrets, by which we were attached to the obligation to draw out its truth, and made guilty for having failed to recognize it for so long" (Foucault, *History of Sexuality*, p. 159).

17. The notion of general economy comes from Bataille, representing one reading of heterogeneity and excess as inseparable from authority. "The science of relating the object of thought to sovereign moments, in fact, is only a *general economy* which envisages the meaning of these objects in relation to each other and finally in relation to the loss of meaning. The question of this *general economy* is situated on the level of *political economy*, but the science designated by this name is only a restricted economy, . . . The *general economy*, in the first place, makes apparent that excesses of energy are produced, and that by definition, these excesses cannot be utilized. The excessive energy can only be lost without the slightest aim, consequently without any meaning. It is this useless, senseless loss that *is* sovereignty" (Georges Bataille, *L'Expérience intérieure* [Paris: Gallimard, 1954], p. 233; quoted in Derrida, "From Restricted to General Economy: A Hegelianism without Reserve," in *Writing and Difference*, trans. A. Bass (Chicago: University of Chicago Press, 1978), p. 271). This sovereignty, this authority, this excess lost without meaning, represents the age of injustice, older than any utilization, that haunts every use, every rule, every work.

18. Charles Sanders Peirce, "How to Make Our Ideas Clear," in *Collected Papers*, ed. C. Hartshorne and P. Weiss (Cambridge: Harvard University Press, 1931–35), 5.388–410; reprinted in *Philosophical Writings of Peirce*, ed. J. Buchler (New York: Dover, 1955), p. 38.

19. In *Euthyphro*: "Euthyphro, you think that you have such an accurate knowledge of things divine, and what is holy and unholy, that, in circumstances such as you describe, you can accuse your father? You are not afraid that you yourself are doing an unholy deed?" (Plato, *Euthyphro* 4e). By what authority can

you bring your father to trial for such a questionable crime? If not the gods' authority, then reason's authority.

20. Michel Foucault, *The Order of Things* (*OT*) (New York: Vintage, 1973), p. 169.

21. The idea of sublimation in Freud rests on units of affect and cathexis that can be transferred from one object of desire to another without loss. Pleasure and pain compose an economy of exchange and substitution not only in Freud but in Bentham and Mill. Saussure's view of language as differences provides a theory of phonemic and syntactic units that can be exchanged for each other. The universality of social law presupposes an economy under which each act and person comprises an equivalent unit without difference under law. What of this lack of difference under law?

22. We return to this question in an entirely different way in chaps. 9 and 10.

23. Told in Michel Foucault, *Discipline and Punish*, trans. A. Sheridan (New York: Vintage, 1979), pp. 3–6.

24. Michael Polanyi, *Personal Knowledge* (London: Routledge & Kegan Paul, 1958), p. 65.

25. See also: "Yet I do not enter this commitment unconditionally, as shown by the fact that I refuse to follow both the tradition and authority of science in its pursuit of the objectivist ideal in psychology and sociology. I accept the existing scientific opinion as a *competent* authority, but not as a *supreme* authority, for identifying the subject matter called 'science.'" (Polanyi, *Personal Knowledge*, p. 164).

26. Also:

> Just as in the order of representations the signs that replace and analyse them must also be representations themselves, so money cannot signify wealth without itself being wealth. But it becomes wealth because it is a sign; whereas a representation must first be represented in order subsequently to become a sign.
>
> Hence the apparent contradictions between the principles of accumulation and the rules of circulation. At any given moment of time, the number of coins in existence is determined. (Foucault, *OT*, p. 177)

27. "Such analyses show how value and exchange interlock; there would be no exchange if there were no immediate values.... But the exchange creates value in its turn, and in two ways. First, it renders useful things that without it would be of slight utility or perhaps none at all:.... On the other hand, exchange gives rise to a new type of value, which is 'appreciative': it organizes a reciprocal relation between utilities, which parallels the relation to mere need; ... " (Foucault, *OT*, p. 198).

28. Here Foucault offers no acknowledgment of Sade's misogyny. In *The History of Sexuality*, vol. 1, Foucault's discussion of Sade has a different ring, closer to violence and death, still without reference to gender except within sexuality: "In Sade, sex is without any norm or intrinsic rule that might be formulated from its own nature; but it is subject to the unrestricted law of a power which itself knows no other law of its own; if by chance it is at times forced to accept the order of progressions carefully disciplined into successive days, this exercise carries it to a point where it is no longer anything but a unique and naked sovereignty: an unlimited right of all-powerful monstrosity" (Foucault, *The History of Sexuality*, p. 149). Such an unrestricted law of power represents the monstrosity of injustice, whatever its powers.

29. "The prosperities of *Juliette* are still more solitary—and endless" (Foucault, *OT*, p. 211).

30. This discussion of Polanyi's view of traditional authority continues in chap. 9.

Chapter V. Subjection's Abjection

1. Martin Heidegger, "The Origin of the Work of Art" (*OWA*), in *Poetry, Language, Thought*, pp. 22–23.

2. See here, n.4, chap. 1, especially.

3. And *adikia*'s "reck": see chap. 1, p. 2.

4. But emphasized elsewhere, especially where he speaks of genealogy as the "insurrection of subjugated discourses" (Michel Foucault, "Two Lectures," in *Power/Knowledge*, trans. and ed. C. Gordon [New York: Pantheon, 1980]). Even here, as the subjugation and insurrection testify to injustice, we wonder at the subordination of pain and suffering within the positivities of discourse.

5. Even in Levinas, amid obsession and passivity, the subject is thrown down under the world's responsibilities, supporting rather than abjecting.

May we hear the subjection of authority in that wonderful passage in *The Archaeology of Knowledge* defining "us"? "[The diagnosis] establishes that we are difference, that our reason is the difference of discourses, our history the difference of times, our selves the difference of masks. That difference, far from being the forgotten and recovered origin, is this dispersion that we are and make" (Michel Foucault, *The Archaeology of Knowledge*, trans. Alan M. Sheridan Smith [New York: Pantheon, 1972], p. 131). May we understand, when archaeology passes into genealogy, insurrection, that this dispersion of differences composing us delimits another subjection, masked and dispersed, another authority?

6. Michel Foucault, *Discipline and Punish* (*DP*), p. 74.

7. Fyodor Dostoevsky, *Notes from Underground and The Grand Inquisitor* (*NU*), trans. R. E. Matlaw (New York: Dutton, 1960), p. 18.

8. Julia Kristeva, *Powers of Horror: An Essay on Abjection*, trans. L. S. Roudiez (New York: Columbia University Press), 1982, p. 209.

9. Michel Foucault, "Nietzsche, Genealogy, History," in *Language, Countermemory, Practice*, p. 150.

10. "The nature of these rules allows violence to be inflicted on violence and the resurgence of new forces that are sufficiently strong to dominate those in power" (Foucault, "Nietzsche, Genealogy, History," p. 151).

11. Lyotard, *The Differend* (*D*), p. 77. See p. 318 for the full quotation.

12. "This is what a wrong [*tort*] would be: a damage [*dommage*] accompanied by the loss of the means to prove the damage. This is the case if the victim is deprived of life, or of all his or her liberties, or of the freedom to make his or her ideas or opinions public, or simply of the right to testify to the damage, or even more simply if the testifying phrase is itself deprived of authority" (Lyotard, *D*, p. 5). "The title of this book suggests (through the generic value of the definite article) that a universal rule of judgment between heterogeneous genres is lacking in general" (Lyotard, *D*, p. xi).

13. In Foucault's words: "Ideology is not exclusive of scientificity.... By correcting itself, by rectifying its errors, by clarifying its formulations, discourse does not necessarily undo its relations with ideology" (Foucault, *Archaeology of Knowledge*, p. 186).

14. Also in Levinas, between the Saying and the Said, *Dire* and *Dit*.

15. Also: "And linkage must happen 'now'; another phrase cannot not happen. It's a necessity; time, that is. There is no non-phrase" (Lyotard, *D*, p. xii).

16. Jean-François Lyotard, *Le Différend* (Paris: Minuit, 1983), p. 90; Lyotard, *D*, p. 55.

17. "First then we observe that some things always come to pass in the same way, and others for the most part. It is clearly of neither of these that chance is said to be the cause, nor can the 'effect of chance' be identified with any of the things that come to pass by necessity and always, or for the most part. But as there is a third class of events besides these two—events which all say are 'by chance'—it is plain that things of this kind are due to chance and that things due to chance are of this kind" (Aristotle, *Physics* 2.196b).

18. G. W. F. Hegel, *The Logic of Hegel* (the *Encyclopaedia Logic*) trans. W. Wallace (Oxford: Oxford University Press, 1892), p. 282.

19. "Meant for remission, sin is what is absorbed—in and through speech. By the same token, abjection will not be designated as such, that is, as other, as something to be ejected, or separated, but . . . as the point where the scales are tipped towards pure spirituality. The mystic's familiarity with abjection is a fount of infinite jouissance" (Kristeva, *Powers of Horror*, p. 127).

20. Whitehead's evil.

21. "Since the time when we recognized the error of supposing that ordinary forgetting signified destruction or annihilation of the memory-trace, we have been inclined to the opposite view that nothing once formed in the mind could ever perish, that everything survives in some way or other, and is capable under certain conditions of being brought to light again, . . . " (Sigmund Freud, *Civilization and Its Discontents*, trans. J. Riviere, International Psycho-analytical Library [London: Hogarth Press, 1953], p. 15).

22. "The aggressiveness is introjected, 'internalized'; in fact, it is sent back where it came from, *i.e.* directed against the ego. It is there taken over by a part of the ego that distinguishes itself from the rest as a super-ego, and now, in the form of 'conscience,' exercises the same propensity to harsh aggressiveness against the ego that the ego would have liked to enjoy against others. The tension between the strict super-ego and the subordinate ego we call the sense of guilt; it manifests itself as the need for punishment" (Freud, *Civilization and Its Discontents*, p. 105).

23. The nihilism that represents "our sole opportunity." This representation of the beginning of *The Will to Power* appears in Gianni Vattimo, *The End of Modernity*, trans. J. R. Snyder (Cambridge, England: Polity Press), 1988, p. 19.

24. Fyodor Dostoevsky, *The Brothers Karamazov* (*BK*), trans. C. Garnett (New York: Modern Library, 1950), p. 279.

25. I owe this phrase to Michael Kreek, to whom I express gratitude for many valuable discussions.

26. Power is everywhere; not because it embraces everything, but because it comes from everywhere. (Foucault, *History of Sexuality* [*HS*], p. 93).

—Power is not something that is acquired, seized, or shared, . . .
—Relations of power are not in a position of exteriority with respect to other types of relationships . . . but are immanent in the latter; . . .
—Power comes from below; . . .
—Power relations are both intentional and nonsubjective. . .
(Foucault, *HS*, pp. 94–95).

27. Continuing: "Hence there is no single locus of great Refusal, no soul of revolt, source of all rebellions, or pure law of the revolutionary. Instead there is a plurality of resistances, each of them a special case; resistances that are possible, necessary, improbable; others that are spontaneous, savage, solitary, concerted, rampant, or violent; still others that are quick to compromise, interested, or sacrificial; . . . " (*HS*, p. 96).

28. Foucault, "Truth and Power," in *Power/Knowledge*, p. 133.

29. Continuing: "But the body is also directly involved in a political field; power relations have an immediate hold on it; they invest it, mark it, train it, torture it, force it to carry out tasks, to perform ceremonies, to emit signs. This political investment of the body is bound up, in accordance with complex reciprocal relations, with its economic use; it is largely as a force of production that the body is invested with relations of power and domination; but, on the other hand, its constitution as labour power is possible only if it is caught up in a system of subjection (in which need is also a political instrument meticulously prepared, calculated and used); the body becomes a useful force only if it is both a productive body and a subjected body" (Foucault, *DP*, pp. 25–26).

30. "To establish the reality of a referent, the four silences must be refuted, though in reverse order: there is someone to signify the referent and someone to understand the phrase that signifies it; the referent can be signified; it exists. The proof for the reality of gas chambers cannot be adduced if the rules adducing the proof are not respected" (Lyotard, *D*, p. 16).

Chapter VI. Monstrosity's Madness

1. Lyotard, *The Differend* (*D*), p. 32.

2. Jean-François Lyotard, "What is Postmodernism?," Appendix to *The Postmodern Condition: A Report on Knowledge*, trans. G. Bennington and B. Massumi (Minnesota: University of Minnesota Press, 1984), p. 82.

3. Foucault, *The Order of Things* (*OT*), p. 156. Also: "On the basis of the power of the continuum held by nature, the monster ensures the emergence of difference. This difference is still without law and without any well-defined structure; the monster is the root-stock of specification, but it is only a sub-species itself in the stubbornly slow stream of history" (ibid.). "In Sade, sex is without any norm or intrinsic rule that might be formulated from its own nature; but it is subject to the unrestricted law of a power which itself knows no other law of its own; . . . a unique and naked sovereignty: an unlimited right of all-powerful monstrosity" (Foucault, *History of Sexuality*, p. 149).

4. Michel Foucault, *Madness and Civilization* (New York: Random House, 1965), p. v.

5. Immanuel Kant, *Critique of Judgment*, trans. J. H. Bernard (New York: Hafner, 1951), p. 91.

6. Jacques Derrida, "Parergon," in *The Truth in Painting*, trans. G. Bennington and I. McLeod (Chicago: University of Chicago Press, 1987), p. 125.

7. Simplicius, *Physica*, 164, 16 (DK 59 B 3); in Robinson, *An Introduction to Early Greek Philosophy* (Boston Houghton Mifflin, 1968), pp. 177, 178. Robinson mentions Zeller's reading of the text, giving the reading, "for it is impossible that what is should cease to be through being cut" (p. 323). This cut joins Anaximander and Derrida.

8. See p. 52, for the full quotation.

9. Stephen Jay Gould, *Wonderful Life: The Burgess Shale and the Nature of History* (*WL*) (New York and London: Norton, 1989); reviewed by R. C. Lewontin, "Fallen Angels," (G), *New York Review of Books*, 14 June 1990, pp. 3-7.

10. In Gould's words: "For species that can be classified within known phyla, Burgess anatomy far exceeds the modern range. . . . But the Burgess Shale also contains some twenty to thirty kinds of arthropods that cannot be placed in any modern group. Consider the magnitude of this difference: taxonomists have described almost a million species of arthropods, and all fit into four major groups; one quarry in British Columbia, representing the first explosion of multicellular life, reveals more than twenty additional arthropod designs" (Gould, *WL*, p. 25). Gould's account remains controversial.

11. In Lewontin's words, "Walcott is described as having a 'deeply conservative and traditional perspective on life and morality,' a perspective that naturally extended to his view of dead animals. Nor, Gould implies, could we expect anything else from someone who was the head of the Smithsonian Institution, president of the National Academy of Sciences, founder, together with President Wilson, of the National Research Council, and generally the intimate of America's upper-class elite" (Lewontin, *G*, p. 6).

12. "In scientific scholarship, there are two patterns for a high status life. One is to be the discoverer and inventor of something that reverberates through the current structure of knowledge, or at least to make consistent, significant contributions to the fundamental structure of problems of the field. The second, sometimes flowing from the first, but not always, is to become part of the political hierarchy of the field, influencing bureaucratically what one no longer can nor never has influenced by the substance of one's scholarship" (ibid.).

13. "Charles Doolittle Walcott, at the time of his discovery of the Burgess Shale, was already at or near the peak of his professional status. . . . he simply did not have the time or psychic energy to carry out the minute dissection of the squashed fossils that would have been necessary. . . . Status and success were

already his and would continue throughout his life irrespective of any scientific discovery he might make" (ibid.). Gould himself agrees with the problem of fame and time: "How could the Burgess Shale possibly have fitted into this caldron, this madhouse of imposed and necessary activity? Walcott needed his summers in the Canadian Rockies for collecting—if only as therapy. But he could never find time for scientific study of the specimens in Washington" (Gould, *WL*, p. 251).

14. This is a reading of Thomas S. Kuhn's *The Structure of Scientific Revolutions* (Chicago: University of Chicago Press, 1962).

15. Michel Foucault, "The Discourse on Language," trans. Rupert Swyer, Appendix to *The Archaeology of Knowledge*, pp. 223–24.

16. Even Popper's view of falsification, at a "metametatheoretical" level, may be read as suggesting that the monstrosities of disconfirmation delimit the possibilities of science far more than any confirmations, any repetition of order. (Karl R. Popper, *The Logic of Scientific Discovery* [London: Hutchinson, 1959]).

17. Luce Irigaray, *Speculum of the Other Woman*, trans. Gillian G. Gill (Ithaca: Cornell University Press, 1985), pp. 13–14. Her quotations and page references are from Sigmund Freud, "Femininity," in *New Lectures on Psychoanalysis*, from *The Standard Edition of the Complete Psychological Works of Sigmund Freud*, ed. J. Strachey, 24 vols. (London: Hogarth Press, 1953–74), 22:112–35.

18. Quoted in Gould, *Wonderful Life*, p. 291.

19. René Descartes, *Meditations* (*M*), vol. 1, trans. N. K. Smith (New York: Modern Library, 1958), p. 177.

20. Jacques Derrida, "Cogito and the History of Madness" (*CHM*), in *Writing and Difference*, trans. A. Bass (Chicago: University Of Chicago Press, 1978), p. 35.

21. Jacques Derrida, "Violence and Metaphysics: An Essay on the Thought of Emmanuel Levinas," in *Writing and Difference*, p. 138. See also: "There can be an order of priority only between two determined things, two existents. Being, since *it is nothing* outside the existent, a theme which Levinas had commented upon so well previously, could in no way *precede* the existent, whether in time, or in dignity, etc. Nothing is more clear, as concerns this, in Heidegger's thought. Henceforth, one cannot legitimately speak of the 'subordination' of the existent to Being, or, for example, of the ethical relation to the ontological relation. . . . The thought of Being (of the existent) is radically foreign to the search for a principle, or even for a root (although certain images lead us to believe this, occasionally), or for a 'tree of knowledge': it is, as we have seen, beyond theory, and is not the first word of theory. It is even beyond all hierarchies" (p. 136).

22. Derrida suggests that Foucault overreads Descartes's relation to madness, that after putting madness aside (in relation to what Derrida calls "natural

doubt"), Descartes readmits it as an equal among other deceptions. "Now, the recourse to the fiction of the evil genius will evoke, conjure up, the possibility of a *total madness*, . . . a madness that will bring subversion to pure thought and to its purely intelligible objects, to the field of its clear and distinct ideas, to the realm of the mathematical truths which escape natural doubt" (Derrida, *CHM*, pp. 52–53). In Descartes's own words: "How do I know that I am not myself deceived every time I add 2 and 3, or count the sides of a square, or judge of things yet simple, if anything simpler can be suggested?" (Descartes, *M*, p. 179). "I shall consider myself as having no hands, no eyes, no flesh, no blood, nor any senses, but as falsely opining myself to possess all these things" (Descartes, *M*, p. 181). I imagine I am deceived, either according to God's will or that of a malignant power—a monster—first in all external things of sensory experience, then including my sensory relation to the body, but also in thinking two plus three or counting the sides of a square. Shall we take this as madness itself?

23. Oliver Sacks, *A Leg to Stand On*, reprinted as one of four books in *Awakenings* (*A*), *A Leg to Stand On* (*L*), *The Man Who Mistook His Wife for a Hat and Other Clinical Tales* (*H*), and *Seeing Voices* (*SV*) (New York: Quality Paperback Book Club, 1990), p. 85.

24. "From the vast space of his creation, the Chimaera arose, rose up from the depths in majestic splendor, all milky-white, furrowed, like Moby Dick— except, unbelievable!—he had horns on his head, and the face of a vast browsing animal." "Now, outraged, he turned his gaze on me—with immense bulbous eyes, like the eyes of a bull, but a bull which could draw the whole river into his mouth, and with a vast scaly tail as big as a cedar" (Sacks, *L*, p. 57).

25. He gives a wealth of examples. Patients with Parkinson's disease live in a "strange and deeply paradoxical world," described by a patient as a relation to space and time: "It's not as simple as it looks. I don't just come to a halt, I am still going, but I *have run out of space to move in*. . . . You see, *my* space, *our* space, is nothing like *your* space: our space gets bigger and smaller, it bounces back on itself, and it loops itself round till in runs into itself" (Sacks, *A*, p. 339). Parkinsonian patients lack spatial and temporal measure, live in chaos, a disorder with another order without congruence with ours.

Or consider the man who mistook his wife for a hat. "He reached out his hand and took hold of his wife's head, tried to lift it off, to put it on. He had apparently mistaken his wife for a hat! His wife looked as if she was used to such things" (Sacks, *H*, p. 11). He was a musician with no sense of body or image apart from music. "I think that music, for him, had taken the place of image. He had no body-image, he had body-music: this is why he could move and act as fluently as he did, but came to a total confused stop if the 'inner music' stopped." "Schopenhauer speaks of music as 'pure will.' How fascinated he would have been by Dr. P., a man who had wholly lost the world as representation, but wholly preserved it as music or will" (Sacks, *A*, p. 18).

26. Sacks quotes Nietzsche on the abyss: "If you stare into the abyss, it will stare back at you." Yet the silence of the abyss Sacks faces, his scotoma, does not look back. "Outwardly, then, there was soundlessness and noise, and inwardly, simultaneously, a deadly inner silence—the silence of timelessness, motionlessness, *scotoma*, combined with the silence of non-communication and taboo. Incommunicable, *incommunicado*, the sense of excommunication was extreme" (Sacks, *L*, p. 110). This, for us, represents the ex- of general economy.

27. "The writing of sovereignty places discourse *in relation* to absolute non-discourse. Like general economy, it is not the loss of meaning, but, as we have just read, the 'relation to this loss of meaning.' It opens the question of meaning. It does not describe unknowledge, for this is impossible, but only the effect of unknowledge" (Derrida, "From Restricted to General Economy: A Hegelianism without Reserve," in *Writing and Difference*, p. 262).

28. And perhaps general economy becomes Restricted Economy.

29. Speaking of "justice in itself, if such a thing exists, outside or beyond law" (Derrida, "Force of Law," *Cardozo Law Review* 11 [1991]: 945).

30. "Locke's *Essay Concerning Human Understanding* stands in a peculiar relation to the tradition that it founded. On the one hand, the school known as associationism, represented most prominently by David Hartley, depended on Locke's assertion that ideas are derived from experience. The principle by which these ideas were said to be governed, moreover, was designated by a phrase lifted out of the fourth edition of Locke's *Essay*, 'the association of ideas.' On the other hand, the use of *association* to name a central principle of rational thought altered the meaning it had in Locke's work, in which it referred to a thought process subversive of normal reasoning and described as a 'madness'" (Cathy Caruth, *Empirical Truths and Critical Fictions* [Baltimore and London: Johns Hopkins University Press, 1991], p. 1). The account of madness here in Locke derives from Caruth's striking reading.

31. John Locke, *Essay Concerning Human Understanding* (New York: Dover, 1959), bk. 2, chap. 23, p. 527.

32. See the detailed reading of *Phaedrus* in chap. 9.

33. Jacques Derrida, "Plato's Pharmacy," in *Dissemination*, trans. B. Johnson (Chicago: University of Chicago Press, 1981)..

34. See chap. 9, especially pp. 219–21; 246–47. Could the discourse that "drifts all over the place" circulate in the mad monstrosity of a general economy?

35. Aeschylus, *Ajax*, trans. R. C. Trevelyan, in *The Complete Greek Drama* (*CGD*), ed. W. J. Oates and E. O'Neill, Jr. (New York: Random House, 1938), p. 325, lines 295–303.

36. Levinas asks, "What is Hecuba to me? Am I my brother's keeper?" (Emmanuel Levinas, *Otherwise than Being or Beyond Essence* [*OB*], trans. A. Lingis [The Hague: Martinus Nijhoff, 1981], p. 117). We add to Levinas's obsession, hostage to the other, monstrosity and madness.

37. Euripides, *Hecuba*, trans. E. P. Coleridge, in *The Complete Greek Drama*, ed. Oates and O'Neill, p. 812, lines 253–56.

38. Martha Nussbaum speaks of many of these things in *The Fragility of Goodness* (*FG*) (Cambridge: Cambridge University Press, 1986). We might have called our book, or another, "The Monstrosity of Goodness."

39. "Lo! I am come from out the charnel-house and gates of gloom, where Hades dwells apart from gods, I Polydorus, a son of Hecuba the daughter of Cisseus and Priam. . . . but now am I hovering o'er the head of my dear mother Hecuba, a disembodied spirit, keeping my airy station these three days, ever since my poor mother came from Troy to linger here in Chersonese" (Euripides, *Hecuba*, p. 907, lines 1–25).

40. It shows up in Levinas as *monstration* (Levinas, *OB*, p. 23).

41. Jacques Derrida, "*Geschlecht* II: Heidegger's Hand" (*G*), in *Deconstruction and Philosophy*, ed. J. Sallis (Chicago: University of CHicago Press, 1987), p. 166.

42. Martin Heidegger, "What Calls for Thinking," in *Basic Writings*, ed. D. Krell (New York: Harper & Row, 1977), p. 357.

43. Immanuel Kant, *Critique of Judgment*, trans. J. H. Bernard (New York: Hafner, 1951), pp. 100–101.

44. Derrida, "Parergon," p. 125.

45. Take heart; thou art safe from the suppliant's god in my case, for I will follow thee, alike because I must and because it is my wish to die; for were I loth, coward should I show myself, a woman faint of heart. (Euripides, *Hecuba*, p. 814, lines 342–44).

After pleading to be spared, Iphigenia speaks in the same noble voice.

> O, kill me not untimely! The sun is sweet!
> Why will you send me into the dark grave?
> I was the first to sit upon your knee,
> The first to call you father, first to give
> Dear gifts and take them.
> (Euripides, *Iphigenia in Aulis*, II,
>   p. 323, lines 1259–62).

> I have been thinking, mother,—hear me now!—
> I have chosen death: it is my own free choice.

> I have put cowardice away from me.
> Honour is mine now. O, mother, say I am right!
> (Euripides, *Iphigenia in Aulis*, II,
> p. 329, lines 1374–77).

46. Nussbaum describes this understanding as follows: "[B]oth Choruses insist on the importance to assessment of our distinction between reparable and irreparable crimes, arguing that some offenses are so severe in their effects that their commission, even under situational constraint, must be followed by a serious punishment" (Nussbaum, *FG*, p. 41). Some offenses are so severe that they must be avenged. Some vengeances, justly provoked, must be punished. Injustice remains.

47. These themes are discussed in relation to the Greeks in Nussbaum, *The Fragility of Goodness*. They appear in similar form in contemporary African narratives. See here, chap. 11.

48. Nussbaum, *FG*, p. 37. See chap. 7, pp. 185–86.

49. Nussbaum summarizes this insight without monstrosity: "We are asked to see that a conflict-free life would be lacking in value and beauty next to a life in which it is possible for conflict to arise; that part of the value of each claim derives from a special separateness and distinctness that would be eclipsed by harmonization" (Nussbaum, *FG*, p. 81). In *Hecuba*, however, injustice cries out its monstrosity: "Neither of them [Hecuba or Polymestor] could endure to be human, with the openness to risk that that condition requires. Doggishness arrives as a welcome gift, a release. They embrace it. If *we* find it foul, we are forced to ask what human life could be happier" (Nussbaum, *FG*, p. 417). Monstrosity arrives in many forms, here as animal, a recurrent Western prejudice. It arrives here as the happiest possibility within injustice, telling, showing, remaining together with injustice. With the end of *nomos*, with law in time, injustice remains in its monstrosity without restitution.

50. Ernst Bloch, *Natural Law and Human Dignity* (*NLHD*), trans. D. Schmidt (Cambridge: MIT Press, 1986), p. 248.

51. See chap. 11, pp. 281–85.

52. Michel Foucault, *I, Pierre Riviére, Having Slaughtered My Mother, My Sister, and My Brother . . . : A Case of Parricide in the Nineteenth Century* (New York: Pantheon, 1975). Riviére was put to death.

53. Foucault's *Discipline and Punish* addresses these issues, asking us to think about the ways in which our Law and Reason work, not upon the criminal, sane or mad, but upon those who would be neither criminal nor mad.

54. As Amartya Sen points out, eighty to one hundred million women who might have been expected to live have died in the second half of the twenti-

eth century (Amartya Sen, "More than One Hundred Million Women are Missing," *New York Review of Books*, 20 December 1990, pp. 61–66).

Chapter VII. Law's Force

1. Paul Shorey's translation of *Republic* in *Plato: The Collected Dialogues*, trans. Hamilton and Cairns (Princeton, N.J.: Princeton University Press, 1969), sounds an anachronistic voice. I keep it here, without returning to the Greek as I do elsewhere, because the disparity of the voice so forcefully echoes Thrasymachus's accusations toward Socrates.

2. "I knew it and predicted that when it came to replying you would refuse and dissemble and do anything rather than answer any question that anyone asked you" (Plato, *Republic* 337a).

3. What restitution?

4. H. L. A. Hart, *The Concept of Law* (*CL*) (Oxford: Clarendon Press, 1961), p. 7.

5. Michel de Montaigne, "We Should Meddle Soberly with Judging Divine Ordinances," Essay 32 in *The Complete Works of Montaigne*, trans. D. M. Frame (Stanford, Calif.: Stanford University Press, 1958), p. 162.

6. Montaigne, "Of Experience," in *The Complete Works of Montaigne*, p. 821.

7. Blaise Pascal, *Pensées*, trans. W. F. Trotter (New York: E. P. Dutton, 1932), p. 84.

8. David Hume, *A Treatise of Human Nature*, ed. L. A. Selby-Bigge (Oxford: Oxford University Press, 1888), III, I, p. 457.

9. Immanuel Kant, *Critique of Judgment* (*CJ*), trans. J. H. Bernard (New York: Hafner, 1951), p. 11.

10. In Derrida's reading: "justice isn't justice, it is not achieved if it doesn't have the force to be 'enforced'; a powerless justice is not justice, . . . " ["Il est juste que ce qui est juste soit suivi (autrement dit, le concept ou l'idée du juste, au sens de justice, implique analytiquement et a priori que le juste soit 'suivi,' *enforced*, et il est juste-aussi au sens de justesse-de penser ainsi); il est nécessaire que ce qui est le plus fort soit suivi (*enforced*)"] (Derrida, "Force of Law: The 'Mystical Foundation of Authority'" (*FL*), *Cardozo Law Review* 11 (1991): 937.

11. The passage continues: "If it were not possible to communicate general standards of conduct, which multitudes of individuals could understand, without further direction, as requiring from them certain conduct when occasion arose,

nothing that we now recognize as law could exist. Hence the law must predominantly, but by no means exclusively, refer to *classes* of person, and to *classes* of acts, things, and circumstances; and its successful operation over vast areas of social life depends on a widely diffused capacity to recognize particular acts, things, and circumstances as instances of the general classifications which the law makes."

12. Stanley Fish, "Force" (*F*), in *Doing What Comes Naturally* (Durham and London: Duke University Press, 1989), p. 505. Fish presents a court decision more direct than Hart on the dangers of arbitrariness, in *Cargill Commission Co. v. Swartwood*. (198 N.W. 1924): "Were it otherwise, written contracts would be enforced not according to the plain effect of their language, but pursuant to the story of their negotiation as told by the litigant having at the same time being the greater power of persuading the trier of fact. So far as contracts are concerned the rule of law would give way to the mere notions of men as to who should win law suits. Without that [the prol evidence] rule there would be no assurance of the enforceability of a written contract. If such assurance were removed today from our law, general disaster would result" (*Cargill*, p. 538; Fish, *F*, p. 507).

13. Also, "Once the rule of recognition recedes into practice, it becomes not a matter of fact, but of interpretation, and the way is open to exactly the situation Hart hopes to avoid, the situation in which the law is what the courts say it is; for if one locates the rule by looking 'to the way in which courts identify' it, then the actions of the court come first and rule second" (Fish, *F*, p. 512).

14. Derrida, "Force of Law"; Walter Benjamin, "Critique of Violence" (*CV*), in *Reflections*, ed. P. Dementz (New York: Harcourt Brace Jovanovich, 1986), pp. 277–300.

15. Also, "Mythical violence is bloody power over mere life for its own sake, divine violence pure power over all life for the sake of the living" (Benjamin, *CV*, p. 297).

16. Speaker and hearer can reciprocally motivate one another to recognize validity claims because the content of the speaker's engagement is determined by a specific reference to a thematically stressed validity claim, whereby the speaker, in a cognitively testable way, assumes
    with a truth claim, obligations to provide grounds
    with a rightness claim, obligations to provide justification, and
    with a truthfulness claim, obligations to prove trustworthy.
(Jürgen Habermas, *Communication and the Evolution of Society*, trans. T. M. McCarthy [Boston: Beacon Press, 1979], p. 70).

17. In a similar way, Gadamer seems to speaks of the authority of text and tradition:

What is necessary is a fundamental rehabilitation of the concept of prejudice and a recognition of the fact that there are legitimate prejudices, if we want to do justice to man's finite, historical mode of being.

We can, then, bring out as what is truly common to all forms of hermeneutics the fact that the sense to be understood finds its concrete and perfect form only in interpretation, but that this interpretative work is wholly committed to the meaning of the text. Neither jurist nor theologian regards the work of application as making free with the text. (Hans-Georg Gadamer, *Truth and Method* [New York: Seabury, 1975], p. 297).

If the heart of the hermeneutical problem is that the same tradition must always be understood in a different way, the problem, logically speaking, is that of the relationship between the universal and the particular. (*Truth and Method*, p. 278).

Prejudices rule with necessity and, in some cases, legitimacy, and if we hope to reflect human finiteness, we must accept both necessities. Gadamer appears to fear what Hart and the *Cargill* court fear, that if we make "free with the text" meaning will collapse, even as he recognizes that every same, text or tradition, can and will—if not "must"—be "understood in a different way." The understanding is different, suggesting that the tradition and the text are different. History gives us understanding of the same tradition and the texts that constitute it through the differences it unfolds, suggesting that nothing can impose necessity on the sameness of any text or tradition.

We see how quickly Gadamer moves from the necessities of difference in historical and textual understanding to the universal. Necessity presupposes a universal, not even a general, rule. The understanding sought in tradition and text, the meaning history gives to reading and writing, looks to universality. Yet Gadamer claims to accept the principle that guides Derrida's view of iterability, that the repetition demanded by writing and reading, by history and tradition, belongs to its differences, and that these differences cannot be regulated except in virtue of another repetition whose iteration repeats differences. The circulation of the universal meaning of tradition and text disposes of any universality it may have except under law, disposing as well of any necessity. As Fish says, in issues of interpretation and meaning, nothing can be regarded as settled.

18. See the preceding note for Gadamer's reading of truth and tradition.

19. "It is always possible one could speak the truth in a void; one would only be in the true, however, if one obeyed the rules of some discursive 'policy' which would have to be reactivated every time one spoke" (Foucault, "The Discourse on Language," pp. 223–24).

20. "An address is always singular, idiomatic, and justice, as law (*droit*), seems always to suppose the generality of a rule, a norm or a universal imperative"

(Derrida, *FL*, p. 949). Perhaps law's generality works in a different space from universality, with a different force and authority.

21. We may express this authority in terms of two principles:

We can say anything we wish to say in any language.
The language in which we speak or write determines what we say.

See my *The Limits of Language* (New York: Fordham University Press, forthcoming), for a detailed discussion of how these and other related principles aporetically coexist and conflict in relation to language.

22. "Since the origin of authority, the foundation or ground, the position of the law can't by definition rest on anything but themselves, they are themselves a violence without ground. Which is not to say that they are in themselves unjust, in the sense of 'illegal.' They are neither legal nor illegal in their founding movement. They exceed the opposition between founded and unfounded, or between any foundationalism or anti-foundationalism" (Derrida, *FL*, p. 943).

23. No "and so on" appears in the French: "3. Conséquence: la déconstruction a lieu dans l'intervalle qui sépare l'indéconstructibilité de la justice et la déconstructibilité du droit, de l'autorité légitimante ou légitimée" (p. 944).

24. See also: "one would not speak of injustice or violence toward an animal, even less toward a vegetable or stone. An animal can be made to suffer, but we would never say, in a sense considered proper, that it is a wronged subject, the victim of a crime, . . . What we confusedly call 'animal,' the living thing as living and nothing else, is not a subject of the law or of *droit*" (Derrida, *FL*, p. 951); "In our culture, carnivorous sacrifice is fundamental, dominant, regulated by the highest industrial technology, as is biological experimentation on animals—so vital to our modernity. As I have tried to show elsewhere, carnivorous sacrifice is essential to the structure of subjectivity, which is also to say to the founding of the intentional subject and to the founding, if not of the law, at least of *droit*, the difference between the law and *droit*, justice and *droit*, justice and the law here remaining over an abyss" (Derrida, *FL*, pp. 951–53).

25. See here, chap. 1, p. 3 and chap. 3, pp. 41–42.

26. Jacques Derrida, *Of Spirit*, trans. G. Bennington and R. Bowlby (Chicago: University of Chicago Press, 1987), p. 37.

27. See chap. 1, p. 2, especially n. 4.

28. Trinh T. Minh-ha, *Woman, Native, Other: Writing Postcoloniality and Feminism* (Bloomington: Indiana University Press, 1989), pp. 98–99. See chap. 1, p. 000, for the full quotation.

29. Nussbaum, *The Fragility of Goodness* (Cambridge: Cambridge Univer-

sity Press, 1986), p. 37. She is paraphrasing Walter Burkert. As close as she comes, however, she fails to recognize Derrida's insight that this sacrifice of animals marks another immemorial injustice.

30. Jacques Derrida, "Restitutions," in *The Truth in Painting*, trans. G. Bennington and I. McLeod (Chicago: University of Chicago Press, 1987), p. 281. See chap. 8, pp. 202–204.

31. Søren Kierkegaard, *Fear and Trembling*, trans. W. Lowrie (Garden City, N.Y.: Doubleday, 1954): "Abraham cannot be mediated, and the same thing can be expressd also by saying that he cannot talk. So soon as I talk I express the universal, and if I do not do so, no one can understand me" (p. 70). "Either there is an absolute duty toward God, and if so it is the paradox here described, that the individual as the individual is higher than the universal and as the individual stands in an absolute relation to the absolute/or else faith never existed, because it has always existed, or, to put it differently, Abraham is lost, ..." (p. 91).

32. Emmanuel Levinas, *"Un Droit infini,"* in *Du Sacré au Saint. cinq nouvelles Lecture talmudiques*, pp. 17–18; quoted in Derrida, *FL*, p. 959.

33. Derrida's aporias:

> 1. *First aporia: épokhè and rule.*

. . . .

In short, for a decision to be just and responsible, it must, in its proper moment if there is one, be both regulated and without regulation: it must conserve the law and also destroy it or suspend it enough to have to reinvent it in each case, rejustify it, at least reinvent it in the reaffirmation and the new and free confirmation of its principle. . . .
. . . It follows from this paradox that there is never a moment that we can say *in the present* that a decision *is* just. . . . (Derrida, *FL*, p. 961)

> 2. *Second aporia: the ghost of the undecidable.*

. . . .

The undecidable is not merely the oscillation or the tension between two decisions, it is the experience of that which, though heterogeneous, foreign to the order of the calculable and the rule, is still obligated—it is of obligation that we must speak—to give itself up to the impossible decision, while taking account of law and rules. A decision that didn't go through the ordeal of the undecidable would not be a free decision, ... (Derrida, *FL*, p. 963)

3. *Third aporia: the urgency that obstructs the horizon of knowledge.*

. . . .

But justice, however unpresentable it may be, doesn't wait. It is that which must not wait. To be direct, simple and brief, let us say this: a just decision is always required immediately, "right away." . . . The instant of decision is a madness. (Derrida, *FL*, p. 967)

Monstrosity's madness.

Chapter VIII. Idolatry's Authority

1. Friedrich Nietzsche, *Twilight of the Idols* (*TI*), in *The Portable Nietzsche*, trans. W. Kaufman (New York: Viking, 1968).

2. Friedrich Nietzsche, *Thus Spake Zarathustra* (*Z*), in *Portable Nietzsche*, p. 128.

3. Jacques Derrida, "Tympan" (*T*), Introduction to *Margins of Philosophy*, trans. Alan Bass (Chicago: University of Chicago Press, 1982), p. xiii.

4. Gianni Vattimo, *The End of Modernity* (*EM*), trans. J. R. Snyder (Cambridge: Polity Press, 1988), pp. 2–3.

5. See n.16, this chapter.

6. "[P]erhaps, someone will ask, whether women are under men's authority by nature or institution? . . . there has never been a case of men and women reigning together, but wherever on the earth men are found, there we see that men rule, and women are ruled, and that on this plan, both sexes live in harmony. . . . one may assert with perfect propriety, that women have not by nature equal right with men: but that they necessarily give way to men, and that thus it cannot happen, that both sexes should rule alike, much less that men should be ruled by women" (Benedict de Spinoza, *A Theologico-Political Treatise and A Political Treatise*, trans. R. H. M. Elwes [New York: Dover, 1951], pp. 386–87). See chap. 3, pp. 57–60.

7. Michel Foucault, "What Is an Author?" in *Language, Counter-memory, Practice*, trans. D. F. Bouchard and S. Simon (Ithaca, N.Y.: Cornell University Press, 1977), p. 138. The line is quoted from Samuel Beckett, *Texts for Nothing*, self-translated (London: Calder & Boyars, 1974), p. 16.

8. "[T]he 'author-function' is tied to the legal and institutional systems that circumscribe, determine, and articulate the realm of discourses; it does not operate in a uniform manner in all discourses, at all times, and in any given culture; it is not defined by a spontaneous attribution of a text to its creator, but through a series of precise and complex procedures; it does not refer, purely and

simply, to an actual individual insofar as it simultaneously gives rise to a variety of egos and to a series of subjective positions that individuals of any class may come to occupy" (Foucault, "What Is an Author?" pp. 130–31).

9. See chap. 7, pp. 174–75, where Derrida speaks of this authorization in relation to Walter Benjamin's "Critique of Violence."

10. Jacques Derrida, "Restitutions" (*R*), in *The Truth in Painting*, trans. G. Bennington and I. McLeod (Chicago: University of Chicago Press, 1987), p. 281.

11. Martin Heidegger, "The Origin of the Work of Art," in *Poetry, Language, Thought*, trans. A. Hofstadter (New York: Harper & Row, 1971), p. 33.

12. At first: "But each time I've seen the celebrated passage on 'a famous picture by Van Gogh' as a moment of pathetic collapse, derisory, and symptomatic, significant" (Derrida, *R*, p. 262). Later: "The 'pathetic' paragraph on the silent call of the earth is consonant, in another correspondence, with this or that letter of Van Gogh" (Derrida, *R*, p. 368). The ambiguity of the pathos of the authority vested in the famous paragraph on the celebrated picture reflects a secret correspondence with the measure of authority and injustice, before all time, all measure, present in time as subjection.

13. Irigaray, *Speculum of the Other Woman*, p. 135.

14. G. W. F. Hegel, *Lectures on the Philosophy of Religion*, trans. E. B. Speirs and J. B. Sanderson (London, 1895), vol. 2; reprinted in *Hegel on Tragedy*, ed. A. Paolucci and H. Paolucci (New York: Harper & Row, 1962), p. 312.

15. He once refers to Deleuze.

16. "Perhaps I know the Germans, perhaps I may even tell them some truths. The new Germany represents a large quantum of fitness, both inherited and acquired by training, so that for a time it may expend its accumulated store of strength, even squander it. It is *not* a high culture that has thus become the master, and even less a delicate taste, a noble 'beauty' of the instincts; but more *virile* virtues than any other country in Europe can show. . . . One will notice that I wish to be just to the Germans: I do not want to break faith with myself here. I must there also state my objections to them, One pays heavily for coming to power: power *makes stupid*" (Nietzsche, *TI*, p. 506). See p. 192 here for the end of the passage. I too wish to be just to the Germans, in the name of injustice.

17. Jean-François Lyotard, *Heidegger and "the jews"*, trans. A. Michel and M. Roberts (Minneapolis: University of Minnesota Press, 1990), pp. 4–5.

18. Martin Heidegger, *Identity and Difference* (*ID*), trans. J. Stambaugh (New York: Harper & Row, 1969), p. 101.

19. Walter Benjamin, "Theses on the Philosophy of History," in *Illuminations*, trans. H. Zohn (New York: Schocken, 1969), p. 256.

20. Michel Foucault, "Nietzsche, Genealogy, and History," in *Language, Counter-memory, Practice*, p. 151.

21. "The past carries with it a temporal index by which it is referred to redemption. There is a secret agreement between past generations and the present one. Our coming was expected on earth. Like every generation that preceded us, we have been endowed with a *weak* Messianic power, a power to which the past has a claim. That claim cannot be settled cheaply" (Benjamin, "Theses," p. 254). How cheaply to resist catastrophe!

22. R. Guardieri, "Les Sociétés primitives aujourd'hui," in *Philosopher: les interrogations contemporarines*, ed. C. Delacampagne and R. Maggiori (Paris: Fayard, 1980), p. 60; quoted in Vattimo, *EM*, p. 158.

Chapter IX. Science's Spell

1. "Since the object of pure scientific knowledge cannot be other than it is, the truth obtained by demonstrative knowledge will be necessary" (Aristotle, *Posterior Analytics* 73a). "Demonstrative knowledge must rest on necessary basic truths; for the object of scientific knowledge cannot be other than it is" (*Posterior Analytics* 74b). "When the objects of an inquiry, in any department, have principles, conditions, or elements, it is through acquaintance with these that knowledge, that is to say scientific knowledge [*epistēmē*], is attained. For we do not think that we know a thing until we are acquainted with its primary conditions or first principles, . . ." (Aristotle, *Physics* 184a).
All proceed from preexistent knowledge.

2. Now no one deliberates about things that are invariable, nor about things that it is impossible for him to do. Therefore, since scientific knowledge involves demonstration, but there is no demonstration of things whose first principles are variable (for all such things might actually be otherwise), and since it is impossible to deliberate about things that are of necessity, practical wisdom cannot be scientific knowledge nor art; not science because that which can be done is capable of being otherwise, not art because action and making are different kinds of thing. The remaining alternative, then, is that it is a true and reasoned state of capacity to act with respect to the things that are good or bad for man. (Aristotle, *Nicomachean Ethics* 1140b)

Scientific knowledge is judgment about things that are universal and necessary, and the conclusions of demonstration, and all scientific knowledge, follow from first principles (for scientific knowledge involves apprehension of a rational ground).... If, then, the states of mind by which we have truth and are never deceived about things invariable or even variable are scientific knowledge, practical wisdom, philosophic wisdom, and intuitive reason, and it cannot be any of the three (i.e. practical wisdom, scientific knowledge, or philosophic wisdom), the remaining alternative is that it is *intuitive reason* that grasps the first principles. (Aristotle, *Nicomachean Ethics* 1141a)

3. "We must, as in all other cases, set the observed facts before us and, after first discussing the difficulties, go on to prove, if possible, the truth of all the common opinions about these affections of the mind, or, failing this, of the greater number and the most authoritative; for if we both refute the objections and leave the common opinions undisturbed, we shall have proved the case sufficiently" (Aristotle, *Nicomachean Ethics*, 1145b).

4. "Now of these characteristics that of knowing all things must belong to him who has in the highest degree universal knowledge; . . . ." And these things, the most universal, are on the whole the hardest for men to know; . . . And the most exact of the sciences are those which deal most with first principles; . . . But the science which investigates causes is also *instructive*, in a higher degree, for the people who instruct us are those who tell the causes of each thing" (Aristotle, *Metaphysics* 982a20–29).

5. "How will wisdom, regarded only as a knowledge of knowledge or science of science, ever teach him that he knows health, or that he knows building?" (Plato, *Charmides* 170c).

6. "[S]ince for everything that has come into being destruction is appointed, not even such a fabric as this will abide for all time, but shall surely be dissolved, and this is the manner of its dissolution. . . . there will come a time when they will beget children out of season" (Plato, *Republic* 546ab).

7. Francis Bacon, *Novum Organon*, in *The English Philosophers from Bacon to Mill*, ed. E. A. Burtt (New York: Modern Library, 1939), p. 25. See also "I have realized that if I wished to have any firm and constant knowledge in the sciences, I would have to undertake, once and for all, to set aside all the opinion which I had previously accepted among my beliefs and start again from the beginning" (René Descartes, *Meditations*, vol. 1, trans. N. K. Smith [New York: Modern Library, 1958], p. 17).

8. John Locke, *An Essay Concerning Human Understanding*, ed. Alexander Campbell Fraser (New York: Dover, 1959), vol. 1, p. 121.

9. David Hume, *A Treatise of Human Nature*, ed. L. A. Selby-Bigge (Oxford: Clarendon, 1888), p. 187.

10. David Hume, *An Inquiry Concerning Human Understanding* (New York: Liberal Arts, 1955), p. 137.

11. Jean-Luc Nancy, "The Inoperative Community," in *The Inoperative Community*, trans. P. Connor, L. Garbus, M. Holland, and S. Sawhney (Minneapolis: University of Minnesota Press, 1991), p. 40.

12. The Greek does not appear to have the Latin sense of "lover" despite its extraordinary relevance to the dialogue. It does preserve the sense of "self" as in self-knowledge and the sense of privacy, as in private person. We find ourselves between public and private.

13. We revisit Plato's pharmacy, with a different prescription. (Jacques Derrida, "Plato's Pharmacy" *(PP)*, in *Dissemination*). I hope to follow Derrida by reading *Phaedrus* differently, by reading Plato and Derrida differently, perhaps to give a more disturbing reading of *pharmakeia*'s relation to science's authority, in relation to any authority. "Plato's Pharmacy" reads *Phaedrus* in the light of the rules of its game. "A text is not a text unless it hides from the first comer, from the first glance, the law of its composition and the rules of its game. A text remains, moreover, forever imperceptible. Its law and its rules are not, however, harbored in the inaccessibilty of a secret; it is simply that they can never be booked, in the *present*, into anything that could rigorously be called a perception" (Derrida, *(PP)*, p. 63).

What rules? What game? And why into a perception? Or rather, in our reading, do we find Pharmakeia's magic turning our gaze into a different kind of perception?

14. Robert Graves, *The Greek Myths,* vol. 1 (Baltimore: Penguin, 1955), pp. 168–72.

15. Derrida reminds us that "the ceremony of the *pharmakos* is thus played out on the boundary line between inside and outside, which it has as its function ceaselessly to trace and retrace" (Derrida, *PP*, p. 133). This, indeed, replays Socrates incessantly as our *pharmakos*, circulating with Pharmakeia.

16. This doubling in the play of Pharmakeia turns upon Orithyia, giving another side to Derrida's reading of her tragedy, "the scene where that *virgin* was cast into the abyss, surprised by death *while playing with Pharmakeia.* . . . Through her games, Pharmacia has dragged down to death a virginal purity and an unpenetrated interior" (Derrida, *PP*, p. 70).

And what of Eurynome?

17. Even Derrida, in "Plato's Pharmacy," does not suggest that the dialogue may present a profound if deeply critical understanding of science's authority.

18. Continuing, "Again, it is argued that a lover ought to be highly valued because he professes to be especially kind toward the loved one, . . . it is obvious

that he will set greater store by the loved one of tomorrow than by that of today, . . . " (231c).

"And really, what sense is there in lavishing what is so precious upon one laboring under an affliction . . . ?" (231d).

"If you are to choose the best of a number of lovers, your choice will be only among a few, . . . " (231e).

"Again, a lover is bound to be heard about and seen by many people, consorting with his beloved and caring about little else, . . . " (232b). "[I]t is doubtless the lover who should cause you the more alarm, for he is very ready to take offense, and thinks the whole affair is to his own hurt" (232c).

"A lover more often than not wants to possess you before he has come to know your character . . . and that makes it uncertain whether he will still want to be your friend when his desires have waned, . . . " (233a). "It ought to be for your betterment to listen to me rather than to a lover, for a lover commends anything you say or do, even when it is amiss, . . . " (233b).

"[T]he proper course, surely, is to show favor not to the most importunate but to those most able to make us a return. . . . " (233e).

19. "[F]or the outcome of each action depends upon how it is performed. If it is done rightly and finely, the action will be good; if it is done basely, bad. And this holds good of loving, for Love is not of himself either admirable or noble, but only when he moves us to love nobly" (Plato, *Symposium* 181).

20. "You see then what this ancient evidence attests. Corresponding to the superior perfection and value of the prophecy of inspiration over that of omen reading, both in name and in fact, is the superiority of heaven-sent madness over man-made sanity.

"And in the second place, when grievous maladies and afflictions have beset certain families by reason of some ancient sin, madness [*mania*] has appeared among them, and breaking out into prophecy has secured relief . . . and in consequence thereof rites and means of purification were established, . . . " (Plato, *Phaedrus* 244e).

"There is a third form of possession or madness, of which the Muses are the source. . . . if any man come to the gates of poetry [*poiēsis*] without the madness [*mania*] of the Muses, persuaded that skill [*technē*] alone will make him a good poet, then shall he and his works of sanity with him be brought to nought by the poetry [*poiēsis*] of madness [*mainomenōn*], . . . " (*Phaedrus* 245).

21. See my *Metaphysical Aporia and Philosophical Heresy* (chap. 2, especially pp. 72–77), where I discuss the consequences of understanding human *ergon* and *aretē* in *Republic* as belonging to *technē*, represented as one overarching human excellence.

22. "All soul [*psychē*] is immortal, for that which is ever in motion is immortal" (Plato, *Phaedrus* 245c).

"Let [the soul] be likened to the union of powers in a team of winged steeds and their winged charioteer. . . . With us men, . . . one of them is noble and good, and of good stock, while the other has the opposite character, and his stock is opposite" (*Phaedrus* 246b).

"All soul has the care of all that is inanimate, and traverses the whole universe, though in ever-changing forms. . . . one that has shed its wings sinks down until it can fasten on something solid, and settling there it takes to itself an earthy body which seems by reason of the soul's power to move itself. This composite structure of soul and body is called a living being, . . . " (*Phaedrus* 246c).

23. Also: "But when one who is fresh from the mystery, and saw much of the vision, beholds a godlike face or bodily form that truly expresses beauty, first there come upon him a shuddering and measure of that awe which the vision inspired, ..."

"Wherefore as she gazes upon the boy's beauty, she admits a flood of particles streaming therefrom—that is why we speak of a 'flood of passion'—whereby she is warmed and fostered; . . . ."

"And behind its bars, together with the flood aforesaid, it throbs like a fevered pulse, and pricks at its proper outlet, and thereat the whole soul round about is stung and goaded into anguish; . . . ."

"At last she does behold him, and lets the flood pour in upon her, releasing the imprisoned waters; then has she refreshment and respite from her stings and sufferings, and that moment tastes a pleasure that is sweet beyond compare" (Plato, *Phaedrus* 251–52).

24. Socrates' words seem colored: "He that is on the more honorable side is upright and clean-limbed, carrying his neck high, with something of a hooked nose; in color he is white, with black eyes; . . . . The other is crooked of frame, a massive jumble of a creature, with thick short neck, snub nose, black skin, and gray eyes; hot-blooded, consorting with wantonness and vainglory; shaggy of ear, deaf, and hard to control with whip and goad" (Plato, *Phaedrus* 253e). We may grant him every Greek's prejudice toward appearance, tall and white more beautiful than dark and short. Yet we wonder at such a concession, since Socrates so seldom follows any prejudice without irony and is by no means upright and clean-limbed himself. In *Republic* where he takes up the question of women guardians exercising naked together with the men, he moves from calling it "the funniest thing" (Plato, *Republic* 452b) to the claim that "the women and the men, then, have the same nature in respect to the guardianship of the stage, save in so far as the one is weaker, the other stronger" (*Republic* 456). We may emphasize that he continues to call women weaker than men "as a class" (*Republic* 457b). But the principle he follows belies every normative gender distinction: "if it appears that the male and the female sex have distinct qualifications for any arts or pursuits, we shall affirm that they ought to be assigned respectively to each. But if it appears that they differ only in just this respect that the female bears and the male begets, we shall say that no proof has yet been produced that the woman differs from the man for our purposes, but we shall continue to think that our guardians and their wives ought to follow the same pursuits" (*Republic* 454e). The same pursuits rep-

resent the fundamental premise of the dialogue, a monolithic and undivided human virtue rather than one multifarious and complex. (See my *The Ring of Representation*, chap. 2.) The principle stated here would apply to any human virtue: that gender differences must be shown to entail differences of virtue and work, otherwise they and other generic differences are irrelevant to the good. The irony toward standard Greek views of gender differences is clear. Why should we assume it would not apply as well toward national and racial differences? Socrates repeatedly tells us tales from elsewhere, granting Egypt and Atlantis considerable authority regardless of the color of their citizens' skins. Such a tale appears later in *Phaedrus* 274–75. Perhaps we can respond to cultural biases when they appear in works that largely belie them that they represent not a deeper truth on either side—for or against the bias—but the imperishability and endurance of cultural and social forms. For if Socrates had described the nobler steed as dark and stocky, the ignobler as tall and white, what truth would we have gained? Socrates himself, the most beautiful of human beings, is physically ugly.

25. We may puzzle over whether this entire speech, unlike the earlier one, represents a violent sexual act, even a rape, so that the image of sexual restraint is overcome by pulling, forcing, violence, shame, and horror, by blood. How can blood be introduced into a scene of sexual compulsion without the thought of rape?

26. "And when they lie by one another, he is minded not to refuse to do his part in gratifying his lover's entreaties; yet his yokefellow in turn, being moved by reverence and heedfulness, joins with the driver in resisting. And so, if the victory be won by the higher elements of mind guiding them into the ordered rule of the philosophical life, their days on earth will be blessed with happiness and concord, ... And when life is over, with burden shed and wings recovered they stand victorious in the first of the three rounds in that truly Olympic struggle. . . . " (Plato, *Phaedrus* 256b).

27. "Then may she not justly return from this exile after she has pleaded her defense, whether in lyric or other measure?" (Plato, *Republic* 608d).

28. We are reminded of Heraclitus' view of *dikē*, as *polemos*.

29. "All soul has the care of all that is inanimate, and traverses the whole universe, though in ever-changing forms. . . . " (Plato, *Phaedrus* 246c). See n.22, this chapter.

> 30. All things, so it ran, that are ever said to be consist of a one and a many, and have in their nature a conjunction of limit and unlimitedness. This then being the ordering of things we ought, they said, whatever it be that we are dealing with, to assume a single form and search for it, for we shall find it there contained; then, if we have laid hold of that, we must go on from one form to look for two, if the case admits of there being two, otherwise

for three or some other number of forms. . . . But we are not to apply the character of unlimitedness to our plurality until we have discerned the total number of forms the thing in question has intermediate between its one and its unlimited number. It is only then, when we have done that, that we may let each one of all these intermediate forms pass away into the unlimited and cease bothering about them. (Plato, *Philebus* 16e)

31. "Now since virtue cannot be taught, we can no longer believe it to be knowledge, so that one of our two good and useful principles is excluded, and knowledge is not the guide in public life" (Plato, *Meno* 99b).

32. Socrates appears to tell us directly: "if you have anything else to say about the art of speech, we should be glad to hear it, but if not we shall adhere to the point we made just now, namely that unless the aspirant to oratory can on the one hand list the various natures among his prospective audiences, and on the other divide things into their kinds and embrace each individual thing under a single form, he will never attain such success as is within the grasp of mankind" (Plato, *Phaedrus* 273de). This success returns us to the public world where the art, the *technē*, of discourse belongs. All these disclosures, these oppositions, belong to discourse's *technē* representing its political movement, its public life, in that sense close to modern science. How can we take such a public knowledge and influence to belong to Socrates? How can we suppose that he can avoid them?

They certainly belong to Lysias and Pausanias. "Then we may feel that we have said enough about the art of speech, both the true art and the false" (*Phaedrus* 274b). "But there remains the question of propriety and impropriety in writing, that is to say the conditions which make it proper or improper" (*Phaedrus* 274b).

33. Here we differ with Derrida, who tells us that Socrates thus adopts the major, decisive opposition that cleaves the *manteia* of Thamus: "*mnēmē/ hypomnēsis*, the subtle difference between knowledge as memory and nonknowledge as rememoration, between two forms and two moments of repetition: . . ." (Derrida, *PP*, p. 135). And what if this represented no opposition but an endless circling?

34. Derrida warns us that the parent here is the father [*patros*], waxing ecstatic at Plato's domesticity. "This scene has never been read for what it is, for what is at once sheltered and exposed in its metaphors: its *family* metaphors. It is all about fathers and sons, about bastards unaided by any public assistance, about glorious, legitimate sons, about inheritance, sperm, sterility. Nothing is said of the mother, but this will not be held against us. And if one looks hard enough as in those pictures in which a second picture faintly can be made out, one might be able to discern her unstable form, drawn upside-down in the foliage, at the back of the garden" (Derrida, *PP*, p. 143).

How else can we read the legitimacy of writing?

35. Not to mention the seriousness of play, dissolving gravity's rainbow. "Plato thus plays at taking play seriously" (Derrida, *PP*, p. 157).

36. "[A]ny work, in the past or in the future, whether by Lysias or anyone else, whether composed in a private capacity or in the role of a public man who by proposing a law becomes the author of a political composition, is a matter of reproach to its author . . . " (Plato, Phaedrus 277d).

"On the other hand, if a man believes that a written discourse on any subject is bound to contain much that is fanciful, that nothing that has ever been written whether in verse or prose merits much serious attention—and for that matter nothing that has ever been spoken in the declamatory fashion which aims at mere persuasion without any questioning or exposition—that in reality such compositions are, at the best, a means of reminding [*hypomnēsin*] those who know the truth, . . . " (278a).

"[I]f any of them has done his work with a knowledge of the truth, can defend his statements when challenged, and can demonstrate the inferiority of his writings out of his own mouth, . . . " (278d).

"A name that would fit him better . . . would be 'lover of wisdom,' [*philosophon*] or something similar" (278e).

"[O]ne who has nothing to show of more value than the literary works on whose phrases he spends hours . . . will rightly be called a poet [*poiētēn*] or speech writer or law writer" (278e).

Yet there is nothing wrong or shameful about writing itself.

37. "The truth of writing, that is, as we shall see, (the) nontruth, cannot be discovered in ourselves by ourselves. And it is not the object of a science, only of a history that is recited, a fable that is repeated. The link between writing and myth becomes clearer, as does its opposition to knowledge, notably the knowledge one seeks in oneself, by oneself" (Derrida, *PP*, p. 74).

We wonder at the opposition to knowledge.

Chapter X. Witches' Science

1. "The systematic development of truth in scientific form can alone be the true shape in which truth exists" (Hegel, *Phenomenology of Mind*, p. 70). "The truth is the whole. The whole, however, is merely the essential nature reaching its completeness through the process of its own development. Of the Absolute it must be said that it is essentially a result, that only at the end is it what it is in very truth; and just in that consists its nature, which is to be actual, subject, or self, becoming, self-development" (pp. 81–82).

2. Jean-François Lyotard, *The Postmodern Condition: A Report on Knowledge* (*PC*), trans. G. Bennington and B. Massumi (Minneapolis: University of Minnesota Press, 1984), p. 29.

3. Jean-François Lyotard and Jean-Loup Thébaud, *Just Gaming* (*JG*), trans. W. Godzich (Minneapolis: University of Minnesota Press, 1985), p. 16.

4. We will come to death. For Derrida reminds us that "The fear of death is what gives all witchcraft, all occult medicine, a hold" (Derrida, "Plato's Pharmacy," in *Dissemination*, p. 120).

5. "The distinction between a private and a public sphere of life corresponds to the household and political realms, which have existed as distinct, separate entities at least since the rise of the ancient city-state; . . . .

"In our understanding, the dividing line is entirely blurred, because we see the body of peoples and political communities in the image of a family whose everyday affairs have to be taken care of by a gigantic, nation-wide administration of housekeeping" (Hannah Arendt, *The Human Condition* [*HC*] [Chicago: University of Chicago Press, 1958], p. 28).

6. Michael Polanyi, *Personal Knowledge* (*PK*) (London: Routledge & Kegan Paul, 1959), p. 53.

7. Michael Polanyi, *Knowing and Being* (Chicago: University of Chicago, 1969), p. 133.

8. See what this becomes in a reading of Polanyi directed toward a religious authority.

> The attitude of doubt and scepticism towards tradition and authority and belief, has not only affected the realm of science but has spilled over into society and caused a civic predicament. (Alexander Thomson, *Tradition and Authority in Science and Theology* [*TAST*] [Edinburgh: Scottish Academic Press, 1987], p. 24).

The art taken as model for science and theology represents not *poiēsis* but *technē*, or rather, a *technē* without *poiēsis*, fearing a *poiēsis* without *technē* even as *technē*'s rules fail to provide security.

> Rules of art can be useful, but they do not determine the practice of an art; they are maxims, which can serve as a guide to an art only if they can be integrated into the practical knowledge of the art. They cannot replace this knowledge. (Polanyi, *PK*, p. 50).

The civic predicament restores the authority of science to the city, to political practice and practical judgment, in all its excessiveness. We recognize the *poiētic* in *technē* as the threat of anarchy even as we know that we can pursue neither *praxis* nor *epistēmē* by rules. Before this threat of anarchy, we throw ourselves down under, subject ourselves to authority, claiming that we have the authority to do so.

> We can learn a skill, and receive the premisses of science only in imitating someone who is a recognised authority in science, and by practice. (Thomson, *TAST*, p. 26).

Science's innocence rules.

9. Michael Polanyi and H. Prosch, *Meaning* (Chicago: University of Chicago Press, 1975), p. 184.

10. "In Jesus Christ we are confronted with the reality of God's self-revelation. This is our conviction which we must plainly state at the outset. We cannot in a detached impersonal way demonstrate the truth of this conviction. Jesus Christ carries with Him His own authority which calls forth from us our convictions and belief. We are submitting ourselves to the self-authenticating authority of the Truth itself" (Thomson, *TAST*, p. 107). Polanyi deserves no more than anyone to be subjected to his follower's misreadings—if they are misreadings. We wonder at the excessiveness of traditional authority in any form, remaining within what both Polanyi and Thomson reject, unrelenting suspicion of the injustices of authority.

11. Hans-Georg Gadamer, *Truth and Method* (New York: Seabury, 1975), p. 258.

12. Michel Foucault, "Two Lectures," in *Power/Knowledge*, trans. and ed. C. Gordon (New York: Pantheon, 1980), p. 83.

13. Hans-Georg Gadamer, "The Universality of the Hermeneutic Problem," in *Philosophical Hermeneutics* (*PH*), trans. D. E. Linge (Berkeley: University of California Press, 1976), p. 11.

14. "[B]y subjugated knowledges one should understand something else, something which in a sense is altogether different, namely, a whole set of knowledges that have been disqualified as inadequate to their task or insufficiently elaborated: naive knowledges, located low down on the hierarchy, beneath the required level of cognition or scientificity" (Foucault, "Two Lectures," p. 82). "What [the genealogical project] really does is to entertain the claims to attention of local, discontinuous, disqualified, illegitimate knowledges against the claims of a unitary body of theory which would filter, hierarchise and order them in the name of some true knowledge and some arbitrary idea of what constitutes a science and its objects. Genealogies are therefore not positivistic returns to a more careful or exact form of science. They are precisely anti-sciences" (p. 81).

15. Michel Foucault, *The Archaeology of Knowledge*, trans. Alan M. Sheridan Smith (New York: Pantheon, 1972).

16. Jean-François Lyotard, *Heidegger and "the jews"* (Minneapolis: University of Minnesota Press, 1990), p. 5.

17. Gaston Bachelard, *The New Scientific Spirit*, trans. A. Goldhammer (Boston: Beacon Press, 1984), pp. 31–32.

18. Gaston Bachelard, *The Philosophy of No*, trans. G. C. Waterston (New York: Orion Press, 1968), p. 35.

19. Kathryn Pyne Addelson, "The Man of Professional Wisdom," in *Impure Thoughts* (*IT*) (Philadelphia: Temple University Press, 1991), p. 62.

20. Steve Fuller, *Social Epistemology* (*SE*) (Bloomington and Indianapolis: Indiana University Press, 1988), p. 4.

21. Foucault, "Truth and Power," in *Power/Knowledge*, p. 133.

22. A space filled with violence. "In choosing violence—and that is what it's all about from the beginning—and violence against the father, the son—or patricidal writing—cannot fail to expose himself, too" (Derrida, "Plato's Pharmacy," p. 146). Perhaps not just the father's or son's violence, not just against the father, but against Pharmakeia.

23. An example close to Arendt: "We have to beware thinking that all the different partial perspectives provided by different conceptual approaches to the world can somehow be coordinated and merged to arrive at a single, consistent, total view of the world" (Patrick Wilson, *Second-hand Knowledge: An Inquiry into Cognitive Authority* [Westport, Conn.: Greenwood Press, 1983], p. 7). Leading to monstrosity: "An authority on authorities is one who can be trusted to tell us who else can be trusted. He need not himself be learned in the fields in which he can identify the authorities. It is enough that he has some way of telling who deserves to be taken as having cognitive authority" (Wilson, *Second-hand Knowledge*, p. 179). Who might possess such monstrous authority but a librarian, natural enough since Wilson's book addresses the epistemic authority of librarians? Do we find missing any sense of danger? A dose of skepticism keeps us safe. "Contrary to perpetual misunderstanding, the skeptic is not debarred from action or work; the one thing he does not do is to take a position as to whether what appears to be so really is" (Wilson, *Second-hand Knowledge*, p. 195). Contrary to everyone's dream of cognitive authority, the skeptic threatens nothing even when taken to threaten everything. Do we suppose that those who feel threatened by skepticism and relativism know nothing of truth? Or shall we take for granted the monstrosity and menace of skepticism and relativism, where rule and law obscure the menace of their monstrosity? How do we make the commitment necessary within skepticism to take action? How do we accommodate witchcraft and sorcery within our scientific practices?

24. Lynn Hankinson Nelson, *Who Knows* (*WK*) (Philadelphia, Pa.: Temple University Press, 1990), p. 250.

25. Michel Foucault, "Politics and the Study of Discourse," in *The Foucault Effect*, ed. and trans. G. Burchell, C. Gordon, P. Miller (Chicago: University of Chicago Press, 1991), p. 69.

26. Sandra Harding, "The Instability of the Analytical Categories of Feminist Theory," *Signs* 11, no. 4 (1986): 648.

27. Immanuel Kant, *Critique of Pure Reason*, trans. Norman Kemp Smith (London: Macmillan, 1956), p. 573.

28. John Dewey, *Logic: The Theory of Inquiry* (London: George Allen & Unwin, 1938), pp. 3–4.

29. Summarizing:

1. *Logic is a progressive discipline.* . . .
2. *The subject-matter of logic is determined operationally.* . . .
3. *Logical forms are postulational.* . . .
4. *Logic is a naturalistic theory.* . . .
5. *Logic is a social discipline.* . . .
6. *Logic is autonomous.* (Dewey, *Logic*, pp. 14–20)

30. "The force of this proposition may perhaps be most readily understood by noting what it precludes. It precludes the determination and selection of logical first principles by an *a priori* intuitional act, ... It precludes resting logic upon metaphysical and epistemological assumptions and presuppositions" (Dewey, *Logic*, pp. 20–21). It precludes grounding logic upon *a priori* intuitions or metaphysical and epistemological presuppositions. It seems to preclude the dangers of *erōs* and *philia* and the terrors of the witches, that science may never avoid subjection, though it may represent within itself the injustices of its own authority. The social side of science represents order for Dewey within an extraordinary sense of its locality and temporality. "Genuine time, if it exists as anything else except the measure of motions in space, is all one with the existence of individuals as individuals, with the creative, with the occurrence of unpredictable novelties." "Individuality conceived as a temporal development involves uncertainty, indeterminacy, or contingency. Individuality is the source of whatever is unpredictable in the world" (Dewey, "Time and Individuality," in *Experience, Nature, and Freedom*, ed. Richard Bernstein [Indianapolis: Bobbs-Merrill, 1960], p. 239).

31. Is it imagined by Derrida, in his three aporias of justice? Does Derrida recognize the worst in the best? See n.33, chap. 7.

32. "Intelligence is concerned with foreseeing the future so that action may have order and direction" (John Dewey, *Human Nature and Conduct* [New York: Modern Library, 1950], p. 238). "As habits set in grooves dominate activity and swerve it from conditions instead of increasing its adaptability, so principles treated as fixed rules instead of as helpful methods take men away from experience" (p. 238).

33. We find here not a better but a monstrous science. It appears again as heterogeneity in Arendt. "Human distinctness is not the same as otherness—the curious quality of *alteritas* possessed by everything that is. . . . only man can express this distinction and distinguish himself, and only he can communicate himself and not merely something—thirst or hunger, affection or hostility or fear.

In man, otherness, which he shares with everything that is, and distinctness, which he shares with everything alive, become uniqueness, and human plurality is the paradoxical plurality of unique beings" (Arendt, *HC*, p. 156). Otherness and distinctness pass through plurality to uniqueness under another monstrous sign of *Geschlecht*.

34. See chap. 1, p. 6.

35. Alfred North Whitehead, *Process and Reality* (*PR*), corr. ed., ed. D. R. Griffin and D. W. Sherburne (New York: Free Press, 1978), p. 4.

36. Alfred North Whitehead, *Science and the Modern World* (*SMW*) (New York: Macmillan, 1925), pp. 249–50. See the discussion here in chap. 4, pp. 85–88.

37. See my *Perspective in Whitehead's Metaphysics* (Albany: State University of New York Press, 1983), chaps. 9 and 10.

38. Martin Heidegger, "The Age of the World Picture," in *The Question Concerning Technology and Other Essays*, trans. W. Lovitt (New York: Harper, 1977). "The essence of what we today call science is research. In what does the essence of research consist?" "In the fact that knowing [*das Erkennen*] establishes itself as a procedure within some realm of what is, in nature of in history. Procedure does not mean here merely method or methodology. For every procedure already requires an open sphere in which it moves. And it is precisely the opening up of such a sphere that is the fundamental event in research. This is accomplished through the projection within some realm of what is—in nature, for example—of a fixed ground plan [*Grundriss*] of natural events" (p. 118). We may take this already to mark the difference between Heidegger's fourfold and the witches, who threaten the future, threaten another subjection, an injustice somehow missing in Heidegger. "[W]hen man becomes the primary and only real *subiectum*, that means: Man becomes that being upon which all that is, is grounded as regards the manner of its Being and its truth" (p. 128). Man the ground masks his own subjection, masking with it all the forms of his subjugation of others.

39. Alfred North Whitehead, *Modes of Thought* (New York: Capricorn, 1958), p. 2.

40. This understanding of generalization and systematization as critique represents what I find missing in Richard Rorty, whose understanding of critique is largely iconoclastic.

41. Alfred North Whitehead, *Adventures of Ideas* (New York: Macmillan, 1933), p. 341.

42. "In this epoch thought stands in a position of *Verwindung* in regard to metaphysics. Metaphysics is not abandoned like an old, worn-out garment, for it still constitutes our 'humanity' in *geschicklich* terms; we yield to it, we heal our-

selves from it, we are resigned to it as something that is destined to us" (Vattimo, *The End of Modernity*, p. 52).

43. Heidegger, "The Origin of the Work of Art," in *Poetry, Language, Thought*, p. 80.

44. See chap. 4, p. 90.

45. Martin Heidegger, "The Question Concerning Technology" (*QT*), in *Basic Writings*, p. 294.

Chapter Eleven. Justice's Injustice

1. We remember Whitehead's stunning claim (see chap. 3, p. 42), frequently repeated, that expresses a monstrous injustice to Plato and the others, an injustice inseparable from its truth: "The safest general characteristic of the European philosophic tradition is that it consists of a series of footnotes to Plato" (Whitehead, *Process and Reality*, p. 39). How unjust the dream that this might be "safe"!

2. Donald J. Consentino, "Midnight Charter: Musa Wo and Mende Myths of Chaos," in *Creativity of Power*, ed. W. Arens and I. Karp (Washington and London: Smithsonian Press, 1989), pp. 23–26.

3. Michelle Gilbert, "Sources of Power in Akuropon-Akuapem: Ambiguity in Classification," in Arens and Karp, *Creativity of Power*, p. 59.

4. Alma Gottlieb, "Witches, Kings, and the Sacrifice of Identity or The Power of Paradox and the Paradox of Power among the Beng of Ivory Coast," in Arens and Karp, *Creativity of Power*, p. 254.

5. (In a Beng voice, retold by Gottlieb): "Long ago, when it came matriclan X's time to contribute a member to be the chief of village P, the clan elders refused to do so because they did not want to have other clan members killed in witchcraft by the new chief. . . . The king of the region in which village P is located commented to me that P 'could not be a good village' until clan X reinstated itself back into the village chiefship rotation cycle." (In Gottlieb's voice): "and, by implication, permits clan members to be killed through witchcraft by the new chief" (Gottlieb, "Witches, Kings," p. 255).

6. William E. Connolly, "Modern Authority and Ambiguity," *Authority Revisited, Nomos*, vol. 29, ed. J. R. Pennock and J. W. Chapman (New York: New York University Press, 1987), p. 19.

7. Terence Ball, "Authority and Conceptual Change," in Pennock and Chapman, *Authority Revisited*, p. 48.

8. Nancy L. Rosenblum, "Studying Authority," in Pennock and Chapman, *Authority Revisited*, p. 123.

9. Michel Foucault, *The Order of Things: An Archaeology of the Human Sciences* (New York: Pantheon, 1971), p. 26.

10. Told to me by Mary Ellen Collins, who found the voice of the witches on her own: she calls it "God."

11. Kathleen B. Jones, "On Authority: Or, Why Women Are not Entitled to Speak," in Pennock and Chapman, *Authority Revisited*, p. 155.

12. Michel Foucault, "Truth and Power," in *Power/Knowledge*, p. 131.

13. Foucault, "Nietzsche, Genealogy, and History," in *Language, Counter-memory, and Practice*, pp. 150–51.

14. Catharine MacKinnon, "Feminism, Marxism, Method, and the State" (FMMS), *Signs* 8 (1983): 635–58.

15. Ronald Dworkin ("Liberty and Pornography," *The New York Review of Books* (15 August 1991) criticizes MacKinnon's and others' attack on pornography as neglecting Isaiah Berlin's distinction between negative liberty (freedom from obstruction) and positive liberty (empowerment). "It is of course understandable why Michelman and others should want to expand the idea of negative liberty in the way they do. Only by characterizing certain ideas as themselves 'silencing' ideas—only by supposing that censoring pornography is the same thing as stopping people from drowning out other speakers—can they hope to justify censorship within the constitutional scheme that assigns a preeminent place to free speech. But the assimilation is nevertheless a confusion, exactly the kind of confusion Berlin warned against in his original lecture, because it obscures the true political choice that must be made" (p. 15). Dworkin seems unable to recognize that to make a political decision by means of a philosophical distinction represents the unjust cut of *technē*.

Yet he knows perfectly well, even describes in detail, the impossible and intractable subordination of women in his description of why pornography should not be singled out as a unique site of women's subjection. "It seems unlikely that [pornography, especially sadistic pornography] has remotely the influence over how women's sexuality or character or talents are conceived by men, and indeed by women, that commercial advertising and soap operas have. Television and other parts of popular culture use sexual display and sexual innuendo to sell virtually everything, and they often show women as experts in domestic detail and unreasoned intuition, and nothing else. . . . Sadistic pornography, though much more offensive and disturbing, is greatly overshadowed by these dismal cultural influences as a causal force" (p. 14).

He represents the feminist case in forceful terms, yet apparently without understanding the depths of the critique. "Some feminist groups argue, however, that pornography causes not just physical violence but a more general and endemic subordination of women" (p. 14). "Frank Michelman . . . argues that some speech, including pornography, may be itself 'silencing,' so that its effect is to prevent other people from exercising their negative freedom to speak" (Frank Michelman, "Conceptions of Democracy in American Constitutional Argument: The Case of Pornography Regulation," *Tennessee Law Review* 56, no. 291 [1989]: 303–4; "Liberty and Pornography," Dworkin, p. 15). Perhaps American constitutional protection of freedom of speech outweighs the injustice of such silencings. Perhaps the virtue of freedom of speech, to allow the profession of all points of view, including the most heinous, is a requisite for democracy. Perhaps pornography, however revolting, however sadistic, does not deserve to be singled out for the pervasive subordination of women.

Yet what the witches show, MacKinnon among them, including *pharmakeuses* like Michelman, is the injustice of every rational distinction that obscures recognition of the pervasiveness of women's degradation. What if our entire Western, rational, enlightenment tradition, the entire system of law and authority, science and government, subordinated women, silenced and oppressed them? What if we could not draw a line, within our legal system, within our rationality, between sexual intercourse and rape, between freedom of speech and sexual or racial oppression? What if every system of criminal law inevitably fell disproportionately on ethnic minorities? We cannot live without such distinctions in the circulation of justice and law. We cannot live comfortably with such distinctions, as if they perpetrated no injustice.

See also in this chapter, pp. 306–307.

16. "Left to itself, the incalculable and giving (*donatrice*) idea of justice is always very close to the bad, even to the worst for it can always be reappropriated by the most perverse calculation. It's always possible. And so incalculable justice requires us to calculate" (Derrida, "Force of Law," p. 971). See chap. 7, pp. 178–85.

17. "[T]here is never a moment that we can say *in the present* that a decision *is* just. . . . " (Derrida, "Force of Law," p. 961). A decision is obligated "to give itself up to the impossible decision, while taking account of law and rules" (p. 963). "[J]ustice, however unpresentable it may be, doesn't wait" (p. 967). (See chap. 7, pp. n. 33, pp. 348–49.)

18. Especially in my *The Ring of Representation*, but also in my *Metaphysical Aporia and Philosophical Heresy, Inexhaustibility and Human Being, The Limits of Language*, and *Locality and Practical Judgment*.

19. We are repeating the sonorescences of the ring of representation sounding the concordance and discordances of the inexhaustible circulation of things in time, acting and falling into history, representing, in their inexhaustible mirrors, the excesses of each other. See chap. 1, n.15.

20. "Musically," remembering the cicadas, the Mouses (in their Furies), and Musa Wo.

21. We recall Trinh Minh-ha's words concerning The Master's Culture. See chap. 3, p. 45.

22. I am speaking again of *The Ring of Representation*, where ergonality echoes nature's work.

23. See n.15, this chapter. In the same issue (*New York Review of Books*, 15 August 1991, pp. 36–42), Peter Singer describes hostile and sometimes violent German reactions against his being permitted to speak. Understandably moved by remembrances of eugenics and euthanasia under Hitler, some contemporary Germans react with hatred against any attempt to discuss either, even when the context is very different, react with a hatred Singer finds reminiscent of Nazi hatred against Jews. Similarly, discussion and even research on ties between race and crime in the United States evoke passionate opposition to the point of silencing, again understandably from fear that such discussions would be used to bolster racism.

We remember immemorial injustice in four ways:

1. Every tyrannical régime silences oppositional speech and press in the service of its injustices;
2. There is a passion for justice that knows nothing of its own injustice.
3. Freedom of expression is among the greatest of political goods, pervaded nevertheless by the deepest injustices, in particular, that it always circulates among those who have been silenced—women, ethnic minorities, certain classes—and contributes to their silencing;
4. Archaic injustice imposes on us a responsibility without limits for the restitution of the injustices of even the greatest of our practices. Freedom of expression represents a freedom virtually without limits, imposing a continuing responsibility for restitution for the suffering of remaining victims.

24. Do we remember our consciousness of justice's injustice as the contradictions of our unhappy consciousness? "[T]he *Unhappy Consciousness*, the Alienated Soul which is the consciousness of self as a divided nature, a doubled and merely contradictory being." "This unhappy consciousness, divided and at variance within itself, must, because this contradiction of its essential nature is felt to be a single consciousness, always have in the one consciousness the other also; and thus must be straightway driven out of each in turn, when it thinks it has therein attained to the victory and rest of unity" (Hegel, *Phenomenology of Mind*, p. 251). Hegel tells this narrative as a story of the Subject, which must give up its will to Reason to regain its authority. "For giving up one's own will is only in one aspect negative; in principle, or in itself, it is at the same time positive, positing and affirming the will as an *other*, and, specifically, affirming the will as *not* a particular, but universal" (Hegel, *Phenomenology of Mind*, p. 266). The Subject overcomes its alienation by giving up its particularity to law even as Hegel later reaffirms the mere abstraction of universality without the particular, the injustice of

law's justice, the reaffirmation of law's injustice *as* the universality in particularity, as the unending play of universality and particularity, never reappears.

For Hegel never questions the authority of authority, that of which we find ourselves most suspicious, our subjection.

25. "The non-present is in-comprehendable by reason of its immensity or its 'superlative' humility or, for example, its goodness, which is the superlative itself. The non-present here is invisible, separated (or sacred) and thus a non-origin, an-archical. The Good cannot become present or enter into a representation" (Levinas, *Otherwise than Being*, p. 11). See also chap. 1, pp. 11–12.

INDEX

Abjection, 5, 7, 10, 14, 103, 105, 107–109, 114–15, 117, 119–21, 123–25, 196, 200, 204, 296–98, 302, 304, 307, 313–14, 334–36; *see also* Subjection

Aboriginal, 1, 7, 9–11, 27, 39, 43, 69, 79, 81, 88, 91, 122, 180, 281, 312; *see also* Immemorial, Origin

Abraham, 187, 348; *see also* Kierkegaard

Absence, 23–25, 27, 54, 61, 73, 81, 110, 134, 143, 152–53, 175, 178, 183, 250, 255, 261, 274, 279, 290, 303, 317; *see also* Silence

Absolute, 8, 17, 19, 22, 28, 33–34, 59, 68–69, 74–77, 81, 93, 106, 109, 111, 118, 124, 150, 183, 188, 200, 217, 253, 265, 288, 310, 316, 318, 329–30, 341, 348, 358

Absolution, 110, 118, 188

Abstraction, 74–76, 84, 262, 330, 367

Abyss, 29, 31, 71–72, 143–46, 149–51, 273, 285–86, 327, 330, 341, 347, 353

Act, 14, 21, 25–28, 43, 50, 68, 70, 78, 81, 83, 91, 98, 108, 113–14, 129, 143, 155, 164, 170, 201, 234–36, 249–51, 256–58, 290, 301, 308, 320, 323, 325, 328, 330, 333, 340, 351, 354, 356, 361–62, 366

Activity, 73, 79, 83–85, 121, 255–57, 266, 326, 339, 362

Actuality, 74–76, 85–88, 91, 112, 138, 182, 227, 327, 330–31, 350, 358,

Addelson, K., 265–69, 361

Adikia, 1–2, 54, 154, 173, 316, 318, 321–22, 334, 368; *see also* Injustice

Adorno, T., 198

Aeschylus, 38–39, 147–48, 153, 322–23, 341

Africa, 1, 44, 134, 155, 173, 185, 193, 196, 198, 283, 294, 301, 343

Agamemnon, 147, 152–53, 156

Agathon, 219, 240

Age, 1, 5–6, 11–12, 18, 34, 39, 43, 45, 47, 52–53, 55, 58, 61–64, 69, 71–72, 75–76, 81, 87–90, 92–93, 96, 100, 114, 122, 132, 137, 144, 146, 157, 175, 192–93, 195, 200–201, 238, 248, 275, 291, 327–28, 332, 363; *see also* Immemoriality, Time

Agency, 26, 84, 132, 223, 257, 319, 329

Ajax, 147–48, 341

Akuropon-Akuapem, 283, 364
Alcibiades, 197, 219, 227–28
Alētheia, 245, 278; *see also* Truth
Alienation, 9, 68, 141–43, 145, 211, 367
Alterity, 209, 320, 362; *see also* Other, Otherwise
Ambiguity, 26, 97, 154, 230, 242, 244, 251, 253, 257, 265, 267, 273, 278–79, 284–85, 287–90, 292, 295, 303–304, 308, 311, 350, 364
Ammon, 245–46, 324
Anamnēsis, 232
Anarchy, 11, 20, 36, 38, 145, 261, 266–68, 359
Anaxagoras, 130
Anaximander, 1–2, 4, 18, 36, 41, 45, 52, 54, 57, 65, 88, 91, 110, 113, 130, 154, 173, 175–76, 181–82, 187, 201, 228, 309–10, 315–16, 318, 338, 368
Ancient, 1, 11, 16, 27, 38–39, 47, 64, 116, 123, 125, 194, 196, 199–200, 204–205, 331, 354, 359; *see also* Greek, Immemorial
Animals, 21, 23, 44, 57, 66, 77, 100–101, 113–15, 152–53, 120–21, 132, 150, 156, 184–86, 199–200, 221, 263, 288, 293–97, 298–99, 302, 311, 313, 330–31, 338, 340, 343, 347–48; *see also* Monstrosity
Annihilation, 2, 9, 336; *see also* Death
Anthropology, 35, 195–97, 210, 274
Apollo, 1, 15, 36, 81, 89, 192, 199, 236, 298
Apology, 47, 120; *see also* Plato
Aporia, 71, 181–82, 187, 189, 218, 270, 292, 298, 302, 304, 324, 328–29, 348–49, 354, 362. 366
Appearance, 26, 33, 51, 55, 71, 122, 130, 139, 144–45, 155, 196, 207, 220, 222, 233, 238–39, 248, 303–304, 310, 326, 328, 355
Appropriation, 76, 105, 188, 206–208, 210
Aquinas, T., 193
Arbitrariness, 20, 23, 33–34, 59, 63, 68–70, 74–75, 78, 81, 87–89, 96, 113, 119, 145, 153, 156, 164–65, 169, 171, 262, 274, 277, 286, 295, 345, 360
Archaeology, 36, 103, 334
Archaic, 1, 3, 5, 8, 10–11, 19, 25, 27–31, 36, 46–47, 69, 71, 81, 110–12, 114–23, 125, 129, 138–39, 143–44, 147–48, 150, 153–55, 157, 171–76, 178, 180–83, 186, 195, 285, 292, 311–12, 317, 319–20, 330, 367; *see also* Ancient, Immemorial
Archē, 20, 115, 322, 326
Arendt, H., 7–8, 41, 256–57, 267, 304, 309, 318, 323, 359, 361–63
Aretē, 61–62, 228, 232, 282, 305, 328, 354
Argument, 17, 24, 55, 63, 83, 144, 161, 163, 166–67, 203, 214–15, 244, 246, 265, 366; *see also* Proof
Aristophanes, 219
Aristotle, 41, 55–59, 61–63, 112–13, 183, 193, 197, 213–17, 261, 327, 335, 351–52
Armenians, 294, 306
Arrive-t-il?, 189; *see also* Event, Lyotard
Art, 2, 26–28, 47, 49–51, 81, 103, 105, 116, 202, 215, 225, 229, 238–39, 241, 243–45, 248, 250, 257, 259, 264, 271, 276–77, 286, 298, 324, 327–28, 332, 342, 351, 357, 359; *see also* Poiēsis, Technē
Athena, 38, 147, 178, 284, 324
Athens, 39, 47, 51, 128, 164, 197, 221, 223, 225, 237, 281
Atlantis, 246, 324, 356
Auschwitz, 207

Index

Author, 6, 17, 26, 42, 201–202, 219, 349, 358
Authoritative, 29, 32, 48, 51, 56, 66, 127, 134, 168, 171, 174, 215–16, 259, 273, 288, 352
Authority, 1, 3, 5–36, 38–39, 41–52, 54–83, 85–101, 103, 106–15, 119–24, 127–29, 131–40, 143–45, 148–49, 152–57, 160–72, 174–86, 188–89, 191–92, 200–205, 207, 210–11, 213–18, 220, 225, 234–35, 249–50, 252–56, 258–67, 269–74, 276–78, 285–97, 299, 301–305, 307–15, 317–18, 320–21, 326, 329–30, 332–35, 345, 347, 349–50, 353, 356, 359–62, 364–68; *see also* Law, Power, Rule, Sovereignty
Authorization, 14, 26–27, 36, 43, 52, 58, 60–61, 63–66, 68–69, 76, 81, 96, 164, 168, 171, 174, 176–78, 180, 183, 201–203, 254–55, 257, 260, 288, 302–303, 305–306, 329, 350
Autonomy, 9, 254, 259, 273; *see also* Freedom

Babel, Tower of, 270, 272
Bachelard, G., 264, 360
Bacon, F., 322, 329, 331, 352
Bantu, 196
Bataille, G., 332
Beast, 66, 147–48, 152–53, 159, 186, 199; *see also* Animals, Monstrosity
Beauty, 40, 49, 67, 100–101, 146, 210, 213, 218, 223, 233–37, 239, 242, 245, 250, 255, 265, 275–76, 298, 313, 343, 350, 355–56
Beauvoir, S. de, 41
Beckett, S., 349
Becoming, 5, 54, 69, 100, 143, 153, 186, 194, 199, 265–66, 286, 295, 326, 330, 358

Beginning, 2, 6, 12, 41, 44, 69, 74, 81, 106, 125, 196, 205, 209–10, 221, 223, 237–38, 256, 303, 328, 336, 352; *see also* Immemorial, Origin
Being, 2–5, 7–8, 12, 14, 18, 21–22, 27–28, 31–32, 34–35, 40–41, 50–51, 53–55, 57, 68, 70, 75, 83–84, 91–92, 95, 98–99, 102, 105, 108–109, 112–14, 118, 124, 127–30, 136, 138–41, 143–44, 146, 150–51, 154, 166, 168, 188, 197, 201, 204–205, 210–11, 214–16, 221, 223, 229, 232–34, 236–37, 239, 242–43, 245, 247, 250–51, 267, 275, 278, 286, 294, 310–11, 315–16, 318–20, 324, 327–28, 333–34, 336, 338–39, 345–46, 351–52, 355–56, 359, 363, 366–68
Beings, 3, 6, 10–12, 18–23, 25, 32–33, 35, 41, 44, 47, 58, 61, 66, 73, 100, 105–108, 114, 119–21, 133, 137, 146, 153, 186, 213, 232, 240, 250, 257, 260, 265, 270, 276, 293–95, 311, 316, 319–20, 328, 331, 356, 363, 368
Belief, 17, 50, 64, 80, 142, 260–61, 264, 352, 359–60; *see also* Knowledge
Belonging, 19–20, 26–27, 43, 45, 75–76, 88, 93, 98, 109, 120, 123–24, 135, 137, 139–40, 143, 146, 157, 168, 173, 176, 181, 206–207, 238, 269, 272, 285, 309, 320, 354
Benefit, 19, 60, 62, 70, 164, 224–25, 230, 232, 239, 249, 265, 276, 283, 300; *see also* Calculation, Good, Instrumentality, Measure
Beng, 283–84, 364
Benjamin, W., 16, 34, 41, 172–75, 177, 181, 198, 208, 321–22, 345, 350–51

Bentham, J., 67, 69–71, 328, 333
Berkeley, G., 83–84, 331, 360
Berlin, I., 365
Bernal, M., 324
Bernstein, R., 330
Bewitchment, 233, 274, 283, 302; see also Magic, Witchcraft
Biology, 120, 132, 134–36, 347
Bloch, E., 153–55, 310, 343
Blood, 38, 153, 173, 185, 235, 284, 291, 297, 302–303, 307, 311, 314, 340, 356
Bodies, 14, 19, 21, 34–35, 57, 72, 76–77, 83, 118–21, 131, 136, 139, 141–42, 145–46, 149, 151, 234, 236, 240–41, 243, 265, 299, 325, 329, 331, 337, 340, 355, 359–60; see also Embodiment, Materiality
Boreas, 221–23, 253, 256–57
Brauchen, 2, 207
Brothers Karamazov, The, 117, 336; see also Dostoevsky
Buchler, J., 324, 332
Burgess Shale, 131–36, 338–39; see also Gould
Burkert, W., 186, 343, 348

Calculation, 29, 70–71, 134, 189, 225, 232, 234, 239, 279, 290, 297, 337, 348, 366; see also Economy, Measure
Canon, 10, 42, 69, 127, 209, 296, 302, 313, 316, 368; see also Measure
Capitalism, 307–308
Carnivorousness, 152, 184, 199, 299, 347; see also Animals
Caruth, C., 145, 341
Catastrophe, 110, 208–11, 283–84, 287, 294–95, 297, 300, 303, 310, 351
Categories, 112, 128, 151, 226, 317, 361; see also Metaphysics, Philosophy

Cause, 27–28, 38, 55–58, 84, 91, 112, 116–17, 138, 143, 178, 183, 214–15, 217, 235, 265, 293, 329, 335, 342, 352, 354, 365
Cephalus, 160, 218, 222
Certainty, 43, 55–57, 74, 107, 130, 136, 166, 269
Chance, 48, 58, 61, 112–13, 116, 145, 209, 214–16, 326, 334–35
Change, 78–80, 83, 137, 169, 364
Chaos, 94, 141, 145, 223, 287, 340, 364
Charity, 5, 58, 65, 77, 118, 186, 256, 282, 284, 296, 305, 309, 312–13, 317–19; see also Sacrifice, Valor
Charmides, 216, 352
Children, 7, 14, 47, 57, 59–62, 116–18, 165, 170, 216, 236, 247–48, 267–68, 270, 281, 291, 293, 306–308, 310, 352
Christ, 164, 196, 262, 281, 360
Christianity, 152, 165, 173, 182, 191, 197–98
Cicadas, 63, 227, 238, 243–44, 366
Cicero, 15, 63–64, 66, 320, 328
Circulation, 1, 7, 11, 43, 86, 88–90, 92–97, 99–103, 110, 114, 118, 131, 137, 141, 155, 157, 175, 201–202, 220, 225–26, 243–44, 247, 252–53, 256, 258–60, 263, 276–77, 282, 284, 286, 291, 295, 298, 301–302, 304–305, 309–10, 313, 319, 333, 346, 366; see also Economy
Circumstances, 32, 103, 138, 148, 156, 164, 219, 265, 332, 345
City, 48–50, 55, 111, 203, 218–19, 221, 227, 229, 231, 248, 250, 257, 270, 300, 306, 326, 348, 359; see also Polis
Civilization, 78, 116, 139, 173, 276, 310, 321, 324, 330, 336
Cixous, H., 328
Class, 14, 19, 119, 170, 197, 202,

214, 232, 259, 267, 297, 330, 335, 350, 355
Classification, 129, 131–32, 135, 226, 234, 364
Coercion, 15–17, 78, 162–63, 168, 170–72, 235, 292, 299; *see also* Oppression, Violence
Cogito, 111, 124, 143–44, 339; *see also* Descartes
Cognition, 265–66, 360–61; *see also* Knowledge, Science
Coins, 95, 98–99, 333; *see also* Currency
Coleridge, S., 342
Collective, 70–71, 84–86, 88, 208, 254–57, 259, 304
Colonial, 14, 31, 44, 79, 260, 267, 325
Colossal, 129, 151–52, 299, 303
Commandments, 11, 16, 165, 187
Commands, 15–16, 30–31, 63–64, 321
Commitment, 98–99, 258, 260–61, 307, 319, 333, 361
Commodities, 73, 94, 103; *see also* Measure
Commonwealth, 29–31, 156
Community, 6–8, 33, 39, 51, 69–70, 84–86, 114–15, 118, 164, 218, 260, 297–99, 308, 310, 312, 318, 353, 359
Compassion, 53, 288–89; *see also* Charity
Compensation, 4, 42–45, 48, 51–54, 101, 117, 144, 203, 323, 329; *see also* Restitution
Competence, 127, 244, 260, 333; see also *Technē*
Conatus, 91, 327; *see also* Spinoza
Conscience, 98, 266, 336
Consciousness, 9, 76, 269, 310, 367
Consensus, 161, 198, 254, 312
Consequences, 52, 211, 258, 260, 263, 266, 294, 354

Contingency, 18–20, 39, 59–60, 62, 91, 112, 133–35, 137–38, 273, 289, 329, 362
Continuum, 85–86, 88, 331, 337
Contrast, 20, 62, 76, 135, 220, 239–40, 244, 254, 330
Control, 33, 138, 140, 160, 169–71, 208, 221, 226, 259, 272–73, 293, 301, 355; *see also* Domination, Power
Corporeality, 250; *see also* Materiality, Matter
Correspondence, 71, 106, 202, 350, 354
Covenant, 17, 23, 25–27, 39; *see also* Debt, Justice
Creativity, 87–88, 273, 364; *see also* Whitehead
Creator, 66, 97, 220, 349; *see also* God
Crime, 96, 107, 121, 148, 152–57, 170, 290–92, 333, 343, 347, 367
Criminal, 114, 154, 156, 186, 197, 343, 366
Criteria, 110, 113, 168–73, 255, 273
Critique, 16, 19, 43–44, 46–47, 54, 58, 70, 77, 80–81, 108, 124, 136, 140, 154, 172, 188–89, 200, 209, 216, 220, 224, 266, 268, 270, 275, 307, 309, 321–25, 329, 338, 345, 350, 363, 365
Culture, 3, 14, 45–47, 78, 80–81, 185, 201, 204, 208–10, 260, 269, 299, 302, 324, 347, 349–50, 356, 365, 367
Currency, 94, 96–98, 220
Custom, 2, 64, 145, 166, 217, 325

Damiens, 96
Danger, 13, 18–22, 60, 75, 78–81, 122, 142, 159, 163–65, 172, 185, 191, 198, 230, 249, 252, 255–57, 259–61, 264, 271–74, 276, 279–80, 283–85, 288, 297, 299–305, 307, 314, 361; *see also* Risk

Death, 16, 18, 21–22, 32, 35, 47–48,
  50–51, 102, 122, 132, 137, 139,
  145–47, 152–54, 159, 164, 169,
  171, 186, 191, 201, 209, 211,
  218, 221–22, 225, 235, 238, 240,
  247, 250, 252, 257–58, 260, 262,
  281–82, 284, 292–94, 303,
  305–306, 309–10, 334, 342–43,
  353, 359
Debt, 1, 3–4, 6, 12, 69, 78, 100, 122,
  157, 173, 185–86, 198, 271,
  286–87, 296, 301, 303, 309, 312,
  317; see also Justice, Restitution
Deception, 62, 141–43, 145, 214,
  229, 249, 300, 340
Decision, 70, 74, 98, 187–88, 259,
  275, 293, 345, 348–49, 365–66
Deconstruction, 175–84, 290, 299,
  309, 323
Deferral, 11, 46, 155, 173, 175, 189,
  292, 307
Deleuze, G., 44, 350
Delphi, 222, 227–28, 256
Democracy, 18, 50, 74, 198, 201,
  293, 307, 366
Demon, 128, 141, 143–44, 149–50,
  153, 156, 271, 299
Demonstration, 128, 149–50, 153,
  156, 214, 262, 293, 327, 351,
  258, 360
Departing, 43, 195
Derrida, J., 16, 41, 44, 90, 129,
  140–43, 145, 149–52, 172–82,
  184–89, 194, 196–98, 202–205,
  230, 245–46, 263, 290, 292, 309,
  315–18, 321–23, 330, 332,
  338–50, 353, 357–59, 361–62,
  366, 368
Descartes, R., 31, 42, 139–41, 143–44,
  146, 216, 269, 339–40, 352
Desire, 5, 10, 18–20, 23–26, 28, 31,
  35, 48–50, 53, 55, 63, 65–66, 72,
  77, 91–92, 96, 98, 100–102, 120,
  132, 146–47, 152, 163, 213–14,
  218–19, 221, 223–36, 238–39,
  243, 246–54, 256, 265, 270–71,
  285–86, 290–93, 296, 300–304,
  311, 313–14, 317, 322, 327, 329,
  333
Despair, 118, 165, 309
Destiny, 3–4, 41–42, 76, 138,
  154–55, 194, 196, 198, 206–208,
  210–11, 277–80, 293, 296, 300,
  316, 328, 368
Destruction, 31–33, 38–39, 73, 137,
  170, 181, 191, 260, 272, 280,
  282, 294, 305, 308, 336, 352
Determinateness, 61, 74, 85, 88, 91,
  112, 143, 170, 273, 331, 362
Dewey, J., 78–81, 196, 198, 272–74,
  330, 362
Dialectic, 60, 89, 210, 233
Dialogue, 28, 53–54, 166, 216,
  218–19, 221, 226–27, 229–31,
  233–38, 240, 244, 249–50, 353,
  356
Differences, 7–9, 19–20, 32, 35, 51,
  57, 62, 65, 59, 71, 95–100,
  109–10, 112–13, 128, 136, 138,
  150, 155, 162, 177, 181, 188,
  197, 205–206, 227, 238, 241–43,
  245–46, 251–52, 262, 269, 271,
  286, 290, 295, 297, 304–305,
  310, 318, 324, 328, 333–34,
  337–38, 346–47, 350, 357, 363
Différance, 140, 175
Différend, 9–10, 90, 109–15,
  120–25, 127–28, 286, 311, 318,
  335
Dikē, 1–2, 11, 24, 27, 240, 316,
  321–22, 356, 368
Dionysus, 36, 48–49, 81, 89, 117,
  192, 194, 198–200, 236, 262,
  269, 298, 301–302, 304
Diotima, 219–20, 225, 250
Dire, 170, 335; see also Levinas
Discipline, 56, 107, 118, 132, 135,
  265, 333–34, 343, 362

Discourse, 9, 53–54, 60, 66, 89, 92, 102, 123, 128, 140, 160–61, 163, 173, 177, 194–95, 201–203, 219–21, 223–24, 226–28, 231, 236–37, 240, 244–45, 247, 254, 263, 286, 288, 326–27, 332, 334–35, 341, 357–58, 361; *see also* Language

Disorder, 2, 18, 20, 69, 88–89, 137, 141–42, 144–45, 223, 276–77, 296, 340

Dispersion, 16, 21, 24, 45, 74, 131, 202, 207, 217, 240, 257, 271–72, 317, 330, 334

Dissemination, 259, 341, 353; *see also* Derrida

Dit, 335, 344; *see also* Levinas

Divine, 22, 37–38, 48, 63, 91, 152, 164–65, 171, 173–75, 177–78, 187, 195, 224–26, 228–35, 238–41, 243, 246, 249, 296, 298–300, 308, 332, 344–45; *see also* God

Divinity, 152, 198, 200, 219, 222, 229, 232, 235, 238; *see also* God

Domination, 8, 40–41, 80, 89, 108–109, 115, 209–10, 271, 279, 289–92, 297, 302–303, 310–11, 314, 337

Dostoevsky, F., 107–108, 117, 335–36

Doubt, 15, 33, 37, 42, 62, 101, 111, 141, 163, 169, 171–72, 176, 183, 221–22, 228–29, 259, 340, 359

Droit, 8, 69, 152, 175, 179–81, 187–88, 299, 322, 346–48; *see also* Loi

Duty, 25, 68, 70, 73, 259, 276, 325, 348; *see also* Law, Obligation, Responsibility

Dworkin, R., 15–16, 31, 321, 365–66

Earth, 33–34, 44, 75, 117, 133–34, 185, 225, 235–37, 278, 283–84, 295, 329, 349–51, 356

Economy, 71, 85, 92–98, 100–103, 107, 110–13, 115, 118–19, 124, 130–32, 136, 139, 141, 143–44, 156–57, 175, 178, 180, 182, 186, 194–95, 197, 201–202, 223, 231, 250–52, 256–57, 260–62, 268, 271–73, 277, 279, 282, 286–87, 291–92, 294, 298, 301–13, 332–33, 337, 341; *see also* Calculation, Measure

Ecstasy, 224, 229, 248–50, 357

Effectiveness, 60, 109, 258, 268

Effects, 92, 107, 118, 217, 266, 289, 343

Efficacy, 19, 47, 109, 119, 132, 160, 255, 276, 329–30

Egypt, 41, 44, 198, 237, 245–46, 324, 356

Ekstasis, 277, 279

Emancipation, 4, 45–47, 78, 89, 124; *see also* Freedom

Embodiment, 76, 120, 134, 234, 250, 253, 303; *see also* Bodies, Materiality

Emergence, 34, 39, 41, 106, 123, 141, 207, 211, 337

Emerson, R., 323

Empirical, 19–20, 22, 62, 141, 216, 329, 341

Empiricism, 93, 145, 217

Enchantment, 47, 236, 238, 253, 271–72; *see also* Magic, Witchcraft

Endlessness, 1, 5–6, 9, 11–12, 18, 28, 36, 42, 45, 48, 65, 71–72, 94, 96, 99–100, 103, 109–10, 114, 116–19, 130–31, 144, 153, 155, 175, 178, 181–83, 186, 206, 252, 286–87, 292, 301, 306–14, 330–31, 334, 357

Ends, 19, 27, 71, 107, 164, 172, 191, 236, 282, 286

Engels, F., 267

English, 2, 69, 176–78, 184, 196, 198, 205–208, 229, 295, 315, 322, 324, 329, 331, 352, 368

Enlightenment, 19, 43–44, 69, 114, 140, 198, 216, 263–64, 308, 366
Environment, 260, 293–94, 330
Epic, 132–33, 324
Epistemic, 21–22, 50, 71, 80, 83, 92, 138, 166, 216–18, 225, 254, 264, 285, 361; *see also* Knowledge, Science
Epistemology, 218, 265–66, 361; *see also* Knowledge, Science
Epistēmē, 50, 55–57, 213–14, 222, 232, 238, 242–43, 351, 359
Epoch, 87, 210, 269, 275, 277, 331, 363
Equality, 10, 18–26, 32–33, 35, 58–59, 62, 123, 297
Er, 178, 238
Ereignis, 127, 206–208, 210
Ergon, 12, 56, 61, 297, 354
Ergonality, 9, 12, 296, 302, 304, 313, 317, 322, 367
Erinyes, 28, 38–39, 96, 111, 114, 156–57, 178, 284, 299, 302–303, 305–306, 308–309, 313
Erotic, 223, 227, 231, 234–36, 244, 246, 248–51, 256–57, 267, 278
Eros, 77, 146, 218–19, 221, 224–25, 232, 235–44, 246–47, 250, 252, 254, 256, 258, 267, 271–72, 276, 279, 285, 290–91, 299, 303–304, 308, 362
Errancy, 3–4, 42
Error, 3, 9, 25, 214, 336
Essence, 3, 11, 21, 36, 41–42, 54–55, 58, 77, 83, 91, 150–51, 167, 173, 175, 210–11, 262, 274, 278–79, 295, 316, 320, 326–28, 330–31, 363, 368
Eternal, 38, 55–56, 87, 117, 192–93
Ethics, 2, 7, 50, 55–58, 74–75, 91, 140–41, 167, 186, 214–15, 224, 255, 266–67, 275, 282, 289, 295–96, 303–304, 312, 316, 320, 326–31, 351–52, 363, 365, 368

Ethnic, 297, 366–67
Eumenides, 147, 299, 303, 322; *see also* Erinyes, Furies
Euripides, 148, 242–43, 342–43
European, 2, 42, 44, 47, 152, 184, 201, 281, 306, 350, 364
Eurynome, 223, 253, 353; *see also* Orithyia
Euthyphro, 160, 164–66, 216, 245, 332
Event, 40, 127, 129, 138, 143, 156, 206–207, 210–11, 214, 267, 274, 305, 308–10, 319, 330, 335, 363
Evidence, 42, 63, 121, 128, 150, 156, 170, 218, 268–69, 275, 345, 354
Evil, 6, 19, 23, 29, 53, 86–88, 100–101, 115, 117, 139, 166, 229, 235, 274–76, 282–83, 322, 327, 336, 340
Evolution, 131–32, 134–37, 345
Exaltation, 39, 108, 114, 117, 236
Excess, 18, 23–24, 33, 42, 44, 46, 48–50, 52, 54–55, 58–59, 61, 63, 65–66, 69, 71–73, 83, 93, 96–97, 101–102, 112, 116, 123, 135–36, 145–47, 149, 151–52, 155, 180–81, 179–81, 187–88, 213, 216–17, 221, 232, 234–36, 251, 253, 258, 263, 267, 269–70, 276, 289, 291–92, 298, 301, 303–304, 308–309, 312, 314, 323, 329, 332, 347, 366
Exchange, 70–71, 94–98, 100–103, 107, 111, 202, 233, 246, 260, 297, 304, 322, 333
Exclusion, 46, 57, 86, 88, 98, 115, 132, 156, 180, 203, 206, 207, 275, 279, 323, 335, 357
Existence, 9, 43, 45, 74, 78, 84, 87, 91, 99, 114, 127, 144, 168–70, 172, 182, 208–209, 214, 274–75, 277, 290, 323, 329, 333, 362; *see also* Being

Index

Exodus, 200, 321
Experience, 14, 21, 51, 58, 70–71, 79–81, 93, 105–106, 129, 140–42, 144–46, 166–67, 188, 217–18, 234–35, 243, 258, 267, 270, 274–75, 313, 330, 340–41, 348, 362
Experimentation, 95–96, 266, 347, 384
Expert, 254, 262, 265, 268, 285
Expression, 8, 18, 43, 59, 62, 137, 155, 197, 216, 275, 307, 329, 367
Extension, 80, 83–88, 133, 258, 299, 331

Face, 7, 11, 17, 26, 63, 102, 142, 155, 172, 177, 182–83, 197, 199, 237, 263, 311, 318, 320, 340, 355
Facts, 48, 56, 86, 128, 139–41, 167, 263–64, 352
Failure, 61, 99, 101, 164, 276
Faith, 144, 277, 348, 350
Fate, 38, 63, 93, 128, 310–11
Father, 1, 164, 166, 282, 321, 332–33, 342, 357, 361
Fear, 16–18, 20–24, 27, 59, 64, 159, 162–64, 166, 171–72, 192, 199, 236, 260–61, 263–64, 305, 346, 348, 359, 362, 367
Female, 44–46, 62, 136, 267, 283, 288, 306, 325, 328, 339, 355; *see also* Gender, Woman
Feminism, 1, 266–69, 319, 361, 365
Fiction, 26, 29–30, 58, 145, 340–41
Finite, 35, 80, 91, 105, 128, 149, 151, 182, 189, 205, 235, 322, 329–30, 346; *see also* Limit
Fish, S., 171–74, 184, 345–46
Flesh, 142, 148, 191, 340; *see also* Bodies, Embodiment, Materiality
Force, 2, 7, 10, 16–17, 33, 50, 56, 58, 63, 68, 73, 76, 79, 81, 83–84, 96, 103, 108–109, 116, 121–22, 128, 143, 153, 155–57, 159–76, 178, 181, 186, 201, 207, 215, 217–18, 226–27
Forgetting, 2, 9, 32, 41, 111, 118, 124, 128, 131, 178, 191, 195, 198, 205, 233, 238, 243, 263–64, 281, 284, 294–95, 305–306, 316, 328, 368
Forgotten, 2, 5, 11–12, 41, 109, 111, 122, 124, 128, 155–56, 196, 206, 220, 227, 244, 264–65, 286, 316, 328, 334, 368
Fortune, 56, 61
Foucault, M., 10, 17, 29, 35–36, 41, 44, 89, 92–97, 99–103, 105–107, 109, 113, 118–20, 129–31, 135–36, 140–41, 143–44, 149, 173, 177, 196, 198, 201–202, 209, 225, 262–63, 265–66, 269, 287, 289, 315, 318–19, 321–22, 327, 332–37, 339, 343, 346, 349–50, 360–61, 368
Foundation, 14, 16, 32, 69, 71, 78, 80, 106, 166–69, 172, 174, 176, 178–81, 183, 195–96, 216, 272, 299, 321, 326, 345, 347
Frame, 42, 206, 208, 219–20, 233–34, 266, 344, 355
Freedom, 10–11, 22–23, 32, 34, 50, 71–73, 75–77, 88, 102, 112–13, 124, 135, 155, 167, 202, 255–56, 267, 299, 307, 311, 316, 329–30, 335, 365–67; *see also* Autonomy
French, 69, 128, 149–50, 176–78, 184, 196–98, 205–207, 254, 263–64, 297, 315–16, 319, 347, 368
Frenzy, 49, 147–48, 224, 305
Freud, S., 116–17, 136, 308, 310, 333, 336, 339
Friend, 148, 189, 218, 222, 227–28, 231
Frost, R., 138–39

Fuller, S., 224, 265, 361
Furies, 38–39, 111, 147, 305–306, 308, 310, 366; *see also* Erinyes, Eumenides
Future, 78–79, 85–86, 112, 116, 120, 155, 208, 216, 236, 276, 282, 284, 292–94, 301, 323, 325, 358, 362–63; *see also* Temporality, Time

Gadamer, H–G., 177–78, 261–64, 345–46, 360
Geist, 106, 185, 278–79, 315, 318, 323, 368
Gender, 19, 65, 170, 267–69, 288, 290, 292, 297, 307, 328, 334, 349, 355–56; *see also* Sex, Sexuality
Genealogy, 262, 334–35, 360
Generality, 29, 87–88, 143, 169–71, 275, 306, 331, 346–47
Generation, 29, 102, 200, 276, 351
Genesis, 270
Genres, 110, 122–23, 156, 286, 335
Geophilosophy, 198, 206–207, 263
German, 2–3, 41, 69, 106, 121, 150, 152, 177, 184–85, 191–94, 196–99, 205–207, 263–64, 293, 295, 297, 303, 307, 315–16, 323, 350, 367–68
Geschick, 3, 42, 196, 206–207, 209–11, 277–79, 363; *see also* Destiny
Geschlecht, 77, 133, 150, 152, 185, 263, 293–94, 297, 299, 303–305, 307, 311, 323, 330, 342, 363; *see also* Gender
Gestell, 206–208, 210, 277–78, 280
Ghost, 5, 148, 187, 317, 348
Gift, 77, 131, 146, 148, 150, 152, 186, 210, 229, 231–32, 263, 295, 299, 304, 307, 343
God, 1, 11, 24, 31, 39–40, 48, 64–67, 69, 84, 86–89, 91, 93, 117–18, 131, 142, 144, 146, 148, 152, 156, 165–66, 174, 182, 187–88, 191–200, 204–205, 211, 215, 223–25, 228–29, 232–33, 236–39, 241, 245, 250, 261, 269–75, 279, 281, 287, 296–99, 308, 320–21, 333, 342, 348, 355
Goddess, 40, 56, 223, 237, 241, 261, 324
Good, 47, 62–63, 67, 134, 147–48, 153–57, 165, 189, 224, 230, 240–41, 248–49, 251–52, 265, 271, 275, 279, 288, 295, 300–301, 312, 314, 342–43, 368
Goods, 29, 34, 97, 100–102, 224, 367
Gould, S., 131–35, 137–38, 338–39
Governance, 29, 32, 50, 63, 74, 139, 144, 201, 217, 287, 341
Government, 21, 32, 50, 121, 163, 201–202, 205, 322, 366
Greatness, 19–22, 24, 32, 41, 43, 56, 60–63, 66–67, 71, 77, 85, 88, 93, 96–97, 101, 119–20, 124, 129–30, 137, 140, 142, 147, 149, 151, 153–54, 156, 160, 163–66, 171, 181–82, 185, 189, 192, 201–202, 206, 211, 215, 229, 232, 246, 238, 241, 245, 255, 257, 261, 284, 294–95, 303, 310, 320, 326, 337, 345, 354, 367
Greeks, 1–3, 31, 41–44, 46, 56, 58, 105–106, 119, 147, 152–56, 160, 165, 173, 185–86, 194, 196–98, 205, 213, 223, 229, 253, 255, 283–84, 294–95, 304–306, 310, 315–16, 322, 324–25, 341–44, 348, 353, 356, 368
Ground, 15, 19, 26, 28, 55, 66, 70–72, 77, 80–81, 87, 91, 96, 99, 105–106, 132, 136, 165, 167, 179, 187, 231, 257, 271, 274, 277, 320, 345, 347, 352, 362–63
Guardieri, R., 209–10
Guilt, 2, 10, 38, 96, 111, 116–17,

128, 153–55, 164, 173, 237, 296, 308–11, 332, 336
Gulliver's Travels, 97
Gunman, 161–62, 168, 170–73, 283

Habermas, J., 176–78, 345
Habitats, 199, 293
Habits, 79, 169, 217, 362
Hand, 22, 56, 76–77, 97, 100–101, 150, 164, 166, 169, 193–95, 203, 217, 231, 236, 243, 252, 263, 278, 283, 299, 323, 326, 330, 333, 337, 340–41, 357–58; *see also* Bodies, *Geschlecht*, Gift
Happiness, 5, 7, 49, 67, 70–71, 108, 162, 295, 310–12, 343, 356
Harmony, 67, 86, 117, 188, 242–43, 313, 317, 349
Hart, H., 161–62, 164, 168–72, 344–46
Hartshorne, C., 332
Healing, 45, 124, 206–207, 210, 280, 310
Health, 32, 48, 156, 215, 243, 322, 329, 352
Heaven, 164, 225, 229, 232, 235–37, 252, 270, 288
Hebrew, 41, 173, 287
Hecuba, 12, 147–49, 152–54, 199, 342–43
Hegel, G., 8, 42, 69, 71, 74–78, 110, 112–13, 117, 124, 183, 185, 193, 196, 198, 204–205, 253–54, 277, 310, 318, 329–30, 332, 335, 341, 350, 358, 367–68
Hegemony, 43, 46–47, 115, 268
Heidegger, M., 2–4, 41–43, 77, 90, 105–106, 117, 124, 140, 149, 176–77, 181, 185, 192–95, 197–99, 201–203, 205–209, 263, 277–79, 315–16, 320, 322–23, 330, 332, 342, 350, 360, 363–64, 368
Heraclitus, 24, 27, 39–41, 197, 219, 315, 321–22, 356, 368

Heresy, 42–43, 298, 324, 328–29, 354, 366
Hermeneutics, 89, 209, 262–63, 346, 360
Hermes, 40, 245, 324
Heterogeneity, 7–8, 46, 86–87, 89, 92, 100, 110, 112–13, 123–24, 131, 170, 185, 211, 256, 268, 275, 286–87, 299, 302, 304, 307, 332, 335, 348, 362
Heterosexuality, 236, 290
Hierarchy, 19, 91, 214, 266, 270, 332, 338–39, 360
Highest, 3, 15, 41, 63, 87, 106, 146, 152, 155, 185, 193–94, 196, 198, 200, 205, 236–37, 261, 283, 298, 316, 347, 352, 368
History, 3–5, 8–10, 15–16, 20, 23, 27, 31–34, 36, 41–42, 48, 53, 58–59, 64–66, 71, 77–78, 82, 90, 99, 108, 110–11, 114, 116, 121–22, 129, 132–35, 137–38, 140, 143, 149, 156–57, 166, 172, 175, 179, 185, 187, 189, 193, 201, 205–206, 208–11, 218, 220, 246, 249, 252, 255, 258, 262, 269, 272, 277, 281, 284, 296, 302, 308–309, 313–14, 319, 323, 325, 334–35, 337–39, 346, 351, 358, 363, 366
Hitler, 3, 41, 193, 297, 323, 367; *see also* Germany, National Socialism
Hobbes, T., 12, 17–36, 55, 59–60, 66, 68–69, 74–75, 77–78, 99, 106, 123, 145, 195, 261, 303, 321, 329
Holocaust, 193, 198, 297, 306, 310
Holy, 146, 164–66, 332
Homogeneity, 45, 123–24, 185, 304, 315, 368
Hope, 1–2, 14, 17–19, 23–24, 30, 36–38, 41, 43, 46, 61, 79, 82, 97–98, 108–109, 118, 150, 155, 173, 175, 178, 201, 205–207,

Hope *(continued)*
  250, 268–69, 272, 278–79, 284, 286–90, 292–95, 310–11, 318, 346, 353, 365
Honor, 128–29, 194, 198, 220, 238, 248, 343
Human, 6, 10–11, 14, 17–29, 32–37, 40, 44, 47–48, 51–52, 56–58, 61–62, 64, 66, 71, 73, 75, 77–78, 80–81, 89, 96, 100, 107–108, 113–21, 125, 133–34, 136, 139, 150–53, 156, 165, 168, 170–71, 173, 178, 185–86, 188, 193, 197, 199, 201, 205, 208–13, 216, 218–19, 225, 232–33, 240, 250, 254, 257, 260, 262–63, 265, 270–71, 276, 289, 293–95, 298, 305, 307–308, 311, 318–20, 324, 330–31, 341, 343–44, 346, 352, 354, 356, 362–63, 366
Humanism, 188, 209–10, 298
Hume, D., 141, 145, 167–68, 217–18, 254, 344, 352
Hypokeimenon, 106, 252
Hypomnēmasis, 233, 245–46, 252, 264

Ideals, 15, 49, 58, 61, 74, 107, 193–94, 259, 269, 333
Identity, 8–9, 16, 43, 95–100, 110, 112–13, 131, 162, 198–99, 206, 227–28, 282, 284, 309, 316–17, 350, 364, 368
Ideology, 9, 119, 132, 255, 263, 265, 307–308, 335
Idolatry, 103, 192–200, 202, 204–205, 207, 209, 211, 253, 285, 287, 299
Idols, 103, 157, 189, 191–97, 199–202, 204–205, 207–209, 211, 261, 349
Iliad, 201
Image, 2, 9, 42, 70, 135, 217–18, 234–36, 238–41, 247, 269, 339–40, 356, 359

Imaginary, 10, 167
Imagination, 72, 135, 137, 145, 205, 260, 285
Immeasurable, 7, 12, 19, 23, 27, 41, 93, 100, 198, 317, 330
Immemoriality, 1–2, 4–5, 11–12, 27, 31–32, 34, 43, 70, 88, 91–92, 96, 106, 111, 114–19, 128, 144, 154–55, 172–76, 178–83, 186–88, 195, 201, 241, 272, 276, 279, 282–84, 286, 290–91, 294–96, 301–302, 304–305, 309–13, 315, 318, 348, 367
Immortality, 64, 232–36, 240, 247, 250–51, 254–55, 354
Imperfection, 11, 143, 259, 265
Imperialism, 44, 325
Impossibility, 10, 53, 58, 70, 90, 98, 116–17, 122, 182–84, 187–88, 204, 214, 292, 313, 324
Improper, 16, 245, 321, 357
Inanimate, 232, 254, 355–56
Incalculable, 187, 189, 290, 366; *see also* Immeasurability
Indeterminateness, 54, 61, 72, 88, 97, 273, 329–31, 362
Individuality, 20, 25, 35, 50, 67–71, 74–76, 84–86, 91, 94–95, 101, 112, 124, 129, 138, 169, 170–74, 177, 183, 188, 205, 257, 270, 273–74, 293–94, 299, 304, 307, 313, 329–30, 348, 350, 357, 362
Inequality, 10, 20, 22, 24
Inescapability, 4, 8–10, 14, 20, 27–28, 30, 32, 34, 40, 51, 54, 60, 65, 69, 73, 77–77, 86–87, 89, 92, 103, 106, 108–13, 123, 147, 152, 157, 171, 178, 182, 186–87, 189, 252, 258, 264, 269, 271–72, 281, 286, 289, 291–95, 305, 310, 317
Inevitability, 37, 106, 133, 180, 208, 252, 265, 294
Inexhaustibility, 2, 9, 11–12, 46, 49, 54, 58–59, 61–63, 66–67, 69, 72,

85–86, 89, 91–92, 96, 100, 102–103, 121, 155, 157, 173–75, 181, 224–25, 227, 231, 247, 251–52, 258, 264–65, 269–70, 273–74, 284, 286, 288–89, 292, 296, 301–302, 304–305, 307–313, 317, 322, 330, 366
Inferiority, 13–14, 34, 59, 62, 66, 73, 99, 298, 358
Infinite, 9, 23, 33, 45–46, 48, 63, 78–79, 91, 117, 130, 149–51, 171, 182–83, 188, 204, 227, 247, 251, 330, 336
Ingredients, 139, 301, 317–18
Injustice, 1–12, 14–15, 17–18, 22, 24–25, 27–31, 33–45, 49, 51–52, 58–63, 65, 69–71, 73, 75–79, 81–82, 85–94, 96, 99–101, 103, 106–107, 109–31, 135, 137–40, 143–45, 147–50, 152–57, 161–64, 166, 170–84, 186–89, 191, 195, 201, 207, 221, 228–30, 240–41, 249–52, 255–56, 259, 263–69, 271–76, 279, 281–96, 300–15, 317–22, 324, 326–27, 330, 332, 334, 343, 347–48, 350, 363–64, 366–68
Innocence, 111, 121, 128, 139, 153, 160, 183, 272, 305, 307–308, 359
Inquiry, 93, 239, 263, 265, 269, 272–73, 316, 351–52, 361–62; *see also* Knowledge, Science
Insanity, 141, 305; *see also* Madness
Instrumentality, 17–19, 21–24, 27–29, 73, 96, 100, 107–109, 114, 116–18, 161, 166, 169, 176, 184, 186, 255, 269, 279, 285, 295, 297, 307–308, 310–311, 323, 337; *see also* Calculation, Economy, *Technē*
Insurrection, 4, 43–44, 106, 262–63, 265, 334
Interpretation, 133, 164, 171, 230–31, 239, 261, 324, 345–46

Intimacy, 99, 149, 218, 221, 223–24, 226–27, 229, 231, 236, 240, 248–51, 257, 266, 290–95, 300, 303–304, 338; *see also* Love, Private
Intuition, 56, 72, 129, 151, 214–15, 329, 365
Ion, 232, 238
Iphigenia, 152, 342–43
Ipseity, 316, 368
Irigaray, L., 136, 197–98, 203, 318, 328, 339
Irony, 42, 93, 194, 197, 271, 295, 355–56
Irrationality, 29, 87–88, 199, 240–41, 261, 266, 269, 274; *see also* Rationality
Isaiah, 365
Iterability, 181, 346

Jews, 2, 65, 152, 173, 185, 188, 197, 206, 263, 294, 297, 306, 316, 328, 360, 367–68
Job, 15
Jouissance, 2, 7, 115, 295, 304, 306, 336
Joy, 63, 115, 118, 145, 276, 310
Judgment, 9, 17, 33, 38–39, 50, 90, 110–11, 113, 120–24, 167, 170, 181, 184, 223, 247, 255, 260–61, 266, 273, 299, 317, 319, 321, 327, 335, 338, 344, 351, 359, 366
Justice, 1–2, 4–7, 10, 12, 15–16, 18–20, 23–28, 30–31, 33–34, 36–41, 43, 45–49, 51, 53–55, 57, 59–60, 63–65, 67, 69–70, 74, 77–78, 81, 88, 92, 96, 100, 109–11, 114–15, 117–18, 120, 122–23, 128, 144, 147, 150–51, 153–56, 159–60, 163–64, 167–68, 170–84, 187–89, 195, 201, 203, 205, 224, 229–30, 240–41, 248–49, 251–52, 255, 263, 269, 271–74, 276, 279, 281,

Justice *(continued)*
    283–84, 286–87, 289–95,
    299–315, 320–22, 326–27, 341,
    344, 346–47, 349, 362, 366–68
Justification, 15, 32, 73, 78, 110,
    114, 127, 155, 173–75, 177, 182

Kafka, F., 16, 28, 32, 69, 96, 111,
    116–17, 153, 321
Kant, I., 7–8, 35, 42, 67, 69, 71–74,
    110, 129, 151, 167, 182, 193, 196,
    198, 205, 269–70, 318, 329, 338
Kierkegaard, S., 42, 187, 189, 348
Killing, 19, 34, 49, 114, 116, 147,
    153, 155–56, 186, 199, 260,
    281–84, 296, 306, 342, 348, 364
Kind, 25, 76, 89, 100, 103, 122, 143,
    160, 162, 188, 192, 203, 208,
    221, 228, 236, 240, 243–44, 247,
    252, 257, 269, 271–72, 278–79,
    330, 335, 353, 365
Kindred, 139
Kinds, 16, 48, 71, 83, 96, 101, 119,
    131, 134, 168, 248, 330, 338,
    351, 357
King, 22, 50, 63, 139, 223, 245,
    283–84, 321, 364
Kinship, 129, 218, 283
Knowledge, 30, 40, 47, 55–56, 58,
    71–72, 80–81, 96, 98–100, 103,
    105–106, 129–30, 156–57,
    164–66, 168, 172, 213–16,
    218–23, 226–27, 230, 232, 240,
    242–43, 245, 247–52, 254,
    258–60, 262, 265, 268–69, 271,
    274, 285, 296, 298, 301–302,
    313, 318–19, 327, 329, 331–34,
    337–39, 349, 351–52, 357–61
Kristeva, J., 328, 335–36
Kuhn, T., 135, 339

Labor, 34–35, 135, 257, 265, 298,
    323, 325

Lack, 9, 20, 55, 58, 61, 64–65, 69,
    81, 90–91, 93, 98, 110, 113, 123,
    155, 172, 174, 176, 180–81,
    184–85, 224, 228, 238–41,
    250–53, 265–66, 270,
Lagado, 97–98
Language, 3–4, 6, 16, 47–48, 95, 97,
    100, 109, 115–16, 120, 128–29,
    134, 137–38, 148–50, 155, 160,
    163, 168, 173, 176–78, 180,
    182–88, 195–96, 198, 235,
    240–41, 254–55, 263, 270,
    272–73, 276, 278, 289, 297, 299,
    302, 304, 313, 315–16, 318, 320,
    332–33, 345, 347, 349, 366, 368
Law, 1–2, 4–6, 8, 10–21, 23–34,
    36–41, 43–74, 77–81, 85, 87–89,
    92–96, 99–101, 103, 106–11,
    113–25, 127–28, 131, 134, 137,
    139, 143–44, 147, 149, 151–52,
    154–57, 160–62, 165–89, 194,
    209, 213–14, 219, 225, 229, 248,
    250–54, 257–58, 263–64,
    266–67, 272, 275, 277, 281,
    284–86, 289–316, 319, 321–23,
    325–27, 329, 333–34, 337, 341,
    343–48, 353, 358, 361, 365–68
Legislation, 12, 48, 95, 167, 328–29
Legitimacy, 9, 13–14, 59, 69, 110,
    121, 162–65, 170–71, 179,
    247–48, 254–55, 263, 265–66,
    283, 346, 357
Legitimation, 68–69, 74, 76, 89, 110,
    113, 115–16, 162, 179, 254–55,
    298
Leibniz, G., 7, 66–67, 83–86, 318,
    328, 331
Leviathan, 27–28, 321; *see also*
    Hobbes
Levinas, E., 2–3, 7, 11–12, 100, 140,
    175, 180–81, 184, 188, 198,
    311–12, 316, 318–20, 327–28,
    334–35, 339, 342, 348, 368
Liberation, 10, 14, 50, 59, 78, 119,

135, 155, 273, 298–99, 306
Liberty, 17, 22–27, 32–33, 68–69, 254, 311, 329, 365; *see also* Freedom
Life, 6, 14, 16–18, 21, 23–25, 28–29, 32–35, 48–50, 60, 63, 74, 76–78, 80, 94, 101–102, 108, 114, 116, 120, 129, 131–37, 140–41, 143, 145, 154, 156, 165–66, 170, 182, 186, 198, 228, 232, 235–40, 242–43, 248, 250–52, 256, 268, 271, 276, 282, 285, 290, 292–94, 303, 310–11, 319, 323–26, 328–30, 335, 338–40, 343, 345, 356–57, 359
Limits, 1, 9, 12, 14, 18–25, 28, 33, 35, 37, 47, 50–51, 67, 72, 79–80, 83, 85, 87–88, 95–97, 101, 122, 128–29, 131, 136, 140, 149, 181–82, 186–87, 199–200, 204–205, 213, 217, 219, 234–35, 238–39, 260–61, 263, 265, 272, 274, 277, 292, 305, 312, 320, 329, 347, 366–67
Lingis, A., 316, 319–20, 368
Literature, 1, 78, 80, 128, 166, 193, 286
Locality, 9, 12, 81, 270, 272–74, 296, 302, 304, 309, 311, 313, 317, 322, 362, 366
Locke, J., 12, 29–36, 59, 66, 69, 72–73, 76, 144–48, 193, 216–18, 322, 341
Logic, 79, 134, 268–69, 272–73, 335, 339, 362
Logos, 1, 8, 40, 272, 297
Lorde, A., 9, 41
Loss, 87, 94, 100–102, 121–22, 128, 142, 144–45, 194, 202, 205, 223, 251, 258, 285, 293–94, 309–10, 332–33, 335, 341
Love, 37, 53, 100, 118, 146–47, 197, 218–21, 223–29, 231, 234–41, 245, 248–51, 256, 258, 265, 278, 290–92, 294–95, 300, 354

Lyotard, J-F., 2, 8, 89–90, 109–11, 113–15, 120–24, 127–28, 135, 156, 181, 185, 197, 206, 254–55, 263–64, 273, 286, 316, 318, 328, 331, 335, 337, 358, 360, 368
Lysias, 218–20, 222–24, 226, 237, 239, 243–44, 250, 265, 357–58

MacKinnon, C., 290, 292–93, 308, 365–66
Madness, 1, 17, 64, 88, 127, 129, 139–53, 156–57, 189, 223–24, 226, 229–41, 243–55, 257–58, 267, 272–73, 276–80, 285, 287, 295, 299–302, 304–305, 308–10, 321, 339–42, 349, 354
Magic, 24, 47, 222–26, 230–31, 233, 236, 238–42, 244, 249, 251–54, 257–58, 260, 262, 264–65, 267, 269–71, 273, 276–77, 279–80, 282, 285, 287–89, 292, 295, 300–302, 304–306, 308, 311, 353; *see also* Witchcraft
Magnitude, 84, 151, 338
Male, 103, 136, 152, 184, 204, 283, 288, 290–91, 303, 355; *see also* Gender
Mania, 77, 146, 148, 224–26, 234, 238, 241, 243–44, 247, 250, 254, 256, 276, 285, 354; *see also* Madness
Marx, K., 69, 307–308
Marxism, 119, 155, 259, 267, 308, 324, 365
Masks, 26, 69, 106, 110, 160, 198, 207, 262, 266, 268–70, 276, 278, 284–87, 289, 298, 301, 304, 324, 334, 363
Mastery, 8, 10, 34, 45–46, 57, 59, 68, 76, 185, 230, 239, 242, 249, 257–58, 262, 297, 300, 302, 313
Materiality, 66, 80, 84, 94, 96–97, 100, 142, 234, 270, 284, 286, 316, 368; *see also* Bodies, Matter

Maternity, 316, 368
Mathematics, 94, 98, 108, 151, 268, 340
Matter, 6, 8, 21–22, 38, 60, 65, 72, 83–84, 100–101, 113–14, 125, 141–42, 171, 191, 201, 203, 241–42, 245, 256, 317, 331, 333, 345, 358; *see also* Materiality
Meaning, 7, 23, 89, 95, 97, 144, 149, 160, 181, 200, 206, 209, 218, 234, 240, 255, 263, 270, 279, 296, 318, 320, 322, 328, 332, 341, 346, 360
Measure, 1, 4, 6–8, 10–12, 18–20, 22–29, 31–40, 42–43, 45–46, 51–54, 58–61, 63–64, 66–67, 70–76, 81–89, 92–96, 98, 100, 102–103, 106–107, 109–11, 113–17, 120, 122–24, 127–28, 131, 150–56, 173–75, 177–78, 181–82, 186, 188, 203, 222–25, 230, 232, 234, 238–39, 241, 245, 249, 260, 267, 290–91, 294–97, 300, 302, 308–11, 313, 322, 326, 329, 340, 350, 355–56, 362; *see also* Calculation, Economy, *Technē*
Medicine, 215, 222–23, 231, 242–44, 259, 262, 296, 359
Memory, 1–2, 11, 31, 117, 119, 129, 137, 145, 148, 157, 175, 178, 185–88, 195, 197, 208, 218, 220, 226, 229–30, 232–34, 245, 247–52, 263, 286–88, 296, 299–302, 309, 313–14, 318, 336, 357
Menace, 15, 223, 230, 236, 242, 249, 251, 254, 256–57, 265, 279, 283, 297, 300–301, 361; *see also* Danger
Mende, 293, 364
Meno, 47, 50, 56, 164–65, 216, 228–29, 233, 239, 242, 357
Messiah, 209, 211, 300, 351
Metaphysics, 5, 55–56, 63, 66–67, 82–83, 85, 194, 196, 210, 213, 215–16, 225, 264, 318, 324, 328–29, 339, 352, 354, 362–63
Mill, J. S., 67, 69, 71, 322, 329, 331, 333, 352
Mimēsis, 90, 116, 220, 226, 301–302, 305
Mind, 14, 19, 21, 56, 63, 75–77, 83–84, 111, 131, 133, 149, 169, 173, 175–76, 205, 207, 214, 216–17, 220, 228, 239, 254, 264, 277, 318, 321, 324–25, 329, 336, 352, 356
Minos, 51, 326
Modernity, 8, 31, 42, 89, 95, 101, 105, 131, 171, 195–96, 200, 204–206, 208–209, 216, 218, 225, 253–54, 257, 259–60, 262, 272, 276–79, 298, 307, 321–22, 329–32, 336, 338–39, 347, 349, 357, 362–64
Monadology, 84–86, 331; *see also* Leibniz
Monstration, 128, 149–50, 153, 342
Monstre, 129, 149
Monstrosity, 80, 103, 108, 120, 125, 127–57, 171, 173, 177–78, 181–83, 186, 189, 194, 196–200, 207, 210, 235, 253, 275–77, 285–89, 290, 293, 295, 297, 299, 302–306, 312–14, 334, 337, 341–43, 361–64
Montaigne, M., 165–69, 176, 344
Montesquieu, B., 66, 328
Morality, 65, 167–69, 200, 259, 266, 338
Mother, 116, 148, 155, 170, 199, 281–82, 310, 312, 324, 342–43, 357
Motion, 83–84, 213, 331, 354
Mourning, 11, 18, 39, 48, 69, 79, 122, 145, 148, 211, 213, 284, 296–97, 300, 331, 354
Musa Wo, 281–82, 284–85, 293, 299,

303–305, 308–309, 313–14, 364, 366
Muses, 146, 157, 205, 227–28, 232, 238–39, 244, 293, 299, 305, 308, 354
Music, 22, 227, 238–39, 242–43, 286, 298, 301, 305, 328, 340
Mystical, 16, 103, 166, 168, 172, 174, 176, 178–79, 181, 183, 299, 321, 345
Mythic, 10, 18, 37, 154, 173–75, 177–78, 187, 299, 305, 345
Mythology, 1, 59, 154, 222, 255

Name, 4, 28, 39, 41, 46, 49, 56, 61, 65, 74, 78, 90, 109–11, 113, 116, 128–29, 145–46, 148, 150, 165, 171–72, 174–75, 195–96, 199, 202, 204, 215, 224, 236, 253, 255, 269, 271, 281, 294, 308–309, 321, 328, 332, 341, 350, 354, 358, 360
Nancy, J–L., 218, 318, 353, 364
Narrative, 15, 17, 30, 81, 89, 96, 105–106, 114, 116, 120, 132–36, 138, 143, 155, 183, 194–95, 226, 228, 230, 235, 249, 255, 289, 300, 305, 343, 367
National Socialism, 197–98, 259, 323, 367
Natural, 20, 23–25, 27–29, 31, 34, 36, 55, 57–59, 61, 63, 66, 71, 75, 80, 87, 89, 95, 100–101, 108, 120, 133, 136–37, 139, 142, 155, 167–68, 172, 183–84, 186, 213, 240, 258, 273, 276, 297, 311, 340, 343, 361, 363
Nature, 4, 6–9, 12, 15, 17–19, 22–33, 35–37, 39, 42, 51–53, 55–68, 72, 74–77, 84, 86–92, 98, 101–103, 106, 108, 110–13, 115, 119, 122, 125, 131, 134, 136–37, 139, 144–45, 151, 163, 167, 171–75, 186, 208, 213–16, 218, 221–22, 225, 227, 229–31, 233, 237, 239, 243–44, 248–49, 251, 254, 266–67, 272, 274, 276–77, 279, 297–98, 300–305, 311–14, 316–17, 319–20, 322, 330, 334–35, 337–38, 344, 349, 355–56, 358, 362–63, 367
Necessity, 18, 37, 55–57, 61, 66, 74–75, 91, 111–13, 120, 124–25, 133–34, 137–39, 176, 178, 182–83, 188, 207, 210–11, 213–15, 217, 274, 276, 289, 298, 303, 305, 311–12, 321, 335, 346, 351
Need, 24, 35, 68, 101, 155, 161, 231, 247, 256, 267, 271, 276
Nietzsche, F., 8–9, 15, 17, 38, 41–43, 47, 87, 89, 92, 109, 116–17, 124, 160, 164, 191–201, 205–209, 220, 262, 281, 305, 335, 341, 349–50
Nihilism, 117, 135, 193, 209, 294, 336
Nomos, 1, 8, 51, 288, 343, 364–65
Non–Western, 19, 41–47, 119, 133, 206, 268, 291, 295–97, 324
Normality, 13–15, 18–20, 35, 108, 115, 132, 150, 265, 270, 297, 341
Normativity, 14–15, 297
Norms, 15, 20, 34, 38, 40, 51–52, 81, 116, 187, 287–88, 321
Number, 52, 56, 99, 101, 130, 138, 215, 330, 333, 352, 354, 357
Nussbaum, M., 186, 342–43, 347

Obedience, 15–16, 30, 39, 49, 56, 63–64, 66, 69, 73, 169, 187, 215–16, 261, 276, 330
Objectivity, 99, 143, 257, 265–67, 272
Obligation, 12, 21, 71–72, 98, 168–69, 176–78, 180, 183, 252, 257, 286, 298, 319, 332, 348, 366

Oblivion, 12, 32, 40–43, 106, 118, 121–22, 141, 192, 248, 278, 296, 301, 303, 308, 320; *see also* Forgotten
Odysseus, 132, 147–48, 241
Oedipus, 156
Old, 1, 4–6, 8, 10–14, 18, 23, 25, 27–29, 33–37, 40, 46, 52–54, 58, 64–65, 71, 75, 77–78, 81, 85–93, 95, 97, 100–101, 103, 107, 109–10, 115, 118, 120, 124, 127, 130–31, 140, 144, 146, 155, 157, 192–93, 104–105, 211, 219–20, 231–32, 283, 287–88, 291, 296, 308–309, 311–12, 326, 332, 363; *see also* Age, Time
Oppression, 8, 20, 22, 58, 60–61, 78–81, 114, 119, 121, 155–56, 171, 173, 181, 188–89, 208–209, 252, 258, 260, 262, 265–67, 272–74, 289, 292, 297, 306–307, 310, 366
Order, 2–4, 18–20, 27, 29, 32, 34, 36, 42, 56, 63, 67, 69, 78–79, 85, 87–89, 91–92, 94–97, 99, 102, 105–106, 123, 136–38, 141, 143–45, 149, 151, 154, 159, 173–74, 185, 194, 205, 215, 223, 228–29, 239, 248, 251, 258, 274, 277, 281, 290, 296, 320, 322, 333–34, 337, 339–40, 348, 360, 362
Orders, 16, 67, 91, 122, 162, 215
Ordinance of time, 1, 27–28, 37–38, 40, 54, 60, 65, 69, 91, 96, 114, 315, 344, 368; *see also* Anaximander, Injustice
Oresteia, 28, 74
Origin, 1, 31, 43, 63, 73, 75, 81, 102, 105, 133, 173, 179–80, 187, 197, 202, 277, 318, 325, 328, 332, 334, 347
Orithyia, 221–23, 245, 256, 267, 272, 290, 293, 295, 302, 305–306, 353

Other, 3–4, 6–8, 10–12, 14, 17–19, 22, 24, 27, 30, 40–45, 47, 52, 54, 58, 63, 65, 67–68, 70–71, 73, 76–77, 79, 86, 91–93, 96, 100–102, 106–107, 112, 116, 118, 121, 130, 141–43, 145, 147, 149, 156, 161, 165, 173, 178, 184–86, 188, 193, 196, 198–200, 213, 219–20, 224, 227, 231, 233, 235, 255, 261, 263, 267–68, 273–74, 281, 284–85, 287, 294, 303, 306, 310, 312, 316, 319–20, 325–26, 335–37, 363–65, 368
Overcoming, 29, 42, 51, 54, 63, 66, 77, 116–17, 119, 125, 145, 174, 191, 196, 206–207, 233, 238, 246, 277, 312, 316, 356

Pagan, 255, 273
Paideia, 240, 248
Pain, 2, 16, 22, 70, 81, 109, 115, 137, 171, 181, 186, 199, 273, 286, 295, 303, 306, 333–34; *see also* Suffering
Parents, 47, 57, 59, 62, 116, 165, 199, 236, 247, 307
Parmenides, 5, 40, 52–54, 197, 317, 323, 326–27
Pascal, B., 166–68, 176, 344
Passion, 221, 223–24, 226, 234, 236, 238, 243, 248, 250, 367
Payment, 4–6, 12, 41, 48, 52, 54, 65, 69, 100, 114, 117, 123, 131, 137, 154, 173, 178, 183, 185–87, 203, 209, 290, 310–11, 323, 350; *see also* Restitution
Peace, 17–18, 24, 37–38, 40, 147, 235–36, 276, 289, 297, 304, 312–13, 322
Peirce, C., 93, 332
Perfectibility, 8, 22–23, 95, 97, 225–26, 230, 249, 295, 298, 300
Perfection, 6, 11, 22, 32, 34, 51, 57, 63–64, 66–67, 70, 96–97, 107,

193, 220–21, 232–33, 240, 296, 298, 313, 326, 346, 349, 354
Perspective, 7–8, 78, 80, 134, 267, 338, 361, 363
Persuasion, 56, 160, 215, 259, 261, 313, 358
Phaedrus, 48–49, 77, 146–47, 150, 216, 218–24, 226–53, 255–58, 264, 267, 271, 278, 296, 300–301, 324, 327–28, 341, 353–58; *see also* Plato
Pharmakeia, 77, 221–22, 223–26, 229, 232, 235–36, 242–44, 247–57, 260, 264–65, 267, 271, 273–80, 284–93, 295–96, 300–306, 308–11, 313–14, 353, 361
Pharmakeus, 223, 233, 252–53, 257–58, 260, 262, 264–66, 268, 270, 282, 295, 366
Pharmakidos, 256, 268
Pharmakis, 264, 270, 295
Pharmakon, 49, 147, 223, 230, 241, 245, 251–53, 255, 257, 262, 264–65, 268–73, 278, 282, 285, 289–90, 292, 299, 305
Pharmakos, 223, 252–53, 258, 260, 262, 264–65, 268–70, 282, 295, 305, 353
Phenomenology, 253, 318, 358, 369
Philebus, 52, 131, 241, 357
Philia, 53, 218–19, 221, 256, 258, 267, 272, 299, 303–304, 362
Philosopher, 42, 53, 194–95, 202, 204, 233–35, 240, 250–51, 255, 272, 320, 322, 329, 331, 351–52; *see also* Philosophy
Philosophy, 5, 9, 14, 42, 44, 47, 49, 52–53, 65, 74, 78, 80–82, 89–90, 128, 159, 161, 166, 172, 191–92, 194, 196–97, 204–206, 208, 211, 218–20, 222–23, 227, 232–34, 236, 243, 245, 250, 254, 271, 274–75, 281, 315, 323–24, 329–30, 350–51, 360, 368

Phrase, 59, 87, 109, 111, 113, 120–21, 123, 154, 156, 169, 286, 335–37, 341, 358; *see also* Lyotard
Phronēsis, 214–15, 255
Physics, 57, 89, 101, 112, 213–14, 268–69, 274, 279, 335, 351
Physis, 112, 243–44, 252, 279, 297, 302, 313
Place, 2, 9, 18, 24, 30, 37, 48, 58–60, 71, 75–76, 78, 85, 91–93, 95, 97, 99, 108, 116, 130, 142, 146, 154, 159, 165–66, 172, 179, 182, 191, 202, 204, 207, 209, 218, 221, 223, 226–27, 231, 236, 246–47, 249, 266–67, 274–75, 282–83, 286, 293, 307, 309, 315, 317, 321, 328, 332–33, 340–41, 354, 365, 368
Plato, 5, 25, 28, 40–42, 44, 47–55, 57, 61–62, 73, 128, 131, 146, 159–66, 193, 197, 213, 216, 218–29, 231–33, 235–48, 254, 281, 301, 317, 325–28, 332, 344, 352–58, 364
Play, 9–11, 42–43, 46, 51, 55, 77, 97, 109, 112, 118, 131, 136, 148, 152, 205, 221, 223, 235, 240, 256, 266, 271, 276, 279, 284, 288, 293, 296, 301–306, 308, 310–11, 313, 319, 324, 353, 358, 368
Pleasure, 70–71, 95, 115, 118, 234, 236–39, 328, 333, 355
Plenitude, 58–59, 61, 63–66, 72, 75, 84–85, 91–92, 96, 102, 130–33, 136–37, 277, 330
Plurality, 52, 84, 201, 211, 240–41, 287–88, 299, 329, 337, 357, 363
Poetry, 146, 205, 219–20, 222, 232, 238, 242, 260, 271, 275, 278, 286, 324, 332, 354, 358; see also *Poiēsis*
Poiēsis, 29, 36, 56, 98, 223–24, 230–32, 234, 236, 238–39,

Poiēsis (continued)
　242–45, 249–53, 255, 257–58,
　260, 262, 264–65, 267, 270–73,
　275–80, 282, 285–86, 288–89,
　291, 294–305, 308–14, 354, 359
Polanyi, M., 98–100, 103, 257–61,
　263–64, 333–34, 359–60
Polemos, 1, 7, 11, 27, 53–55, 178,
　322, 356
Polis, 27–28, 40–41, 51, 164, 238,
　250, 256, 271, 305
Political, 9, 18, 29, 32, 40, 49–51,
　57, 62–63, 78, 92, 106, 109, 119,
　121, 128, 133, 156, 169, 173,
　185–86, 192, 215, 219, 229, 248,
　255, 259, 268–71, 282–86, 287,
　289–90, 296, 300, 303–304, 312,
　327, 332, 337–38, 349, 357–59,
　361. 365, 367
Polymestor, 148, 152–53, 343; *see
　also* Hecuba
Polyxena, 148, 152
Pornography, 293, 307, 365–66
Possibility, 9, 14, 20–21, 28, 31,
　43–44, 54, 59, 73, 80–81, 87–89,
　91, 93, 95, 106, 109, 113–14,
　121, 123–24, 127–28, 132,
　135–37, 138–39, 141, 146, 153,
　155, 160, 167–68, 172, 176–79,
　182–83, 185–86, 189, 194,
　203–207, 209, 211, 213, 217,
　233–35, 237–39, 254–56, 259,
　262, 265, 268, 273, 277–78, 292,
　303, 306, 308, 318, 327, 329,
　339–40, 343
Postcoloniality, 298, 319
Posthistory, 298
Postmodernity, 89, 105, 135, 195,
　199, 204, 208–209, 255, 298,
　331, 337, 358
Post-historical, 205, 209–10
Potentiality, 85–88, 331
Pouvoir, 121, 319; *see also* Power
Poverty, 130, 139, 156, 290

Power, 8, 10, 14–16, 18–29, 32–35,
　39, 45, 59, 62–63, 65–67, 72–75,
　84, 91–92, 95–96, 98, 106–109,
　112–13, 115, 118–19, 121, 129,
　138, 141, 146, 160–61, 163–64,
　168, 170, 173, 191, 202, 205,
　217, 221, 225, 227–31, 234, 241,
　248–52, 255, 265–66, 280,
　283–85, 287, 289–90, 293, 296,
　300–304, 313–15, 317, 319,
　321–22, 329–30, 334–37, 345,
　350–51, 355, 364, 368
Practice, 8, 22, 30, 33, 56, 60, 70,
　78–79, 81, 94–95, 99, 101, 109,
　168, 245, 266, 269, 273, 276, 283,
　285, 304, 318, 325, 345, 349, 359
Praxis, 60, 66, 81, 108–109, 267,
　286, 289, 292, 312, 359
Prejudice, 124, 167, 262, 316, 343,
　346, 355, 368
Principle, 22, 71–72, 83, 88, 96, 137,
　144, 172, 200, 213–14, 257, 262,
　327–29, 339, 341, 346, 348,
　355–56, 367; *see also* Law, Rule
Private, 51, 62, 86, 168, 170, 218,
　220, 223, 227, 229–31, 236, 238,
　247–49, 256–57, 266–68,
　292–93, 298, 300, 302–304, 313,
　353, 358–59; *see also* Public
Privilege, 11, 15, 19–20, 22, 24,
　41–42, 88, 90–91, 99, 106, 118,
　122, 133, 140, 149–50, 183–85,
　188, 202, 210, 271, 277–79,
　306–307, 320
Production, 44, 47, 97–98, 100, 123,
　325, 337
Profession, 220, 227, 264, 266, 338,
　361, 366
Progress, 89, 132, 136, 203,
　208–209, 225, 284, 289
Prohibition, 37, 64, 143, 160
Proof, 42, 101, 115, 121–22,
　127–28, 133, 144, 149–50, 153,
　156–57, 203, 254, 277, 337, 355

Proper, 3, 16, 23, 41, 55–56, 99, 150, 173, 207, 216–17, 224, 245, 258, 262, 316–17, 321, 328, 347–48, 354–55, 357, 368
Property, 23, 33–35, 70, 72–73, 76–77, 97–98, 162, 169, 181, 228, 267, 272, 287, 298, 330
Prophecy, 227, 230, 232, 234, 249, 300, 354
Proportion, 7, 35, 37, 45, 67, 71, 132, 322–23
Propriety, 2, 4, 8, 10, 35, 41, 55, 57, 115, 157, 210, 216, 258, 298, 349, 357; *see also* Proper
Proximity, 7, 12, 23, 28, 37, 60, 81, 109, 114, 117–18, 142, 151–52, 182, 188, 213, 230, 234, 240, 245, 252, 256, 278–79, 283–84, 312, 315, 320, 368
Prudence, 68
Psychē, 138, 240, 243, 247, 354; *see also* Soul
Public, 7, 16, 29, 80, 84, 86, 169–71, 218, 220, 224, 229–31, 238, 242–43, 247–48, 252, 254, 256–57, 259, 267, 272, 285, 292–93, 298, 300, 302–304, 309–10, 313, 321, 335, 353, 357–59; *see also* Private
Punishment, 34, 73, 96, 107, 114, 116–19, 152–57, 162, 169, 284, 315, 322, 336, 343, 368

Race, 14, 19, 170, 267, 291, 297, 323, 356, 366–67
Radiance, 8, 142, 218
Radical, 102, 155, 195–96, 199, 209–10
Rape, 116, 223, 245, 267, 272, 290–95, 303, 305, 308, 356, 366
Rationality, 30, 35, 42, 66, 73–74, 79–80, 87, 89, 108, 116, 124, 144, 149, 200, 205, 208, 217, 261, 264–66, 268–69, 274–75, 301, 303, 305, 329, 341, 352, 366; *see also* Knowledge, Reason
Reality, 6–7, 44, 50, 67, 72, 94, 112, 115, 120, 122–23, 127–28, 206, 220, 229, 231, 257–58, 264, 267, 270, 298–99, 318, 321, 323, 331, 337, 358, 360
Reason, 1, 5, 8, 15–17, 19, 24–33, 43–44, 46, 56, 63–64, 66, 68, 73–75, 77–79, 81, 86–88, 93, 103, 107–108, 115, 121–23, 127, 129–30, 134, 139–41, 144–46, 149, 151–57, 160–61, 163–64, 166–68, 172, 174, 183, 185–86, 195, 199–200, 204–205, 211, 214, 216–18, 222–23, 234, 260–61, 264, 266, 269–70, 274–75, 277, 285, 288, 294–97, 299, 301, 304–309, 310–13, 318, 329, 333–34, 343, 352, 354–55, 367–68; *see also* Rationality
Recht, 8, 69
Recollection, 187, 232–33, 245–47, 250–51, 255; *see also* Memory
Recompense, 45, 88, 100, 114, 228; *see also* Restitution
Rectification, 45, 110–11, 326; *see also* Restitution
Redemption, 208–209, 211, 300, 351
Regard, 13, 71, 73, 84, 103, 112, 135, 153, 160, 165, 186–87, 210, 222, 228, 260, 270, 363
Regulation, 107, 120–21, 140, 188–89, 238, 273, 325, 348, 366; *see also* Rule
Relation, 1–2, 5–7, 11–14, 18–20, 25, 29, 35–36, 44, 49–55, 62–63, 66, 69, 71–74, 76–79, 85–86, 91, 94–95, 97–98, 102, 106–107, 111, 117–18, 122, 124, 129, 131–32, 135–36, 140, 147, 151, 155, 159, 168, 181–82, 188, 201, 206, 208, 216–18, 224–27, 231, 233–35, 238, 241, 248, 263, 266,

Relation *(continued)*
    275, 293, 311, 315–16, 320, 322, 324–25, 327, 332–33, 339–41, 343, 347–48, 350, 353, 368
Relativism, 260, 271, 301, 361
Religion, 173, 194, 197, 264, 275, 350, 359
Reparation, 4, 12, 18–19, 28, 30, 110, 116, 143, 154, 315, 368; *see also* Restitution
Repetition, 4, 40, 43, 61, 63, 94, 103, 123, 136–37, 141, 147, 152, 176, 183, 185, 192, 206–207, 214, 220, 226, 229, 233, 239, 247, 249–51, 279, 282, 284, 296, 299–300, 304–306, 315, 324, 339, 346, 357, 368
Representation, 2, 9, 17–20, 24–30, 40, 44, 46–47, 50–52, 60–61, 63–64, 68–69, 71–73, 77–79, 81, 84–90, 92, 94–103, 111–15, 119–21, 124, 128–32, 134–35, 143–44, 149–51, 155, 160, 164, 166, 168–70, 175, 180–81, 184–87, 195, 200–201, 207, 215, 218, 220, 226, 230–32, 237, 244, 250–52, 256–57, 265, 273–87, 290–93, 295–96, 301–308, 313–17, 321–24, 328, 333, 336, 340, 356, 362, 366–68
Republic, 28, 48–50, 52, 61–62, 67, 146, 159–64, 216, 218–20, 232, 234, 238, 251, 257, 330, 344, 352, 354–56; *see also* Plato
Resistance, 21–23, 27, 50, 61, 78, 80, 109–10, 118–19, 133, 205, 263, 289, 337
Responsibilities, 7, 178, 183, 334
Responsibility, 3–4, 7, 11–12, 27, 79, 98, 100, 111, 121, 140, 153, 156–57, 167, 178, 182–84, 186–88, 206–207, 271, 292, 296, 298, 303, 311–12, 316–20, 323, 330, 334, 348, 367–68

Restitution, 1–2, 4–6, 9, 11–12, 36–37, 39–43, 45–46, 48–54, 58, 60, 65, 69, 78, 81, 88–89, 92, 100–101, 109–12, 116–21, 123–25, 131, 139, 143–44, 153, 155–57, 173–75, 177, 181–83, 185–87, 203, 209, 276, 284, 286, 290, 292, 294, 296, 301–302, 304–15, 318, 322–24, 326, 343–44, 367–68
Retribution, 6, 11, 43, 111, 155, 171, 173, 178, 310
Rights, 19, 24–26, 29, 69–70, 73, 107, 225, 293, 299, 311, 365
Risk, 60–62, 79–80, 93, 99, 171, 194–95, 273, 325–26, 343
Rousseau, J., 67–69, 328
Rules, 3, 7, 12, 14, 17–18, 22, 24, 26–27, 29–33, 37–48, 50–51, 53, 57, 64, 66, 69, 73–75, 77–80, 85–86, 89–90, 92–93, 96, 99–100, 106–108, 110–11, 113, 118, 120–25, 127, 134–35, 144–45, 155–56, 160–72, 177–78, 182, 185, 188, 197–98, 200, 207, 209, 215–17, 222, 224–25, 230, 235, 238, 243, 249, 251–52, 254–55, 257–58, 265–67, 269, 271–76, 281–83, 287–89, 296, 300–301, 303, 306–307, 310–11, 325–26, 332–35, 337, 345–46, 348–49, 353, 356, 359, 361–62, 366

Sacks, O., 141–43, 146, 149, 340–41
Sacred, 15, 174–75, 177, 324, 368
Sacrifice, 5–6, 65, 86, 92–93, 100–103, 109–10, 118, 121, 152–53, 184–86, 202, 223, 253, 258, 262, 264, 266, 272, 282–84, 293–96, 301–302, 305, 309, 311–13, 317–19, 337, 343, 347–48, 364
Saddest, 149

Index

Samson, 195, 204
Santayana, G., 42, 324
Sappho, 220
Schapiro, M., 202–203
Science, 30, 35–36, 42–43, 50, 55–56, 71, 80–81, 89–90, 92–96, 98–101, 103, 108, 111, 116, 121, 132, 134–36, 150, 156–57, 166–68, 183, 211, 213–18, 220–23, 225, 230, 232–34, 237–44, 247–80, 282, 295, 298, 300–302, 307, 325, 327, 329, 331–33, 338–39, 351–53, 357–63, 366; *see also* Knowledge, Rationality
Self–knowledge, 222–23, 231, 244, 254, 256, 277, 353
Semasis, 90, 110–12, 121, 247, 319
Sex, 10, 61, 118, 120, 136, 225, 268–69, 290, 293, 297, 328, 334, 337, 355
Sexuality, 62, 65, 79, 102, 118–20, 136, 231, 234–37, 267, 269, 290–95, 297, 302–303, 305, 307, 314, 319, 325, 328, 334, 356, 365–66
Significance, 4, 7, 136, 146, 240, 326–27, 329–30, 338, 350
Signs, 30, 97, 99, 101, 119, 122, 136, 150, 174–75, 240, 288, 326–27, 329–30, 333–34, 337, 361, 363, 365
Silence, 2, 45, 109, 111, 115–16, 120–23, 128–29, 143, 154–56, 246, 273, 319, 341, 366
Skepticism, 167, 217, 251, 259–61, 301, 361
Slavery, 14, 20, 22, 33–34, 41, 57–59, 60–61, 79, 193, 199, 256, 267, 284, 291, 294, 297, 302, 306, 313, 323
Social, 19, 24, 44, 68, 70, 80, 119, 132, 155, 160, 169–70, 209, 265–66, 268, 271, 273, 284–85, 320, 325, 328, 333, 345, 356, 361–62
Socialism, 206, 211, 307, 323
Society, 14, 18, 21, 24–25, 28, 64, 70, 87, 92, 119, 155, 159, 174, 186, 199–200, 219, 259, 265, 271, 275–76, 282, 284, 289, 292–93, 321, 332, 345, 359
Socrates, 5, 28, 30, 47–53, 61, 63, 108, 120, 128, 131, 146–47, 149, 159–61, 163–66, 197, 218–29, 231–47, 249–51, 253–58, 262, 267–68, 271–72, 277, 281, 305, 322, 326, 344, 353, 355–57; *see also* Plato
Sophia, 53, 222–23, 232, 234, 241–42, 245
Sophocles, 242–43
Sorcery, 253, 255, 257, 265, 267, 269, 272, 279, 285, 295, 306, 308–309, 311, 361
Soul, 6, 19, 36, 57, 67, 76, 83, 124, 145, 232–36, 240, 243, 245, 247, 250, 254–55, 316, 331, 337, 354–56, 367–68
Sovereignty, 17–29, 20–22, 24–29, 32, 50, 68–69, 73–76, 106, 114–15, 123, 129, 132–33, 135, 156, 162, 169, 171, 174, 195–96, 199, 202, 270–71, 283, 298, 303, 329–30, 332, 334, 337, 341
Space, 3, 9, 16, 26, 50, 54, 56, 87, 94–95, 110, 117, 129, 143, 152, 156, 160, 177, 187, 267, 278, 286–87, 292–93, 295, 309–10, 325, 340, 347, 361–62
Speaking, 3, 6, 16, 19–20, 45, 61, 93, 105, 111, 113, 115, 122, 137, 140, 148, 184, 201–202, 219, 231, 239, 244, 254, 264, 267, 275, 278, 297, 316, 320, 341, 346, 367–68
Species, 120, 132, 134, 153, 294, 338

Speech, 21, 143, 150, 176, 219–20, 223–29, 231–32, 234–37, 239–41, 243–44, 247, 250, 255, 263, 288, 297, 307, 324, 336, 356–58, 365–67
Spinoza, B., 57–59, 61, 91, 198, 311, 327, 349
Spirit, 15, 66, 83–84, 89, 124, 185, 192–94, 204–205, 225, 228, 247, 253, 298, 315–16, 318, 323, 328, 342, 360, 368
Spirituality, 185, 192, 225, 228, 336
Spivak, G., 44–45, 324–25
Stambaugh, J., 206–208, 350
State, 13, 17–19, 21–22, 24–30, 32–36, 57, 59, 62–64, 68–69, 73–78, 106, 120, 155, 160, 174, 178, 202, 215–16, 218, 237, 260, 277, 290, 293, 297, 305, 317, 319, 321, 324, 329–30, 350–51, 360, 363, 365
Statesman, 49–51, 241, 325; *see also* Plato
Strife, 1, 11, 24, 27, 31, 34, 37–38, 40, 52–54, 57, 155, 315, 321, 368; *see also* Polemos
Structure, 14, 29, 80, 98, 143, 152, 172, 179, 233, 337–39, 347, 355
Subaltern, 44–46, 60, 298, 324–25
Subject, 5, 13–14, 17, 21–22, 26–27, 30, 44, 47, 68, 73, 89, 103, 105–108, 114–15, 118–21, 123, 125, 152, 165, 178, 188, 196, 198–99, 202–204, 207, 209, 224, 239, 248, 252, 254, 256–57, 260, 282, 295, 298, 302, 304–305, 314, 316, 320, 325, 332–34, 337, 347, 358–59, 367
Subjection, 5, 7–8, 10, 14–17, 22, 26, 44, 59–60, 103, 106–11, 113–15, 117–25, 157, 185, 196, 200, 204, 254, 261, 272, 276, 281, 285, 287–90, 296–98, 301–304, 307, 310–13, 320, 334, 337, 350, 362–63, 365, 368
Subjectivity, 11, 74–75, 77, 99, 105, 185, 270, 316, 320, 347
Subjugation, 3–4, 8, 14, 46, 58, 60, 62, 106–109, 114–15, 125, 262, 267–69, 272, 274, 289, 297, 307, 334, 360, 363
Sublime, 8–9, 71, 109, 149, 151–52, 186, 229, 299, 318
Subordination, 20–21, 24, 34, 118, 306, 334, 339, 365–66
Substance, 75, 83–84, 215, 234, 331, 338
Substitution, 70, 94–98, 100–101, 304, 333
Suffering, 2–4, 7, 45, 71–72, 79–81, 108, 110–11, 113–18, 121–22, 127, 135, 156–57, 162, 171–72, 178, 181, 185–86, 188–89, 289, 302, 306, 309, 313, 334, 355, 367
Superiority, 8, 13–14, 22, 24, 33–34, 58–59, 61–62, 66, 73, 99, 160–61, 169, 174, 210, 215, 232, 234, 243, 248, 254, 258, 260–62, 281, 298, 354
Supersensible, 71, 270
Suspicion, 3, 7, 14, 45, 111, 157, 174–75, 262–63, 296, 302–303, 306, 312, 360
Symposium, 48–49, 146, 219, 222, 225, 227, 231, 237, 354; *see also* Plato

Technē, 8, 26–33, 36, 40, 47–49, 54–61, 64, 66, 69–70, 73, 75–76, 79, 81, 95, 102, 106–107, 109, 113–14, 123, 150, 157, 164, 166, 174, 184, 220, 224–25, 230, 232, 234, 237–58, 260, 262, 264–80, 282, 284–86, 288–91, 293–98, 300–305, 307–14, 354, 357, 359, 365; *see also* Art, Instrumentality, Measure

Technicality, 19–20, 27–28, 70, 73, 244, 259, 262, 265, 268, 271, 274, 285
Technology, 107, 201–202, 206, 276–80, 297, 347, 363–64; see also *Technē*
Teleology, 58, 296, 307–308, 311, 313
Temporal, 2, 52–53, 65, 78–79, 124, 150, 216, 274, 274, 179, 340, 351, 362; *see also* Time
Terror, 20, 23–24, 27–28, 68, 78–79, 156, 193, 264, 298, 303; *see also* Danger, Monstrosity
Theuth, 239, 245, 324
Thrasymachus, 28, 31, 159–64, 166, 243, 322, 344
Timaeus, 324, 328; *see also* Plato
Time, 1–2, 4–6, 8, 10–12, 18–19, 27–28, 30–31, 34, 36–40, 42–43, 45, 48, 50–55, 59–60, 65, 69, 71, 75–76, 79, 85–96, 98–100, 103, 109–20, 122–25, 128–29, 135, 139, 142–45, 147, 152–57, 166, 172–73, 175–78, 181–82, 184–85, 187–89, 191–93, 195–96, 201, 205, 210, 217, 222–23, 227, 235–36, 238, 248, 257, 263, 268, 273–74, 276–79, 283, 286–88, 292–93, 296, 299, 301–302, 307, 309, 311–15, 322, 326–28, 333, 335–36, 338–40, 343, 345–46, 350, 352, 362, 364, 366–68; *see also* History
Tradition, 4–5, 19–20, 23, 32, 41–44, 46, 63, 69, 81, 93–95, 98–99, 103, 112, 119, 128, 146, 163, 185, 196, 199, 211, 222, 234, 245, 258–59, 261–62, 281, 293, 324, 333–34, 338, 341, 345–46, 359–60, 364, 366
Tragedy, 89, 154, 194, 219, 242, 313, 322, 343, 348, 350, 353
Translation, 2, 149, 208, 210, 344

Trial, The, 16, 164, 240, 281, 321–22, 333; *see also* Kafka
Trinh, T., 41, 45, 185, 198, 319, 367
Truth, 1, 3–5, 7–9, 12, 15–17, 19–20, 26–30, 32, 36, 39–41, 43, 45–48, 50–56, 62–66, 73–74, 76, 78, 80, 86–90, 92–93, 95–96, 98–101, 103, 105–12, 114, 118–19, 121–22, 128, 132–38, 140, 142, 144–46, 149, 153–57, 160–61, 163–68, 173, 177, 180–83, 185, 189, 191, 193, 195, 200, 202–203, 205, 211, 216, 218, 220–22, 224–37, 239–41, 244–52, 254–62, 264–67, 269–79, 281–82, 284–86, 289–90, 294–302, 304, 308, 311–13, 317, 319, 325, 327, 329, 332, 342, 345–46, 348, 351–52, 356, 358, 360–61, 363–64
Tychē, 56, 61, 112, 145
Tyranny, 50, 63, 68, 194

Ultimate, 21, 31, 73, 75, 87–89, 93, 169–70, 174, 178–79, 253, 261, 274–75, 318, 328
Uncanny, 5, 110, 141–42, 152
Understanding, 6–8, 18, 27–28, 41, 51, 68, 71, 78–81, 86, 89–90, 99, 106, 108, 117, 119, 124, 133, 135, 144, 165, 167, 173, 185, 216, 222, 232, 256, 258, 262–63, 287, 290–91, 305, 322, 330, 341, 343, 346, 352–54, 359, 363, 365; *see also* Knowledge, Science
Universality, 21, 23, 29, 56, 59, 67, 71–72, 74–75, 81, 89, 98, 101, 109–110, 124, 145, 161, 170–71, 178, 180, 183–84, 187–88, 200, 209, 217, 257, 259, 263, 274, 289, 315, 321, 324, 327, 329, 333, 335, 346–48, 351–52, 367–68
Universe, 7, 63, 66–67, 84, 86–87, 109, 142, 209, 225, 274–75, 313,

Universe *(continued)*
331, 355–56
Unjust, 4, 8, 10, 18, 24, 28, 39–40, 49, 58, 60, 69, 88–89, 103, 116, 128, 162–63, 170–71, 178, 181–84, 189, 207, 252, 256, 264, 272, 287, 290–91, 295, 304, 308, 312, 314, 322, 347, 364–65; *see also* Injustice
Unpresentable, 109, 111, 128, 349, 366
Unreason, 30, 88, 140, 144–46, 258, 260, 285, 295, 305, 308
Untruth, 5, 27, 30, 45, 53–55, 65, 88, 111, 181, 234, 251, 255, 264, 273–75, 279, 285, 301–302, 327; *see also* Truth
Utility, 69–71, 80, 161, 221, 224–25, 299, 328–29, 333

Valor, 5, 186, 282, 284, 286, 296, 305, 309, 312–13, 317–19; *see also* Charity, Sacrifice
Values, 70, 101–102, 167, 187, 192–94, 229, 333
Van Gogh, V., 202–203, 317, 350
Vattimo, G., 195–96, 198, 205–11, 277, 336, 349, 351, 364
Vengeance, 2, 11, 39, 74, 96, 147–48, 152, 154–56, 178, 256, 284, 298, 310–11, 322
Verwindung, 206–11, 277, 300, 363
Victims, 2, 109–18, 120–22, 128–29, 148, 162, 150, 153, 155–56, 170, 184–85, 299, 306–308, 310, 312, 318, 335, 347, 367
Violence, 9, 16–19, 28–35, 37–41, 50, 69–70, 78, 80–81, 89, 91–92, 109, 111, 116, 123, 141, 153–56, 169–75, 177–78, 182, 185–87, 209–10, 235, 290–95, 297, 299, 302–303, 305, 307, 310, 314, 318, 321–22, 334–35, 339, 345, 347, 350, 356, 361, 365

Virtue, 7–8, 14, 19–20, 34, 42, 47, 49, 53–54, 56–57, 59, 61, 63, 65, 67, 72, 77, 84, 86, 92–93, 96, 102–103, 106, 112–14, 118, 129, 136, 152–53, 165–67, 180, 205–206, 213, 215, 218, 233, 239, 242–43, 245, 257, 282, 289, 298, 305, 325, 327, 330, 346, 356–57, 366

War, 11, 20–25, 27, 29–30, 33, 37–38, 40, 79, 89, 116, 121, 128, 130, 132, 147, 155, 164, 170, 192–93, 209, 279, 289, 294, 297, 321, 329
Wealth, 30, 62, 89, 94–102, 287, 306, 308, 333, 340
Western, 1, 3–4, 8–10, 12, 14, 20, 23, 41–42, 44–47, 69, 72, 82, 85, 93, 95, 107–108, 112, 114, 118–19, 124, 140, 185, 191, 195–96, 204, 206, 209–10, 153, 260, 281–84, 291–93, 296–97, 301, 304, 310, 316, 324, 343, 366, 368
Whitehead, A., 6–7, 41–42, 47, 83, 85–88, 90, 94–95, 97, 101, 112, 196, 198, 274–76, 313, 318, 322, 331, 363–64, 336, 363–64
Wisdom, 48, 53, 55–56, 63, 66, 146, 157, 165, 214–15, 227, 242, 245, 264, 275, 306, 327, 351–52, 358, 361
Witchcraft, 47, 233, 253, 256, 260, 267, 270–73, 278, 282–83, 285, 287–88, 292, 306, 309, 311, 359, 361, 364
Witches, 139, 157, 253, 256–57, 264, 266–72, 274, 282–84, 287–89, 291–93, 295, 298–99, 302, 310–11, 362–66
Witness, 111, 113, 121, 123–25, 128, 161, 185, 200, 262, 286
Wittgenstein, L., 198, 319

Wizards, 223, 253, 256, 258, 265–66, 274, 295, 299; *see also* Witches

Woman, 45, 49, 61, 116, 170, 193, 196, 202, 281, 293, 318–19, 325, 328, 339, 342, 355; *see also* Gender, Man

Women, 7, 57–62, 65, 103, 152, 156, 185, 191, 193–94, 197–98, 213, 234, 236, 256–57, 267–68, 274, 288, 290–92, 294, 306–308, 328, 343–44, 349, 355, 365–66

Work, 6–7, 9, 12–13, 22, 27, 30, 33, 35, 37, 39, 41, 44, 48, 56, 61, 63, 66, 71, 74, 80, 87, 89–90, 105, 108, 116, 118–19, 131, 133, 136, 141, 143–44, 156, 163, 169, 173, 201–203, 205, 216, 218–19, 236, 240, 244, 264–66, 277, 286–87, 289, 297–98, 305–306, 309, 316–17, 325, 332, 341, 343, 346, 356, 358, 361, 367–68

World, 2, 6–9, 14, 31, 35, 37, 45, 58, 60, 66–67, 69, 74–75, 85–87, 89–90, 92–93, 113, 117, 121, 130–31, 133–34, 142, 157, 159, 171, 198, 206, 208, 210, 223, 232, 234–35, 238, 243, 250, 252, 254–56, 261, 263, 266–68, 270–72, 274–75, 287, 289–90, 293, 297, 303–306, 308, 310, 312–13, 319, 328, 330–32, 340, 357, 361–63

Writing, 6, 18, 21, 29–30, 43, 48, 64, 80, 129, 140, 146–47, 150, 153, 156, 171, 177, 183, 201, 218–20, 223–24, 226, 229–30, 233, 237–40, 242–51, 255, 287, 297, 300, 307, 318–19, 324, 341, 346, 357–58

Wrong, 13, 24, 30, 38, 41, 47, 51, 70–71, 73, 77, 90, 110, 113–15, 121, 123–25, 127–28, 145, 156, 162, 185, 203, 228, 237, 245–47, 297, 299, 326, 335, 358

Zarathustra, 194, 196, 349
Zeno, 5, 52, 326
Zeus, 37, 40, 161, 237, 245, 324